Streaming Music, Streaming Capital

Streaming Music,

Eric Drott

Streaming Capital

DUKE UNIVERSITY PRESS *Durham and London* 2024

© 2024 DUKE UNIVERSITY PRESS
All rights reserved
Printed in the United States of America on acid-free paper ∞
Designed by Matthew Tauch
Typeset in Garamond Premier Pro
by Westchester Publishing Services

Library of Congress Cataloging-in-Publication Data
Names: Drott, Eric, [date] author.
Title: Streaming music, streaming capital / Eric Drott.
Description: Durham : Duke University Press, 2024. | Includes bibliographical references and index.
Identifiers: LCCN 2023025131 (print)
LCCN 2023025132 (ebook)
ISBN 9781478025740 (paperback)
ISBN 9781478020998 (hardcover)
ISBN 9781478027874 (ebook)
Subjects: LCSH: Music trade—Technological innovations. | Sound recording industry. | Streaming audio. | Music and the Internet. | BISAC: MUSIC / Business Aspects | SOCIAL SCIENCE / Media Studies
Classification: LCC ML3790 .D77 2024 (print) | LCC ML3790 (ebook) | DDC 338.4/778—dc23/eng/20231027
LC record available at https://lccn.loc.gov/2023025131
LC ebook record available at https://lccn.loc.gov/2023025132

**For Marianne,
as always**

Contents

Acknowledgments ix

Introduction
→ 1

CHAPTER ONE
Streaming Music
→ 22

CHAPTER TWO
Streaming Capital
→ 63

CHAPTER THREE
Music as a Technology of Surveillance
→ 101

CHAPTER FOUR
Counterfeiting Attention in the Streaming Economy: Spam, Click Fraud, and Fake Artists
→ 144

CHAPTER FIVE
Streaming, Cheap Music, and the Crises of Social Reproduction
→ 193

Epilogue
→ 235

Notes 255
Bibliography 307
Index 331

Acknowledgments

Writing a book may often feel like a solitary undertaking, but believing that this is actually the case is to suffer from a misapprehension. While it is my name that appears on the spine of this volume, this book would not have been written without the support, encouragement, and intellectual stimulation of countless others.

Special thanks to friends and colleagues who read earlier drafts of the book, either in part or as a whole: Holly Watkins, Marie Thompson, Jonathan Sterne, Ben Piekut, Sumanth Gopinath, and Kyle Devine. I feel incredibly fortunate to have benefited from such brilliant and generous interlocutors, whose feedback was enormously helpful in shaping, refining, and in some cases obliging me to radically reconceptualize the arguments advanced in the pages that follow.

In addition, my thinking on both streaming and music's complex relation to capitalism more broadly owes a great deal to the conversations I've had over the past decade with a wide range of people, including fellow academics, journalists, activists, industry personnel, students, and many, many others. While this list is no doubt incomplete, I would in particular like to express my deep appreciation to the following people: Georgina Born, David Brackett, Kaleb Goldschmitt, Nick Seaver, Robert Prey, Joe DeGeorge, Tom Hodgson, Paula Harper, Noriko Manabe, Christopher Haworth, Jonathan Goldman, Melina Esse, Bryan Parkhurst, Stephan Hammel, Michael Birenbaum Quintero, Danielle Fosler-Lussier, Peter Schmelz, Michael Gallope, Brian Kane, Amy Cimini, Matthew Gelbart, Seth Brodsky, Martin Scherzinger, Tom Johnson, Max Ritts, Bob Sturm, Clara Latham, Saskia Gregg, Tatiana Koike, Glenn McDonald, Brian Miller, Jairo Moreno, Megan Steigerwald Ille, Evie McNeil, Eamonn Bell, Jedediah Sklower, Jean-Julien Aucouturier, and James Deaville.

I also had the good fortune to be able to share an earlier version of much of this book's contents in conferences, workshops, and invited presentations over the better part of the past decade. Many thanks to Georgina Born and David Brackett for inviting me to participate in the "New Directions in Musical Genre" conference they held at McGill in 2014; Cécile Verschaeve, for asking me to give the keynote address at the 2015 meeting of L'Association pour un Colloque Étudiant sur les Musiques Populaires in Paris; Michael Gallope and Naomi Waltham-Smith, for encouraging me to take part in the panel they convened, "The Political Economy of Sound," in 2016 for the American Comparative Literature Association annual meeting; Bryan Parkhurst and Stephan Hammel, for the panel they organized on music and historical materialism for the joint meeting of the American Musicological Society (AMS) and the Society for Music Theory in fall 2016; Jennifer Iverson for asking me to give a paper on streaming as part of a panel on music and radio at the 2016 meeting of AMS; Paula Harper, Eamonn Bell, and Ralph Richard Whyte, for graciously inviting me to give the keynote address at the 2017 Columbia Music Scholarship Conference; Danijela Spiric-Beard, for inviting me to share my work at the "Music and Socialism" conference she organized at the University of Nottingham in 2017; Jonathan Goldman, for according me the honor of giving the annual Conférences de Prestige at the Université de Montréal in 2019; Sarah Waltz, for inviting me to speak to her students at the University of the Pacific in 2021; Kyung Young Chung and Yi Eun Chung, for extending to me the privilege of giving a keynote address at the 2022 "Differentiating Sound Studies" conference held at Hanyang University; and the students and faculty in the music departments at Northwestern University, Harvard University, the University of Chicago, the University of Minnesota Twin Cities, Cornell University, and the University of Pennsylvania. The feedback and conversations generated at these events were a source of inspiration, and I owe a debt of gratitude to everyone who took the time to engage with me and my work.

I am also remarkably fortunate to have colleagues at the University of Texas at Austin whose support and camaraderie over the years has been gratifying more than words can say: Chelsea Burns, Jim Buhler, Robert Hatten, John Turci-Escobar, and Marianne Wheeldon. Thanks as well to the members of the University of Texas Provost's Authors Fellowship cohort whose conversations and feedback during the darker days of the pandemic were instrumental in helping me see this book to fruition: Ben Brower, Erika Bsumek, and Kirsten Cather.

The students in the seminar I taught on streaming platforms in spring 2022 helped breathe new life into the subject of this book, just as I was putting the finishing touches on the manuscript: Issa Aji, Alejandro Cueto, Jacob Einarsson, Lorena Ferrer, Dimitris Gkoulimaris, Qifang Hu, Seokyoung Kim, Geli Li, Anna Piatigorsky, and J. A. Strub. Their feedback on the portions of the book I shared with them in class was remarkably helpful in honing some of the arguments in the home stretch of the writing process.

Support for my work was provided by two research leaves granted by the University of Texas at Austin. Thanks to the Walter and Gina Ducloux Fine Arts Faculty Fellowship I received in spring 2018 I was able to draft much of chapter 4, while the Provost's Authors Fellowship I received during the academic year 2020–2021 gave me the time and energy to draft much of the introduction and chapter 1 of this book.

I am extraordinarily grateful to Ken Wissoker for his time and patience in seeing me through the submission and review process at Duke University Press. Thanks as well to Kate Mullen, who has been a tremendous help in shepherding me through the various stages of the production process, as well as Cathy Cambron, whose keen eye in copyediting the book has improved the writing immeasurably.

Saved for last is the person to whom I owe the most, my wife, Marianne, who has been an unflagging source of support, encouragement, feedback, and (when necessary) gentle prodding throughout the long process of writing this book. I count myself extraordinarily lucky to have such a partner in my life. This book is dedicated to her.

Introduction

Since 2010 or so, a significant change has taken place in recorded music's commercial circulation. Following music's move online in the late 1990s, the spread of file sharing epitomized by Napster, and the development of a commercial market for digital downloads spurred by Apple's introduction of the iTunes store in 2003, the period since 2010 has witnessed a shift away from the downloadable audio file as the primary object of musical commerce. The digital download, which still treats music as a discrete entity to be bought, sold, and possessed, has been displaced by something more fluid, seemingly more in line with music's status as a paradigmatically temporal art form. This something is the *stream*. An indication of the dominant position cloud-based streaming has attained can be seen in the market share for recorded music it now commands. After several years of steady growth, streaming passed an important threshold in 2015, with the global revenue generated by services such as Spotify, Deezer, and Apple Music for the first time exceeding sales of either digital downloads or physical recordings. By 2019, the total number of streams had passed the one trillion mark per annum; and while some industry observers have expressed concern that the market is approaching saturation ("peak streaming"), far more likely is that slowing growth in the United States and Europe will be offset by expanding markets in Latin America, Africa, and south Asia.[1] The growth of streaming has in turn reinvigorated a moribund recording industry: after years of declining revenue, which finally bottomed out in 2014, global recorded music revenues began to rebound in 2015.[2] By 2021 the maturation of the streaming sector had finally pushed global recording industry revenue past the highwater mark last set in the late 1990s.[3] As one major label executive put it, "thanks to [streaming]—especially Spotify, I would say—we were taken out of the dark times."[4]

The significance of streaming's impact cannot be measured solely in terms of market share or corporate balance sheets, however. If the advent of sound recording in the late nineteenth century enabled musical sound to be objectified, facilitating its subsequent commodification at an ever-expanding scale, the rise of streaming promises to be no less far-reaching in its effects. In certain respects, streaming's impact may prove even more consequential than that of the much-ballyhooed MP3. Whereas the latter still adheres to a logic of possession inherited from the universe of physical goods, streaming operates according to a very different logic, one based on temporary and conditional access. For listeners, music becomes something rented rather than owned. What they get in ceding the rights and privileges that come with the purchase of a physical recording is access to a virtual musical archive of unimaginably vast proportions. "No. More. Limits." Such was the promise made to potential users by one advertisement for Spotify, the latest iteration of the "ideology of plenitude" that music companies have long used to attract customers.[5] For major record labels, the promise of streaming was the promise to transcend limits of a different kind. After more than a decade of declining revenue, conveniently blamed on the alleged piracy "epidemic" that Napster and other file-sharing sites set in motion, the new business model of renting access to music offered rights holders a source of income that was both stable and predictable. Just as important, it provided them with a means of reimposing control over their intellectual property, and did so in a way that made it appear as if it was something other than a form of control.

If major labels and a handful of superstar artists have fared well under this new dispensation, for many working musicians the balance of streaming's benefits to costs has been less clear-cut. On the positive side of the ledger, streaming has helped lower barriers to entry considerably. In contrast to terrestrial radio stations and brick-and-mortar record stores, music platforms impose few restrictions on the amount or kind of material that can be posted to their services. Lowering barriers further are digital distributors such as CD Baby and DistroKid, which make it easy for artists to bypass labels and self-release their music on streaming platforms. In addition, the fact that services such as Spotify, Apple Music, and SoundCloud operate across national markets brings the possibility of reaching a truly global audience closer to reality for many musicians than had been the case in the past. Yet it is at this point that streaming's benefits become difficult to distinguish from its costs. For the possibility of reaching a global audience has as its corollary the fact that the competition musicians face is equally global in scale. As studies of superstar economies over the years have underlined, the larger the market in which cultural producers are compelled to compete, the more likely that winner-take-all tendencies will concentrate wealth—symbolic as well as economic—in the hands of a few top earners.[6]

This is not the only upside that becomes hard to distinguish from a downside. Consider the shift from an ownership model to an access model of music distribution that streaming inaugurates. For independent and major label artists alike, this new model holds out the possibility of recovering a fraction of the income that might have hypothetically been lost to file sharing, had streaming not displaced MP3 downloads as the primary medium of music's commercial circulation. And yet the guaranteed minimums written into the licensing agreements that major labels have signed with most major platforms mean that they will receive an outsize share of streaming revenue no matter what, shoring up their dominant position in the market for recorded music (in 2021, for instance, streaming platforms generated $16.9 billion for the record industry worldwide, $12.8 billion of which went to major labels).[7] If agreements like these leave a smaller slice of the pie to be split among a vast number of independent musicians, it isn't as if artists signed to major labels necessarily fare much better. Far from being relegated to the analog past, the dubious accounting practices that have long been synonymous with the record industry have been updated for the streaming era. This includes counting streams as sales rather than as licensed performances (which in many record contracts results in artists receiving a less favorable royalty split)[8] and continuing to deduct from artist payments expenses that have little relevance for digital music (such as breakage, a holdover from the days of physical distribution).[9] Viewed from this angle, streaming isn't simply a technology of music distribution; it is also and more significantly a technology of wealth redistribution, allowing value to be rerouted away from musicians to tech monopolists on the one hand and copyright monopolists on the other.

Also important is the way streaming restructures the manner in which artists are paid. No longer are recordings unbundled into just a collection of individual audio files, a transformation Apple's iTunes music store instigated when it began selling individual MP3s for $0.99 apiece. With streaming, tracks undergo an even more radical disaggregation, being unbundled into a series of transient streams. This renders the payment that artists receive equally piecemeal: royalties that would have been earned up front from the sale of an album or an MP3 file are now dispersed across the longer span of time it takes to accrue the equivalent, as calculated in the number of individual streams. While a number of factors determine the exact amount a given artist will earn from streaming—which streaming service is being considered, the overall size and distribution of the revenue pool out of which an individual service pays royalties, whether an artist is signed to a label or self-releasing, if the advance one has received from a record company has been recouped or not, and so on—on average the typical royalty earned per stream ranges somewhere between $0.004 and $0.01. To be sure, such micropayments can add up over time. Particularly for older, established artists, or those in possession of large music catalogs (two variables that often go hand in hand), streaming payments can amount to meaningful income. By the same token, however, those in possession of the largest catalogs—namely, major labels and publishers—will be the biggest beneficiaries of the streaming model. For younger, less established musicians, or those working on the margins of the mainstream music industry, the situation couldn't be more different. A representative survey of UK musicians conducted in December 2020 indicates that 80 percent of music creators earn less than £200 ($264) per annum from streaming.[10] And even if over the long run a recording might end up earning the same amount from streaming as from physical sales, for many musicians this prospect is cold comfort. "People don't eat in the long run," Harry Hopkins famously remarked. "They eat every day."[11]

Furthermore, the same technical infrastructure that makes streaming viable as a method of music distribution (music's digitization, the expansion of wireless connectivity, the proliferation of mobile devices) also allows for the accumulation of vast quantities of data: data about music, data about music use, and data about its users. The information gathered can then be exploited in a variety of ways. As a source of competitive advantage among platforms, this information functions as the raw material that fuels the various services platforms offer potential customers, notably those involving the customization of the listening experience (music recommendations, personalized radio stations, exercise playlists that sync to users' gait, and so on). But these data constitute a valuable asset in their own right, one that can be used to attract advertisers or monetized via partnerships with data brokers and other third parties. In either case, the exploitation of data for commercial purposes also alters how music is ordered and listeners are interpellated. With the increased customization of music recommendations and the growth in playlists organized as much by mood or activity as by musical genre, categories and modes of address characteristic of broadcast media (such as radio) or the sale of mass-produced recordings lose some of their rhetorical force. Or perhaps it would be more accurate to say that such modes of address are disavowed, even as they continue to operate in the background. The same may be said for broad classes of music, such as genres and radio formats. These too appear to have been disaggregated into a mass of individual tracks and data points, just as the broad publics convened by mass media and mass-produced commodities have dissolved into a collection of users and user attributes. But the seeming individuation of music on one side and listeners on the other may be more of an ideological effect than anything else. Streaming generalizes music as an aggregation of particulars, at the same time as it hails the public as a series of atomized individuals.[12]

Streaming Music, Streaming Capital seeks to shed light on some of the transformations music has undergone thanks to streaming's ascendancy from the late 2000s to the present. These are changes that have profoundly reordered music's social, technical, aesthetic, and economic bases. Yet simply considering streaming's effects on music would be insufficient without at the same time taking into account music's effects on streaming—in particular, how certain legal forms, social relations, and cultural values embedded in music's governing institutions have shaped the possibilities and limits of this new socioeconomic regime. This dialectic is perhaps most pronounced in chapter 3, which examines how entrenched understandings of music's privileged relation to psychic interiority have informed its use as a means of tracking users' shifting moods, affects, and states of mind. If music is believed to plumb the depths of our souls, then what better resource is there for surveillance capitalists to exploit in their drive to know everything they can about us, both inside and out? Nor is music's use as a technology of surveillance the only instance in which the imprint of musical discourses, practices, and traditions may be discerned. Other examples include practices of playlisting inherited from radio and other broadcast media; the persistence of classed and racialized categories in the organization of music's circulation, however disguised or submerged these might be; the bifurcated ontology that has long enacted music as both process and object, service and good; skeuomorphic callbacks to older formats and playback technologies within the design of platform interfaces; the fluid and shifting boundary between what constitutes attentive and distracted modes of listening; conventions surrounding cover songs and the economic logics governing them; the quotidian use of music for therapeutic purposes; and the obduracy of musical time—both the time of its creation and the time of its reception—in the face of social acceleration. These are but a few of the conventions, practices, and discourses that have shaped streaming, even as these have been transvalued in turn by this new model of musical distribution.

A New Political Economy of Music

What streaming *does to* music, then, is shaped by what music *does for* streaming. That music mediates streaming as much as streaming mediates music is a premise that guides this book. But as important as this mutual mediation may be, as both a real process and methodological principle, attention to the interplay of streaming and music should not lead us to ignore the ground on which it unfolds. This is the ground constituted by capitalism in its current stage of development. Important in this respect is the way in which the ascendancy of digital platforms (and the tech sector more generally) represents a response to the crises that have afflicted the capitalist world-system since the 1970s and that have intensified since the financial crisis of 2008: a long-run tendency toward stagnation; declining rates of productivity and profitability; and a drying-up of attractive sites of private investment. While digital technologies and recourse to so-called multisided markets may abet platform capitalists in their efforts to break out of this economic impasse, what is critical is the broader strategy of accumulation that these technologies and models advance. Following Brett Christophers, one might describe it as an approach that prioritizes "making money by having" over "making money by doing."[13] The platform, by this account, is both a symptom of and force for the consolidation of monopoly power in recent years, which has enabled the extraction of monopoly rents to flourish in its wake.[14] In standard models of capitalist development, promulgated by economists on the right as well as the left, rent and rentiers are typically regarded as residual holdovers from a precapitalist, feudal past. Capitalism, we are told, displaced the source of value from land productivity to labor productivity. As this new mode of production developed, the manufacture of goods and services became the principal site for the accumulation of capital, with the surplus generated by labor captured by those who own the means of production, that is, the capitalist class. Such narratives overlook a key fact: while it may have been in the interest of capitalism as a system to promote market competition, it has always been in the interest of individual capitalists to minimize competition as much as possible, to dominate markets rather than compete in them. As Immanuel Wallerstein puts it: "Capitalists do not want competition, but monopoly. They seek to accumulate capital not via profit but via rent. They want not to be bourgeois but to be aristocrats."[15] This drive is all the more pronounced in an era such as ours. With growth sluggish and opportunities for profitable investment diminishing, accumulation through production (of goods, services, value) looks less and less attractive compared to accumulation by other means—above all through the redistribution of wealth that control over scarce resources affords.

Helping this epochal shift along has been a suite of policies that have been pursued under the banner of neoliberalism: the deregulation of business and financial activity, the weakening of labor protections, the lowering of barriers to trade and the international flow of capital, the relaxation of antitrust enforcement, the strengthening of intellectual property regimes, and monetary policies that have fueled speculative bubbles and asset-price inflation, among others. Despite championing free, competitive markets in theory, in practice neoliberal policy has had the opposite effect. By removing obstacles to competition, both within and across nation-states, neoliberalism has encouraged the concentration of economic and political power at a global scale, ushering in a new era of transnational monopoly capitalism.[16] For illustration of this tendency, one need look no further than the music industry, which has undergone a series of consolidations since the 1990s. In the United States, the loosening of ownership caps occasioned by the Telecommunications Act of 1996 resulted in a wave of acquisitions, with numerous local radio stations coming under the control of conglomerates such as Cumulus and Clear Channel (later rebranded iHeartMedia). Similarly, the Federal Trade Commission's 2010 decision to green-light the merger of Live Nation and Ticketmaster meant that within ten years' time the new company had come to dominate a number of interlinked markets (ticketing, concert promotion, talent management, venue management).[17] Meanwhile, at a global level, mergers and acquisitions within the recording industry led to a further tightening of the oligopoly that has long dominated the sector, with the five major labels in existence in the late 1990s whittled down to just three twenty years on. The same is true of music publishing, whose market by the end of the 2010s was largely divided among four firms (Sony/ATV, Universal, Kobalt, and Warner/Chappell).[18]

The rise of digital platforms is another expression of the broader trend toward monopolization and rent extraction. Perhaps this is putting it too mildly; better would be to say that platformization is not just an expression but the leading edge of this tendency. Tellingly, the principal representatives of platform capitalism—major tech firms such as Amazon, Google, and Facebook, as well as streaming services like Spotify and Netflix—have also become the main representatives of concentrated corporate power in the years since the 2008 financial crisis, with each occupying a dominant position in its respective market. What these companies share in common is ownership over some virtual space where different kinds of social and commercial transactions take place.

Like other monopolists, the exclusive control those companies enjoy over a given asset means that they are in a position to obtain superprofits via the rents they can charge for its access or use. This is evidently the case with tech giants such as Google and Amazon, which rank among the world's most profitable companies. But it is also true of a company such as Spotify, despite the fact it has seldom turned a profit in all the years it has been in operation. Spotify's problem is that its monopoly is built on the back of another, as the rents it charges users for its services are invariably consumed by other rents it is obliged to pay—namely those demanded by rights holders, to license use of the valuable asset that is music. Spotify's saving grace is that it has been kept afloat by still other forms of rent, generated by a different class of assets—namely those held by investment banks, private equity, institutional investors, and other representatives of finance capital.

While recourse to new forms of monopoly power and rent extraction represent one response to the declining growth and stagnation that has characterized the capitalist world-system since the 1970s, it is not the only one. A second response—one that is critical to the arguments traced in this book—involves the increasing expropriation of resources, use values, and forms of work not of capital's making, but that nonetheless prove useful to it. Helpful for understanding this dynamic are the "nonreductive account[s] of capitalist production" that have been developed over the decades by Marxist feminists, ecosocialists, theorists of racial capitalism, and other heterodox thinkers and activists.[19] Critical is their contention that capitalism, despite appearances to the contrary, is marked by incompleteness, inconsistency, and a disavowed dependence on a variety of outsides.[20] Julie Graham and Katherine Gibson, writing jointly under the pseudonym J. K. Gibson-Graham, have observed for instance how the hegemony enjoyed by "capitalocentric" discourses ends up rendering non- or extracapitalist forms of economic activity invisible:

> When we say that most economic discourse is "capitalocentric," we mean that other forms of economy (not to mention noneconomic aspects of social life) are often understood primarily with reference to capitalism: as being fundamentally the same as (or modeled upon) capitalism, or as being deficient or substandard imitations; as being opposite to capitalism; as being the complement of capitalism; as existing in capitalism's space or orbit.[21]

Capitalism may be dominant, but that doesn't mean it is all-encompassing. The capitalist economy is neither coextensive with society as a whole, nor with the "economy," to the extent that this domain can be analytically separated from the various fields of activity with which it is entangled. Existing alongside a number of alternative regimes of exchange, circulation, and valuation, capitalist processes nevertheless outweigh and always threaten to absorb these alternatives.

Significantly, the relation between the capitalist economy and its various noncapitalist others is not one of inert and indifferent coexistence. Rather, the two continually interact and inflect one another, their relation shifting from one historic conjuncture to the next. An increasingly common shape this relation takes is for resources generated *outside* capitalism to furnish the stuff out of which monopoly power *within* it is made. Given declining opportunities for productive investment, an attractive (because cheap) method for establishing a monopoly is to identify some source of work or wealth standing outside the formal economy, lay claim to it (which usually involves getting state power to recognize and enforce this claim), and thereby transform this resource into an asset over which a given corporation has exclusive control. One can see this process play out in the exploitation of natural resources, as state concessions enable extractive industries to turn the "free gifts" of nature into durable sources of rent. It also plays out in connection with creative activity, including music, as intellectual property law enables the copyright industries to turn the "free gifts" of human nature into equally durable sources of rent. Still another place where this extractivist dynamic is at play in streaming is in the data that platforms capture from user interactions, thanks to the terms and conditions to which individuals are obliged to assent to use their services. Once harvested, such data become yet another valuable asset over which platforms enjoy a monopoly, which they can then share, trade, sell, rent, or exploit as they see fit.

Yet this is not the only way capitalism and its others relate to one another. Critically, capital doesn't simply colonize its others. Nor does it simply dominate them. Dominant and dominating capital may be; but it is also *dependent*. Thus, while it is important to remain clear-eyed about the central role that capital accumulation plays in ordering social life, it is equally important to situate this overarching imperative vis-à-vis the extraeconomic conditions on which it relies. As Nancy Fraser has argued, the "'economic foreground' of capitalist society requires a 'non-economic background,'" with processes of social reproduction, the work of nonhuman nature, and the infrastructures provided by political institutions figuring prominently among the underlying conditions that make capital accumulation possible in the first place.[22] Without a continuous supply of ecosystem services, institutional supports, and the unpaid work of caring, capital's incessant drive to valorize value would come to a standstill. But because the resources that capital draws from outside itself and puts to work are treated simply as given, there is a tendency for the extracapitalist systems on which it depends to be steadily run down. Fraser summarizes the dynamic: "Capitalism's economy . . . stands in a relation of *denial* vis-à-vis its background conditions. It disavows its dependence on them by treating nature, social reproduction, and public power as 'free gifts,' which are inexhaustible, possess no (monetized) value, and can be appropriated ad infinitum without any concern for replenishment. . . . And that is a built-in source of potential instability, a recipe for periodic crises."[23] To be underlined is that these and other background conditions are not simply given but are themselves made—and, more specifically, made background. If they are external to capitalism, it is because they are externalized by capitalism. By this account, the capitalist law of value is not simply a mechanism of incorporation, which fundamentally alters that on which it acts (via commodification, the transformation of labor processes, the subjection of all sorts of things to the property form, and so on). It is also a mechanism of abjection, which likewise alters that on which it acts (via depreciation, expropriation, dispossession, and so on).

A basic claim I make in this book is that music is not simply transformed into yet another good, service, or asset within modern capitalist economies. While certain of music's material embodiments can be, have been, and will continue to be commodified and assetized, music at the same time functions as yet another "'non-economic' background condition" that the economy relies on, without acknowledging or accounting for this reliance. Music's excorporation from capitalism is as important as its incorporation, its decommodification as important as its commodification. Music's significance for capital, in other words, does not reside wholly in the brute fact that it, too, is something that can be produced for sale on the market or that can be transformed into an asset for which rents may be charged. Rather, music's significance resides as much in its ability to serve as an extraeconomic resource. And one of the main tasks for which music qua resource is enrolled is the necessary yet systemically devalued work of social reproduction. I explore this issue in chapter 5, but for now social reproduction may be provisionally defined as comprising all those activities and processes that, by sustaining life on a daily and intergenerational basis, indirectly help to sustain capitalism, by replenishing the special commodity that is labor power. In music sociology, the aspect of social reproduction that has received the most attention to date consists of the various forms of class and social stratification that music helps inscribe and reinforce.[24] But given that music is nonrepresentational as well as representational, acting just as much on an affective and physiological level as it does at the level of meaning or identity, it may also play a more direct role in the work of care, as a tool for adjusting moods, facilitating social interactions, calibrating sleep cycles, extending or intensifying workouts, and so forth. Like other resources put to work in the reproduction of individuals and communities, music also serves as a resource for their reproduction as a source of labor power. This has long been the case with respect to manual labor, with music not just serving to coordinate and energize physically strenuous activities but also helping people unwind, relax, and replenish themselves at the end of the day. But considering the increasing centrality of affective, communicative, and other forms of so-called immaterial labor in deindustrializing societies, as the economic center of gravity shifts from manufacture to services, there is the additional need for individuals' affective, communicative, and cognitive energies to be continuously replenished—a need that music, with its ability to alter moods, facilitate interaction, and focus the mind, is well-positioned to satisfy.

Like capitalism's other others, music stands in a profoundly ambivalent relation to the economy, being situated at once inside and outside its frontiers, continuously drawn into and expelled from its churning vortex—whence the well-founded perception that music, like other art forms, represents an "economic exception," or possesses its own "exceptional economy."[25] Historically, a number of factors have impeded music's unproblematic subjection to the logic of capital accumulation. For one, the property form isn't straightforwardly applicable to music in the same way it is to other ordinary products, like a bolt of linen or a pound of wheat. For another, it is difficult to reorganize musical labor—or any other form of artistic labor—in line with capitalism's drive to increase productivity (in Marxian terms, artistic labor resists "real subsumption"). From this perspective, the history of music's insertion into processes of capital accumulation is the history of the social, legal, and technical fixes that have been devised to surmount these difficulties, reducing music's economic ambivalence enough to make it compatible with the demands of capital accumulation. Copyright offers one such fix: as a legal apparatus that imposes the property form on music, it makes what might otherwise take the form of a public good behave like a private one instead.[26] Technologies of mechanical reproduction offer another. True, they may fatally undermine the "aura" that shrouds the unique artwork, as Walter Benjamin famously maintained.[27] But these same technologies also make it possible to achieve efficiencies in the industrial process of musical reproduction that are otherwise ruled out in the artisanal processes of musical production. And even if these and other "fixes" to music's economic exceptionality prove only partly successful, the broader social and aesthetic values that are attached to music can nonetheless drive the development of other adjacent sites and activities that are productive of economic value (instrument manufacture, consumer electronics, publishing, the production and sale of ancillary merchandise, and so on).[28]

Streaming may likewise be understood as providing a solution to the challenges posed by music's ambivalent economic status, challenges that have been amplified by technologies of digital reproduction and networked communication. It is not just that sales of recorded music plummeted in the first decade of the new millennium, but that this downturn appeared to augur a pair of broader and potentially catastrophic crises: in the property form imposed on music by means of copyright and, by extension, in the continued viability of recorded music's commodity status. To shore up their faltering position during this prolonged downturn, major record labels pursued a number of avenues: claiming a cut of artists' earnings from touring and merchandise as part of "360 deals"; increased sync licensing of music for use in television and film; seeking out new sites of commodification (for example, ringtone sales); and most notoriously, bringing lawsuits against listeners alleged of copyright infringement, in order to disincentivize file sharing.[29] It was in this context that streaming emerged in the late 2000s as a potential response to the industry's purported woes. Streaming presented an answer to a number of unresolved questions plaguing the industry: how to reprivatize audio files that digitization had transformed into quasi-public goods; how to reintroduce into the new, digitally mediated condition of musical abundance a semblance of scarcity; how to turn difficulties in commodifying digital music from a problem into an advantage, by using music to commodify other things instead; and how to transform payment for recorded music from an irregular, unpredictable, and one-off event into something continuous and predictable. Yet streaming's success in overcoming impediments to digital music's reinsertion into the circuit of capital introduced a new set of problems and contradictions. Perhaps the most notable has to do with the infinitesimal royalty payments recording artists, composers, and songwriters receive under this new model, a cause of much public concern and critique. Of course, one might respond to critiques like these by pointing out that the financial situation of most musicians was hardly much better in the prestreaming, predigital music industry. If nothing else, such a response has the merit of being true. But to say that what has changed are the mechanisms by which musicians are underpaid, with the fact of their underpayment remaining a stubborn constant, shouldn't lead us to believe that this state of affairs is inevitable, that the skewed distribution of wealth and economic power that typifies music under capitalism is an eventuality to which we have no choice but to be resigned. Nor is this the only harm that streaming either produces or perpetuates. We might also cite its recourse to rampant consumer surveillance; its disaggregation of listening publics and music communities; its exacerbation of winner-take-all dynamics, with superstars gaining outsize attention and income at the expense of smaller, independent artists; and, not least of all, the negative environmental impacts generated by such a resource- and energy-intensive method of music consumption.[30] The cost of cheap and abundant music, it turns out, is quite high.

Mapping the Streaming Ecosystem

Since music streaming platforms are many different things, this book touches on a wide range of subjects over the course of its pages: soundalikes, metadata errors, interface design, clickwork, network architectures, sleep playlists, streaming fraud, recommendation algorithms, and listening metrics, to name but a few. Given the eclecticism of the topics covered, the materials I draw on are equally eclectic, encompassing marketing and promotional materials put out by streaming companies; coverage of music platforms in the business press, trade journals, and mass media outlets; data gleaned from application programming interfaces (APIs) and other backend sources; comments and discussions on community forums; earnings reports and financial disclosure statements; leaked contracts; patents; information gathered from the various ancillary markets that feed into—and off—digital music services (data aggregation, music distribution, promotion services of varying degrees of legitimacy, and so on); playlist formatting and design; "platformized" musical production (for example, pseudopersonalized tracks or soundalike covers); as well as insights derived from conversations, casual and otherwise, that I've had over the years with former and current employees of streaming services, record industry personnel, musicians, users, data analysts, and activists, among others.

The foregoing should give some sense of the empirical base on which *Streaming Music, Streaming Capital* rests, an archive supplemented by the growing body of secondary literature on streaming that I have drawn on and learned a great deal from in the course of writing this book.[31] But if I range across a wide and variegated assortment of materials and topics in what follows, it isn't in order to revel in eclecticism for its own sake. Rather, an overriding aim of this book is to trace the mediations connecting seemingly disconnected phenomena, in an effort to discern the underlying conditions that make their movements possible. To a certain extent, this impulse follows from my background and training as a music theorist, even if the kind of theorizing I pursue in this book bears little resemblance to music theory as it is commonly understood. It also follows from my commitment to a broadly Marxist understanding of the musical economy, albeit one that draws on a wide and varied mix of traditions (social reproduction theory, Frankfurt School critical theory, value-form theory, autonomist Marxism, ecosocialist thought, as well as more standard forms of Marxist political economy). But most important of all, the expansive approach I take to streaming derives from a decisive feature of the platform economy itself. Namely, as economic power has become ever more concentrated in the hands of an ever-smaller tranche of corporate bodies over the past twenty-odd years—a tendency of which platforms are both a cause and effect—the boundaries that once separated ostensibly distinct spaces and sectors (finance, tech, the music industries, and so on) have perforce eroded. Of course, the more such sectoral differences are blurred, the more it becomes clear that their prior delineation wasn't necessary but contingent, a product of the resistance thrown up by forces strong enough to hold back or even reverse capital's drive toward concentration (government regulation, interfirm competition, inherited custom, but above all labor struggles). But even if capitalism's drive to subsume anything and everything under the sun is hardly new, this makes it all the more necessary for studies of music streaming—or of music and capitalism more generally—to avoid restricting themselves to *just* music, or *just* the music industry, as the latter is conventionally construed. At least, these studies cannot limit themselves in this way if they wish to do justice to the way music is imbricated in socioeconomic processes that extend well beyond its conventional boundaries. Indeed, this is one of the key insights shared by both social reproduction theory and ecosocialist thought: that objects, activities, and forces ostensibly placed beyond the pale of a given socioeconomic system are often necessary to secure this system's ongoing existence, shaping what transpires within its legislated boundaries in profound if indirect ways.

For this reason, any effort to model music's insertion into the streaming ecosystem needs to consider its "material and technological enabling conditions."[32] But such an effort also has to explore the material conditions that music enables in turn. For once it is taken up and mediated by digital platforms, music can have effects in sites far removed from the server farms whence audio files issue, the devices on which these files are played back, or the bodies they touch once they are translated into sound waves. Kyle Devine has identified one such effect, describing the largely disregarded (because largely externalized) environmental impacts for which streaming is responsible (greenhouse gas emissions, destructive forms of resource extraction, and so on). To this distant, dispersed impact others may be added. One concerns how users' seemingly solitary listening activity may indirectly shape what musics others will encounter, which in turn determines how much compensation artists and rights holders are liable to receive. Another concerns how the data collected from platforms about people's listening behaviors may be recycled by third parties and put to use for purposes that seem to have little clear or direct connection to music as such (for example, credit card ratings and insurance pricing). Still another concerns how the use of music as a means of social reproduction may serve as a means of holding in check the costs of sustaining both life and labor power. And yet another concerns how this enactment of music as a form of cheap care hinges in turn on suppressing the cost of music—which is tantamount to suppressing the cost of musical labor. Pertinent in this regard is an arresting observation Martin Daughtry has made in connection to the far-flung environmental effects for which music performance may be responsible. "While all performances begin," Daughtry writes, "no performances truly end; rather, they all taper off, in an asymptotic decrescendo of sorts, as the various bodies that they manipulate and transform and unleash eternally continue to make pathways through—and exert effects within—the aggregate body called 'environment.'"[33] The same may be said of music as streamed, with the difference that the real and virtual bodies it sets in motion make pathways that do not just traverse those ecosystems conventionally categorized as non- or extrahuman but move through all sorts of nominally human ecosystems as well, whether economic, technological, social, infrastructural, or musical.

Despite the expansive range of issues addressed in this book, despite the attempt to trace the often obscure interconnections linking them, *Streaming Music, Streaming Capital* doesn't purport to provide a comprehensive account of the streaming ecosystem. To attempt such a thing would be quixotic, since any totalizing theory of streaming—or of anything else, for that matter—will necessarily come undone under pressure of future developments. In the case of streaming, barring a major, systemic change to the economy, either the industry will adapt in coming years to heightened interfirm competition, government regulation, ecological crisis, inflationary pressures, and intensifying labor activism, or the industry will fail. And assuming it does adapt, this will almost certainly involve the colonization of new spaces and the forging of new interconnections between them, beyond those I identify in the pages of this book. Indeed, as multisided markets, platforms are precisely in the business of forging such interconnections, striving to leverage them to their benefit through the opportunities for arbitrage they open up.

Hence, in light of the fluid and still-unfolding character of my book's subject, the best I can hope to offer readers is a rough and provisional sketch, one that seeks to identify a number of the streaming ecosystem's key interlocking features and that endeavors to make some sense of the logic underpinning their articulation. Some of these features and interconnections include how copyright monopolies at once underwrite streaming (via licensing agreements) and depend on it (for the protection and valorization of their IP); how the ideological construction of the stream, its framing as something necessarily ephemeral, obscures the constitutive role of copyright; how the ideological work performed by the ostensible ephemerality of the stream helps bind users as well as artists to platforms; how the different user groups convened by platforms not only function as assets but are also put to work to produce still other assets, most notably data (about music, about users); how the personalized curation services used to justify extensive data collection are paralleled by the promise made to advertisers of providing equally personalized forms of ad targeting; how the economic imperative to amass data leads platforms to frame music as an accessory for living, a means for self- and social reproduction; how entreaties that seek to get users to treat music as such—as a resource for the ongoing reproduction of life and labor power—are facilitated by the way the platform model effectively transforms music into a privatized public good, as something that can be given away on condition users have first paid an obligatory toll; how this strategic and above all partial decommodification of music has as its corollary the effective decommodification of musical labor; and so on. To these may be added the ramifying interconnections that relate what takes place in and around platforms to broader forces beyond them: how the rentierism that underpins both platforms' and copyright holders' business models is motivated by the declining profitability of the global economy in recent decades; how platforms, through their data collection practices, function as tributaries to a much broader data economy; how the transformation of music into a means of social reproduction is facilitated by the steady rise of the cost of care elsewhere in the economy; and so on.

Each chapter of this book addresses a different piece of this larger puzzle. Chapter 1, "Streaming Music," begins with the question of what streaming makes of music. To explore how platforms transform music to make it fit for streaming, chapter 1 draws on the mediation theory elaborated by Georgina Born and others in order to examine some of the key mediations that platforms put into play. Streaming services enact music as many different things: as data, metadata, intellectual property, and much else besides. Taken together, this constellation of features conspires to make what is ultimately a change in music's political and economic condition appear otherwise, as if it were a change in its being imposed by a novel technological system. Stream versus download, object versus event, music as good versus music as service—such commonplace dichotomies, which undergird popular narratives about the changes wrought by streaming, deflect attention away from a more significant mutation for which music platforms are responsible: the transformation of digital copies from durable to disposable goods, a transformation that exploits digital reproduction's enactment of recorded music as a quasi-public good at one level to paradoxically reinscribe music within the regime of private property at another.

Chapter 2, "Streaming Capital," turns to the specific form of industrial organization that music platforms embody—what the business literature refers to as "multisided markets"—and considers the implications this form has for the value accorded to both music and musical labor. Thanks to the particular way in which platforms orchestrate flows of data, attention, and revenue, music comes to assume a peculiar economic status within the spaces that streaming services manage. As noted earlier, users of streaming platforms never pay directly for music; all they pay for is access to the virtual enclosure where a vast archive of recorded music is housed.[34] Yet the decommodification music undergoes once it is no longer stamped by exchange value appears this way only on one side of the platform, the side that faces end users. For other agents, situated on other sides of streaming's multisided market—record labels, publishers, as well as platforms themselves—music remains thoroughly commodified. The ambivalent status that the architecture of platforms confers on music, being neither wholly commodified nor wholly decommodified, in turn gives rise to a peculiar form of fetishism: not commodity fetishism but what might be called noncommodity fetishism, in which what is misrecognized is not the source of the value that is ascribed to a commodity but the source of the nonvalue that is ascribed to a noncommodity—in this case, music. On streaming platforms, music appears as simply *there*, as something that is free for the taking—provided, of course, that users have paid a fee to access the privatized space where music is now contained.

If the first two chapters provide a broad overview of streaming platforms and their organization, chapters 3 and 4 turn to the individual circuits of production, exchange, and accumulation that they catalyze. Chapter 3, "Music as a Technology of Surveillance," is concerned with the exchanges that take place between platforms and an assortment of advertisers, data brokers, and other third parties. Especially among stand-alone services such as Spotify, Deezer, and Pandora (both before and after its acquisition by Sirius XM), the need to develop alternative means of extracting value from customers has led them to aggressively assetize user attention and data. Marketing campaigns directed not to end consumers but to prospective advertisers and investors are particularly revealing in this regard. What these campaigns highlight are the particular affordances that music alone possesses. Not only is music said to provide privileged insight into listeners' innermost selves, but it also serves as an ideal tracking device. By pervading the everyday lives of listeners, accompanying them across a variety of social and physical spaces, music offers platforms and the third parties with whom they partner a means by which information about listeners' everyday lives may be collected, aggregated, and put to work. Significant in this regard is the growing popularity of playlists organized by mood, activity, or context (for example, music for workouts, for singing to in the shower, for sleep). Playlists of this type provide platforms with a proxy by which they can infer users' moods, activities, and contexts. And even if the accuracy of such inferences is questionable, music's use as a technology of surveillance nevertheless has far-reaching consequences. It is not merely that this affords a microtargeting of advertising that runs parallel to the microtargeting that characterizes music recommendation. In addition, the fact that platforms share such data with various third-party partners, including major data aggregators such as WPP and Acxiom, means that the information that platforms collect not just about users' musical behaviors but by means of their musical behaviors may feed algorithmic systems in far-flung sectors of the economy (credit rating, insurance pricing, risk assessment, and so on).

In chapter 4, "Counterfeiting Attention in the Streaming Economy," the focus shifts to another side of platforms' multisided markets, the side that faces artists. In particular, the chapter examines how the technical infrastructures and economic incentives put in place by streaming platforms have encouraged certain actors to develop strategies to exploit various quirks and loopholes of this new mode of music distribution, leveraging them to their advantage. These include musicians, who, in response to platforms' low payout rates, have been compelled to use whatever means they can to eke out whatever income they can. Three cases in particular are considered. One concerns so-called musical spam, in particular knockoff cover versions of popular hits, which exploit weaknesses in platforms' discovery tools to siphon off a portion of the attention (and royalties) that the originals would otherwise attract. A second concerns so-called click fraud, as rights holders aim to improve the "discoverability" of the music they own and ultimately the share of revenue they are due by resorting to alternative means of procuring streams—in particular, by purchasing them in bulk from gig workers and click farms located in the Global South. Finally, the third case study examines the controversy that erupted in 2017, when it was revealed that Spotify had paid professional music producers, working under pseudonyms, to create tracks for the platform's mood and activity playlists, presumably as a way of reducing the overall share of revenue it was obliged to share with rights holders (above all the three major labels). Together, the different kinds of imposture at play in these three cases shed light on a more fundamental imposture that underpins the entire streaming economy, as platforms pass off quantitative metrics as qualitative judgments, and equate digital signals with the engagement they allegedly index.

Following the examination of different aspects of the platform model in chapters 3 and 4, the last chapter, "Streaming, Cheap Music, and the Crises of Social Reproduction," takes a broader view of streaming and its socioeconomic impacts. Chapter 5 does so by returning to the increasing prominence of mood-, activity-, and context-based playlists on streaming platforms. Much has been written on the effects of such playlists. For some authors they are the agents by which music is transformed into "neo-Muzak"; for others, they are nothing more than an extension of long-standing practices that treat music as a medium for self-regulation and self-care. This chapter offers an alternative perspective on this phenomenon, reading it through the lens of social reproduction theory. Besides being a technology of the self or of surveillance, music on streaming platforms is in addition a technology of social reproduction. It acts, in other words, as a tool or resource by which users can perform some of the tasks necessary to maintain themselves and others—work that is, at one and the same time, necessary to maintain both themselves and others as sources of labor power. Framed in this way, as a device for helping people to get through the day, music also serves as one of the many devices that prepares them to go to work the next. Facilitating this change in music's use value for listeners is the partial decommodification it undergoes on streaming platforms, discussed in chapter 2. As a form of "cheap culture," streaming media are made particularly attractive as a resource for managing the deepening crisis of social reproduction, a crisis brought on by the rising cost of care work on the one hand and the increasing shifting of these costs onto individuals and households as a result of neoliberal austerity politics on the other. Yet the more platforms frame music as a resource for living, the more the living of musicians is threatened. Cheap music, after all, depends on a cheapening of musical labor. The result is a crisis of reproduction specific to the world of music, with many musicians no longer able to support themselves through their music, which more often than not amounts to an inability to reproduce themselves as musicians.

To close, the epilogue to the book picks up where the preceding chapter leaves off, by considering different interventions that have been proposed in response to the difficulties many musicians and music communities confront at present. To this end, I work through a number of proposals, ranging from the more modest to the more far-reaching: increasing the minimum payout rates guaranteed to artists, changing the revenue-sharing model utilized by services, developing platform cooperatives, and transforming platforms into public utilities, to name a few. Which of these is preferable, as well as which is feasible, depends on the broader field of political possibility and the balance of forces within this field—which is simply another way of saying that any meaningful transformation of the music economy cannot occur in isolation but must be tied to broader transformations in the economy as a whole. But which path or paths are to be pursued also depends on what kind of future we want. Is the goal a reformed streaming economy? A poststreaming economy? Or a postprecarity and postscarcity musical economy, a possibility that is hard to imagine without it being a postcapitalist economy at the same time?

Chapter One

Streaming Music

Streaming platforms, we are often told, owe their growth since 2010 to the convenient, near-instantaneous, and frictionless access to music they provide. To the extent this is true, it is ironic that the first thing prospective users encounter on downloading a service's app is not music but a barrier. Rarely can audio files be streamed straightaway. Hindering access is a sign-up page, an obligatory point of passage for anyone wishing to use a service. Such pages serve at least two functions. First, they compel users to create an account and thus enter into an economic and legal relationship with the platform. Second, they present a variety of entreaties to do exactly that—to sign up for the service whose use they impede.

A common feature of such appeals is their maximalist rhetoric. The Indian-based platform JioSaavn, for instance, boasts that it will deliver "All Your Music," while Tidal—launched by Jay-Z and other artist-investors in 2015—qualifies this claim, promising "All Your Favorite Music."[1] Such assertions are not new. The service Rdio, which operated from 2010 until going bankrupt in 2015, announced it would provide "all the songs you want," while the subscription-based service MOG (2009–2014) offered "Unlimited Music on Demand." Supporting such claims are the size of platform catalogs. By the end of 2022, Amazon and Apple Music professed to have more than 100 million titles in their databases, Spotify 90 million, and JioSaavn approximately 80 million.[2]

The all-inclusive, all-embracing experience streaming platforms say they provide is not just a matter of catalog size. Comprehensiveness is defined qualitatively as well as quantitatively. This is clear from the tagline that announced the launch of Apple Music's streaming service in 2015: "All the ways you love music. All in one place" (see figure 1.1).[3] Nor do services stop at aggregating audio files, seeking to aggregate listening subjects as well. In late 2019, for instance, Spotify's pitch to first-time visitors centered as much on listeners as what they listen to: "Music for Everyone. Millions of Songs." Time and space are likewise spanned by such universalizing appeals. Almost every site features some variant of the now-standard trope of making music available to listeners "anytime, anywhere."[4] In the case of Pandora, this trope is invoked via an image of unfettered mobility: "Take your music with you wherever you go."[5] In the case of the French platform Deezer, the prospect of music consumption without end is cast as a kind of ersatz companionship ("Always with you").[6]

Together, these solicitations paint a picture of a world in which every song or piece of music is accessible to everybody, all the time, everywhere. The language they speak is one of absolutes, their lexicon populated by words like "all," "every," and "always." Within this discursive frame, streaming is the means by which this experience of repleteness can be obtained. "Everything Music": such is the way Nigerian-based service Boomplay puts it.[7] Granted, exceptions to such exaggerated claims are easy to find. For starters, the nominally comprehensive libraries of streaming services are still riddled with gaps, especially in connection with older recordings or musics that stand on the margins of the record industry. In addition, claims to universal access are belied by the actually existing barriers—social, technical, and economic—limiting such access. What these claims presuppose without acknowledging is the existence of network infrastructures having

1.1 Apple Music advertisement (2015)

sufficient bandwidth to support streaming and ownership of devices such as smartphones, to say nothing of a dependable electrical grid.[8] Nor are streaming services as free and frictionless as they present themselves to be. As profit-seeking enterprises, streaming platforms, through their demand for payment—whether in money or attention—transform what is ostensibly unrestricted access to music into something conditional and economically contingent. Discrimination in access to goods and services on the basis of ability to pay may be so ubiquitous under capitalism that it has become second nature. But it remains a form of discrimination nevertheless.

Such limitations call into question the promise streaming platforms make of a musical experience unburdened by any limits whatsoever. Yet because these are all external limits, contingent rather than necessary, they hold out the possibility of eventually being surmounted. More tracks can always be added, internet access can always be expanded, and so on. In this, streaming encapsulates a dynamic characteristic of capitalism more broadly, its need for a "barrier in order to constitute itself as infinitely expanding."[9] Yet there is another, more intractable limit that streaming confronts. The guarantee of providing users with "all the music, all the time" (as an early Spotify advertisement put it) runs up against the fact that an audio stream is scarcely all that music is or can be. Helpful in this connection is Georgina Born's observation that music is "the paradigmatic multiply-mediated, immaterial and material, fluid quasi-object, in which subjects and objects collide and intermingle."[10] A stream is but one of the many media through which music may be embodied, circulated, and experienced, alongside live performances, sheet music, MIDI files, earworms, vinyl records, and half-remembered snatches of tunes, among others. And no less than the music it mediates, a stream is likewise a "multiply-mediated, immaterial and material, fluid quasi-object." Streaming's mediation of music is shaped by the particular constellation of mediations that constitute streaming in turn.

If platforms are to render music in the form of a stream, in other words, they must also render it as other things besides: as property, as data, as metadata, as something interfaced (and as an interface itself). In this chapter, I examine these different mediations in turn. Each has its own history and logic, as well as its own distinctive set of sociomaterial possibilities and constraints—which means that streaming's establishment as a technology, economic model, and cultural form hasn't been the outcome of a single, linear process. Rather, it has resulted from the confluence of a number of distinct yet entangled developments. Some of these developments platforms helped to catalyze. Most, however, were the product of longer-term and larger-scale transformations that platforms have either benefited from or opportunistically seized on.

To make streaming a viable alternative to both file sharing and MP3 sales, then, platforms have had to accomplish a number of things:

- secure licenses from rights owners
- develop or obtain access to infrastructures capable of supporting the near-instantaneous transfer of audio files
- ensure files were labeled and indexed with sufficient accuracy to permit their location and retrieval
- design interfaces that disguised their mediation of music just enough to create the illusion of immediate, frictionless access
- persuade users that streaming necessarily involves a form of real-time data transmission, leaving no durable trace in its wake

Many of the mediations through which music passes en route to becoming a stream aren't new or unique to streaming. To take one example, the rendering of music as data has a history that stretches back through the MP3 and other compression formats to the audio files that were first written onto compact discs in the 1980s—and, before that, to developments in pulse code modulation in decades prior. What has changed with streaming is which mediations in particular are articulated with one another and how they are combined. Furthermore, while the resulting assemblage may be messy, heterogeneous, and multimodal—and this in spite of the sleek facade that most platforms project—there is a logic and intentionality governing the different, partial aspects of music that platforms cobble together. If streaming formats music in a particular way, it is chiefly to make the online circulation of music feel fluid and seamless, even while it remains highly regulated and constrained. Access to music is to appear as "frictionless" as possible. Yet this is only to be the case within the virtual space of the platform, whose boundaries are guarded by forms of technical and legal "friction" that services strive to uphold (as evinced by the sign-up pages discussed at the opening of this chapter). Thus, the different moments I examine over the course of this chapter can all be seen as working together to maintain this precarious balance between a vivid experience of immediacy and limitlessness, and an obscure(d) reality of withdrawal and limitation. Data networks allow music to be separated from users and stored remotely, while the networks' architecture works to collapse this distance and hence the lag between file request and delivery. Metadata is hived off from audio data, even as it is appended to the latter with the intention of facilitating its discovery. Shrink-wrap licenses minimize the number of contractual agreements users need to enter into, even as their extensive terms and conditions make this into a change of degree not kind. And interfaces are designed to minimize any extraneous information or controls that might delay musical gratification, even though the interface itself is an insuperable limit that stands between users and the musical abundance that platforms promise.

This chapter, then, considers some key conditions that underpin streaming. By sketching their histories, interrogating their logics, and examining their mutual imbrications, I hope to shed light on what streaming makes of music. If one answer to this question highlights how streaming makes it seem as if music is always there for listeners, ready to hand—despite being increasingly withdrawn, both legally and technically—another concerns the way streaming transforms music from a thing into a flow, from a good into a service. This latter characterization has become part of the conventional wisdom surrounding streaming, which is understandable, since it captures something vital about streaming's peculiar phenomenology. But as I will argue toward the end of this chapter, transformations in music's status that are routinely ascribed to streaming are more apparent than real. The reason is that streaming, in addition to being a technical protocol or business model, is more importantly an ideology. The figure of the stream furnishes a schema that frames people's relation to music, tacitly foreclosing other relations. Within this schema, the stream appears as a fleeting transmission from platform to user, one that dissipates as soon as it is produced and consumed, lending it features typically associated with the economic category of the service rather than the good. Platforms, consequently, assume the guise of service providers, with the real-time, on-demand delivery of streamed music being the principal service they provide. One upshot of this figure is that the stream comes to appear as if it is categorically distinct from more durable formats, such as the digital download. Yet critical interrogation of the stream as both material process and ideological construct tells a different story: one in which the fluid and fleeting character of the stream is not necessary but contingent, its evanescence is due not to technical exigencies but economic imperatives, and the boundary separating stream from download is not crisp but blurred. Indeed, if streaming "works," in the sense of making music readily and immediately accessible to users, the reason is that it often doesn't involve much actual streaming, as this technology is popularly understood. Often, what is passed off as a stream is just a special kind of download: a digital copy that has been designed to be disposable, a "single-use product" whose built-in perishability remakes a good (or thing) in the image of a service (or flow).[11] In this way, the ideology of the stream not only helps to bind users and artists alike to the platform. It also naturalizes this relation of dependency, making it appear as a technological constraint, and not as an expression of economic and political power.

Music as Intellectual Property

Before anything else, music on streaming platforms takes the form of intellectual property. The centrality of rights management to the record industry long predates streaming. Already in 1987 Simon Frith had noted that "for the music industry the age of manufacture is now over," as record companies "are no longer organized around making *things*" but instead "depend on the creation of *rights*."[12] Frith's observation was prescient. It was also premature. The sale of CDs, tapes, and other "old media" remained the core of the record industry's business through the 1990s and into the first decade of the twenty-first century, delaying its transformation from a manufacturing to a copyright industry. Throughout this period, the intellectual property embodied in a song or master recording continued to function primarily as an input to production, a form of fixed capital used in the manufacture of material objects. It was only the development of audio compression formats (such as the MP3) and the subsequent spread of online file sharing circa 2000 that sounded the death knell for the "age of manufacture." And it was only the threat posed to record labels' principal asset—their intellectual property—that made apparent the sector's full-fledged transformation into a copyright industry. The separation of audio files from the containers that hitherto stored them (CDs) revealed the degree to which music's excludability (a precondition for its commodification) had been backstopped by a particular kind of material embodiment. Once this backstop disappeared, the artificial scarcity that copyright law imposes in principle became hard to enforce in practice.

For much of the decade following Napster's debut in 1999, the record industry's response to the threat posed by file sharing was twofold. One involved a technical fix, in the form of digital rights management (DRM), which used code to restrict access and reimpose excludability. The other involved a legal fix, using lawsuits targeting file-sharing sites as well as individual listeners, in an effort to stem both the supply of and demand for illicit MP3s. By the end of the 2000s, the industry had a new target for litigation: music streaming services. Notably, several platforms got their start by making unlicensed content freely available to listeners, a strategy that allowed them to quickly expand their user base and strengthen their position in subsequent negotiations with rights holders. Such was the case, for instance, with Deezer, Grooveshark, Baidu, and—most notably—Spotify.[13] As before, major labels and trade industry groups such as the Recording Industry Association of America (RIAA) and International Federation of the Phonographic Industry (IFPI) pursued aggressive legal actions against these companies, accusing them of infringement. But in contrast to the lawsuits the record industry brought against Napster, Kazaa, and other file-sharing sites earlier in the decade, by 2008 or so, the aim was no longer to shut down platforms. Rather, such actions functioned as leverage in negotiating favorable licensing deals, which typically ended with Sony, Universal, Warner, and EMI each receiving a substantial portion of the revenue generated by platforms, usually along with an ownership stake.[14] As one observer noted in 2008, "[the] companies that are most often rewarded with licenses are the ones that got big on illegal actions.... It's hard to advise entrepreneurs to follow the law because it's unlikely they'll get off the ground."[15]

For streaming services, their main concern early on was securing licensing agreements, considering that the post-2000 downturn in recorded music sales did not fundamentally alter the major labels' continued market dominance. Getting labels on board didn't resolve all of the fledgling streaming industry's licensing issues, however. The reason is that every recording is not just a recording, but a recording of a particular song or composition. Hence, besides obtaining licenses for recordings (master rights), platforms are also obliged to obtain licenses for the underlying compositions (publishing rights). Though the exact percentage varies from one market to the next, generally speaking between a fifth and a quarter of all streaming revenue paid out to rights holders goes to the owners of publishing rights, with the rest going to the owners of the master rights on the recording. This uneven distribution of revenue reflects an uneven distribution of economic power, as the displacement of sheet music by records as the principal medium of music's commodification in the middle decades of the twentieth century ensured the recording sector's ascendancy over the publishing industry (in actuality, the boundary between these two sectors is blurred, given that all three major labels have publishing arms that are equally dominant in the publishing sector—Sony Music Publishing, Universal Music Publishing, Warner/Chappell).

Given this ascendancy of record labels and master rights, streaming services have often treated publishing rights as an afterthought. The result has been a series of lawsuits charging that platforms—Spotify in particular—have failed to secure all the licenses necessary to use songs licitly. In the United States, at least, some relief for these legal troubles was provided by the passage of the Music Modernization Act (MMA) in 2018, which sought to update and simplify an antiquated mechanical licensing system. For songwriters and publishers, the MMA promised a speedier, more efficient, and more reliable system for obtaining payouts from digital music platforms. For platforms, the MMA promised a less complex set of legal hurdles to navigate in clearing licenses. But the legislation offered platforms something equally valuable: safe harbor protection against future copyright infringement claims, retroactive to January 1, 2018.[16] Small wonder, then, that Spotify and other streaming services vigorously lobbied in support of the bill, since it effectively preempted future litigation coming from songwriters and rights holders. Small wonder that the three major labels did as well, since by 2018 the bulk of their revenue was coming from online streaming. And yet the passage of the MMA hasn't brought to an end the legal wrangling around publishing rights. In 2019, Eight Mile Style, LLC, publisher of Eminem's music, filed a suit against Spotify, alleging not only copyright infringement but also that the retroactive shielding of the platform against such claims represented "an unconstitutional taking of Eight Mile's vested property right."[17] Meanwhile, in 2019 Spotify, along with Google, Sirius XM, and Amazon Music, filed an appeal to the 2018 decision of the Copyright Royalty Board (CRB) to raise the statutory rate on mechanical licenses by 44 percent. Unsurprisingly, many artists were incensed by the decision of Spotify et al. to appeal the CRB's ruling, seeing it as an attempt to bolster the earnings of platform operators at the expense of songwriters and composers.[18] Writing on Instagram, songwriter Justin Tranter castigated the platforms in question, noting that "without songs these tech companies [would] have nothing to stream/sell. Shameful."[19]

If music's enactment as intellectual property remains the object of intense economic, legal, and symbolic struggle, much of this struggle takes place in courthouses and conference rooms far removed from the day-to-day experience of end users. In contrast to the battles around file sharing in the aughts, which pitted an oligopolistic music cartel against ordinary listeners, the current tug-of-war pits one set of corporations (tech companies) against another (copyright companies). For listeners, the result is to deflect attention from music's enactment as intellectual property, making it appear as if it were simply there, ready to hand. With platforms assuming responsibility for securing licenses—or dealing with the legal fallout when they fail to do so—users are absolved from having to concern themselves with the niceties of copyright law. The main license addressed to them is the end user license agreement (EULA), which must be accepted before access to most platforms, along with the music they host, will be granted.[20] By contrast, music's mediation by copyright, ubiquitous though it may be, is experienced only indirectly. As a legal infrastructure, copyright exhibits a key feature of all infrastructures, being "only revealed in its moments of breakdown and failure."[21] One might encounter copyright's constraints in the form of a track withdrawn from a site's catalog at the behest of its rights holders or as an invisible limit that restricts what users can do with music. Or one might encounter it in the simple fact of being bound to the platform, unable to remove audio files from the "digital enclosure" that services have erected.

Music as Data

Like music's rendering as intellectual property, its rendering as data has a history that predates the advent of streaming. As Jeremy Wade Morris has observed, many listeners first encountered music as data when the compact disc was launched in the early 1980s, even if its packaging and playback technology ensured that this encounter was indirect: the "CD commodity," he writes, "was only musically digital," being encased in "nondigital packaging."[22] It was only after home computers were transformed into multimedia devices in the late 1980s and 1990s that individuals could directly access the files stored on CDs.[23] By the late 1990s and 2000s the proliferation of compression formats (MP3, AAC, and so on) helped entrench datafied music's place in people's everyday lives, thanks to the necessity of managing the audio files that increasingly populated people's hard drives and mobile devices.

Discussions of music's rendering as digital data usually highlight a cluster of qualities attributed to this change: interactivity, compressibility, acceleration, configurability, replicability, and so on. Streaming platforms avail themselves of many of these attributes of datafied music in one way or another, though they often do so in constrained and attenuated forms. For instance, the manipulability of digital audio that has given rise to various "recombinant" or "configurable" musics (mashups, remixes, and so on) is primarily manifest on streaming services in terms of the potentially endless contextualization and recontextualization to which tracks are subject, as they move in and out of playlists, album track listings, search results, radio feeds, and so forth.[24] What is changeable is not so much tracks themselves but the contexts in which they are heard.[25] A more consequential attribute of datafied music for streaming is its replicability. Just as the speed, ease, and cheapness with which digital audio files can be reproduced helped drive file sharing in the early 2000s, so too have streaming platforms drawn on these same qualities to produce an ostensibly "frictionless" musical experience. No less than file sharing or digital downloads, streaming is fundamentally a technology of digital reproduction. I will expand on this point at the end of the chapter; for now, it is enough to recall that on clicking play, an audio file is copied to a buffer on a user's device. The main difference is that the copy generated tends to be transferred piecemeal, and is stored in the buffer only for a short period of time—often (though not always) for only as long as it takes to play back the track.

Replicability is vital not just for the listener-facing front end of streaming services but for their backend operations as well. Platforms store duplicate copies of the same recording for a number of reasons. One is the need to make tracks available in different file formats, to accommodate different devices and subscription tiers. Tidal's basic tier, for instance, streams audio files encoded using the lossy compression format AAC, while its pricier HiFi tier streams files encoded in the lossless FLAC format (starting in 2017, some of these were also encoded using the proprietary MQA codec for "high-res" audio).[26] More significantly, multiple copies of the same audio file are routinely distributed across the devices and servers that platforms stitch together, to minimize the delay between a file request and the point when enough data has been received to initiate playback. Until 2014, Spotify, for instance, used a peer-assisted architecture, building on the model pioneered by file-sharing sites such as Napster and Kazaa. Users clicking on a song would have their file request satisfied by data drawn from a combination of three sources: the cache of the user's device (if they had recently played the track), the caches of other users' devices (if they, too, had recently played the track), and Spotify's remote servers.[27] Where, exactly, audio data would be pulled from, and in what proportion, were determined by algorithms that calculated which particular configuration would minimize lag.

Other platforms have adopted different setups to reduce the delay between file request and playback. The most common approach forgoes the peer-assisted character of Spotify's pre-2014 architecture, favoring a less "flat" and more hierarchical server-client topology. Here, too, however, audio files are not simply transferred from a data center to a user's device but are assembled from data drawn from a mix of local caches and remote servers. Such is the approach taken by Pandora, Deezer, and Tidal (not to mention Spotify, after it abandoned its peer-assisted model in 2014). Achieving speeds comparable to peer-to-peer networks requires some work-arounds. One is to disperse copies of audio files on server farms spread across the parts of the world where a platform does business.[28] Given its focus on the North American market, for instance, Pandora long relied on a single data cluster in Oakland, California.[29] By contrast, by 2016 Deezer's global ambitions obliged it to operate four data centers across the globe: two in its home country of France, one in the United States, and one in Singapore.[30] Meanwhile, streaming services integrated into larger platforms (such as Amazon Music Unlimited and YouTube) have at their disposal the globe-spanning infrastructures these companies have built out over the years. Nor is it just Amazon's or Google's streaming services that utilize such global infrastructures. By the late 2010s, a number of stand-alone streaming sites had moved their data to space leased on the cloud computing services operated by these same tech giants. Such is the case with Spotify and Pandora: both have ceased operating their own data centers, opting to rent space on Google Cloud instead.[31]

The geographic dispersion offered by situating data centers in different regions of the world goes only so far in cutting down the lag time separating the moment a user presses play and when the music starts. To further shorten the distance between audio files upstream and devices downstream, digital media providers have increasingly looked to content delivery networks (CDNs) to bridge the gap. CDNs are geographically distributed clusters of servers that cache files sent from centralized data centers to the edges of a network, bringing content physically closer to end users. Historically, CDNs have been mainly operated by third-party firms, such as Akamai and Limelight, from which others rent access.[32] From 2015 on, however, a notable trend has been the development of private CDNs, owned and operated by content providers, reserved for their own operations. As is typical for the tech sector, ownership of private CDNs is concentrated in the hands of large tech firms (Google, Amazon, Facebook, Microsoft).[33] Whether the dominance of CDNs by companies such as Amazon and Google will confer a competitive advantage on their own streaming services, at the expense of stand-alone platforms like Spotify, Tidal, or Deezer, remains unclear. In any event, the use of CDNs—whether third-party or privately owned—likewise relies on the replication at scale that music's datafication affords. Indeed, a common feature of all these different network topologies (client-server, peer-assisted, CDN-assisted) is their proliferation of digital copies of files to speed their delivery to users. These copies are distributed across the entire network, found on server farms located in different corners of the globe, in the caches of local CDNs, and in the memory of users' devices. Without this proliferation of digital copies, streaming platforms' promise of a seamless musical experience would be a dead letter.

Yet the speed and seamlessness achieved by replicating audio files en masse comes at a cost. Friction is minimized by displacing it elsewhere, externalizing it beyond the virtual enclosures that platforms command. The digital reproduction of audio files may appear immaterial and instantaneous. In reality it is anything but. Despite the seeming insubstantiality of datafied music—especially compared to the bulk and tangibility of tapes, vinyl records, and CDs—the countless copies of audio files that streaming platforms multiply do, in fact, take up space. As Kyle Devine puts it, "digitalization ≠ dematerialization."[34] Digital audio files are not dissolved into the ether, as the imagery of cloud computing might suggest. It is just that their materiality is dispersed across devices, servers, fiber-optic cables, CDNs, and other infrastructures that link these objects together. "Digital infrastructures and devices are absolutely material," Devine remarks, adding that "digital files are themselves also material (albeit microscopically so)."[35] The copying of files consumes time and energy as well. The gap separating file request and file delivery may be measured in milliseconds, and the amount of electricity required for the transfer of a single MP3 may not amount to much. In the aggregate, however, streaming is an energy-intensive affair. Consider Spotify. According to its 2018 sustainability report, the six data centers the company continued to own and operate consumed roughly 7,600 megawatt hours per year, equivalent to three hundred thousand tons of carbon emissions. By 2021, the company's continued growth and expansion into new markets had caused its carbon emissions to rise to approximately three hundred fifty thousand tons, despite its alleged commitment to achieving "net zero" emissions by 2030.[36] Even these self-reported figures tell only part of the story, however. The

2018 report notably excluded from its estimates the energy used in operating the servers Spotify began leasing from Google Cloud in 2016, where a significant portion of Spotify's data processing now takes place (the 2021 report omits any mention of its outsourcing of data processing to Google Cloud). Nor do these figures take into account the energy use required by the CDNs that connect the service's backend and individual users.[37] And, as the uptick in carbon emissions from 2018 to 2021 evinces, the ease, speed, and low cost at which datafied music may be reproduced, a condition of streaming's commercial viability, may simply encourage a more profligate use of streaming services—which would amount to a more profligate use of the resources these services consume.

Music as Metadata

A user visiting Spotify's artist page for the 1990s Zouk group Energy circa 2020 would have been greeted by a curious sight.[38] At first glance the page seemed unremarkable. Its layout adhered to the standard format established on Spotify by the late 2010s. At the top, the group's name was given in large, bold font, alongside an artist image. Below were a series of tabs ("Overview," "Fans also like," "About," "Concerts"), with a list of the group's most popular tracks rounding out the header. The bulk of the page presented the group's albums, in reverse chronological order, followed by singles, EPs, and compilations at the bottom of the page (missing was a list of playlists the group appeared on, presumably because they didn't appear on any). What made Energy's artist page curious was not its form but its content. For instance, the thumbnail artist image showed not a picture of the group, nor of one of their releases, but an image of a pile of buttons, each stamped with the logo for the band Energy. The problem was that the logo was for a different band of the same name—not the Antillean Zouk group but a punk outfit from the United States. Similarly, while the list of most streamed tracks a little lower down the page featured two tracks by the band ("Tempo 106," from their 1993 album *Bich' bich'*, and "Pasyon," from their 1994 album *Chayé*), the rest was a heteroclite mix of disco polo, Malay pop, mid-90s house music, and prog rock. Scrolling further down the page made it clear why. While the two full-length albums on the page were indeed by the Zouk band, the singles, EPs, and compilations presented a jumbled assortment of music: "Ingiusta," by the Italian rapper Isisan; "Ada Diri-mu," by the Malay vocal group Soutul Amal; plus the compilations *Disco Polo New Hits no. 3*, *Balearic Soft Prog Essentials*, *Jazz Rock, Blow Up Disco vol. 3: Back to Italodisco*, and *Sono Zouk*, among others. What these recordings shared in common was that somewhere or other within the artist name, the word *energy* could be found.

This sort of confusion was not restricted to Spotify. A fan looking for music by the same group on Tidal, Deezer, and other platforms circa 2020 would have come up with similar results. This might have been a problem for aficionados of Zouk, who would have had a hard time discovering the band's music (on Spotify, doing a search for *Energy* turns up at least twenty-three other artists by this name, with little to distinguish them; see figure 1.2). It would also have presented a problem for the band, whose music would have had a hard time being discovered. Partly this is the misfortune of being a little-known or defunct group that has chosen a very common word for its name. But it is also—and more significantly—a problem of metadata.

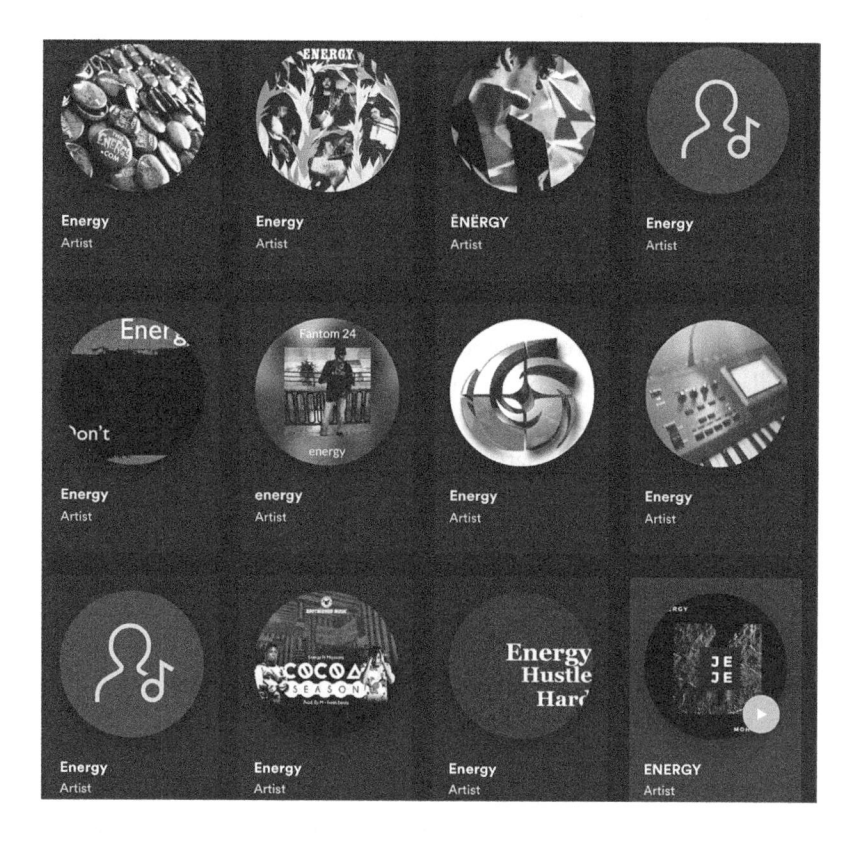

1.2 Search results for Energy on Spotify

The term *metadata* is of recent vintage, coined by computer scientist Philip Bagley in 1968 to refer to data that describes other data.[39] As regards digital audio, the distinction seems intuitive: what counts as data in this instance is a digitized representation of a sound recording, while what counts as metadata is whatever information accompanies, identifies, or describes this audio data (title, duration, artist, and so on). Yet this distinction, which suggests that metadata is somehow peripheral to audio data, fails to do justice to how much metadata conditions both the existence and experience of music on digital platforms. As Maria Eriksson remarks, "metadata is deeply involved in producing musical experiences and *making music happen*."[40] Musical metadata takes a number of different forms. At a basic level are the metadata that identify a recording and distinguish it from other recordings in a platform's database. Commonly referred to as "descriptive metadata," this category covers things such as track title, album title, artist name, release date, genre, and so forth. Also included in this category are the "persistent identifiers" used to track products: the International Standard Recording Code (ISRC) assigned to each sound recording; the International Standard Musical Work Code (ISWC) assigned to each underlying composition; the Universal Product Code (UPC), a twelve-digit code used to identify trade goods, whose most familiar guise is the barcode accompanying most tangible goods (including physical recordings); and so forth.[41]

The importance of such identifying descriptors is not to be underestimated. Without them, it would be nearly impossible to locate a recording among the tens of millions that populate streaming catalogs. While music's rendering as data ensures its rapid retrieval and playback, its rendering as metadata ensures there is something to be retrieved and played back in the first place. The presence and accuracy of such metadata is thus a necessary condition for the use value latent in digital audio to be realized—which in turn is a necessary condition for the realization of whatever exchange value it might possess ("digital files, as unlabeled chunks of code, are a tough sell," remarks Morris).[42] The same goes for a second type of metadata, alternately referred to as administrative or ownership metadata. While this category includes technical information about audio files, it also provides information about copyright ownership and the revenue splits to which parties are entitled. Such metadata aid streaming platforms in identifying rights holders and distributing to them whatever revenue they are legally entitled to.[43] But despite the economic and symbolic importance of metadata, ensuring its accuracy has proven challenging. The quality of the metadata associated with digital recordings has been a persistent source of concern, for both streaming services and the music industry more broadly. By the end of the 2010s, the sense of crisis had reached the point that what was widely referred to as the industry's "metadata problem" had come to be blamed for many of the troubles facing artists: difficulties in getting their music discovered by audiences, in receiving proper recognition for their work, and—most important—in receiving fair remuneration for the use of their music on streaming platforms. An article published in *The Verge* in 2019, for instance, reported that one indie musician had lost $40,000 in royalty payments, thanks to errors in the ownership metadata appended to his recordings.[44]

The sources of the industry's metadata problem date back to the 1980s and 1990s. Because the main form of digital music at that time, the CD, came packaged with booklets where relevant credits and commercial identifiers could be printed, little effort was made to append metadata to digital audio files, beyond the bare minimum (track number, duration).[45] It was only once CD burners and CD-rewritable drives became widely available in the late 1990s that industry and consumers alike began to grasp the consequences of this oversight. Efforts to address this lack came from a number of quarters. Some involved grassroots initiatives, such as Compact Disc Database (CDDB) and ID3 tags, both of which were developed in the mid-1990s as a means by which listeners could access, add, and edit the metadata for the audio files ripped from CDs.[46] Other responses to the metadata problem were more institutional or corporate. Some companies hired people to tag audio manually; such was the case with Microsoft's short-lived MSN Music Search Engine in the late 1990s and (more famously) Pandora's Music Genome Project.[47] Increasingly, however, the appending of metadata to audio files was automated, using techniques developed by researchers active in the relatively novel discipline of music information retrieval (MIR). At first, efforts in this direction employed machine listening to cluster and tag music on the basis of audio features, as a way of organizing music catalogs according to sonic similarity (the idea being that tracks that were sonically similar likely belonged to the same genre). By the second half of the 2000s, the coterie of techniques used to tag audio had expanded to encompass other variables (patterns of music use, linguistic descriptors, emotion, context, and so on), reflecting a belated recognition that sonic similarity is not always the most relevant factor in predicting taste.

By the mid-2010s, technologies capable of manufacturing and collecting metadata at scale had become a key pillar of the digital music economy. One symptom of their significance was to be seen in the growing number of data scientists employed not just within streaming services but across the entire music industry.[48] Another symptom was the emergence of a burgeoning metadata sector, as a growing number of start-ups got into the business of harvesting, processing, and analyzing metadata. Examples include Next Big Sound, Musimap, Musicmetric, Assai, Soundstr, Chartmetric, Soundcharts, Auddly, Jaak, Senzari, Sodatone, Indify, and the Echo Nest, among others. But perhaps the clearest indication of the rapidly appreciating value of metadata can be seen in the intense commercial maneuvering over music analytics start-ups. Beginning in 2014, a flurry of acquisitions occurred, with Spotify buying out the Echo Nest and Seed Scientific, Pandora acquiring Next Big Sound, and Apple Musicmetric.[49] While the pace of acquisitions slowed some after 2015, they did not cease. In 2018 alone, Warner Music acquired Sodatone, Apple bought Shazam and Assai, and Spotify purchased Loudr.

Yet even as the growth in the music analytics sector attests to metadata's importance to the digital music economy, the sector's rapid growth has threatened to exacerbate the very problem that individual businesses seek to address. In contrast to the situation circa 2000, by the late 2010s the problem was not necessarily a deficit in metadata but the excessive quantities of it churning through the industry. With competition over the collection, generation, and storage of metadata intensifying, so too has the chance of errors and inconsistencies. Industry actors are cognizant of this perverse dynamic. "Creating multiple databases will not solve the metadata issue," argues Niclas Molinder, founder of Auddly, a Swedish company backed by songwriter Max Martin and musician Björn Ulvaeus (of ABBA fame), whose mission is to create "a new music industry infrastructure where the data is clean, transparent, and correct for everyone."[50] According to Molinder, the existence of rival systems for metadata collection increases the "high risk of human errors," at the same time as it "prevents transparency."[51] "Different people inputting, changing, and syncing data from different sources," he remarks, "make it extremely difficult to keep data continuously matched between the databases."[52] For a company such as Auddly, the preferred way of resolving the inconsistencies in music information that market fragmentation has helped bring about is to have the company's service become so widely adopted that it effectively becomes "the entire industry's transparent reference"—standardization through market dominance, as it were.

But if cornering the music analytics market represents one way to go about regularizing metadata, it isn't the only way. Another, less competitive and more collaborative approach is presented by the Digital Data Exchange (DDEX), an organization created by a consortium of music industry stakeholders in 2006, whose purpose is "to develop a single set of standard message formats for the business-to-business communication of information between organizations operating in the digital music value chain."[53] By guaranteeing the uniformity of administrative metadata, DDEX thus hopes to smooth the flow of information (and money) between publishers, labels, aggregators, metadata companies, and so on. Yet despite the group's best efforts, adoption of its standards remains voluntary. Lacking the hard power to impose its conventions, DDEX has instead relied on the soft power of persuasion. In 2019, a video posted to its website's home page sought to convince musicians and industry personnel that uniform data records were not just useful but desirable.[54] Toward the beginning of the video, Barak Moffitt, executive vice president for content strategy and development at Universal Music Group, suggests that "we should call metadata sex, so everyone knows they need it." Following Moffitt's comment, the video's title—"Metadata: You Know You Want It"—fades in against a backdrop of wah-wah guitar, synth bass, and other hallmarks of so-called porn groove.[55] But even were a video like this to succeed in imbuing metadata with a degree of libidinal energy, it is unclear that this would be enough to overcome the competitive pressures militating against the adoption of a shared, industry-wide reference for metadata. As the group itself has acknowledged, "even though DDEX standards have been developed and published, data between some individual partners is still being communicated using various proprietary formats."[56] What this stubborn reality underlines is that the metadata problem is ultimately a collective action problem. Standing against the industry's common interest in standardizing metadata is the self-interest of individual companies and economic actors, for whom metadata's dispersal into conflicting proprietary forms may serve as a source of competitive advantage.

Until this collective action problem is resolved, the brunt of its effects will fall mainly on those with the fewest resources to cope with it. For the most part, superstar artists are insulated from the difficulties created by bad metadata. The same cannot be said of most rank-and-file musicians. "The streaming services have developed algorithms to make sure that the top of the chart looks clean," explains the music analytics company Soundcharts, adding that "once you take a deep dive on the long tail, all sorts of errors start falling through the cracks."[57] It isn't even necessary to take that deep a dive. According to figures collected by Network of Music Partners, a federation of European performing rights organizations, 96 percent of the top 100 tracks on streaming platforms possessed accurate metadata by 2017. Expanding beyond this tiny sliver of megahits, errors quickly multiplied: among the top 10 percent of tracks hosted on streaming platforms, roughly a third were afflicted with faulty metadata.[58] The most tangible effect of such errors for recording artists, as noted earlier, is a potential loss of revenue. For producers, audio engineers, session musicians, and other recording personnel, inaccurate or incomplete metadata poses an additional problem, as the project-based nature of their work means that the ability to win future employment is contingent on the credits received from prior jobs.[59] Lacking metadata, one lacks credits; and lacking credits, one is likely to lack work.

Less visible but no less problematic is the way faulty metadata may influence the "discoverability" of artists and their music, as the case of Energy exemplifies.[60] The reason is that metadata, in addition to directing royalty payments to rights holders, also determines to whom a given track is displayed—and hence whether it gets played or not. This problem is particularly pronounced for artists whose music is rooted in traditions other than those of Western popular or classical music. In cases such as these, the machine listening techniques that companies like Spotify use to generate descriptive metadata may apply parameters that are wholly inappropriate for much non-Western music (e.g., key, mode, time signature). And the result of such mislabeling may well be to exclude tracks from certain editorial playlists, to the extent that illegibility vis-à-vis the default Eurocentrism of many machine listening algorithms will necessarily place such tracks outside the range of values used to ensure a playlist maintains a consistent mood, vibe, or beat. But even metadata that is nominally correct may still reflect biases that will affect a track's chances not only of being heard but of being heard by certain audiences. Such biases are nowhere more manifest than in the use of genre tags as descriptive metadata, seeing as how musical categories have long been shaped by race and class, segmenting the musical labor market in the process. As music theorist Tom Johnson has shown, the number of genre tags that accrue to artists on Spotify is strongly correlated with the ascribed identity of either an artist or the broader metagenre with which they are affiliated (rock, hip-hop, pop, and so on). Thus, whereas Spotify tags Tame Impala's music with a diffuse assortment of genre labels (Australian alternative rock, indie pop, indie rock, neo-psychedelic, psychedelic rock), as Johnson points out, an artist like Rihanna is confined to a narrower cluster of closely related categories (dance pop, pop, R & B, and urban contemporary)—a fact that significantly downplays the sonic and stylistic diversity of her music.[61] More broadly, artists identified with certain kinds of music (for example, rock) typically accumulate a greater number of genre tags on Spotify than artists associated with other kinds of music (such as pop and hip-hop). Given the ascendancy of omnivorousness as a privileged form of sociocultural distinction, the uneven distribution of genre tags across classed and racialized musical categories such as rock (coded as white) and hip-hop (coded as Black) amounts to an uneven distribution of cultural capital.[62] At the same time, disparities in the genre markers attached to different musics affects their discoverability. The number of tags assigned to an artist affects the number and diversity of other artists they will be linked to, and this in turn shapes the number of paths (or "vectors") that will lead listeners to the artist's music.[63] Like other forms of algorithmic bias, the racist and classist ideologies inscribed in music metadata transform platforms into means not just for reproducing music but for reproducing systems of social domination as well.[64]

Music as Interface

One way of framing the impediments thrown up by metadata errors and biases is provided by platforms themselves, whose prevailing philosophy of interface design casts this or any other obstacle separating users from the object of desire as a source of "friction." Within this paradigm, there is no such thing as good friction. "Frictionless UX [user experience] has now become the new standard" announced one design firm in 2015.[65] This is a sentiment that interface designers employed by streaming services share. A 2019 post to the Spotify Design blog, for instance, describes how "a focus on removing friction should feel familiar to every designer because we do that work every day."[66] Friction, moreover, is to be understood capaciously: "We define friction as anywhere in the user experience where a human struggles in pursuit of their goals."[67] And as the post's authors go on to argue, much of Spotify's popularity is due to its elimination of such encumbrances, both within the app's backend architecture and within its consumer-facing interface: "One key to Spotify's early success was creating a frictionless listening experience. Instead of waiting two minutes to download a specific song, Spotify users could immediately play any song anytime, anywhere. Removing the friction of waiting every time you wanted to play music helped Spotify win over piracy and enabled the streaming revolution to take off."[68]

In actuality, the development of the platform's interface wasn't as smooth as this account would suggest. As a result of the service's initial focus on ensuring that the code, network infrastructure, and licensing agreements were all in place, little attention was paid early on to interface design or aesthetics.[69] One erstwhile member of the company's design team recalled how when they joined Spotify in 2012, "the level of inconsistency and fragmentation shocked me. Up-close, the treatment of type, color, imagery, layout, IA [information architecture], and interactions just didn't seem to align anywhere."[70] It was only in 2013 that the platform underwent a makeover that streamlined the interface. Guiding the redesign was the idea that Spotify should be "content first," since, as one executive put it, "ultimately [music is] what our users are coming to the service for."[71] A related principle was that the interface should strive to "do less," reducing the distance separating users from content.[72] As the same executive explained, users shouldn't have to "use much effort for what they want to do. [The interface] needs to be really slick, it needs to be simple, really getting the user to do what they really want."[73] The contradiction embedded in this statement—between getting someone to do something, and getting them "to do what they really want"—can be read as a symptom of the conflicting imperatives at play in commercial interface design. Rather than simply fulfilling users' desires, the point is to structure these desires, blurring the distinction between what users want and what platforms want them to want.

Far from being distinctive or unique, the sleek facade that Spotify adopted after 2013 resembles other music platforms in its broad contours, stripped of anything extraneous to a service's commercial imperatives, branding strategies, or intended uses. The minimalist style that platforms share is of a piece with the distinctive visual culture embraced by Silicon Valley since the early 2000s, where usability is wedded to technological sophistication, and a promise of hipness, dynamism, and upward mobility is tendered to a mass public for whom many of these attributes are more an aspiration than a reality.[74] Indeed, the uncluttered design of most streaming interfaces may be seen as partaking of the broader "aestheticization of restraint" that became a hallmark of social distinction following the Great Recession of 2008–2009.[75] That streaming has long presented itself as a means by which users could dispense not only with the bulky materiality of CDs and tapes but also with the virtual clutter of messy MP3 collections, suggests that such marketing discourses appeal not simply to the practical benefits of streaming but to a latent form of class politics as well.

Minimalism comes at a cost, however. For Spotify and other platforms to "do less" requires stripping away much of the information and iconography that frames the musical experience. On smartphones, the user interface (UI) provides only a few square inches for the display of text and images, limiting the paratexts that accompany the music. Generally speaking, clicking on a playlist or album calls up just a few pieces of information: a title; a thumbnail image (for example, album covers or the stock photos frequently used for mood or activity-based playlists); a track list; and, depending on the app, a few other miscellaneous bits of information (such as label, release date, or a brief blurb describing a playlist's aesthetic or mood). Tablets and computers, with their larger screens, should in principle allow for a greater number of paratexts, but this is seldom the case. To take one example, the layout of playlists on Amazon Music's desktop application closely resembles the interface of its mobile app, in keeping with the drive to maintain a consistent brand experience across platforms. As on the mobile app, the top of the screen is dominated by the playlist title and accompanying thumbnail image. The playlist "Spa Day," for instance, features an abstract image of waves, on top of which the playlist title is overlaid in bold caps. Below this, in smaller font, is a brief blurb, describing the atmosphere the music is to evoke ("A perfect soundtrack for relaxation and healing"). Also at the top of the screen is the name of the person or corporate entity responsible for compiling the playlist ("Amazon's Music Experts"); the number of tracks it contains (101); and its overall duration (six hours and fourteen minutes).[76] The remainder of the page is devoted to the titles that compose the playlist, along with some other basic information: artist names, the albums from which tracks are drawn, and song timings. While the desktop application offers a little more information than the mobile app, on Amazon Music as on most other streaming services little context is provided for the music on offer. The paratexts that do frame the music revolve around issues of time, identity, and function: how long the playlist is, how long individual tracks are, when the playlist was created and by whom, what effects listening to it will elicit, and so on. The narrow range of concerns addressed tacitly respond to an equally narrow set of questions, hailing the user as someone whose interest in music extends only so far as these implied questions allow.

Not all listeners are content with the interface configuring them so narrowly. The general lack of liner notes, credits, and other paratexts on streaming services has been a recurrent source of complaint, for listeners and artists alike. Enthusiasts of jazz and Western classical music have been particularly vocal in this regard.[77] In a 2013 presentation at the CASH Music Summit in Portland, Oregon, violinist and Future of Music board member Jean Cook decried how streaming platforms "inconsistently and alternately list composers or performers under 'artist' when it comes to classical music."[78] Jazz suffered from similar problems. As an example, Cook pointed to the recording of "Blue in Green" by the Miles Davis Sextet, highlighting that Pandora had failed to "associate Bill Evans with the track in any way," despite his being a coauthor of the song and a performer on its premier recording.[79] Jump ahead a few years, and the same criticisms were being voiced. A post to Spotify's community forum in 2019 described one user's frustrations with "the limited amount of credits on each album," noting that for "people who are big fans of [jazz], knowing who played the piano, drums, or saxophone is a huge part of understanding the music."[80] For journalist Craig Havighurst, the problem with digital music's "death of context" was that it devalued music twice over, first economically, then symbolically. Because "albums are sold and streamed without the credits or liner notes of the LP and CD era," we now find ourselves in an "information-poor environment," one that is ill-suited to transforming casual listeners into hardcore fans or connoisseurs.[81]

The situation was dire enough by 2017 that one music fan saw fit to launch a petition on Change.org, lobbying platforms to do a better job of informing listeners about the music they stream. "Services that stream music currently do not include album liner notes and/or album credits that are usually associated with physical formats of previous generations. THIS IS A TRAVESTY! Not only are people missing the experience reading the liner notes, the artists involved with these recordings are going completely unrecognized."[82] A common refrain in such criticisms is that platforms represent a step backward, compared to the richer experience provided by more immediately tangible formats such as LPs, CDs, and cassette tapes. This narrative—which has become something of a commonplace within discourses on digital music—maintains that digitization has dispossessed music of the sources of textual and iconographic meaning that hitherto shaped its reception. One version is recounted by Morris, in his description of how music's move online meant that "highly crafted artwork, album graphics, and liner notes were reduced to thumbnail images and metadata," paralleling the way in which "high-quality CD sounds were compressed, and excess sonic data were thrown away."[83] Overlooked in such accounts is that the ostensibly richer paratexts that liner notes, album cover art, and the like once provided were themselves already quite limited.[84] Lyrics printed on an album's dust jacket, for instance, may clarify what words a singer sings but not how the singer delivers them. The same goes for other paratexts, no matter how much more tangible or detailed they appear when printed on album sleeves or CD booklets.

That older recording formats are also limited in terms of the paratexts that frame them highlights a contradiction that haunts interfaces in general: namely, an interface's capacity to grant access is contingent on its simultaneous restriction of access. This is a point numerous media thinkers have made. Writing in 1997, Siegfried Zielinski noted that "the interface is something that connects. . . . Otherwise the term would make no sense."[85] But he also observed that this act of connection presupposes a distance that the interface must simultaneously uphold: "the interface is something that separates. . . . Otherwise the term would make no sense."[86] This dialectic is a defining feature of the interface. In the words of Alexander Galloway, interfaces must always be "unworkable" at some level.[87] To succeed at bringing discrete entities into contact, an interface must at the same time fail at this appointed task. The exchanges it affords can only ever be partial.

That there is an insuperable limit that interfaces necessarily confront, no matter how streamlined their design, doesn't mean that digital music platforms have relinquished the dream of fashioning an interface that would eliminate the distance it cannot help but uphold.[88] On the contrary. One symptom of the enduring desire to design an interfaceless interface can be seen in the ongoing efforts to whittle away features and controls deemed to be "inessential," standing in the way of a perfectly frictionless user experience.[89] Another can be seen in the investment that tech companies have made in voice-controlled interfaces since the mid-2010s. But even if smart speakers and home assistants overcome certain barriers put in place by screen-based interfaces, they erect others in their place, transforming the voice—and sound more generally—into barriers in turn. But perhaps the most important way this drive manifests itself is in the way platform interfaces encourage users to run streaming apps in the background while they do other things. By offering so little to draw one's attention, the minimalism of platform interfaces facilitates music's mediation of other activities and situations: workouts, study, sleep, and so on (see chapter 5). And this in turn suggests that the more that the interfaces charged with providing access to music recede, the more music itself comes to act as an interface.

Cast in this role, music exhibits the same ambivalence as other interfaces, simultaneously connecting and separating. This is manifest with respect to music's temporality: not only is audio content delivered to listeners through the medium of time, it is also withheld from them. The large-scale aggregation of audio files on streaming services fosters the impression that this vast archive of recorded music is simply present, an impression their promotional discourses reinforce. Yet because listeners can only access recordings one at a time means that this synchronic collection can be experienced only as a diachronic succession, undercutting the purported givenness of platforms' vast catalogs. A file request may be transmitted to a platform's servers in the blink of an eye, and the file itself buffered on a user's device in fractions of a second; but the act of listening to music cannot be accelerated without fundamentally altering the aesthetic experience (though the speeding up of music on TikTok, in response to the constraints imposed by short-form video, suggests that even this aesthetic norm may be in the process of coming undone).

For rights holders, music's temporality represents an economic obstacle, as royalty payouts are indexed to the number of streams a track accrues—a problem compounded by the industry norm whereby a track counts as eligible for royalties only after thirty seconds of playback.[90] One way of circumventing this barrier to profitability is by making tracks shorter; and it is no coincidence that the average length of a song on the Billboard Hot 100 decreased by about twenty seconds from 2013 to 2018.[91] Short of speeding up music consumption and making it more "productive," the number of tracks streamed can be increased by subdividing listening time into smaller increments. For listeners, the obstacle presented by music's temporality is a different one, since selecting any individual track, album, or playlist from a platform's vast archive means temporarily forgoing every other one on offer. "Friction," in other words, isn't simply to be found in the interface that stands between users and content; it can be and often is constituted by music itself. Even if shrink-wrap EULAs consolidate legal impediments to access; even if the design of network architectures and the geographic dispersal of digital files shrink the lag between file request and delivery; even if metadata makes the vast catalogs of streaming services navigable—even if all these mediations succeed in making streaming frictionless, music presents its own kind of friction. This may be a source of frustration, particularly when one dislikes a track in a playlist. But it may also represent a kind of aesthetic pleasure, as when a song jumps out of the flow and commands one's attention—this too is a kind of friction.

If such friction presents a problem, it is one for streaming services, not necessarily for users. For platforms the imperative is to keep listeners listening, constantly and continuously. Their commercial logic demands that any song that stands out for some reason, whether good or bad, be absorbed back into an unending flow of music. Making autoplay a default setting is one way of achieving this goal. Another is to ensure that individual tracks, playlists, albums, or artists seldom appear in isolation. While paratexts are generally minimized, other things continue to frame music—most notably, other music. On Spotify, for example, below an album's track list there is typically a list of "more albums by [*insert artist's name here*]." Likewise, artist pages feature not only their recordings but also links to other artists and playlists that "fans also like" (see figure 1.3). Recommendations for what to listen to next, these icons also serve as a tacit reminder of the opportunity

1.3 "Fans also like"

Streaming Music → 47

cost incurred by listening to one piece of music rather than another. They index the surplus of music that platforms make available in the abstract but that always remains beyond one's grasp. Clicking on a recommendation will bring one no closer to the musical plenitude that platforms purport to provide. Rather, doing so simply recommences the same process, presenting the listener with still other musics and other recommendations, which lead to still others in turn. As an interface by which a service's catalog may be accessed, music's givenness is also the means by which it is withheld, helping to bind users to platforms by projecting the point when they will deliver on their promise of plenitude into an infinitely receding future.

Music as Stream

"Despite the term having entered common vernacular, 'streaming' remains a distinctly difficult term to accurately and clearly define." So writes Dom Robinson in his 2017 book *Content Delivery Networks: Fundamentals, Design, and Evolution*.[92] Part of the difficulty in defining the stream is that it is, like music, not one but many things, sitting astride a number of domains. Three different definitions of the term *streaming* give some sense of this multiplicity.

1   First, consider Robinson's own definition. At the outset of *Content Delivery Networks*, he sketches a brief history of streaming. He frames this history by asking what problem this technology set out to solve: "To understand streaming," he notes, it is necessary to understand "what it tries to achieve."[93] After taking note of the pioneering work done on voice (and later video) transfer protocols on the Advanced Research Projects Agency Network (ARPANET) in the 1970s and 1980s,[94] his consideration of the commercial expansion of streaming media pivots on the bandwidth limitations of the 1990s, when the vast majority of people still accessed the internet via dial-up modems. Streaming, by this account, was a work-around for sluggish download times. To illustrate this point, Robinson cites MP3 audio. Given a standard telephone modem access speed of 14.4 kbps, "it could take at least as long as the play duration of the file to download—so a 5 minute long piece of music would take often more than 5 minutes between the point of choosing to listen to it, and the point it could be heard."[95] Making

this lag especially egregious was the fact that downloading the entire MP3 before starting playback wasn't strictly necessary. Because files transferred over the internet are disaggregated into packets, a recording is no longer "a discrete item."[96] However, the protocols of the era allowed files to be read only after every packet had been received, checked for errors, and reassembled. So long as the download was incomplete, the "computer itself could not make sense of the file."[97] Yet there was no reason why protocols couldn't be changed to allow playback of files whose download was still in progress. This is precisely what streaming did. Viewed from this angle, streaming is a technology for collapsing time—the time separating file request from file use, desire from gratification.

2   Now consider a second definition of *streaming*. First published in 2002, David Austerberry's *The Technology of Video and Audio Streaming* was mainly addressed to media professionals still coming to grips with digital distribution. Early on, Austerberry explains the basic principles of what, for his readers, was presumably a novel technology: "Streamed media is delivered direct from the source to the player in real-time. This is a continuous process, with no intermediate storage of the media clip."[98] To make things more concrete, Austerberry links streaming to an older technology: "Streaming media has been around for 70 years. The conventional television that we grew up with would be called streaming media if it were invented today."[99] Having established a continuity between old and new media, Austerberry enumerates some key differences. One is that the multidirectional, many-to-many, and interactive architecture of the internet means that servers can adjust to bandwidth fluctuations, still a live issue at the time of the book's writing. Another is that "content can be provided on demand." A third is that the use of digital rights management can ensure that users have only "conditional access to content"—a comment no doubt reassuring to the media professionals for whom the book was intended. But even taking into account all these qualifications, the underlying analogy remained. Just as television is cast as streaming avant la lettre, streaming is cast as little more than an updated version of television's real-time transmission of information.[100]

3   Still another way of understanding streaming is tucked away in a 2011 North American licensing agreement between Sony Music and Spotify (the contract was leaked anonymously in 2015, just as

Streaming Music → 49

Spotify was in the midst of renegotiating its licensing deals with Sony and other major labels).[101] In certain respects, this definition covers similar terrain as Robinson's and Austerberry's. The differences are telling, however. Streaming is here described as a process whereby "any portion of a recording is delivered by means of digital audio transmission, which transmission is substantially contemporaneous with the performance of the recording embodied therein."[102] This description of streaming resembles the others discussed earlier, especially with its emphasis on streaming's "real-timeness." Significantly, however, the Sony-Spotify contract qualifies this characterization: the stream need only be "substantially contemporaneous" with its playback. Streams, the contract further specifies, should be "delivered in an approved format that is designed so that such recording cannot be digitally copied, duplicated or stored in a renderable form in any manner or medium in whole or in part, directly or indirectly (other than any temporary copies used solely for so-called 'caching' or 'buffering')."[103] What was implicit in Austerberry's definition is here made explicit, namely that the "real-timeness" of streaming should serve to constrain the free circulation of digital files. Music is to be consumed more or less at the moment of its transfer—or, to be more exact, at the moment of its (re)production. What Sony's definition of streaming underlines, in other words, is Spotify's contractual obligation to make recorded music appear not in the familiar guise of a durable good but as a transient service. And what it makes clear in addition is that the aim of this transformation is to protect the asset that is Sony's intellectual property, not just by embedding files with DRM but by making music appear evanescent to the listener.

Despite their points of overlap, each of these accounts accentuates a particular aspect of streaming: for Robinson, it is the technological; for Austerberry, the experiential; and in the Sony-Spotify contract, the economic. How are these different dimensions of streaming articulated? To answer this question, a good place to start is with Austerberry's analogy likening streaming to television. Motivating this reference is Austerberry's interest in normalizing streaming for his audience. By situating streaming within a longer historical lineage that stretches back to older broadcast media, he makes the unfamiliar familiar. As such, his analogy operates according to the logic of mediality described by Jonathan Sterne, but with one key difference. Whereas for Sterne *mediality* denotes "the complex ways in which communication technologies refer to one another,"[104] in the case at hand what is critical is the way one communication technology (streaming) doesn't simply refer but is performatively *made to refer* to another (television). Austerberry's invocation of television, in other words, doesn't remediate streaming so much as *premediate* it. It is prescriptive rather than descriptive, providing a frame for how users are to experience the medium in advance. And this is a frame that streaming platforms have reinforced, by borrowing from broadcast media terms such as "playlists" and "radio stations."

Crucial to observe is the normative force of this frame: by obscuring certain features of streaming and bringing others to the fore—above all the putative real-timeness of its transmission—it encourages users to experience streaming likewise. Furthermore, this frame's efficacy hinges on the other mediations discussed throughout this chapter all being in place. Only when licensing agreements are secured, data infrastructures are sufficiently robust, and metadata and interface design collapse the virtual distance separating users from music—only when these conditions have been met can features associated with broadcast media be successfully projected onto streamed media. And inasmuch as streamed media, like broadcast media, are thus imagined to be "delivered direct from the source . . . in real-time," they will presumably exhibit a phenomenology akin to radio or television—what Raymond Williams famously encapsulated in the concept of "flow."[105] The term *stream* itself would already seem to steer us in this direction. Jeremy Wade Morris and Devon Powers, for instance, note how the term conjures images of "mobility, motion, or continuity"—though, as they also note, other connotations of streaming evoke "division, separation, and improved results through removing the extraneous" (as in the educational practice of "streaming" students according to performance).[106] Indeed, it is the term's polysemic richness that lead the pair to regard *streaming* as "a key metaphor for the flow of information in the digital age."[107]

At this point a connection may be made with another aspect of streaming, one touched on in the Sony-Spotify contract—namely, streaming's rendering of recorded music not as a good but as a service. Underpinning this connection is the fact that notions such as *stream* and *flow* are not just media concepts but economic ones, functioning as a key axis along which services are distinguished from goods. What differentiates "flows" from "stocks" (of goods, assets, capital, and so on) is their different temporalities.

Writing at the turn of the twentieth century, the economist Irving Fisher remarked on the need to relate measures of economic activity to that "great 'independent variable' of human existence, *time*." He goes on to note that "when we speak of a certain quantity of wealth we may have reference either to a quantity existing at a particular instant of time, or to a quantity produced, consumed, exchanged, or transported during a period of time. The first quantity is a *stock* (or *fund*) of wealth; the second is a *flow* (or *stream*) of wealth."[108] The stock/flow distinction has since become a mainstay of both mainstream economic theory and everyday accounting. In the United Nations' System of National Accounts framework, stocks are defined as "holdings of assets and liabilities at a point in time," while flows represent "the creation, transformation, exchange, transfer, or extinction of economic value" over time.[109] Applied to goods and services, the stock/flow distinction provides a key axis of differentiation, in that only goods can be held in stock; services cannot. As a rule, the latter assume the form of a flow. Some characteristics of services clarify why. First, as Peter Hill notes, the output of a service activity is not a durable thing but a change in condition.[110] This change may affect a person or legal entity (such as a business), or it may affect an item they possess. Second, while the effects of a service may be enduring, the actual provision of a service lasts for as long as it takes to be performed.[111] In the case of streaming, playing a song has a number of effects, some of which may be ephemeral (a change in mood or heart rate), others less so (the experience of the song). But while some changes wrought by a service may be long-lasting, even permanent, the activity that produces them isn't. While users cannot "unhear" the track that they have streamed and in that sense are permanently changed by the experience, the track's provision and consumption take just as long as the act of streaming does.

From this follows another characteristic of services: their production and consumption generally coincide. By comparison, between the moments when goods are produced, when they are acquired, and when their use value is realized, a series of intervals necessarily intervenes. This remains the case despite the systemic pressure exerted by capital to accelerate the turnover of commodities. The delay between a good's production and its purchase can be shortened but not eliminated. As Hill notes, "goods have to be produced before they can be consumed—their production and consumption are separate and sequential—so that they must enter into inventory, even if only momentarily, after they are produced."[112] The opposite is the case with services: "services cannot be held in stock because a stock of changes is a contradiction in terms."[113] And if the production and consumption of services cannot be separated, then neither can producer and consumer. This fact makes services more relational than goods typically are. This is evident in the case of personal services (such as teaching, personal training, and medical exams), which demand a high degree of interaction—a fact that limits how much their productivity can be increased (see chapter 5). The same also holds for automated services such as music streaming: generally speaking, one can stream a track only if one is connected to a platform or has an established relation with it (for example, by having an active account). By comparison, goods require no direct contact between producer and consumer. Indeed, one of the characteristics of capitalism is its tendency to create an ever-widening gulf between producers and consumers of goods, as seen in the inexorable expansion of what Anna Tsing calls "supply chain capitalism," or the concentration of manufacturing in special economic zones that stretch from Shenzhen to the maquiladoras located along the US-Mexico border.[114]

This overview of some of the traits distinguishing services from goods clarifies what is at stake in descriptions of streaming as the force that moved the record industry away from the sale of goods to the provision of services, or that cast streaming as an extension of the "X as a service" business model to music—or even in the commonplace that holds Spotify, Apple Music, and the like to be "streaming services" (as opposed to "stream producers," "stream distributors," or "stream providers").[115] At the same time, the coupling of the stock/flow and goods/services distinctions also clarifies the economic logic underlying the reimagination of recorded music as a service. As Gavin Mueller notes, the simultaneity of production and consumption in services was instrumental to the record industry's successful "outflanking" of piracy in the late 2000s and early 2010s: "Because no music is stored, issues of the usage rights of audiences, such as fair use, never come into play."[116] Files that are never in one's possession are files that cannot be shared, either licitly or illicitly. Hence one might view streaming as a device by which a phase transition of sorts is induced, such that the solidity of a durable good (a recording) is transformed into a fluid and ephemeral service (the playback of a recording). Music enters the platform as a good licensed from rights holders, and it exits as a flow. Furthermore, the fact that the coincidence of production and consumption entails contact between producer and consumer ensures the "tethering" of streaming users to platforms. As Mueller puts it, streaming relies on users having "continuous access to the servers"—the corollary of which is the streaming company having "continuous access to the listener."[117] In principle, such "continuous access" need last only as long as it takes for a track or playlist to stream. In practice, however, the transience of services—the fact that they produce a change in condition instead of a lasting thing—means that the two-way connection between service producer and consumer must be serially reestablished. In other words, limits on the ability to store audio files outside a platform's "walled garden" (absent stream-ripping software) further chains listeners to this platform. In contrast to downloads, which leave a durable trace within a device's memory, streaming leaves no such trace—apart from what is inscribed in the memory of the listener.

Or so it would seem. Yet is it really the case that streaming leaves no material trace? Recall Robinson's account of streaming's commercial development in the 1990s. In his telling, the impetus behind it was the demand to have files commence playback before transfer was complete. Streaming, by this account, isn't qualitatively different from downloading but is itself a variety of download, just one in which stages otherwise separate (download *then* playback) instead overlap (download *and* playback). But even this technical distinction isn't always observed in practice. Recall as well the allowance made in the Sony-Spotify contract for the creation of "temporary copies" of files, for the purposes of buffering and caching.[118] Such allowances are commonplace among streaming services. From the perspective of rights holders such as Sony, the storage of temporary files on local drives is a necessary evil, countenanced only under certain circumscribed conditions. One is when users listen off-line—as when they are in transit, without access to a wireless signal. Another is when certain files are accessed so frequently that it is more efficient to temporarily store them on a user's device. Still another is when an app "pre-fetches" from the server an audio file that is likely to be played in the near future, perhaps because it is next up in a playlist—or perhaps because (as one patent held by Spotify envisages) "motion, hand/proximity, or heat sensor[s]" on a user's device anticipate where one's finger is about to tap.[119] Given the number of exceptions that allow the downloading and storage of files on users' devices, one has to wonder how exceptional they really are. "The role of caches on end systems should not be underestimated," remarks one network engineer, citing studies that credit caches for reducing web traffic up to 20 percent.[120] The amount of disk space that caches consume also attests to their importance for streaming services. The "high-res" streaming platform Qobuz, for instance, allows users to decide how large a cache they want. Yet the three standard settings on desktop clients range from one gigabyte (the "optimized" setting) to thirty (the "comfort" setting)—the latter some six times the storage capacity of the Apple iPod when it debuted. While Qobuz may be an outlier, given its commitment to lossless compression formats, it's not unusual for streaming caches to occupy several gigabytes of disk space.

The importance music platforms accord to cached files underlines how much of what goes by the name of streamed music is something else entirely. Even when a file is streamed more or less in real time, the process involved is less akin to transmission (contra Austerberry's analogy with television broadcast) than to digital (re)production. A file is still being copied and transferred. The only difference is that the relay of data from remote server to local disk occurs piecemeal. This may result in some segments of a file being overwritten while the track is still being played back, to free up space in the buffer.[121] But not necessarily. And ultimately it matters little if a file is transferred in parts or as a whole, synchronously or asynchronously, linearly or nonlinearly—none of these eventualities alters the fact that, in streaming no less than in downloading, what takes place is that a new copy of a file is produced and written onto a user's device. If this copy is expunged almost as quickly as it is assembled, this is not by necessity but by design. It is not some necessary feature of the technology that causes streams to "perish in the very instant of their performance" (to cite Adam Smith's oft-cited definition of services). Rather, the reason is because they have been programmed to do so.

The more one scrutinizes the stream/download dichotomy—a dichotomy that is the hinge around which popular narratives about the evolution of digital music turn—the less clear-cut it appears. The same is true of the service/good dichotomy that ostensibly distinguishes streaming from downloads (or nondigital media, for that matter). Streaming doesn't transform music from a good into a service. Rather, it makes certain goods (namely, audio files) so short-lived, so disposable, that they effectively mimic the characteristics of services: impermanence, coincidence of production and consumption, and so on. Yet none of these characteristics are simply given; they must be contrived. Given the large number of audio files that streaming platforms store on local devices, there is no need for users to have "continuous access" to their servers, and vice versa. Nor is there a hard and fast reason why the production and consumption of streams must coincide. This fact is made altogether clear by both the (licit) practice of caching and the (illicit) practice of stream-ripping. What these contradictions underline is the need to attend to another aspect of streaming, beyond the technological, experiential, and economic aspects foregrounded in the three accounts discussed earlier. This is its *ideological* character: the way in which the experiential quality of flow makes the ephemerality of the stream appear as if it is a technological exigency, rather than an expression of economic power. As Andreas Aegidius argues, the metaphor of streaming "hides... essential control mechanisms."[122] Cast as a technical protocol, streaming provides cover for a radical reconfiguration of the social and economic relations people have to recorded music, a reconfiguration that disproportionately benefits platforms and rights holders. It is thanks to the misrecognition engendered when streams are cast as categorically different from downloads—when music is cast as a service rather than as a good that has been programmed to self-destruct—that this redistribution of power is normalized.

We might refer to this as the ideology of streaming. It is an ideology that performs a good deal of work for platforms and rights holders. One example of such work may be witnessed in the way the imaginaries woven around the figure of the stream divert attention from the (re)imposition of copyright controls that the digitization of music had once seemed poised to overthrow. Listeners who are persuaded that streaming is a matter of transmission rather than reproduction are listeners who will be dissuaded from sharing files, believing there are no files to be shared. Equally important, however, is the way in which streaming surreptitiously reintroduces the sort of digital rights management technologies that rights holders have long clamored for and music fans have long rejected. Initially integrated into MP3s at the behest of major labels, as a way of restricting the post-sale circulation of audio files, DRM met with such fierce resistance that it ended up being largely abandoned within the digital download market (it helped that Steve Jobs was among those who soured on DRM, considering his role in creating a legitimate mass market for MP3 downloads via the iTunes store).[123] Here as well, the depiction of streaming as a fundamentally different technology from digital downloads has aided rights holders in their efforts to smuggle such controls back in behind users' backs. If a file is already present in one's cache, for instance, "streaming" it doesn't involve the transfer of audio data. Rather, it involves an exchange of cryptographic keys, which, if one is an authorized user, allows the cache to be unlocked and made accessible for playback. No connection means no authorization means no decryption means no playback—and this despite the fact that the file is in one's possession the entire time. That this very different process for accessing music gets lumped under the catchall rubric of streaming means the role played by DRM disappears from view. A tightening of legal controls appears otherwise, as an unavoidable feature of streaming technology.

The same sleight of hand also serves to transform irregular, one-off transactions between buyers and sellers of music into something more lasting, predictable, and consistent. In short, it transforms erstwhile buyers of music into subscribers to a service. But it does more than this: the ideological figure of the stream also rationalizes the durable relation of dependence that ties listeners to platforms, making it appear as if it resulted from the peculiar ontology of the stream. If users are obliged to have "continuous access" to a service to enjoy continued access to music, the figure of the stream suggests that this is due to its apparent evanescence. By making this peculiar kind of digital good vanish almost as soon as it is fabricated, platforms manage to rob it of a key feature conventionally associated with goods: the particular relation they institute between present and future. That goods persist beyond the production process enables them not only to be held in stock for future use but also to act as a stock of future use values.[124] This is evident for storage media such as LPs, cassette tapes, CDs, and even MP3s (provided they lack DRM), all of which guarantee to listeners that musical enjoyment may be repeated or deferred. Put differently, these storage media provide listeners a way of inoculating musical experience against the vicissitudes of time and their own ephemerality.[125] This control may give rise to its own pathologies—most notably, what Jacques Attali described as the tendency for consumers to "stockpile" recordings they never actually get around to enjoying.[126] But if ownership of recordings raises the prospect of the present being sacrificed to a future that may never arrive, streaming turns this dynamic on its head: the perishability of the stream sacrifices the future to a present that is always slipping away. Control is ceded to platforms, who take over from users the responsibility of amassing records.[127] But far from transcending the logic of repetition that, per Attali, fuels the drive to stockpile, streaming marks its apotheosis. If it appears otherwise, it is because users are separated from this stockpile and from the store of future uses it represents.

Another way of getting at the peculiar temporality of the subscription model is through a comparison to another commonplace instrument of late capitalist value extraction: debt. Both can be understood as forms of "secondary exploitation"—that is, exploitation that takes place within the sphere of circulation rather than that of production, and that derives from the unequal ownership of, control over, and access to some asset or resource (such as a stock of copyrighted recordings).[128] At a basic level, what debt permits is a chronological separation of use and exchange: a car, a house, an education, a sum of money—these and other items acquired on credit can be used straightaway, throughout the entire term of the loan's repayment, and beyond (provided one doesn't default). Yet, as many authors have noted, the projection of one's debt obligation into the future allows capital to lay claim to this future, binding it to a fixed schedule of payment and thereby robbing it of some of its openness and indeterminacy.[129] Whereas the up-front purchase of a good involves a sacrifice in the present for a promised gain in the future (namely, the potential uses the good will presumably afford), contracting a debt involves a sacrifice of the future for the present. Here we can see a parallel between the temporality of debt and that of the subscription. The subscription, like debt, functions "as an apparatus that closes and preempts time."[130] Inasmuch as it transforms payment from a one-time occurrence into regularly reiterated event, it too lays claim to some part of the subscriber's future.[131] What is more, the servicing of debt subordinates the lived time of the subject to the homogeneous and abstract time of the calendar, across which are parceled the fixed points when installments come due.[132] Here, too, a connection can be drawn with streaming subscriptions, whose payment schedule likewise transforms the indeterminacy of the future into something regular, predictable, and determinate. This holds true regardless of whether one has a premium (that is, paid) subscription or an ad-supported one. It is simply that in ad-supported tiers, what is claimed is the user's future time and attention, to be paid off at regular intervals by means of the periodic advertisements one is obliged to listen to.

So much for the similarities between subscriptions and debt. What of the differences? Perhaps the most glaring is that with debt there is little choice but to pay; the debtor is obliged to do so, both by law and a problematic ethics that equates indebtedness with moral fault.[133] In the case of subscriptions, by contrast, one is nominally free at any moment to cease payment and reclaim the part of the future that the subscription forecloses. But while this freedom of action is something the subscriber enjoys and the debtor lacks, there is less to it than meets the eye. A variety of inducements, nudges, and other methods of persuasion help keep users locked into an ongoing relation to the platform. The automation of payment—whether by monthly charges to users' credit cards or the surreptitious collection and monetization of data—is arguably the most powerful means of ensuring users' continued capture by platforms. But it is not the only one. Ads touting the merits of streaming, the shrinking number of stand-alone MP3 players on the market, technical hurdles impeding the transfer and playback of audio files on smartphones, the pressure exerted by online retailers such as the relation between their present and future, just as it does for listeners. For the latter, as we've seen, the purchase of a recording entitles listeners to a stock of use values that can be amortized across the lifetime of the medium on which it is inscribed. Money is exchanged in the present for a commodity that promises more or less unfettered future use. For artists, the sale of recordings is similarly front-loaded. They exchange a recording in the present for a different kind of commodity—money—that also promises unfettered future use (all the more so, given money's status as a general equivalent). As industry analyst Mark Mulligan observes, "in the . . . sales model artists would get a large sum of money in a relatively short period of time."[145] But streaming's transformation of music into a service, even if only an ersatz one, transforms the temporality of compensation as well. For listeners, payment and use are no longer separate and sequential but concurrent, while for artists payment no longer precedes use by listeners but comes afterward. Income from recordings, in other words, is no longer front-loaded but distributed unevenly and unpredictably across present and future. Or, as Mulligan puts it, "streaming income is more like an annuity, a longer-term return where the music keeps paying long after release."[146] In principle the same recording may generate the same royalty income via streams as it would through sales, given sufficient time. But everything hinges on what constitutes sufficient time. For anyone lacking access to means of subsistence in the here and now, the same income measured in quantitative terms has a very different value in qualitative terms, depending on whether it is paid up front or parceled out in irregularly spaced micropayments. They may add up to the same amount in the long run, but to cite John Maynard Keynes's famous quip, in the long run we are all dead. And even if certain musicians benefit from the steady drip of payments they receive from platforms (which is especially the case with older or more established artists, who have amassed a large catalog of songs over their careers), the fact that money is no less subject to "constant annihilation" than other necessities of life means that they are bound just as tightly to platforms as listeners are.

• • •

In this chapter I have examined the constellation of features that distinguish streamed music from other, more familiar mediations (live music, notated music, downloaded music, music on vinyl, amateur performance, and so on). Yet to say that music that is streamed is distinctive in many respects is not to say that streaming marks an absolute break with other ways music has been enacted historically, or that music could be enacted under different material conditions. Many of the mediations that play a prominent role in streaming are found in other forms of musicking. Music's rendering as data, as noted earlier, is characteristic not just of streaming services but also of the sound files that are encoded in CDs, minidiscs, MP3s, and countless other digital formats. The same is true of music's representation both through and as an interface. The illustrations adorning Victorian-era sheet music, the particular manner in which notation is engraved, the paratexts in which the "music itself" is embedded—like other interfaces, these separate as well as connect. They provide access to music at the same time as they stand in music's way, creating a gap between musicking subject and musical object that can never be wholly bridged. And so it goes with other mediations that characterize streaming.

What makes streamed music distinctive, then, isn't the particular mediations it convenes but rather the particular way in which they are configured and, above all, how they interact with one another. Consider the last of the mediations discussed in this chapter, the stream as ideological construct. Music's rendering as a stream is more than just a technical matter, insofar as its underlying motivation stems from the drive among rights holders to both maintain and squeeze value from their principal asset, the intellectual property they hold. Conversely, what Aegidius terms the "streamification" of music not only enforces but alters music's status as intellectual property, masking the latter's organizing role by making restrictions on use, circulation, and (re)production appear as technical exigencies rather than a function of economic power.[147] This mutual mediation of streamification and copyright law mediates in turn how metadata function within platforms in determining what appears in users' feeds, what gets streamed, how the revenue generated is partitioned, and so on—which in turn shape the design of interfaces and so forth.

While the different mediations discussed in this chapter are critical to lending streamed music its particular character and texture, they are not the only ones that matter. Equally important are some that have been only briefly touched on so far: music's enactment as a device for the aggregation of user attention and data, as the source and object of various forms of measurement (for example, play counts, churn rate, and "dwell time"), and as a means of social reproduction. These are issues that the rest of this book will take up. But first, the next chapter examines one mediation of particular import for streaming: the mediation of streaming services by a specific kind of industrial organization, one that is designated by the term *platform*.

Chapter Two

Streaming Capital

"Music itself is going to become like running water or electricity."[1] With this sentence, uttered in the course of a 2002 *New York Times* interview, David Bowie gave birth to one of the most durable metaphors of twenty-first-century musical life. True, other claims he made during the same interview haven't aged nearly so well, above all his confident declaration that in ten years' time copyright would be a thing of the past. Also true is the fact that metaphors likening music to water are hardly new: examples range from contemporaneous accounts of Chopin's piano technique to the lyrics of modern pop songs and recent musicological writing.[2] But unlike most uses of the trope, which have tended to operate at an aesthetic or experiential level, Bowie's comment used the figure of water to anticipate the changes that the internet would likely have on music's circulation and on the musical economy more broadly. Bowie emphasized this last point in a piece of unsolicited advice he offered musicians whose livelihoods digitization was about to irrevocably alter: "You'd better be prepared for doing a lot of touring because that's really the only unique situation that's going to be left."[3]

In the years since Bowie's interview was published, the "music like water" metaphor has taken on a life of its own, having been adopted, rejected, and debated by an array of actors, from musicians to tech CEOs to journalists to fans. Certain commentators have taken exception to the metaphor, describing it as a "fallacy."[4] Yet it is not always clear whether it is the metaphor itself that critics find objectionable or the reality it purports to describe. Among proponents of the latter view is industry analyst Mark Mulligan. In a 2019 keynote at Midem (a major industry trade show), Mulligan conceded that in the past twenty years music "*has* become like water." But this change was not without problems:

> There's . . . the unintended consequences of . . . music becoming like water. . . . How many of us go: 'I love the water that comes out of my

tap, I really value it.... I feel connected with water in my tap.' We don't. It's something that we'll miss if it's not there, but it's just a utility. And there's a risk that we've turned it into that, by stripping it of a lot of the context and emotion and cultural identity that music used to have.[5]

Others have been more enthusiastic in embracing both the metaphor and the transformations it heralds. Notable in this regard is the 2005 book *The Future of Music*, by self-described futurists David Kusek and Gerd Leonhard. Greatly expanding on Bowie's offhand comparison, the book has done much to promote the "music like water" metaphor.[6] Indeed, Kusek and Leonhard's treatment of this theme has been so influential that key figures within the music tech sector have adopted it wholesale. In a 2010 interview Spotify CEO Daniel Ek employed the metaphor to describe his aspirations for the then recently launched platform: "We believe that music should be like water. We want music to be everywhere and in every device, in every place.... I should always have music accessible."[7] For Ek, at least, the trope didn't offer a description of how things are so much as a prescription for how they should be, a reality that Spotify would usher into being.

In this chapter I revisit the "music like water" metaphor. My goal is not simply to subject this particular figure of thought to critique—though critiqued it will be. Rather, even as I consider its ideological dimensions, I argue that this metaphor also discloses something important about music's status on streaming services. Namely, it throws into relief the increasingly ambivalent relation streamed music has to the commodity form. In contrast to traditional distributors or retailers, platforms aren't simply or straightforwardly agents of music's commodification. Rather, they commodify and decommodify music at one and the same time. Their success in commodifying music on behalf of certain parties (rights holders) hinges on their simultaneous decommodification of it in relation to others (users). The latter aspect is perhaps most apparent in relation to advertising-supported "freemium" services, where music functions as a "free lunch" used to attract listener attention and generate listener data, which can then be rented to advertisers or shared with data brokers.[8] But even when users pay a monthly fee for a service, they do not pay for music as such. What subscribers pay for is access to the service. Streaming a greater number of tracks incurs no extra marginal cost, just as streaming fewer provides no discount. As a result, the connection between music and exchange value is severed—at least from the standpoint of users.

Yet music's decommodification vis-à-vis users is only part of the story. The reason is not that some people pay hard cash for streaming services, while others don't. Nor is it that music, like most other things, passes in and out of the commodity form across its "cultural biography." While it is true that music "may be treated as a commodity at one time and not at another," what makes streaming distinctive is how it collapses these successive moments.[9] Specifically, the model of the multisided platform enacts music as both commodity *and* noncommodity, and it does so because each of these economic forms is useful in producing and valorizing the assets (data, user base, ad networks, and so on) that stand at the center of the platform business. If music is enacted as a noncommodity, this is true only on the side of the service that faces users, as a way of building up the asset that is a service's user base. Conversely, if music remains a commodity on other sides of the service, in relation to other actors—most notably rights holders—this is because music serves as a critical input for the maintenance and valorization of the asset that is the platform itself. But even if music is only passingly decommodified on streaming services, this nonetheless marks an important change.[10] As Theodor Adorno and others have argued, commodification profoundly reshapes culture, subjecting this paradigmatic expression of the nonidentical and the noninstrumental to the identitarian and instrumentalizing logics of capital. This being the case, even an incomplete and partial decommodification of music promises to be no less profound in its effects.[11] It is this change in music's status that the "music like water" metaphor indexes. And it is for this reason that this chapter reconsiders this metaphor, along with the platform architecture responsible for making this figure of thought a lived reality. The aim is not simply to understand why so many people have been drawn to this trope over the years. It is also to see what this metaphor gets right about music's changed status on streaming platforms and what it gets wrong.

The Future of Music

As the most detailed exposition of the "music like water" trope, laying bare its premises and implications, Kusek's and Leonhard's 2005 text merits a close reading. To clarify music's changed status in the digital age, the authors map three key aspects of water onto music. First, the metaphor describes the present condition of music, with digital reproduction having transformed recorded music from a product defined by scarcity to one defined by plenitude. Readily available, music can flow from any digital device connected to the internet, just as water flows from any faucet connected to a water supply. "Access to music has never been easier," the pair remark, with listeners "completely awash in music."[12] Critically, however, this condition was at the time of their book's publication still only *in potentia*. That music would eventually flow freely like water was, for Kusek and Leonhard, a foregone conclusion, one whose eventual actualization was delayed by purely contingent obstacles: technical limitations, antiquated business models, an overly aggressive application of copyright law, and so forth. Music, by this account, assumes the guise of a Heideggerian "standing reserve," a resource that is simply *there*, waiting to be tapped.[13] That this had yet to occur circa 2005 did not fundamentally alter this status; it just deferred the date when the contradiction between music's novel ontological status and its practical realization would be resolved.

Second, the "music like water" metaphor represented a strategy for how to respond to the declining record sales for which digital reproduction and file sharing were widely blamed. The solution to the traditional record industry's declining fortunes, Kusek and Leonhard contended, was to be found in the model of the utility company. "Along with air," they observe, "water is an absolute essential of life. We do not pay for air—yet—but we do pay for water, and consequently some water utility companies are among the richest companies on the planet."[14] According to the utility model, music, like water, would be "available on a flat-fee basis, or on a very low 'by-the-gallon' fee schedule" (with the option, however, of paying a premium for high-end musical goods, much as one might pay a premium for bottled water). Extending the metaphor further, the pair wonder whether such a change in business model might transform music into just another "part of the cost of living," on a par with other necessities.[15] By and large, this is precisely the model that streaming services subsequently adopted, that of music as a utility or service—albeit with a few crucial differences. Central among these differences is the fact that unlike commercial streaming services, many water utilities are either publicly owned or heavily regulated by government agencies. True, neoliberal initiatives promoting deregulation and the privatization of public goods have led to a rise in privately owned utilities since the 1990s. Meanwhile, in the Global South, multinationals have been buying up water rights for decades, part of a strategy of enclosing resources previously held in common. I'll return to the threats presented by this and other such "new enclosures" later.[16] For now, it's worth noting that the utility model that Kusek and Leonhard advocate for nevertheless raises a prospect that neither they nor technocapitalists such as Ek seem to entertain: the possibility that music, like water, is better conceived as a form of public good than private property.

Also afforded by the "music like water" metaphor is a sense of how this economic relation might be experienced by users. Kusek and Leonhard suppose that such a "flat-fee utility model" would be inexpensive—"next to free," as they put it.[17] Just as monthly payments to water utilities allow access to a seemingly unlimited supply of tap water, a small periodic payment would provide users access to an unlimited supply of recorded music. And much as the fees paid to water utilities "are woven into the fabric of nearly everyone's monetary routines,"[18] the same would be true of music services. In this way, a fee structure that isn't actually free would nonetheless be experienced as such: "It would feel free to us." Setting aside that what "feel[s] free" to some might be experienced differently by those occupying a more precarious socioeconomic position, there is still something peculiar about the consumer phenomenology that Kusek and Leonhard describe. This is evident when, writing in 2005, they try to imagine what it would feel like to be a client of a media service ten years' hence: "It's 2015, and we're paying $59 a month to get all the basic content on the network for free."[19] The exact figures Kusek and Leonhard float are less important than the paradox at the core of their argument: that in paying for something, we somehow get it for free. This is a curious formulation. And while it is tempting to treat it as a slip, to do so would be a mistake. For this paradox speaks to an ambivalence that haunts the economic model they are outlining. It is this ambivalence and the underlying economic model to which the next section turns.

Music Platforms in the Asset Economy

To what extent, then, have streaming platforms made good on the predictions of Kusek and Leonhard? And if streaming platforms have indeed transformed music into something resembling water, how have they done so? To answer these questions, we need to consider the organization of these and other digital platforms, an expansive category that encompasses social networking sites such as Facebook, virtual marketplaces such as Amazon, and digitally mediated services such as Uber and Airbnb.[20] Much has been written on digital platforms, reflecting not just their growing economic significance but also the capaciousness of the word *platform* itself. As Tarleton Gillespie has pointed out, the promiscuous use of the term since the mid-aughts draws much of its power from the discourses it jumbles together: computational, architectural, political, and so on.[21]

Yet the efficacy of platforms isn't just semiotic; it is also material and practical, stemming from a particular form of industrial organization that digital platforms embody, which economists refer to as a *multisided marketplace*.[22] What this term captures is the way platforms mediate the interaction of a number of different economic actors, whom they leverage off one another in order to foster positive feedback loops, otherwise known as "network effects."[23] Streaming services, for instance, convene a number of parties: *artists and rights holders*, who provide the content to be streamed; *advertisers*, who pay for the privilege of accessing user attention; *investors*, who (in the case of stand-alone platforms such as Spotify) may subsidize operations in the here and now in exchange for future returns; and *listeners*, for whom access to music is conditional on payment (of money in the case of paid subscribers; attention in the case of "freemium" users; and personal data in either case). As with other platforms, the success of streaming platforms depends on their success in mobilizing network effects. The more users one attracts, the more revenue generated by subscriptions and advertising, and the more likely artists and record producers will distribute their music on the platform. By the same token, the more music a platform hosts, the greater the number of users it is likely to draw. And such increases in the size of a platform's database of tracks and user base translate into a commensurate increase in the amount of data the platform is able to accumulate, which can be used to enhance the services offered to advertisers as well as record companies—and so on.

As a model for understanding the economic logic of streaming services, that of the platform or multisided market has much to recommend it. But like any model, it inevitably distorts the reality it seeks to describe. This is a point stressed by the authors of *Spotify Teardown*. Among the shortcomings they enumerate are its tendency to offer "a flat rendering of digital markets" and its failure to account for anything that is not contained in the [platform] model."[24] For this reason they contend that the platform concept obscures more than it illuminates and that it should be abandoned in favor of a "properly empirical account of digital markets."[25] Yet it is not at all clear that attending to the various markets in which a firm like Spotify participates addresses the problems they highlight. After all, the figure of the market is no less an abstraction than that of the platform. "Pure" markets exist only in theory, not in practice. Hence it is far from certain whether focusing on markets rather than platforms will generate greater insights, or even whether this change of focus actually represents much of a change, given that the platform model is committed to the primacy of the market (as seen in platforms' definition as multisided markets).[26] Furthermore, by privileging of the moment of exchange, a focus on digital markets obscures other, equally important moments of economic activity (for example, production), at the same time as it elides the way capital cycles between the moments of production and exchange.

To address the limits of the platform model, then, we need to not just scrutinize the markets in which streaming services are implicated but also trace the larger circuits of value that connect the "noisy sphere" of exchange to that of production. While there are continuities between the hidden abode whose workings Marx laid bare in volume 1 of *Capital* and the forms of production that are simultaneously key to and concealed by multisided markets, there are also significant differences. Most notably, the primary concern of streaming platforms isn't so much with the production of commodities to be sold but with the creation, acquisition, and valorization of *assets*: data, databases, user groups, user attention, and above all the platform itself, as a site of investment and appreciation. This is more than just a semantic distinction, as assets have a distinctive logic and social form. Perhaps the most important difference with commodities concerns their temporality. As many thinkers have observed, commodification encourages a peculiar sort of social acceleration.[27] The faster the turnover in products, the higher the profit. Coupled with the need to manufacture demand for the items being sold, this dynamic has the effect of encouraging rapid shifts in fashion, with novelty and innovation valorized—traits evident not just in commercial pop music but also in avant-garde musics of various stripes. By contrast, assets aren't acquired in order to be turned over as quickly as possible. Rather, the point is to hold on to them. To use a term popular in finance, the aim is not to sell assets but to *sweat* them. As Lisa Adkins, Melinda Cooper, and Martijn Konings point out in their book *The Asset Economy*, a long-term, future-oriented bias is built into the asset as an economic form. Theories foregrounding commodification, they argue, view the economy "merely as a series of presents," of one-off transactions. And, "by taking the commodity as the paradigmatic form of the economy," such models lack "a temporal dimension that would allow us to understand uncertainty and speculation as constitutive aspects of economic life."[28] This contrasts with the logic of the asset, which is characterized by "an expectation-driven practice of valuation oriented towards an uncertain future."[29]

One way this change of temporal horizon manifests itself is in the way streaming transforms older music ("catalog," to use music industry parlance) into a durable source of rents. While most labels have long relied on the income generated by popular titles in their back catalog to offset the uncertainties of popular taste, across-the-board upticks in catalog sales happened only occasionally, usually when the development of a new format kicked off a once-in-a-generation format replacement cycle, as occurred with the transition from vinyl to CDs in the 1980s and 1990s. With streaming, however, older releases can continue to generate a steady revenue flow for years and decades after their initial release, inasmuch as revenue depends on use, no longer on one-time sales. So long as people continue to listen to a track or album, it continues to claim a percentage of streaming revenue and will do so until it falls out of copyright. Among other things, the continued economic relevance of older titles has fueled a spree in song catalog acquisitions, as a number of actors have come to recognize the reliable earnings that streaming allows music, as an asset class, to henceforth generate. As a consequence, it hasn't just been traditional music publishers that began paying hundreds of millions of dollars in the late 2010s and early 2020s to buy rights to songs by the likes of Bob Dylan or David Guetta.[30] It has also been boutique investment firms, such as Hipgnosis; asset management companies, such as BlackRock; and pension funds, such as the Michigan State Employee's Retirement System, which has a 90 percent stake in the Concord Music Group, whose holdings include the Rodgers and Hammerstein songbook.[31] And the continued economic relevance of older songs may in turn help to ensure their continued social relevance, since not just media companies but financial firms now have a strong incentive to promote the music in which they have a stake (for instance, via sync licensing), to keep the revenue from their investments flowing.

Related to this fundamental difference in temporal orientation—that is, the long-termism that distinguishes the asset from the short-termism of the commodity—are other salient distinctions. One concerns the valuation of assets as opposed to commodities. While models based on intersecting supply and demand curves are massive oversimplifications, it is nonetheless the case that commodity prices are shaped by a handful of relatively straightforward and above all knowable variables (the market power of a firm, effective demand, costs of production, and so on). By contrast, the fact that assets can generate returns far into the future means that the value attached to them involves a fair amount of guesswork. This helps explain the difficulties associated with pricing assets consistently, especially intangibles.[32] It also helps explain the development of accounting tools that strive to surmount such difficulties, using formulas such as "net present value" and "discounted cash flow" to square the vagaries of the future with the demand for concrete asset prices in the here and now.[33] Still another difference concerns the kinds of labor that asset management entails, compared to commodity production. Assets, like commodities (and anything else for that matter), must be produced. They don't appear out of thin air. And once fabricated or acquired, specific kinds of work are necessary for assets to maintain, inflate, or realize their value. A song fund such as Hipgnosis, for instance, doesn't have to finance the production of new works, as a traditional label or publisher might. But it still has to expend a good deal of effort in ensuring the continued demand for and cultural relevance of the music it possesses. The same goes for streaming services, which have to expend considerable effort toward the upkeep of the asset that is the platform itself, whether by renewing licensing agreements, updating the interface, adding new features, regularly cleaning data sets, and so on. In addition, the protection of assets creates a need for "guard labor," whether real or figurative (for example, IP lawyers).[34] Indeed, one of the core tasks of streaming platforms is to perform such guard labor on behalf of rights holders, by erecting and maintaining the "walled garden" where their IP resides.

Yet to say that assets occupy a central place in the economic logic of streaming platforms isn't to deny the continued importance of commodities. On the contrary: on platforms as elsewhere, commodities remain crucial. Streaming companies produce a wide array of services, for a wide array of user groups. It is simply that these are by and large a means to an end, the means by which a platform's assets may be accessed, monetized, and otherwise mediated. A case in point is the provision of streams, one of the principal services provided by streaming platforms. As noted in chapter 1, streaming is more accurately described as a process of (re)production than of distribution, since platforms will often generate a new copy of an audio file when a song is played. The stream thus functions as the vehicle by which users can access the asset that is the platform's catalog, as well as the specific piece of intellectual property that is the track. Notably, this marks something of an inversion of the position assets occupy in standard Marxian accounts: there it is the asset that is a means to an end, functioning as a capital good that serves as an input for commodity production. To an extent, the limited role accorded to assets follows from the particular conjuncture when Marx was writing. By the mid-nineteenth century, what was arguably the main asset class (land) and the principal group that owned it (rentiers) appeared as holdovers of a vestigial feudal order, one that was being progressively overtaken by a more dynamic capitalist mode of production. That this past might resemble capitalism's future, once global market consolidation and an associated decline in productivity had rehabilitated rentierism as a strategy of accumulation, was a far-off possibility when volume 1 of *Capital* was published in 1867 (also important is that other kinds of asset classes—such as intellectual property—were still in the process of being legally and socially constituted in the mid-nineteenth century).

Furthermore, the digital assets that are central to streaming differ significantly from the more familiar forms of fixed capital used in the production of physical goods and services, inasmuch as their value doesn't depreciate through use but rather appreciates. Whereas tangible assets (for example, plant and equipment) are generally consumed as a consequence of production, slowly but steadily worn down over time, the reverse is true of many intangibles: the more data, algorithms, and other kinds of digital assets are used, the more useful they become. One might conceive of this along the lines of the "cybernetic commodity" first theorized by Vincent Mosco and later updated by Nicole Cohen—that is, in terms of a product that "consists of the information or feedback created from [one's] actions and interactions."[35] But as noted earlier, "cybernetic assets" differ from commodities (cybernetic or otherwise) in that they aren't produced with an eye toward immediate exchange but have a longer-term value for a company that holds on to them, either as inputs to production or as balance-sheet items inflating a company's worth. Add to this the asset price inflation that macroeconomic policy in the United States and other advanced economies has promoted since the 1980s, and it is easy to understand why the production of assets would be equally if not more important than the production of the goods and services for many digital platforms.

Music and the Circuits of Platform Capitalism

Of the inputs that help produce the different assets and ancillary services that are at the core of streaming platforms' business, music is of course key. Like most other factors of production (servers, software, and office space, as well as the labor power of data analysts, sales representatives, curators, and so on), music is obtained on the market, where it assumes the familiar form of the commodity. But it does so in an unfamiliar way, at least compared to the kind of commodification familiar from physical formats such as sheet music, LPs, cassettes, and CDs. One important difference is that the ultimate buyer of recorded music is no longer the individual but the platform. This is a point I will come back to; for the moment, what needs to be underlined is that platforms don't sell music as a commodity to consumers but instead sell access to the asset that is the virtual archive where music resides—a vital if easily overlooked difference. Also important is that platforms do not purchase music per se but license the right to access and use it from labels, publishers, and other rights holders (though many labels, using accounting sleight of hand, classify the income they receive from streaming as sales rather than licensing revenue, which enables them to exploit the splits inherited from older, prestreaming artist agreements, which are much less favorable to artists than the royalties received from licensing).[36]

Connected to this is another difference, having to do with the structure of the market where this exchange takes place. A notable feature of this market is its symmetry, as a small number of large sellers transact with an equally small number of large buyers. Market concentration in the record industry is nothing new. Apart from a few notable periods of market disruption—most famously during the 1950s and 1960s, with the emergence of rock'n'roll—for much of its history the recorded music industry has been dominated by a handful of major labels. This remains the case today: if anything, the sector's post-2000 downturn encouraged further consolidation, with the five major labels of the late 1990s having been reduced to just three by the 2010s. Music publishing has undergone a similar concentration in recent decades. Four firms now dominate the market, with three of these—Sony ATV, Warner Chappell, and Universal—being part of the same corporate entities as the three major labels.

Notably, a high level of market concentration can also be found on the other side of the transaction. As figures 2.1–2.3 indicate, the market share of the three major streaming services (Spotify, Apple, and Amazon) by the late 2010s was roughly equivalent to the market share of the three major labels and the four major publishers, with roughly two-thirds of their respective markets under the control of just three to four leading companies.[37] Oligopoly in the supply of commercial music is matched by oligopsony on the demand side. To a certain extent, this concentration among buyers

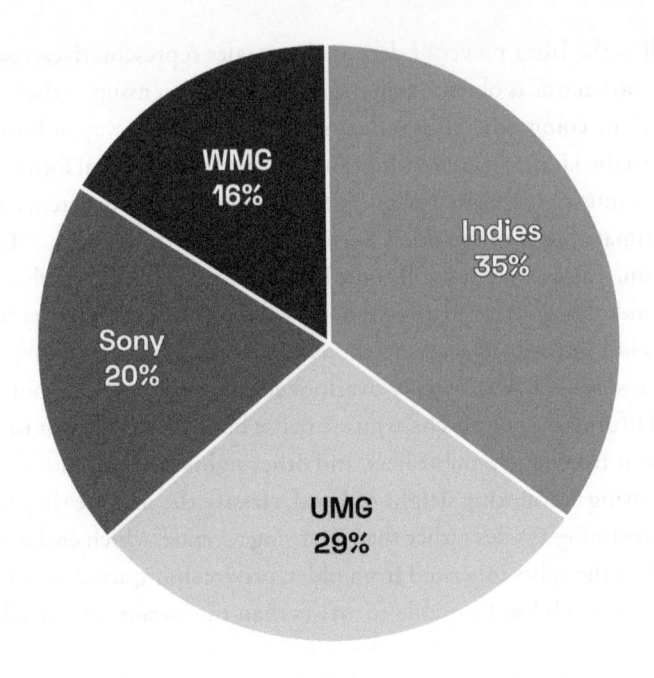

2.1 Global market share for recorded music, first half of 2019

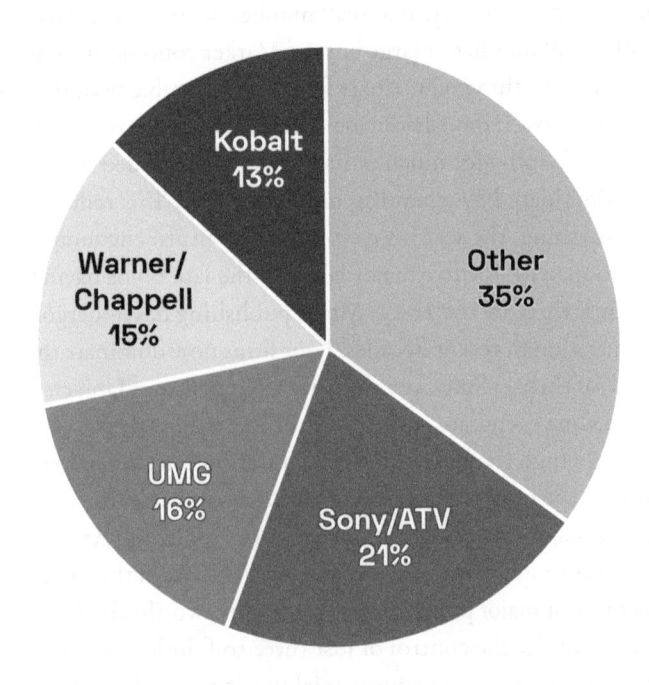

2.2 Global market share for music publishing, first half of 2019

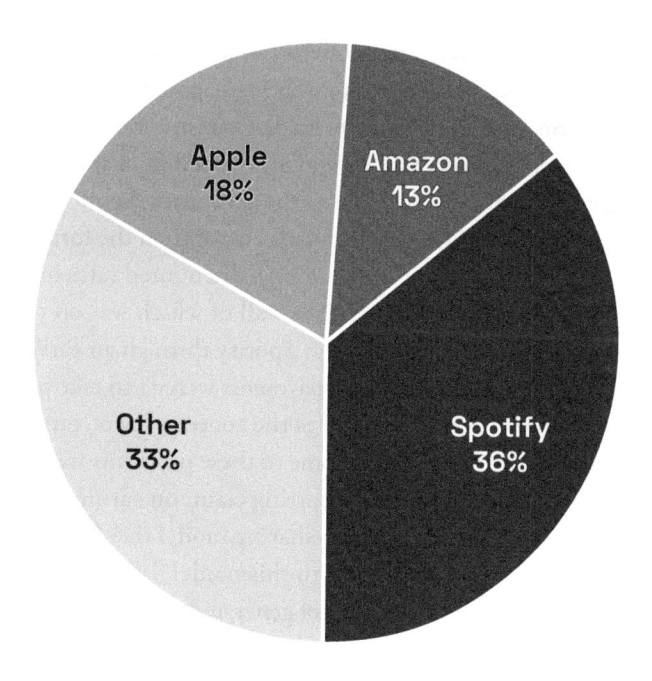

2.3 Global market share for leading streaming platforms, first half of 2019

of recorded music is part of a longer historical trajectory, beginning with the eclipse of small, independent retailers by progressively larger chains and outlets over the course of the 1980s and 1990s (Tower Records, Virgin Music, HMV, Walmart) and culminating in the early 2000s in the near monopoly over the MP3 market that the iTunes store enjoyed for a short period following its debut. Given this recent history, the somewhat less concentrated market for streaming could be seen as marking an improvement in the competitive environment for record labels, giving them greater leverage in negotiating digital distribution deals than they had in the first decade of this century.[38] Even so, the market concentration of streaming platforms, as buyers of recorded music, remains quite high, particularly by historical standards. This fact, coupled with the tight interdependence binding labels and other rights holders to streaming platforms, means that the transactions between these parties have become a site of intense struggle, with protracted and often contentious haggling taking place whenever licensing deals between platforms and major labels are up for renewal (in the United States, a similar struggle can be witnessed whenever the Copyright Royalty Board reviews the statutory rates for mechanical royalties that streaming services are obliged to pay to songwriters and publishers).[39]

Streaming Capital → 75

Complicating the transactions between labels and platforms is the heterogeneous nature of both the items being licensed (digital files, usage rights, and so on) and the payments made to secure these licenses. Here the 2011 contract between Spotify and Sony cited in chapter 1 provides some insight. According to the terms of the agreement, Spotify's payments to Sony were made not just in cash but also in kind: in the form of advertising inventory (equivalent to $9 million), discounted rates on ad buys, and access to certain types of user data—all of which was on top of the ownership stake Sony had obtained in Spotify through an earlier licensing agreement.[40] Furthermore, these payments weren't to take place all at once but were spread across the term of the contract (two years, with the possibility of renewal for a third). Some of these payments were made up front. Others were deferred, as a recurring claim on earnings, using the service-centric (or pro rata) revenue-sharing model that has historically been the industry norm. According to this model, labels are entitled to a percentage of the overall royalty pool generated during the course of an agreed-on reporting period, corresponding to the share of streams a label's catalog is responsible for having generated during this same period.[41] One upshot of this model is that it renders the price of recorded music variable, fluctuating according not only to use but also to how platforms measure and tabulate use—a fact that endows streaming services with a particular brand of "metric power" (see chapter 4).[42] Thus the same catalog, accruing exactly the same number of streams across different reporting periods, may nonetheless carry a different price, should the aggregate number of streams go up or down. What matters is not the absolute number of plays a track accrues but the relative market share it commands, making competition for user engagement a zero-sum game. Curbing this fluctuation in music's price are provisions that grant major labels guaranteed minimums, setting a floor below which revenue shares cannot fall. Similarly, "most favored nation" clauses ensure that the advance one major label receives from the platform is equivalent to those negotiated by the other majors.[43]

Other notable features distinguish the commercial transactions that take place between labels and platforms—including, notably, that the principal unit of exchange is the catalog (or aggregated bundles of catalogs), rather than the individual song or album.[44] Yet arguably the most significant transformation concerns the way music's status shifts from one side of the transaction to the other. While it is true that, for both record labels and platforms, music appears as a commodity in the act of exchange, that does not mean it appears as the same *kind* of commodity. As

Marx's formula for the expanded circuit of capital indicates (M –C … P … C′ –M′), there are commodities and there are commodities. Not a single thing, the commodity form is at least two: an input (C) and an output (C′), a factor of production and merchandise. For record companies, recordings assume the second of these aspects, that of a finished product. Incidentally, this is how Adorno and others have long tended to understand music's commodity status: as a product produced for exchange on the market, whose concrete specificity is subordinated to this end. For streaming platforms, music remains a commodity, albeit one that is purchased rather than sold. And it is a commodity that is purchased because of its utility as a capital good to be set to work in production.

As for what music is used to produce, it is not one but a number of distinct yet interconnected assets, mediated by services addressed to the different sides of the "multisided market" that platforms organize. The most prominent of these is what the general public accesses, the platform as library or archive. This is the virtual space where audio files are not only aggregated and stored but also made ready for consumption, via an entire suite of services that mediates users' access to this archive. These include the core service of producing one-off copies of files on demand (streams). But these services also include various forms of algorithmic filtering; the framing of music by means of paratexts; the provision of different tools to save, like, and/or share music—in short, many of the mediations discussed in chapter 1, in connection with the various ways streaming formats music.

A second asset produced by means of music consists of the very users who are drawn to the platform by means of music. The asset that is a service's user base is of obvious value to rights holders, being the means by which they are able to generate rents from their IP. To that end, platforms provide a number of additional services that mediate rights holders' access to audiences. These include the promotional activity performed by playlists and other types of curation; the (limited) sharing of data about who is consuming music, where, when, and how; and the act of digital reproduction, which record labels effectively outsource to platforms (compare this to the era of mechanical reproduction, when major labels owned vinyl pressing plants and/or CD manufacturing facilities, as part of a vertically integrated production process). But perhaps the most important task that platforms perform for rights holders is that of rent collection. The percentage of the revenue that platforms retain (roughly 30 percent) represents the rent they receive in exchange for the rent they collect. Hence, if platforms are beholden to rights holders because of their monopoly on copyrighted music, rights holders are beholden to platforms because of their monopoly over the valuable resource that is their user base.

Some sense of this precarious balance of forces can be gleaned from the promotional royalty rate that Spotify unveiled with great fanfare in late 2020. According to the scheme, selected tracks could obtain favorable placement on users' personalized recommendations, in exchange for a reduced royalty rate.[45] In light of the interlocking monopolies that platforms versus rights holders wield, this proposed promotional rate amounted to a price hike on the rent that Spotify charges labels and artists. Defending the scheme, Spotify argued that a relative reduction in royalty rates may still result in an absolute gain, should the promotion a track receives end up boosting its overall number of streams. "It does *not* mean lower royalties," one company executive insisted. "If a track is performing well, rightsholders can see a positive ROI [return on investment]."[46] What this argument leaves out, however, is the collective action problem the plan creates for artists and rights holders. Either some fraction of artists forgoes the promotional rate and risks losing a share of user attention (and revenue) to those participating in it, or everyone participates, in which case the benefits of favorable placement are nullified, even as royalties are reduced across the board.

Besides artists and rights holders, another clientele for whom a platform's user base represents a valuable asset are advertisers and data brokers. In services that have ad-supported tiers (such as Spotify and Deezer), user attention is aggregated, packaged according to the services' demographic and psychographic specifications, and rented out to digital advertisers. Along similar lines, the personal information of all users, premium and freemium alike, is valorized via opaque "third-party partnerships" that platforms enter into with data aggregators and data brokers. This aspect of the streaming economy is the focus of chapter 3, so fuller discussion of it will wait until then. For now, the main thing to be highlighted is how platforms' monopolization of their user base's attention helps in building up still other assets—in particular the advertising marketplaces that certain platforms (for example, Spotify and Amazon) have established. As with other digital assets, this is a cybernetic asset, whose value (in both use and exchange) increases the more it is used.

There is still another asset that platforms produce, one that is particularly important for stand-alone services: namely, the platform itself. Here the link between commodification and assetization is particularly tight, as the share price a platform can command on the market in the present is directly linked to expectations about whether its future value is likely to either appreciate or depreciate. Whence another thing that platforms need to manufacture: expectations. The case of Spotify is exemplary. As the authors of *Spotify Teardown* observe, from its official launch in 2008 to its public offering ten years later, the company generated a good deal of hype about its growth potential. One way it did so was by positioning itself as a tech firm, not as a music or media company, which enabled Spotify to benefit from the widespread belief among investors that the tech sector represented a site of boundless growth. One effect of this self-identification was to bind the company ever more closely with US-based capital markets; another was to bring it in line with the model of venture capital–fueled expansion that is a hallmark of Silicon Valley start-up culture. The result, write the book's authors, was that by the time of its 2018 listing on the New York Stock Exchange, "Spotify [was] neither particularly Swedish nor particularly about music."[47] This is true enough, but only up to a point. While music may not have been the end to which Spotify's business was geared, it was still an important means to achieving its principal end—that is, the company's self-valorization as an asset. Spotify has used music to help inflate its value as a potential investment in a couple of important ways. One has been to highlight music's importance for the accumulation of data, one of digital capitalism's most prized resources. A video addressed to potential investors released just prior to its public listing in 2018 highlighted the intimate personal information that music alone allows Spotify to collect. Citing the considerable amount of time that users (especially younger ones) spend on the platform, Spotify boasted that "we know all about the moods, moments, mindsets, and tastes of our 100% logged-in audience."[48] In this telling, music is valuable not just on account of what it reveals about the outward-facing, public aspects of people's identities (such as their tastes in music) but also because of what it reveals about their inner lives, about the "moods" and "mindsets" that would otherwise remain hidden save for the uniquely revealing insights that music—and music streaming—afford (more on this point in chapter 3).

In addition, music has contributed to Spotify's self-valorization via the narratives it has allowed the company to weave about its past, present, and future. In the same prospectus for investors, Spotify recounts the by-now familiar tale of the record industry's post-2000 decline and revival. A video titled "The Big Picture" hits all the major landmarks: the industry's 40 percent drop in revenue from 1999 to 2014, the (alleged) responsibility of "rampant piracy" for this decline, digitization's role in breaking "the music ownership model," and the negative impact all of the above had on musicians and musical culture ("artists and their creativity suffered").[49] The reversal of this downward spiral is credited to Spotify, which "leveraged major technological trends and innovations to help change the way people enjoy and discover music."[50] Within this rescue narrative, music plays a crucial if passive role, cast as the object through which the heroic interventions of Spotify emerge. Music needed to be saved from the forces threatening its existence, and Spotify was the author of its deliverance. Furthermore, a large part of what ailed the record industry was its commitment to an outdated business model. As a result, Spotify's cure comes at a cost: the old must die (or be killed off) for the new to be born. As such, the narrative related in the video plays on tech-libertarian fantasies of disruption, with their appeal to the purifying force of economic violence. For Spotify to be cast in the role of disrupter, it needed something to disrupt. And for it to kick-start a process of accumulation, it needed an industry where the circuit of capital was at risk of grinding to a halt. In both cases, music provided the necessary pretext for Spotify's past interventions, which at the same time provide the condition of possibility for its future growth.

And yet. If it is true that music plays a key role in the self-valorization of a company such as Spotify, it is also true that to play the part of the record industry's savior-cum-disrupter, the company also needed to place itself at a remove from the legacy music industry—whence the benefit of Spotify's self-representation as a tech firm. Given the widespread belief that tech companies are uniquely positioned to benefit from the "demand-side economies of scale" that network effects generate, a company that successfully presents itself as a platform makes itself all the more attractive for investors, conjuring an image of ineluctable market dominance.[51] Often, the result is a self-fulfilling prophecy: the more money investors pump into firms on the basis of this promise, the more likely it is to come to pass. At the same time, the prospect that platforms' in-built tendency toward monopoly will eventually allow them to extract outsized rents leads many investors to overlook persistent shortfalls in earnings (long the case with Spotify). But even if this monopoly position is never fully secured, the influx of capital catalyzed by the promise of its inevitability allows services like Spotify to keep the prices they charge customers artificially low. Such price-suppressing tactics are of a piece with the strategy pursued in the 2010s by many venture capital–backed tech platforms, such as Uber, which prioritized growth over profits. But while this investor-financed strategy of discounting the price of subscriptions may have subsidized the user-facing side of the platform, allowing subscriptions to be priced lower than they might otherwise be, it has had the additional effect of discounting the price of musical labor, as the share of the revenue artists receive has been suppressed along with the revenue that platforms need to earn via subscriptions.

Platforms, then, produce a number of distinct outputs. These assets are then rented to a number of distinct clienteles, each mediated by a variety of services performed by the platform:

- the archive that the listening public pays rent to access
- the user base that rights holders pay platforms to monetize
- the user data and attention that is sold or rented to advertisers and data brokers
- the service itself, as either part of a larger platform ecosystem (for example, Amazon, Apple, Google) or as an object of speculative investment in its own right (Spotify)

Far from simply organizing a series of markets that they oversee, it is more accurate to say that music platforms actively catalyze and manage a range of flows: of music, data, attention, and not least of all capital, in the form of rents paid and rents received. For this reason, a better image than the multisided market to describe the working of platforms is that of a drive gear, which, when set in motion, transmits its energy to other gears with which it is meshed: it is the movement of the platform's specific circuit of capital that sets in motion the other circuits with which it is interlocked. At least this is how streaming platforms seek to position themselves vis-à-vis the different parties with whom they transact. In practice, platforms have encountered significant challenges in shifting the balance of power that disadvantages them relative to certain clients or business partners. As Robert Prey notes, while platforms such as Spotify wield a certain "curatorial power," to the extent that placement on one of their proprietary playlists can prove pivotal for a track's commercial success, this power is not absolute; rather, it is "contingent upon the relative position of a platform in relation to its competitors and the markets it is dependent on—including the market for music."[52] That platforms' power over musicians and record companies is tempered by their dependence on the very same partners and rivals may help explain why so many platforms have had such a hard time turning a profit. Rights holders in particular, and above all the major labels, have long held considerable leverage over streaming platforms. For services integrated into larger conglomerates (such as Apple Music or Amazon Music Unlimited), losses on streaming services pose no real problem. They can simply be absorbed, perhaps by treating streaming as a loss leader that helps drive customers to other, more lucrative parts of their business (hardware in the case of Apple, Prime subscriptions and retail sales in the case of Amazon). For stand-alone platforms, such difficulties have generally been resolved via periodic infusions of capital from investors, acquisition by some larger concern, or—in certain cases—bankruptcy.[53]

From Capitalist Circulation to Social Circulation

In addition to the various circuits of capital that streaming services coordinate, another distinct yet closely coupled circuit opens out onto the space of "general" or "social" circulation, the branching trajectories that goods, services, and other outputs traverse once they exit the market. Often, these circuits are treated as mere extensions of commercial exchange and consumption. But as research in economic anthropology, commoning, and "diverse economies" have all highlighted, even societies where capital dominates are not entirely or exclusively *capitalist*. Rather, an array of alternative, extracapitalist economies coexist within, alongside, and against a dominant capitalist economy. These run the gamut from neofeudal arrangements to "actually existing" communism (David Graeber's term for the kind of sharing that is a matter-of-fact feature of everyday social life); from regimes built around "accumulation by dispossession" and expropriation (of natural resources, prison labor, devalued assets, domestic work, and so on) to communities organized around gift exchanges; from the informal economies that predominate within many countries of the Global South to collectively managed commons.[54]

One reason such noncapitalist economies manage to persist, despite capital's quest to annex anything and everything external to it, stems from capital's dependence on such externalized others. From these others, it draws critical resources that it can neither produce itself nor do without.[55] In addition, the combined force of law, custom, and economic reason enables such noncapitalist spaces to endure and even thrive, albeit under highly circumscribed conditions. Consider an ordinary good, such as a piece of furniture. Its purchase ratifies its status as a commodity. But once purchased, it can become something else. While its buyer may treat it as private property, they may also lend it to a friend, give it as a gift, bequeath it to their heirs, or treat it as a common-pool resource (often the case among members of a shared household). The piece of furniture can also reenter the sphere of commercial exchange, by being resold at a yard sale or thrift store. In short, once a commodity exits the circuit of capital, it can enter into all sorts of other kinds of noncapitalist or extracapitalist economic processes and get enacted as all sorts of other economic entities: as a gift, an inheritance, a piece of common property, and so on.

Copyright complicates matters. In the case of a physical recording, such as a vinyl LP, a copyrighted good can undergo many of the same transformations as an ordinary good. It too can be treated as private property, a lendable object, a gift, a piece of common property. Recordings can also reenter the sphere of market exchange, thanks to the doctrine of first sale in US jurisprudence and the underlying principle of "exhaustion" (whereby copyright holders cede certain rights on selling a copy of a work). Legal precedents like these enable the existence of secondary markets where used books, records, DVDs, and other copyrighted goods can be exchanged.[56] Yet the fact that a copyrighted good such as an LP has a dual status—existing as both a physical object and the medium for a copyrighted work—means that its circulation is subject to additional restrictions. To begin with, copyright law limits the number of copies one can make and distribute. Public broadcast is also ruled out, unless one obtains the requisite license. The same goes for sampling a recording in another composition. In short, which postpurchase uses of a copyrighted good are legally sanctioned—and hence, which extracapitalist circuits it is able to move through—aren't simply given. Rather, they are the outcome of political-economic decisions and hence political-economic struggles. Historically, the record industry may not have been happy about the existence of secondary markets for used records, regarding them as a source of unwanted competition.[57] Yet the balance of legal and political forces meant that labels had little choice but to accept their existence. Likewise, sample-based hip-hop artists may have objected to the restrictions that copyright placed on their ability to draw on older recordings, but the record industry's legal and lobbying efforts were such that they had little choice but to find alternative forms of expression.[58]

With the ascendancy of digital music, many of the physical features that had long backed up the legal constraints of copyright law no longer apply, thanks to the combination of the internet's decentralized architecture and the ease, speed, and cheapness of digital reproduction. Copyright owners may still have retained the *right* to exclude people from the music to which they had title, but they no longer had the same *capacity* to exclude them—a state of affairs made clear by the file-sharing boom that Napster helped spur.[59] Less immediately apparent was how digital technologies might also extend the control that rights holders enjoy over the postpurchase use of copyrighted goods. But with the record industry's push to embed DRM in audio files in the early 2000s, it became apparent that purchasing an MP3 often meant that instead of purchasing a copy of a recording, one was purchasing only a license for its use, subject to strict conditions and limits (how many copies of a file could be made, on which devices it could be listened to, and so on).[60] The subsequent shift from digital downloads to streaming has pushed this tendency further, imposing even stricter limits on music's circulation. With streaming, all listening is to take place within the confines of the platform. One thing this permits is continuous collection of data on user activity, which may then be monetized in a variety of ways (see chapter 3). By tethering music to streaming services, users find themselves similarly tethered.[61] Another thing streaming ensures is that music's passage from capitalist circulation into general circulation is only ever partial. Unlike physical recordings, which once sold can participate in all sorts of extracapitalist relations, music as streamed would seem to never fully escape the circuit of capital. Even on being played back—which in streaming ideally collapses production, circulation, and consumption into a single moment—music still serves as a means of production for platforms, generating valuable resources in the form of data about users and the music they consume.[62]

The restrictions streaming places on music's circulation are not immune to resistance or circumvention on the part of users. Indeed, if prior industry efforts to curtail the flow of copyrighted material have demonstrated anything, it is that virtually every time a technical fix is developed to limit how people can access and use music, a counterfix neutralizing these restrictions follows shortly behind.[63] In the case of DRM, one counterfix was code that could crack the encryption that blocked the unauthorized use of audio files. In the case of streaming, a different counterfix has come in the form of stream-ripping sites, which allow streams to be recorded and saved to a user's device. Small wonder, then, that once revenue from streaming overtook sales of digital downloads and physical recordings, the record industry began to target such sites, casting them as the new face of music piracy. In its 2017 *Music Consumer Insight Report*, the International Federation of the Phonographic Industry (IFPI) noted that copyright infringement had not disappeared with the decline of file sharing but was "evolving rapidly," with stream ripping flagged as the "dominant method" at present.[64] Lobbying efforts and legal actions undertaken by the IFPI and other trade groups have paid off. In spring 2019, the threat of a lawsuit from the RIAA led one stream-ripping site, YouTubNow, to preemptively shut down its operations, at the same time as the RIAA's Australian counterpart, the Australasian Performing Right Association, won an injunction barring internet users in the country from accessing stream-ripping services (2conv, Flv2mp3, FLVto, Convert2mp3).[65] Meanwhile, in 2018, the office of the United States Trade Representative placed a number of stream rippers (for example, MP3Juices) on its annual list of "notorious markets," likely in response to pressure from the RIAA, IFPI, and other trade groups.[66]

Beyond the counterfixes provided by stream ripping and other technologies, there is a more fundamental way music escapes platforms at the point of playback. In the parlance of media industry personnel, this is the "analog hole" down which all digital media inevitably disappear.[67] This may seem trivial. But it is important, if only because it marks a hard limit on platforms' efforts to colonize users' musical lives. And while streaming is designed to prevent any durable trace from being left behind, it cannot prevent a lasting impression from being made on the medium that is the listener. Imprinted in one's memories, music can circulate in ways other than those prescribed by rights holders or technical protocols. For the same reason, even if the act of streaming generates data on both the music being listened to and the person listening to it, the incorporation of consumption into the circuit of capital isn't absolute. There is invariably a remainder that the data thus generated fail to capture. This isn't simply on account of the sparseness of the signals being relayed (what track is being played, when, for how long, on what device, if it is being skipped, and so on). It is also because the process demands that a fluid and qualitative experience be transformed into a series of reified and strictly quantitative data points (see chapter 3). Add to this the fact that the music listened to may resonate with the user, having an affective, psychological, symbolic, or physiological impact that persists well past the immediate moment of playback, and it becomes clear that the technocapitalist dream of listening's full datafication—or music's full enclosure on streaming platforms—is fated to remain an incomplete project.

Yet just as important as what happens once music exits the platform's walled garden are the conditions under which this exit is permitted to occur. In the case of music that is purchased and owned, be it a physical recording or DRM-less download, its release into social circulation occurs only after payment is made. In contrast, the commercial exchange that releases music from a streaming platform's enclosure—however partially and incompletely—is indirect. This is true not just for "freemium" users, whose payment is made in the form of attention. It is equally true for premium subscribers, who pay in legal tender. Rasmus Fleischer underlines this point in relation to Spotify, when he notes that the monthly fee that subscribers pay is, in fact, "the only price that will ever confront an ordinary user of Spotify."[68] From this follows a pair of conclusions. First, that "the one and only commodity sold to consumers by Spotify is the subscription."[69] And second, that the user of Spotify (or any other subscription service) "does not confront songs or albums as commodities."[70] Even as platforms pay labels and publishers for the right to use their music—thus upholding music's commodity status—music assumes this form only in the exchange between rights holders and platforms. For users it appears differently: as something decommodified. Far from an altruistic gesture on the part of streaming services, a gift they bestow on users, this decommodification of recorded music is a strategic gesture. It is the condition of possibility for other things to be commodified in music's stead, including the service (in relation to paying subscribers) or users themselves (in relation to advertisers and data brokers). It is the condition of possibility as well for the platform's assetization. Far from signaling an emancipation from capitalist social relations, music's transformed status vis-à-vis users heralds a displacement and tightening of these relations.

Insight into streaming's complicated relation to the commodity form can be gleaned through a comparison to the sort of free exchange that the MP3 facilitated. Widely heralded in the early years of the new millennium as the means by which a noncommercial musical gift economy might take root, MP3s shared online may have broken with the commodity form in certain respects, but, as Jonathan Sterne points out, in other respects they remained altogether faithful to this form.[71] Not wholly decommodified, MP3s exchanged on file-sharing sites and stockpiled on users' hard drives occupy a liminal space, behaving not quite as a commodity but not quite as a gift either.[72] For this reason, another term used by Sterne—*demonetization*—better describes the MP3's impact, capturing how file sharing removed the need to pay for music, even as it left intact its commodity status. Even after the launch of the iTunes store, many of the MP3s people acquired may not have been legally purchased, but this did not stop listeners from treating them as private property: "Users may be able to handle MP3s quite differently than the recordings they possess in larger physical forms like records or CDs, but they still talk about MP3s as things—things that are owned, and which offer affordances to their users."[73] Also important was that MP3s were still stamped with a price, if only vestigially. Even if an MP3 could be obtained for free, there is a sense in which this represented a discount on a price it would have commanded if acquired licitly. Apple's iTunes store played a critical role in this connection. Once it established the $0.99 per download rate as a de facto industry standard, it was possible to measure how much "consumer surplus" one enjoyed by obtaining an MP3 gratis—exactly $0.99 worth. Even when acquired outside commercial exchange, MP3s are still stamped with an exchange value. It is just that this value goes unrealized.

As something that can be owned (even in the absence of a tangible object) and that represents an exchange value (even in the absence of commercial exchange), the MP3 demonetizes music without decommodifying it. With streaming, however, matters stand differently. Many of the features that still bind the MP3 to the commodity form appear to be lacking in music as streamed. First of all, the possessive relation to music that the MP3 continued to provide users is further attenuated with the shift to an access-based model of music distribution. Granted, individuals may invest the playlists they create and the files saved to them with a sense of ownership, as ethnographic studies of streaming use indicate. Anja Nylund Hagen, for instance, observes how "the playlist enables ownership of music . . . because it undermines or narrows the impact of the service's shared features and content in the interests of elevating personal music selection."[74] But even if possession is not just a legal but a psychological relation, the "psychological ownership" that streaming affords users doesn't confer any legal rights. Users may feel that the tracks saved to a playlist in some fashion "belong" to them, but that doesn't mean they can dispose of the playlist in the same ways they can dispose of things they legally own—say, by removing files from the platform or retaining them upon closing their account.

More important, music as streamed departs from the commodity form in that it no longer carries a price, even notionally. And this is true regardless of whether one is a paid subscriber or freemium user. Those for whom music continues to carry a price are the platforms themselves: it is they who pay for music, not end users, who pay only for access to the platform. And this price remains the same whether one streams a single track a month or hundreds. "Once the monthly subscription is paid," observes economist Alan Krueger, "the marginal pecuniary cost of consuming music is zero."[75]

This dynamic helps clarify the paradoxical way Kusek and Leonhard describe subscription services, as an exchange where one pays to get something for free. Far from being a logical slip on their part, this formulation captures something essential about streaming services. Music no longer costs the user anything, even if the subscription still does.

Helpful for understanding this change in music's status is the standard economic taxonomy that distinguishes between different kinds of goods: public, private, common, and club. Of these, public goods are characterized by a similar decoupling of use value and exchange value (the same is true of the distinct yet closely related category of common goods). This decoupling follows from two attributes that private goods possess and public goods lack: rivalry and excludability. To say that a public good is nonrival is to say that one's use of it doesn't preclude another's, while to say that it is nonexcludable is to say that access to it cannot be restricted. (Public goods differ from common goods inasmuch as the latter are still subject to rivalry, at least to some extent; a common pastureland that isn't properly managed can be subject to overgrazing, as per Garrett Hardin's famous—if ultimately misleading—fable of the "tragedy of the commons").[76] A paradigmatic public good that exhibits both of these characteristics, nonrivalry and nonexcludability, is a radio broadcast: listening to a given station's broadcast doesn't prevent others from tuning in as well, while access to the station is largely unrestricted—albeit on condition that one owns a radio receiver and is within its broadcast range. As this last point underlines, however, the characterization of a good as excludable or nonexcludable is not a binary, either-or affair. Rather, excludability and nonexcludability exist on a continuum, which is also true of rivalry and nonrivalry.

Like most cultural and information goods, music sits more comfortably in the category of public rather than private goods. The goods that are rivalrous and excludable are the media by means of which music is stored and transported—sheet music, vinyl LPs, and so on; these can be treated as private goods.[77] Yet, as many writers on digital culture have observed, digitization attenuates the material qualities that promote rivalry and excludability, undermining music's ability to function as a private good. Technologies of digital reproduction can generate a virtually limitless number of near-perfect copies of a recording, dispensing with rivalry as a meaningful characteristic of recorded music. Meanwhile, the rhizomatic, many-to-many structure of the internet makes it difficult to stem the free movement of recordings online, dispensing with excludability as well. It was of course these features that fueled the file-sharing boom in the decade after Napster's launch in 1999. But streaming doesn't try to combat this state of affairs by introducing new legal and technical restrictions, as the record industry initially did in response to the post-Napster decline of record sales. Rather, the streaming model happily embraces music's status as a quasi-public good. Streaming doesn't seek to turn back the clock and return recorded music to the condition of a private good. At most, it relocates music in a transitional zone between these two extremes. One way of describing this strategy is to say that streaming transforms music into a *club good*, a category that combines the excludability of private goods with the (relative) nonrivalry of public goods. While technically correct, the term doesn't fully capture the symbolic and above all political dimensions of music's changed status. For even as club goods derive some of their utility from being shared—there's little use or enjoyment in being the sole member of a club—they derive another part of their utility from placing limits on sharing. Excludability ensures exclusivity. By contrast, platforms have no interest in restricting membership. Even if their economic model depends on restricting access, this imperative sits alongside the equally pressing demand to grow their user base as much as possible. Rather than describe music on streaming platforms as a club good, it makes more sense to say that it remains a public good, albeit one from which the public has been effectively dispossessed. Music, in short, becomes a privatized public good.[78]

A similar dissociation of use value and exchange value can be seen in connection with other objects and processes. Such is the case with types of work that fall outside the formal economy but that nevertheless perform socially useful tasks. A case in point is the kind of user-generated content that services such as YouTube or TikTok depend on or the data that users coproduce as a consequence of their interactions with digital platforms. Products such as these, while not forming part of an explicit and quantifiable exchange, still prove useful for capital, performing vital work on its behalf. It is simply that the work thus performed isn't recognized as such. As Jason Moore observes, "capitalism is not merely a system of unpaid costs ('externalities')"; it is also "a system of unpaid work (invisibilities)."[79] Another, paradigmatic example of such invisible and disavowed work is that which is required for social reproduction (see chapter 5). The same goes for the work of ecological systems. As with social reproduction, the work that nature performs and that capital benefits from is seldom recognized *as* work. And as is the case with social reproduction, the denial of its status as work enables the ideological mystification whereby the resources that nature furnishes and that capital enlists in its project of endless accumulation are presumed to be "free gifts," simply there for the taking.

To these sources of un- or underpaid work it is necessary to add another: that which is provided by artistic practice. Defined in opposition to the formal economy, as an activity guided not by the profit motive but by its own, internal logic, music in particular has long managed to carve out a space of relative autonomy. This is most clearly evident in connection with Western classical music, which has developed an extensive system of public financing, indirect subsidy, and charitable giving precisely in order to buffer it from the pressures of the market. Yet the belief that the arts (including music) should not be wholly subordinated to the logic of capital is also operative in more thoroughly commercialized forms of musical production and distribution. Indeed, even artists signed to major labels—which may arguably be considered the beating heart of industrial music production—enjoy a control over their labor process that most workers under capitalism lack.[80] But the freedom won by asserting music's eccentricity vis-à-vis the economy also makes music all the more prone to being expropriated by the very economy it repudiates. The assertion that the true value of music cannot be measured in strictly economic terms is all too easily equated with the belief that music lacks economic value and, as a result, can be treated as yet another free gift—not of nature but of human nature, one that is no less ripe for the taking. The relatively poor remuneration that musicians receive for their services—a historic tendency that streaming has aggravated—is but one symptom of music's institutionalized devaluation. Like the content produced by users of digital platforms, the work of social reproduction, and the "ecosystem services" provided by nature, music's social effects continue to have a significant use value for capital, even as the denial of the work music performs *as work* deprives it of exchange value. It is by means of this decoupling of use from exchange value that capital is able to benefit from the former without having to pay for the latter.

Noncommodity Fetishism (or How Music Is Like Water, and How It Isn't)

We are now in a position to address the questions raised at the outset of this chapter: namely, what do claims of music having become like water get right about the digital music economy, and what do they get wrong?

Notably, water has long figured in political economy as the paradigmatic example of a good whose economic value does not adequately reflect its true social utility. None other than Adam Smith looked to water in *The Wealth of Nations* to illustrate the principle that the two aspects that value assumes under capitalism do not always move in lockstep. "Nothing is more useful than water," he observed. And yet "it will scarce purchase anything; scarce anything can be had in exchange for it."[81] While it is true that objects can acquire an exchange value only if they also have a use value, as Marx would later remark, the example of water showed that the reverse didn't necessarily hold: just because something has a use value doesn't mean that it will also bear an exchange value. "The things which have the greatest value in use have frequently little or no value in exchange," Smith commented, while "those which have the greatest value in exchange have frequently little or no value in use."[82] Subsequent authors further developed the disjunction between use value and exchange value that water was seen to epitomize. For James Maitland, it became the hinge on which another distinction, between "private riches" and "public wealth," pivoted. For David Ricardo, the disjunction was an effect of water's status as one of the "gifts of nature which exist in boundless quantity," which made it available at "no price" to "the brewer, the distiller, the dyer," or to any other producer who used it in the "production of their commodities."[83] And for Jean-Baptiste Say, the disjunction served to indicate which domains fell outside the purview of political economy altogether: "Some items of human consumption are the spontaneous gifts of nature, and require no exertion of man for their production, as air, water, and light.... These are destitute of exchangeable value; because the want of them is never felt, others being equally provided with them as ourselves. Being neither procurable by production, nor destructible by consumption, they come not within the province of political economy."[84]

In their treatment of water, these landmark figures of classic political economy interweave a number of the themes touched on earlier: the dissociation of use and exchange value, which makes water singularly "uncooperative" in the face of efforts to commodify it; the basis of this dissociation in water's status as one of the "gifts of nature which exist in boundless quantity," which is to say, in its nonrivalrous and nonexcludable character on the one hand and in the perception of it as a gift freely given on the other; and its representation as a source not of "private riches" but of "public wealth."[85] It is this self-reinforcing complex of qualities that the "music as water" metaphor maps onto music. But contrary to what writers such as

Kusek and Leonhard would suggest, this mapping is not just constative, not just a purely descriptive account of recorded music's condition in the age of digital media. It is also performative, conjuring into being the very condition it purports to describe. In this connection it is important to bear in mind that the transformations that are said to have made music resemble water are in no way necessary but contingent. If digitization has troubled recorded music's ability to assume the form of a private good, and thus that of a commodity, this too is a feature not of music per se but of one of its many mediations. Under other circumstances, realized by means of other mediations, music can quite readily accommodate itself to the commodity form. This is the case with physical media. And, as we've seen, it is also the case in the relation between platforms and the rights holders from whom they license music.

But it is not just that certain mediations of music are more liable to be commodified and others to be decommodified, or that some are more liable to behave like private goods and others more like public goods. Rather, the variability in music's socioeconomic status underlines the fact that the very qualities that distinguish different kinds of goods—public, private, common, or otherwise—are not essential and fixed, but mutable. While material and technical factors may shape which economic category a given object falls into, equally important are the social practices, ideologies, and institutions that govern their management and use. As Massimo DeAngelis observes, even an item—for instance, a hammer—whose material qualities would appear to make it rivalrous, excludable, and therefore a quintessential private good can be made to behave otherwise. Transforming it into a common-pool resource is simply a matter of changing the relations that organize its social circulation and use: "One person's use of the hammer presents a significant barrier to others who desire to use that hammer at the same time. However, the first user does not *use up* the hammer, meaning that some rival goods can still be shared through time."[86] Whether a thing is treated as a private or public good follows not from its putatively innate qualities but from the social organization of its circulation and use. Similar observations can be made about music. For much of the twentieth century, the need for a physical medium to fix, store, and circulate recordings may have facilitated their enactment as private goods and hence as commodities, but it did not unilaterally impose this status on recorded music. For that to occur, there also needed to be in place ideologies that led people to treat recorded music as such and institutions—above all copyright—that encouraged a possessive relation to records, tapes, and other media, while discouraging alternative kinds of relations. That alternatives were indeed possible is demonstrated in the existence of different kinds of institutions, organized around different kinds of ideologies, however overshadowed these may be by the market's hegemonic status. Public libraries are a case in point. Even if the material qualities of books and records make them rivalrous and thus private goods ripe for commodification, the particular way libraries organize the social circulation of their holdings offers an institutional solution to the challenge of their holdings' physical attributes. As with a hammer, the use of a book or record by more than one person at the same time may be disallowed; but if we expand our temporal horizon beyond this single point and disperse use across its duration, it is possible for an object that would otherwise remain a private good—such as a physical recording—to behave like a public one instead.

What the "music like water" metaphor gets right, then, is the way that music, once mediated by digital streaming platforms, comes to assume many of the attributes habitually associated with public goods, with water serving as a prototype of this category. What the metaphor gets wrong, however, are the reasons music has come to assume these qualities. It is not simply on account of the way digitization allegedly "dematerializes" music, robbing it of the material characteristics that were believed to have hitherto guaranteed its rivalry and excludability. It is also—and more significantly—on account of the particular set of social relations that streaming platforms orchestrate. These are social relations that follow from streaming platforms' simultaneous commodification and decommodification of music: music appears as decommodified only in relation to users, so that the data and attention of these same users can be commodified instead—which in turn enables the recommodification of recorded music elsewhere, in the transactions between platforms and rights holders. Appealing to water in order to make sense of music's changed status therefore has the effect of naturalizing this status, along with the forces that are seen to have brought it about. Revealing in this connection is the way Kusek and Leonhard describe the "becoming-water" of music not as an unheard-of departure but as a return to a normal, even "natural" state of affairs. By this reading, the aberration was the twentieth-century record industry's enactment of music as a durable good: "After more than a century of music being pitched and sold primarily as static products, . . . we are, in a way, returning to [the] early days, and music can once again become more about the experience than the product."[87] At the same time, responsibility for this return is attributed solely to technological factors, whose effects are registered in the physical properties of recorded music. It is digitization and streaming more specifically that are seen to have stripped music of those qualities that hitherto ensured its rivalry and excludability, not the economic imperatives these technologies are harnessed to serve.

That is not the only thing the metaphor gets wrong. Comparisons that characterize music in terms of a natural resource such as water don't simply naturalize attributes of music use, attributes that are in fact a contingent effect of the particular industrial organization that digital platforms adopt. By naturalizing certain attributes of music, the metaphor also naturalizes nature, ascribing ontological fixity to what is ultimately an ideologically freighted way of figuring water. "Water is what we make of it," observes Jamie Linton, though "it seldom stays that way for long."[88] In his telling, the dominant guise that water has assumed under capitalism—the ideological construct he dubs "modern water"—treats it simply as a physical substance, shorn of "ecological, cultural, or social factors." Reduced in this manner, water becomes "an objective, homogeneous, ahistorical entity devoid of cultural content." Further reinforcing this conception of water is its "isolation from people," thanks to "modern techniques of management that have enabled many of us to survive without having to think much about it."[89] At the same time, and much like music, water's status as the paradigmatic public good does not follow straightforwardly from the physical qualities with which it is normatively identified. As Silke Helfrich notes, while drinking water is usually considered a public or common good, it need not be so: "depending on the degree of excludability, drinking water can become any kind of good: common to all of us, private, public, or reserved for an exclusive club."[90] Recent history bears out her point. Efforts to privatize the provision of water are among the hallmarks of the neoliberal era. Then again, so too are social movements that have fought back against the enclosure of this critical means of subsistence, some of which have met with a measure of success (the Cochabamba Water War being a famous example). At the same time, the strain industrialized agriculture places on water systems and pollution from resource extraction and manufacturing—to say nothing of the droughts brought on by anthropogenic climate change—call into question discourses that blithely refer to the "ubiquity of water" as a model for envisaging the ubiquity of music.[91]

Despite the ongoing pressures to enclose, expropriate, and commodify water, despite the economic and ecological processes that are making it an increasingly scarce resource across many parts of the world, the figure of water as one of the "gifts of nature which exist in boundless quantity" has proven remarkably resilient. In its own small way, the "music like water" trope contributes to its persistence. To say that music has or should become like water is not only to project a particular ideological construction of water onto music; it is also to performatively reinscribe onto water the very characteristics that music is said to share with it. The result is a self-reinforcing feedback loop, as a reductive conception of water is put to work in generating an equally reductive conception of music, which bolsters in turn the very conception of water in whose image it was fashioned. Water's putative abundance is reflected and reinforced by music's putative abundance. The radical asymmetry between water's use value and its exchange value is reflected and reinforced by the dissociation of these two aspects of music's value on streaming platforms. And the givenness of water, its characterization as a free gift of nature, is reflected and reinforced by the givenness of music on streaming platforms, its appearance as something that is there for the taking, precisely because it does not require payment in exchange—at least not directly.

This last point is worth underlining, as it is not just the nonrivalry and nonexcludability of digital objects that promote music's decommodification for streaming's users, but the longer-standing ideology that disavows musical labor as labor and that discounts both its value and the value of its products as a result. Just as the work performed by social reproduction and the work of ecosystems are seldom recognized as such, the same goes for the work performed by musicians, which is typically characterized more as play than drudgery, as an escape from labor rather than as a form of labor in its own right. In some cases, it is even characterized as a product of nature—namely human nature, with artistic expression being seen as part of the "species being" that defines humankind. "Milton produced *Paradise Lost* as a silkworm produces silk, as the activation of his own nature."[92] Part of a broader meditation on the distinction between productive and unproductive labor, this remark of Marx's is typically interpreted in order to either uphold or contest the classification of artistic practice as productive or unproductive, or to interrogate the utility of drawing such a distinction in the first place.[93] More significant, however, is the way Marx equates these two kinds of labor, one human, the other nonhuman, and the way this equation removes both from the sphere of economic phenomena: both silkworm and Milton produce not with an eye toward exchange but out of an inner compulsion, which neither has any choice but to obey. In much the same way, the "music like water" metaphor positions music as an exception to the economy, fostering the impression that it is simply given, simply *there*, much in the same way as water is imagined to be. And the more that both music and water alike are taken as given, the less visible becomes the work, whether human or nonhuman, that is required for their production and provision.

We might conceive of this situation by way of analogy to Marx's notion of commodity fetishism: think of it rather as a kind of noncommodity fetishism. In both, work comes to be objectified in the products it creates. And in both, this objectification facilitates a certain misrecognition, whereby value (or a lack thereof) is attributed to the physical properties of the object itself, rather than to the work that produced it and the web of social relations within which this work is embedded. The difference, however, is that in the case of commodity fetishism what is misrecognized is the source of a commodity's value; in the case of what I'm calling noncommodity fetishism, however, what is misrecognized is the source of a noncommodity's nonvalue. In this way, the absenting of value that a noncommodity like water or music undergoes is taken unproblematically as an inherent absence of value. Denied expression in economic terms, whatever extraeconomic values a noncommodity possesses are put out of reckoning, as the work that has brought it into being resists expression in the form of abstract labor—the only kind of labor that counts for capital, because it is the only kind of labor capital is able to count.[94] As a consequence, something like water appears as given rather than made and therefore as inherently "destitute of exchangeable value." In a single stroke, the work of the hydrological cycle is dismissed as work. And to the extent the "music like water" metaphor remakes music in the image of water, music too begins to resemble something simply given, as just another feature of the ambient cultural environment, whose readiness-to-hand for listeners occludes the work of the musicians who produced it.[95]

• • •

If streaming platforms commodify music in relation to rights holders while simultaneously decommodifying it in relation to users, then what are the effects on music and on its use by listeners? One possibility is that users are encouraged to treat music as water long has been: as a utility. Morris and Powers, for instance, observe how "streaming services have . . . eagerly promoted a vision of the future where streaming provides a totalizing 'musical atmosphere' to satisfy any musical need at any moment," thereby playing on the "notion of music and media as a kind of 'utility.'"[96] That there is no extra cost to be borne the more music one consumes not only incentivizes the consumption of more music, in a greater variety of contexts; it also incentivizes this way of engaging with music, by lowering the marginal cost of music listening to zero. At the same time, to the extent "musical needs" are explicitly linked on streaming platforms to other kinds of affective, physiological, or social needs—mood regulation, identity construction, self-care, and so on—music is enacted as a utility in more ways than one. It also approaches the condition of water by being cast as a necessity of life, a resource for the ongoing reproduction of life—which, as we will see in chapter 5, is tantamount to securing the ongoing reproduction of labor power.[97]

Whatever the longer-term impacts of music's simultaneous commodification and decommodification on streaming services, the act of listening is not the only place where the effects of this ambivalent status may be felt. Just as important are its consequences for music production—and hence for music producers. For the overwhelming majority of musicians, music as streamed appears the same way as it does for users: as something decommodified. True, they may receive some remuneration from services. But in most cases the payouts artists receive are so meager that their music appears likewise as something given, though perhaps not given freely or willingly.[98] While a commercial exchange still takes place, for all but a handful of superstar performers the amount of money involved is so negligible as to effectively deprive much recorded music of any semblance of exchange value. In this respect, at least, the decommodification of recorded music amounts to a decommodification of the labor of artists: this, too, is deprived of exchange value, even as it continues to be vested with use value (for record companies, publishers, and streaming platforms, as well as for listeners).

In this respect, the work of musicians resembles that of other kinds of work that, in the words of Leigh Claire La Berge, have been subjected in recent years to "an emptying out of the ... wage relation that nonetheless continues to structure our lives."[99] In addition to unpaid or underpaid work within the cultural industries, La Berge cites internships, prison labor, civic and voluntary work, and the various forms of uncompensated student and peer-faculty work that universities rely on. Musicians, to be sure, have not been idle in the face of this institutionalized devaluation of their labor: some have joined (or formed) unions, others have taken part in lobbying efforts seeking legislative redress, others have urged users to boycott streaming services, and still others have withdrawn their labor by withdrawing their music from offending platforms.[100] Taylor Swift famously resorted to this last tactic in November 2014, when she pulled her entire catalog from Spotify in protest of the way its freemium tier devalued music. ("Music is art, and art is important and rare," she explained in an editorial in the *Wall Street Journal*. "Important, rare things are valuable. Valuable things should be paid for.")[101] Still another approach taken by artists and their advocates has been to appeal to the ethical sensibilities of music listeners, urging them to access music via other, better-paying channels (physical recordings, digital downloads, and so on), or to use services that offer more equitable remuneration to artists.[102] This of course is part of the pitch that Jay-Z and other superstar artists somewhat cynically made to music fans in launching Tidal in 2015, presenting the service as an artist-owned platform that would prioritize the interests of musicians.[103] While it's not inconceivable that calls for ethical music consumption will someday gain traction with listeners, there is little reason to suspect they will do anything other than perpetuate existing economic relations. As critics have pointed out, there are significant limits to what can be achieved by means of fair-trade networks, ethical consumerism, and other forms of "market-driven social justice." Beyond the fact that such interventions represent more of a "symbolic challenge to the principle of market exchange under capitalism" than a "fundamental challenge to the core aspects of commodification," there are other reasons for skepticism: not only does ethical consumption draw on and reinforce an illusory sense of consumer sovereignty, but it also adds a further layer of mystification to those already fostered by commodity fetishism, presenting "the commodity form [as] the solution to its own mystifications."[104]

What these diverse responses to the problem of musical labor's devaluation share in common is a drive to recouple the two forms of value—value in use and value in exchange—severed by streaming's enactment of music as a quasi-decommodified, privately owned public good. This is implicit in Taylor Swift's argument. If art's value is indexed by the price it can command, then music that commands no price has no value—not just economically but symbolically. And yet, as Lee Marshall has pointed out, claims like those that Swift makes about recorded music's diminished value at present rest on some question-begging assumptions. One is that recorded music would be valued higher but for the adverse effect of exogenous forces ("piracy, file sharing, and streaming," according to Swift).[105] But as Marshall notes, exogenous forces were just as likely to have been responsible for artificially inflating the value of recorded music in the past. The aberration, in other words, was the high cost of CDs at the industry's peak in 1999, not the "market correction" that followed. As Marshall observes, "digitization merely revealed ... that [recorded] music is less valued by most individuals than has been assumed."[106] But this is not the only way to interpret Marshall's findings. Perhaps people have valued and continue to value music highly, just in terms other than the dollar amount they are willing to pay for it. Viewed from this angle, the more important assumption that goes unexamined is the yoking of music's sociocultural value to its economic value. The problem, in other words, isn't that the absenting of music's exchange value somehow leads inexorably to a diminution of the symbolic and aesthetic value attached to it. Rather, the problem is that these values are deemed to find expression only through the narrow lens of commercial exchange. In a way, this marks a more significant devaluation of music than the one that Swift denounced, a devaluation that occurs when economic value is claimed as the sole medium through which every other kind of value might be expressed.

Understood in this light, the dissociation of exchange and use value that music undergoes on streaming platforms no longer appears as a problem in search of a solution. On the contrary, it represents a potential solution in its own right—albeit a solution to a different problem, the problem that is the commodity form, with all the mystifications, inequities, and forms of domination that it embodies and perpetuates. I'll return to these questions in the epilogue of the book, questions that concern how the streaming economy might be either reformed or wholly dismantled. But for now, what I want to suggest is that much broader systemic changes are required if the utopian potential of music's decommodification is to be realized. These are changes that go beyond calls to restore to music the exchange value it has lost or to recouple it with the use value from which it has been decoupled. Struggling to recommodify music, in the vague hope that doing so might recommodify musicians' labor in turn, will not suffice. Rather than trying to counteract recorded music's decommodification, a more productive strategy would be to push this tendency further still. In certain respects, this recalls a proposal made by musician and author Damon Krukowski. In a 2013 interview, he argued that it was necessary to face up to the "basic truth" that "no one can own the stream, any more than the air," musicians included.[107] He has subsequently reiterated this point, arguing that a better model than streaming would be one premised on "simply sharing music with one another for free."[108] As Krukowski goes on to observe, other sources of income will have to be found for musicians, to compensate for the revenue lost by forgoing royalties from streaming. And this is certainly a pressing need, one that could (and should) be addressed via increased public funding, some kind of guaranteed income scheme, or the issuance to musicians of ownership shares in the major labels, streaming platforms, and other corporations that profit from their creative work.[109] But such stopgap measures shouldn't take the place of a longer-term strategy of extending decommodification to other spheres, beyond those to which it is restricted at present. The problem, from this perspective, isn't that music and musical labor are decommodified but that so many other things aren't—including, most critically, the means of subsistence that musicians no less than anybody else depend on. The problem, in other words, is not that music and musical labor are positioned as exceptions to the capitalist economy, but that so many necessities of life—food, shelter, health care, education, and so forth—continue to be subject to its rule. Yet until such time as these necessities are likewise decommodified, recorded music's (partial) emancipation from the commodity form amounts to a very different kind of emancipation for music workers, a "liberation" from the possibility of making a living from their music.[110]

Chapter Three

Music as a Technology of Surveillance

"SORRY"

On August 21, 2015, Daniel Ek took the unusual action of posting a message to Spotify's official company blog. The gist of it was summed up by a single word blazoned in all-caps across the top of the page: "SORRY."[1] Prompting the Spotify CEO's act of contrition was mounting public outcry in response to recent changes in the company's privacy policy. What had appeared as a run-of-the-mill update to the platform's terms of service turned out to be anything but.[2] Closer inspection revealed a raft of provisions, which, among other things, would grant Spotify permission to retrieve personal data held on third-party apps such as Facebook; access GPS and other sensors on mobile devices; collect voice commands via built-in microphones; and scan media files on users' devices, including MP3 libraries, photo albums, and address books.[3] This last proviso presented a peculiar complication. Individuals whose contact information Spotify could now access via its users' address books would need to consent to their information being shared, even if they didn't have Spotify accounts themselves. Another provision sought to resolve this problem by making users responsible for obtaining such permission: "Local law may require that you seek the consent of your contacts to provide their personal information to Spotify."[4] Under the terms of the new policy individuals would not only be the targets of Spotify's data collection regime; they would also be its accomplices.

The hue and cry that ensued from this updated privacy policy indicated that Spotify had crossed a line, that which separates forms of corporate surveillance to which people have become inured and those still deemed illegitimate. It is a line that digital media companies have taken pains to blur. In 2011, Pandora came under scrutiny from federal investigators for allegedly obtaining information about users without their consent.[5] In 2016, a class action lawsuit was filed against Tidal by fans claiming they had been lured into subscribing to the platform on the (false) promise that it would be the exclusive outlet for Kanye West's album *The Life of Pablo*. The $84 million suit sought to compensate users for the value of the personal information they had disclosed on signing up. Lawyers for the plaintiffs argued that it was precisely in order to collect such information that Tidal had misleadingly promoted itself as the sole site where Kanye's fans could hear his latest release.[6]

In the case of Spotify, criticism of its abortive data grab stemmed not only from the kinds of information the company was seeking to obtain but also from the uncertain ends to which it would be put. "What kind of media files Spotify will collect from you is vague, and why the company needs it is unclear," wrote one journalist, "but it's doing it regardless."[7] In seeking to quell the furor, company spokespersons sought to assure users that the sole purpose of such aggressive gathering of data was to improve the platform's services. "Spotify is constantly innovating," read one press release, noting that "the data accessed simply helps us to tailor improved experiences to our users, and build new and personalized products for the future."[8] The language of the privacy policy, however, pointed to a different rationale. Significantly, Spotify reserved the right to transmit the data it gathered to various third parties, including its "advertising partners." As one clause explained, such data would allow marketers to "show you more tailored content, including relevant advertising for products and services that might be of interest to you."[9] Apparently, music recommendations weren't the only things Spotify sought to customize. Beyond this, other unspecified third parties—euphemistically referred to as "trusted business partners"—were also granted access to users' personal information. Why Spotify trusted these business partners—and why users should do likewise—went unexplained.

This episode throws into relief a pair of issues explored in this chapter: the importance of data to the economy of online music streaming and the implications that follow from its intensified collection, use, and valorization by companies such as Spotify, Amazon, and others. These developments have been noted by a number of scholars. Tim Anderson, for one, observes that "what differentiates so many music services in the new paradigm [of music distribution] from the older one is the reliance on end user data."[10] Commercial exploitation of user data is of course not limited to music services but characterizes digital media companies more broadly, constituting what some have described as the leading edge of surveillance capitalism.[11] Notable examples include Google and Facebook (now Meta), whose advertising revenue hinges on information gathered about users via search queries and social graphs, respectively.[12] For giant tech firms and streaming platforms alike, such data not only promise to improve the services offered users but also represent an important resource that can be (and often is) monetized more directly. This can happen in a number of ways:

- As a *commodity*, data about users can be exchanged, shared, or sold via the commercial relations that platforms have with third parties, including ad servers, credit agencies, insurance companies, and data aggregators.
- As a *factor of production*, data can be used not only to improve various services but also to better define the users whose attention is rented to advertisers, specifying their demographic and psychographic attributes. For larger tech companies, such as Google or Amazon, this data can also inform what other products in their online marketplaces users should see ads for or be steered toward.
- As an *asset*, user data can contribute to a platform's market valuation, making it a more attractive vehicle for capital investment or acquisition.

More will be said about the first two approaches to monetizing user data over the course of this chapter. As for the third—data as asset—it has been instrumental to the survival of certain platforms, above all Spotify, given the company's persistent inability to turn a profit. Prior to its public listing on the New York Stock Exchange in 2018, the company had been kept afloat largely thanks to periodic injections of capital from private investors. In 2015, for instance, the platform raised $350 million from a group of investors including Goldman Sachs, on the basis of a market valuation of $8.4 billion.[13] By the time it went public, the gap between Spotify's high valuation and negative balance sheet had increased, its valuation by that time exceeding $26 billion. Using traditional metrics—for example, price-earnings (P/E) ratio—such a high valuation would seem hard to justify. Some of the market's bullish assessment follows from the aura that surrounds Spotify due to its identification as a technology firm, one of the few sectors that managed to outpace an otherwise lackluster global economy in the wake of 2008.[14] Another part follows from the dynamics of financial speculation, with asset prices appreciating over the course of the 2010s thanks to loose monetary policies ("asset price Keynesianism") and the self-reinforcing feedback loop of financial bubbles—though hikes in interest rates set by the US Federal Reserve and other central banks beginning in 2022 have deflated this bubble considerably, with Spotify's market cap declining to around $20 billion at the time of writing, after peaking in early 2021 at $69 billion, during the height of the COVID-19 pandemic.[15] But perhaps the most important factor buoying the company's balance sheet has been investors' historic lack of concern in Spotify's short-term profitability. According to the model pioneered by other tech platforms—especially those backed by venture capital and private equity—profits are deferred in favor of a ruthless pursuit of scale. The aim isn't simply to build a viable business but to achieve market dominance. This has been Spotify's strategy, with the company routinely invoking "scale" as a panacea that will resolve many of the challenges it confronts—not just consistent losses but also low payout rates for artists. As a financial statement filed by the company in 2016 asserted, "our model supports profitability *at scale*," adding that "*at scale*, our margins will improve."[16]

In certain respects, the strategy has gone according to plan. In 2009, a year after its public launch, Spotify had attracted 7 million users, with revenues totaling $18.1 million.[17] By 2014 its user base had ballooned to 60 million, with revenues crossing the $1 billion mark.[18] Five years later, in 2019, user figures had reached 271 million worldwide (124 million paying subscribers), with revenues of just over $6 billion.[19] So far, so good. The problem for Spotify is that expenses have risen in lockstep with earnings, with the platform channeling roughly 70 percent of its revenue to rights holders. Given this dynamic, it is hard to see how scale alone will ever deliver the kinds of superprofits that investors expect Spotify to someday generate. One way out of this bind is for Spotify to become so dominant in the streaming market that rights holders—above all the three major labels—come to depend on Spotify more than Spotify depends on them. This increased leverage would then allow Spotify to negotiate down the percentage of its revenue that it is obliged to share. To a certain extent, this has come to pass, with major labels agreeing to a reduced percentage—52 percent as opposed to 55 percent—when licenses were renegotiated in 2017.[20] Another way of reducing dependency on rights holders is to redefine the market. This, too, is a strategy Spotify has pursued, through its move into podcasting following its acquisition of Gimlet and Anchor Media in 2019. By adding a new category of content to the service, the company redefined itself as an audio rather than as a music platform, making Spotify less beholden to music companies than in the past.

The turn to podcasting may benefit Spotify in other ways as well, since music streaming and even the more broadly defined service of audio streaming aren't the only markets that Spotify is angling to dominate. Also of keen interest are markets for audio advertising and for consumer data more broadly. Even though Spotify hasn't made much money from advertising to date, using its ad-supported freemium tier mainly as a means of attracting users who can later be "upsold" to the subscription tier, advertising's relegation to a supporting role in the company's business model isn't set in stone. The examples set by Facebook and Google are important in this connection: not only do they demonstrate the immense profits that can be generated by monopolizing a segment of the online advertising market (search in the case of Google, banner ads in the case of Facebook), but their very success in dominating these ad markets has fueled demand among marketers for newer, cheaper media to exploit, with digital audio increasingly seen as an attractive site for expansion.[21] "Advertisers have always understood the power of audio to connect with audiences both on an emotional level and through the mobile, intimate nature of the medium," announces a 2020 report by the Interactive Advertising Bureau. And "thanks to multiple digital advances . . . , there is now a real opportunity for the digital audio advertising market to thrive."[22] This is an opportunity that Spotify has seized on in redefining itself as an audio platform. Critical to its strategy has been the creation of its own advertising marketplace (the Spotify Audience Network), along with acquisitions building out its infrastructure (for example, ad-insertion firm Megaphone).[23] Equally critical to this strategy has been Spotify's accumulation of data over the years. Viewed from this perspective, Spotify's (and investors') dreams of market domination and monopoly rents, while hardly assured, are perhaps not as far-fetched as might first appear. Even if the company has seldom turned a profit, even if it owns few of the music assets on which its business depends, what it does possess is a massive trove of user data. And this is a valuable asset in its own right, being the ground on which its future prospects of dominating the digital audio ad market are staked.[24]

But even were Spotify never to succeed in monopolizing the market for digital audio advertising, there is another way it might still profit from the stockpile of user data it has amassed: through the company's acquisition by a larger firm with an equally voracious appetite for data. "In many ways, the preferred solution [for Spotify] would be to get sold to someone," music industry analyst Mark Mulligan mused in 2014.[25] While talk of its acquisition subsided after 2015—in part because of its rising market valuation—rumors continued to circulate. An article published in *Rolling Stone* in spring 2019, for instance, listed five potential suitors: Netflix, Facebook, AT&T, Samsung, and Tencent. Furthermore, the postpandemic decline in Spotify's market valuation has made this prospect seem less remote than at any other time in the recent past. Should such a sale ever be consummated, as unlikely as it may seem, then the data that Spotify has accumulated over the years would have proven their worth twice over: not just for their role in the company's relentless assetization of its user base but also for their role in Spotify's efforts at assetizing itself.

In the rest of this chapter, I examine the ways streaming services such as Spotify have positioned themselves in the market for user attention and data by casting themselves as sources of highly precious, because highly personal, information. A number of questions follow from this: What data on users' listening habits do platforms collect, and what do they infer from these data about users' lives beyond the platform? How do services make the data generated via user interactions distinctive—and thus desirable—for advertisers and data brokers? And perhaps most important, why is music deemed so effective for data collection? While consumer surveillance in music streaming has garnered increasing attention of late, less attention has been paid to the distinctive qualities that music is said to possess and that make it particularly useful for consumer profiling.[26] Indeed, claims about music's unique affordances for surveillance abound within marketing campaigns that platforms direct not at prospective consumers, but at prospective advertisers and investors. Such campaigns cast music as a medium that offers streaming platforms, advertisers, and data brokers alike privileged access to listeners' innermost selves. But they also cast music as something that pervades our everyday lives and, for that reason, can function as an ideal tracking device, providing unique insights into who we are, how we feel, what we do, and how these fluctuate from one moment to the next. The value of music, by this account, resides in the intensive and intimate knowledge music reveals of ourselves and our lives.[27] Treated not solely as an asset, music is transformed into a means by which listeners can themselves be assetized, as their attention is parceled into ever more finely gradated segments to be rented to advertisers, while their personal data are rendered ever more personal so they might fetch a higher price. As a means of surveillance, music thus becomes at the same time a means of production, helping to generate the data that are extracted from users' listening activity online.

Music for Rent, Listeners for Rent

Far from marking a clean break with the past, streaming platforms' valorization of user data hearkens back to practices inherited from broadcast media.[28] In this light, the model of the platform or multisided market discussed in chapter 2 isn't as novel as its proponents in the business press might suggest.[29] Indeed, its lineaments can already be discerned in one of the most enduring accounts of the political economy of the media, that of Marxist communications scholar Dallas Smythe. Writing in the 1970s, Smythe argued that the main commercial product of corporate mass media was not content (that is, the music or shows being broadcast).[30] Rather, it was the aggregated attention of the audiences attracted by such content that constituted the real commodities that media companies produce, with advertisers being their principal clientele, not the listening or viewing public (later thinkers have reformulated Smythe's thesis in noting that attention is not actually sold so much as treated as a resource to which access is rented).[31] But if ad-supported media mainly traffic in audience attention, what does that make the content they broadcast? For Smythe, it is simply an expedient for pooling attention in the first place. The songs played on the radio, or the programs aired on television, are what Smythe, following A. J. Liebling, refers to as a "free lunch"—a phrase that already gestures toward the way music and other media would be partially decommodified on streaming services, as a way of commodifying (or assetizing) other things (see chapter 2).[32] In this respect, a traditional commercial broadcaster may likewise be understood as orchestrating a multisided market, one that coordinates three circuits: one that provides programming to audiences in exchange for their attention, another that provides some of this attention to rights holders in exchange for access to recordings, and a third that provides another portion of this attention to advertisers in exchange for money.

Smythe's work has garnered renewed interest in light of recent developments in digital media. The internet, mobile telephony, web 2.0, social media, the proliferation of portable (and now wearable) devices, the "internet of things," home assistants: each of these technologies has opened the way to more intensive methods of monetizing media audiences. Scholars have identified a number of ways this process has evolved with the spread of interactive networks. Particularly important is the increasing precision with which users may be packaged and their attention meted out. A baseline for comparison is provided by the largely indeterminate publics solicited by broadcast media, the object of Smythe's writings. Membership in such audiences depends not on a fixed attribute that individuals share but on an action they perform (listening, reading, watching, and so on). "The existence of a public," Michael Warner observes, "is contingent on its members' activity..., and not on its members' categorical classification, objectively determined position in social structure, or material existence."[33] Yet the fluctuating and uncertain character of mass-mediated audiences that results from this has driven attempts to find some "external way of identifying [them]," of rendering them determinate.[34] One strategy involves the identification of some demographic trait seen to bind audience members together: to the extent demography is correlated with differential patterns of consumption, it is thought to function as an adequate proxy for the amorphous figure of the audience. This strategy not only underpins the long-standing practice among record companies and radio broadcasters to subdivide the music-listening public by race, class, age, and gender. It is also what has driven them to develop ever more finely grained segmentations of the market. In the case of the US record industry, this process has led from the partitioning of the market according to the crude race- and class-based categories operative in the 1920s and 1930s ("race," "old time," and so on) to the more fractured genre space of the early twenty-first century.[35] In the case of the US radio market, this same dynamic has prompted the multiplication of ever more tightly focused radio formats since the 1970s, with Contemporary Hits Radio (the current iteration of Top 40) now coexisting with stations specializing in Rhythmic Oldies, Contemporary Inspirational, and Spanish Tropical, among others.[36]

The need to make the otherwise fluid entities that are audiences more concrete has also driven the development of techniques aiming to measure audience size, composition, and behavior. For both broadcast media and advertisers, the ability to quantify audiences—and to do so with some semblance of objectivity—is vital, for it is only when goods can be quantified that they can be priced in a manner satisfactory to both buyers and sellers. One consequence of this has been the development of a secondary industry devoted to the measure of audience ratings. As Eileen Meehan noted in an important revision to Smythe's model, firms dedicated to the measurement of audiences, such as Nielsen and Arbitron, have proven so successful in interposing themselves between media companies and advertisers that ultimately what is traded is not audience attention per se but ratings—symbolic constructs, usually derived from techniques of statistical sampling.[37] Such statistical approximations have long been a source of conflict among both commercial media outlets and advertising agencies. On the one hand, numerical representations of "average quarter-hour persons," "time spent listening," "audience share," and other artifacts of the ratings industry foster a misplaced sense of confidence in broadcasters as well as advertisers. As Ien Ang remarks in connection to television ratings, such figures give rise to "a sense of concreteness, a sense of ontological clarity about who or what the . . . audience is."[38] On the other hand, the latent awareness that such statistical approximations are precisely that—approximations—makes them a source of anxiety, clouding the "ontological clarity" they promise to bestow. The tension generated by this desire to know the public, a desire whose intensity is heightened by the impossibility of ever attaining such knowledge, has fueled the production of newer and ostensibly improved technologies of audience research over the years: from the telephone polls and audimeters of the 1930s and 1940s to Broadcast Data Systems and the "portable people meters" of more recent decades.[39] Yet the fundamental unknowability of audiences means that each innovation that claims to reliably measure them falls shy of the mark.

With the rise of interactive, networked media, however, a qualitatively different kind of entity may be targeted and rented to advertisers: the attention of determinate users rather than indeterminate audiences. Unlike broadcast media, which transmit messages indiscriminately to individuals dispersed in space and time, interactive media can exploit user log-ins, IP addresses, cookies, and digital fingerprinting to ostensibly connect specific individuals to specific devices and online activities. As a result, streaming sites and other digital media platforms are able to monetize users not as potential members of a supraindividual category such as a public but as individuals. Larger groups may still be formed, by collating different users into demographic tranches whose attention can then be rented or their data shared en masse. But in contrast to the publics convened by technologies of mass mediation, the groups convened by networked technologies are nothing more than an aggregation of otherwise disaggregated individuals. As Anderson notes in connection with Pandora, the platform is able to deliver "specific categories to advertisers as the listener listens," which contrasts with commercial radio's reliance of formats "to find audiences that are based on estimates and projections."[40] Pandora may still rent out access to user attention in bulk, but each demographic package it assembles consists of only those individuals who manifest whatever trait advertisers desire, at whatever time and for however long the individuals happen to exhibit it.

This change in unit is only one way digital platforms have sought to valorize the asset that is their user base. Another involves the expropriation of the activities individuals perform in producing the user-generated content on which many platforms depend.[41] As regards music platforms, such content includes the playlists that users compile on most services, the "likes" or other kinds of explicit feedback they can apply to tracks or albums, or, in the case of upload sites such as YouTube or SoundCloud, music itself. More important, however, is that any kind of online activity generates "content," in the form of potentially useful (and thus valuable) information about the user who performed it. As Mark Andrejevic has noted, interactive technologies permit "the redoubling of user activity in the reflexive form of information about this activity."[42] For streaming platforms, such "reflexively redoubled" information includes relatively conspicuous signals, such as which songs or artists are searched for, which are played, how often, for how long, which are added to playlists, and so on. But this information may also include less conspicuous digital traces that are a by-product of users' online activities, such as the date and time tracks are added (or removed) from playlists, at what point in a track a user skips ahead, the distribution of listening activity across different time scales (days, weeks, months, years), and so forth.

Being the property of the platform that captures and records it, such surplus information may be monetized in turn. The result is a cybernetic asset par excellence (see chapter 2). Coupled with other forms of user information, collected during the registration process (name, address, credit card information, and so on) or from third parties, such "reflexively redoubled" data can generate still more information, through the correlations that emerge from the combination of data sets.[43] Demand for the resulting information stems from a variety of commercial actors, most notably data management platforms, credit reporting agencies, ad servers, and other aggregators of consumer information.[44] I'll have more to say about this market at the end of the chapter. For now, it suffices to note that the use value that consumer data hold for companies such as these resides in the contribution the data make to the construction of detailed profiles of individuals. But even if digital media have made it easier than ever to extract value from users' attention and activity, their efforts to monetize these resources still run up against hard limits. Consider the rendering of user attention as an asset. While interactive technologies promise greater precision in targeting individuals, what is packaged and shared with third parties is no less a representation than the statistical projections used to establish audience ratings and price ad slots in broadcast media. As Smythe already noted in the 1970s, what is traded is not the audience per se, but "audience power," that is, the potential of audiences to attend to advertising. What isn't exchanged—indeed cannot be—is their actual attention.[45] Digital media also package an abstract potential for exchange, the difference being that it is situated at an individual rather than a populational level. As with audiences, what can be monetized is the capacity of users to attend to information. But whether this capacity is realized cannot be guaranteed, only inferred through indirect signals (whether users clicked on a banner ad, whether they muted an audio advertisement, and so on).

The same goes for the user profiles that platforms construct. Their nonidentity with the individuals they purport to represent results from the partial and fragmentary image they fashion of their real-world counterparts, a disjointed outline cobbled together from an array of data points. Such profiles may be associated with specific persons and may be refined through the collection of still more information. But they are only ever piecemeal versions of their real-world counterparts. For this reason, Matthew Crain observes, the task of "confronting information gaps about current and potential customers has always been a fundamental challenge for marketers."[46] No matter how much information is added to profiles, the fact that data are never simply given but are the product of contingent techniques of measurement, recording, and representation means that such profiles do not transparently reflect the users to which they are assigned.[47] Profiles may correspond to users, but they are not equivalent to them.

The persistence of such gaps has driven two trends in the market for consumer attention and information. One concerns the way marketers, data brokers, and digital media companies have endeavored to disaggregate users, transforming them from individuals into what Gilles Deleuze termed *dividuals*.[48] As I have discussed elsewhere, such an understanding of the self as multiple informs work in music recommendation, with analysts at streaming platforms conceiving the "single listener" as containing "many listeners," depending on time of day, activity, and so on.[49] For marketers and media outlets, the appeal of this approach is evident: if the individual is still too inexact a target, then it is necessary to go beyond the individual to something more elemental. Thus, even as the interpellation of the user as a dividuated individual is presented as a means of improving music recommendations for the benefit of users, it also serves the interests of platforms and their third-party partners, by justifying a relentless collection of user data. If one's musical desires fluctuate in response to changes in situation, setting, or mood, then it is across these changing situations, settings, and moods that a service needs to track users, if it is to provide them with a musical flow that matches the continuously evolving contours of their lives.

While the drive toward dividuation seeks to overcome the gap separating users and their profiles, a second trend responds to the stubborn persistence of this gap, by improving the quality of the data that are the stock in trade of advertisers and other buyers and sellers of consumer information. Indeed, *data quality management* has become something of a watchword in digital advertising. Take, for example, the report *Enriching Media Data*, published by the Coalition for Innovative Media Measurement in 2015. The report cites a number of problems with the data advertisers acquire, listing "source credibility, recency, consumer classifications, collection method, [and] representativeness" as perennial matters of concern.[50] Such concern for locating sources of high-quality data has created a situation that media companies—including streaming platforms—have cannily exploited, by trumpeting the unique qualities that differentiate the data they collect from that of rival firms. Such efforts at product differentiation are themselves marketing efforts, directed not toward end consumers but to other marketers, whose business media companies wish to attract. The proliferation of media outlets and the heightened competition for advertising revenue this has engendered mean that in order to sell access to users' attention or personal data, media companies also have to work hard to sell themselves, as purveyors of particularly valuable forms of user attention and personal data.

You Are What You Listen To

How then does intensified competition over user attention and information shape the practices of streaming platforms such as Spotify, Pandora, or Amazon Music? Recall that while end users are an important clientele for multisided markets like those coordinated by streaming platforms, they aren't the only one. Also important are another set of consumers—consumers of user attention and user data. Hence platforms compete not in a single market but in several different ones simultaneously. In the consumer market, the competitive struggle is over the money and attention of listeners, with streaming platforms trying to outflank not only other streaming platforms but also terrestrial and satellite radio stations, video-upload sites, social media, digital music retailers, brick-and-mortar record shops, as well as file-sharing sites. In the market for user data and attention, platforms are locked in a different competitive struggle, whose object is the business of advertisers, data brokers, and other third parties. Their rivals within this market likewise go beyond streaming platforms, encompassing the entire spectrum of media, old and new alike.

Because platforms have to compete against a panoply of media for the business of advertisers and data aggregators, it is imperative that they confer a distinctive value on the data and the attention they generate. Platforms' efforts at product differentiation do not take place in a vacuum but involve the collaboration of a variety of actors.[51] Marketing executives, data analysts, and other personnel in the employ of platforms are important participants in these processes. But also important are the contributions made by nonhuman actors, especially the technologies responsible for capturing and processing listening data; by users, whose attention and interactions are obligatory inputs; by rival platforms, which have an interest in dedifferentiating their competitors' products, casting them as generic goods for which others may be substituted; and not least of all by the discourses that circulate around music, which, by shaping impressions about what our listening activities reveal, also shape impressions about how valuable the data generated by these activities might be.

There are a number of ways platforms impart an aura of uniqueness to the audiences and data they collect. They might tout the size of their user base or the vast quantities of data on listeners the platforms have harvested over time.[52] They might also cite the greater number of user interactions that music elicits relative to other media or the heightened attention that audio, unlike images or text, is purportedly able to command.[53] Of all these strategies, two stand out. One focuses on the techniques of data analysis developed by streaming services. The privilege accorded these techniques is largely a function of their much-vaunted capacity to microtarget individual users and dividuated user-attributes. The second centers on the virtues seen to inhere in the very thing that, by prompting users to engage with platforms, also prompts users to shed data about themselves. This thing is music.

The ostensible aim of data analytics is to index, sort, and match audio files to users, in an effort to provide an ever-improving service for customers. As a result, Morris remarks, such techniques of "infomediation" have become "important vectors on which companies seek to differentiate themselves."[54] Thanks to the proprietary algorithms platforms have developed, they can collate music data with various kinds of user data to achieve mass personalization. This is true even of companies such as Apple or Pandora, both of which in the past have touted the input provided by their human employees (to curate playlists in the case of Apple Music and to tag audio with metadata in the case of Pandora). Of course, such paeans to an ineffable "human touch" serve not only to obscure these companies' similar dependence on algorithmic automation but also to differentiate the assets and services they produce from those of their rivals. The same false dichotomy that opposes "good" human curation to "bad" algorithmic recommendation is also used to distinguish services' ad-targeting capabilities. "Algorithms aren't personal. People are personal," declares the Pandora for Brands website. Just as algorithmic techniques are maligned for failing to provide meaningful music recommendations for listeners, so too are they criticized for their shortcomings in connecting advertisers to targeted audiences.[55]

On the other side of this divide, among platforms that vaunt the prowess of algorithmic systems, a similar parallel is routinely drawn between success in music recommendation and success in targeted advertising. Pertinent here is how music recommendation systems have evolved since the turn of the millennium. Following early efforts focused on content-based recommendation (that is, using machine listening to analyze audio features), later supplemented by semantic analysis and collaborative filtering, beginning in the 2010s increasing emphasis was placed on matching songs to users' fluctuating desires by exploiting data about contingent, situational factors, in particular context and mood. In the case of context-aware recommenders, information gathered from sensors embedded in mobile devices are used to identify patterns in musical behavior that correlate with location, local weather, time of day, heart rate, and so forth.[56] As for music emotion recognition, it typically employs some combination of semantic analysis and machine learning to automatically tag audio files with metadata describing their affective features. And just as these developments allow platforms to replace the promise of an individuated user experience with a dividuated one, they allow a similar pitch to be made to advertisers and data aggregators, offering to target not just individual users but users subdivided by changes in mood, activity, context, and so on. For users, the dream that is conjured is one in which activities ranging from the mundane to the consequential can find a suitable musical accompaniment: "From scrambling an egg to choosing the next leader of the free world, all moments can be made better with music."[57] For advertisers and data brokers, the dream that is conjured is one in which these same activities can either trigger a relevant ad or be registered as part of a detailed user profile.

A short video, addressed to potential advertisers and posted to the Pandora for Brands portal in 2015, makes this parallelism clear. Accompanying an image of a garishly colored gumball machine, a woman's voice cheerily asks viewers to hearken back to the frustrated desires of childhood: "Remember when you were a kid, staring at that big gumball machine, and all you wanted was to get your hands on the bright blue berry-flavored gumball? Imagine a world where you can finally ask for and receive the exact gumball you want, and get it in real time."[58] Like music consumers, advertisers are guaranteed they will get exactly what they want, when they want it. But whereas for the listener the object of desire dangled before one's ears is a piece of music perfectly attuned to whatever context or state of mind one happens to be in, for advertisers this object is none other than the in/dividuated listener, the "bright blue berry-flavored gumball" the voice-over invokes (significantly, the listener is figured here as something to be chewed up and spit out). Later in the same video, Pandora specifies what, exactly, has brought to the brink of realization advertisers' dream of "reach[ing] the right audience, with the right contextual messaging, at the right place and time": it is the mass of information on individual listening activity that the platform has collected over the years, overtly for the purposes of refining the delivery of music to users, covertly for refining the delivery of user data and attention to third parties. "Pandora has one of the largest logged in user bases," the video announces, "and our rich targeting capabilities are driven by insightful data points, such as music listening preferences, that we have been processing from our listeners for nearly a decade."[59] Generally speaking, such uses of listening behavior aren't widely publicized. It is mainly in trade magazines, advertising expositions, and other professional contexts that platform employees are more open about the affinities linking customized music recommendation to customized marketing. A tweet by one Spotify executive during an ad expo in 2016 is representative: "Our algorithms build hugely successful listening experiences.

We are using the same expertise to build our ad products."[60] Along similar lines, a product manager at Pandora boasted in an interview that the company "has invested a lot of time and resources to developing the music genome project," which has borne fruit in the "great data asset that we now use for our advertising systems as well."[61] Here as elsewhere, the precision with which the desire of users can be anticipated is presented as a proxy for the precision with which the desire of advertisers can be realized.

Developments in mood- and context-based recommendation take on a particular significance in light of this interest in real-time microtargeted advertising. If information about who one is, what one is doing, or how one is feeling can be marshaled to match the "perfect song" with the "perfect moment" (as one Spotify promotion puts it), then the same techniques can be harnessed for advertising and data collection, albeit in reverse. Instead of using contextual information to identify songs or playlists appropriate for a particular user in a particular situation, songs or playlists may be used to infer what context or setting users find themselves in. The reversibility of these relations follows from the big data ideology that subtends much of the work done in music recommendation. A core tenet of this ideology maintains that if a correlation between two variables is supported by a sufficiently large body of data, then knowledge of the one is tantamount to knowledge of the other. Whether variations in music preferences are actually motivated by context or mood matters little. As big data advocates are wont to argue, causal explanation may have been necessary in "a small data world," where limited sample sizes had to be supplemented by theoretical models that compensated for a lack of adequate information.[62] But in a "big data world," appeals to causal mechanisms can be dispensed with. The quantity of data available is such that correlations are of sufficient predictive reliability to make them adequate as bases for action, rendering causal models—or any kind of theory—obsolete: "Petabytes allow us to say: 'Correlation is enough.' We can stop looking for models. We can analyze the data without hypotheses about what it might show."[63] In contrast to the one-way movement that leads from cause to effect, correlation admits to a bidirectional traffic between any two variables having a statistically significant relationship. Using contextual data to infer musical preferences or using data on musical preference to infer context—either is equally valid. At least this is what the correlationist doctrine that rules data analytics would have us believe.

Working backward from users' streaming activity to identify the emotional and environmental factors presumed to motivate it remains more of an aspiration than a reality.[64] But there are more straightforward ways that platforms can use listening behavior to draw inferences about listeners' mood or context in the meantime, via the growing list of mood-, activity-, and context-based playlists on streaming services. Interviewed for *Advertising Age* magazine in spring 2015, as part of the launch of Spotify's new "playlist targeting" initiative, vice president for advertising Brian Benedik noted that the company increasingly uses "playlists as a proxy for the activity or mood you're in."[65] As a press release explained, "when users hit play on one of the billions of playlists on Spotify, they often signal a common activity or mood—like workout or chill." Such signals make it possible for brands to "target unique audience segments based on streams from Spotify's 1.5 billion-plus playlists, from workout enthusiasts and commuters to millennials, parents and more."[66] By tracking which activity- or context-based playlists users listen to on a regular basis, more granular audience segments may be assembled and more elaborate user profiles constructed. For instance, a person who listens to a running playlist every morning might be identified as a jogger, while someone who makes a habit of listening to sleep playlists in the small hours of the night might be identified as an insomniac. Not only does playlist targeting encourage the multiplication of interest-based, lifestyle, and psychographic audience segments that can be rented out to advertisers, it also expands the range of attributes that may be added to user profiles, increasing their detail and thus their potential value.[67]

As it happened, playlist targeting was just the beginning. In 2016 Spotify expanded its exploitation of user data by moving into programmatic advertising, a technique that employs automated auctions to enable advertisers to bid on users' attention in real time (in this case on the basis of the music or playlists individuals happen to be listening to).[68] With the launch of an ad-supported freemium tier in fall 2019, Amazon took this process a step further, allowing ads not just to be targeted in real time but to be acted on as well.[69] In the FAQ section of its audio advertising portal, Amazon assures potential clients that banner ads accompanying audio spots are "clickable," making it possible for listeners to buy goods immediately on hearing their sales pitch.[70] For both Amazon and Spotify, as well as for other ad-supported streaming services, activity- and mood-based playlists function as a stand-in for users' activities and moods. But unlike methods of playlist targeting that seek to identify the stable features that define users across time, programmatic advertising operates on an altogether different temporal horizon. The aim is to address users at precisely those moments when they are deemed most receptive to an advertising pitch. Playlists function as the means of determining when that moment may be, based on what individual users are doing or how they are feeling at that very instant. As a writer for *Advertising Age* describes it, the approach looks past audience segments, even past the individual, in order to target users as they are fractionated across the moments that comprise everyday life: "Activity categories . . . such as workout . . . will allow a sportswear brand to play an audio ad while someone's on their morning run. . . . And mood categories like happy, chill and sad will let a brand like Coca-Cola play on its 'Open Happiness' campaign when people are listening to mood-boosting music."[71] The shift here is from being to event, from a focus on the allegedly invariant features that constitute one's identity to the transient occurrences, activities, and states of mind that compose the unfolding of our lives. But whether used to figure durable features of our selves or to monitor more short-lived actions or affects, playlists function as a means whereby music consumption taking place *within* the digital enclosure erected by streaming platforms can be used to track who we are, how we feel, and what we do *outside* this digital enclosure.

These developments in the targeting and profiling of listeners bring us to the second major way that streaming platforms distinguish the user and data assets they exploit. Underpinning claims made about the value data analytics impart to these assets is a more basic claim about the value of the data being analyzed. As streaming services aver, these are data that only music can generate. The data's distinctive value derives from music's distinctive properties—specifically, from the intimate relation people have with music. This relation is both extensive and intensive. It is extensive, given music's role in accompanying all sorts of quotidian activities. This is partly a function of technological innovations that have progressively detached music from fixed sites of performance or playback (sound recording, miniaturization, audio compression, and so on). Such developments have created conditions propitious for the development of what Anahid Kassabian has dubbed "ubiquitous listening," a way of attending to music that is characterized by its inattentiveness. Instead of "listening to" music, as Kassabian notes, its ubiquity encourages us to instead "listen 'alongside,' or simultaneous with, other activities."[72] The reverse is also true: just as a quotidian activity may distract from the music accompanying it, music can serve just as well to distract from whatever activity it accompanies (often the case in connection to work, workouts, and other kinds of tedious or strenuous occupations).

Yet if technological innovations are partly responsible for the spread of both ubiquitous music and ubiquitous listening, they are not wholly responsible. The distracted listening that is so often regarded as a peculiarly modern phenomenon has ample precedents in cultures predating sound recording.[73] Conversely, even after radio, phonography, and other technologies of musical reproduction had ushered in an era of relative sonic abundance, distracted modes of listening "alongside" other everyday activities did not ineluctably follow; rather, they were the subject of fierce debate and contestation.[74] Individuals had to become habituated to music in the background, acculturated into a world where disattending to music is not just accepted but unexceptional. Yet this normalization of "listening alongside" is hardly a natural or necessary development. Indeed, as Noriko Manabe has observed, part of the reason that music streaming services initially encountered greater difficulties in establishing a market in Japan had to do with the different practices surrounding radio use and, more broadly, the different culture of listening these practices instantiate. If in the United States the development of genre-specific radio formats and embedded technologies (such as the car radio) encouraged listeners to engage with music broadcast over the air while undertaking other activities, in Japan the more heterogeneous character of radio programming and the absence of a comparable "car culture" militated against such distracted listening. As one of Manabe's informants, an executive at Warner Music Japan, explains: "Americans and Japanese don't listen to music in the same way. Americans spend more time in cars and listen to the radio while they drive. But in Japan, radio's not as central as it is in the U.S. . . . People in Japan don't have as much of a history of listening to music in a passive manner."[75] Much as listeners have to be taught to listen attentively, they also have to be taught to listen inattentively, to treat music as an adjunct to some other action.

Streaming services, like radio broadcasters before them, have played no small role in this peculiar education of the senses. Consider the way activity- and mood-based playlists are foregrounded on the user interfaces of certain platforms, such as Spotify or Google Play Music prior to its absorption into YouTube's premium music service (see figures 3.1 and 3.2). Even if this design to some extent responds to listeners' habitual use of music as a "technology of the self," it cannot help but have a feedback effect, encouraging listeners to engage with music less as an autotelic activity and more as an accessory to something else (a question I'll explore further in chapter 5). Also relevant is the way music is framed in the marketing

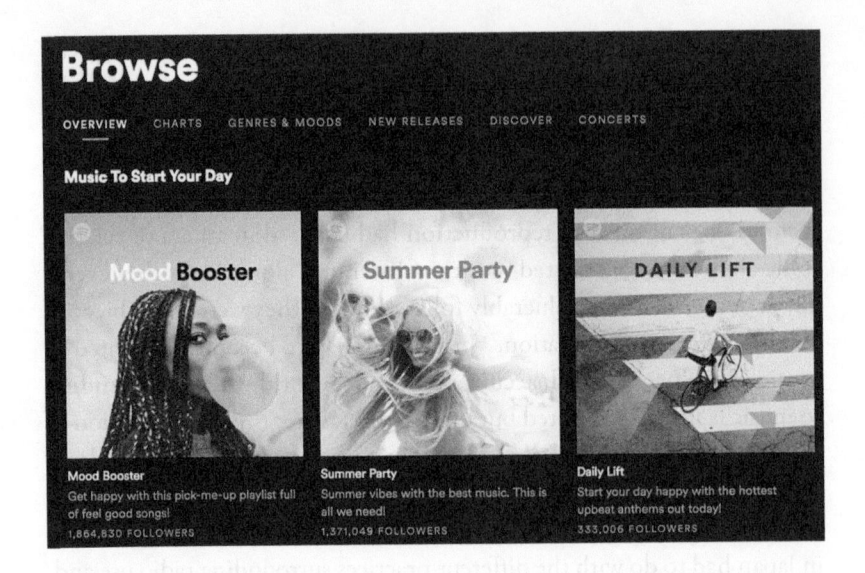

3.1 Mood and activity recommendations on Spotify

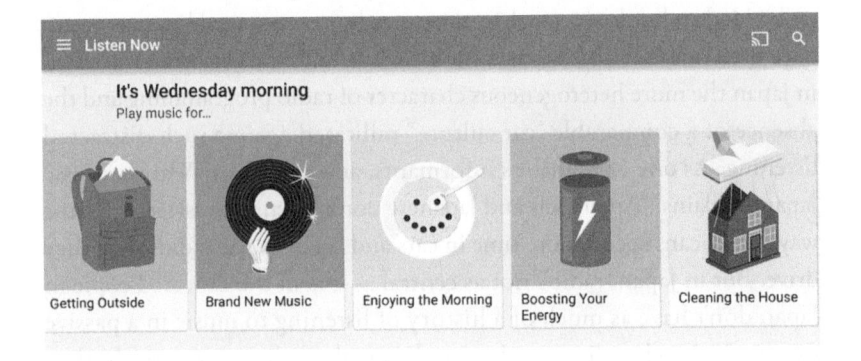

3.2 Mood and activity recommendations on Google Play Music

discourse of streaming platforms. Symptomatic is the subtle yet significant shift that has taken place in the promise of providing listeners with music "anytime, anywhere," a discursive trope whose role in selling mobile music to consumers has been incisively analyzed by Sumanth Gopinath and Jason Stanyek.[76] The image of consumer emancipation this phrase conjures, an image of individuals empowered to listen to whatever music they want, whenever and wherever they want, has in recent years become less a promise than an injunction: the trope of music "anytime, anywhere" is increasingly eclipsed by that of music "every time, everywhere." What was once a matter of choice is recast as a matter of fact. "Now playing everywhere"—such is the pledge that Spotify makes to its partner brands, a guarantee that it can reach its tens of millions of users "when they're most engaged," whenever this might be, "from morning to night."[77]

This pervasiveness of music, both real and perceived, underwrites the claims platforms make about music streaming's usefulness for consumer surveillance. Likewise, it is music's capacity to insinuate itself into every corner of people's lives that distinguishes the data generated by virtue of this surveillance. At the same time as listeners are induced to use streaming music to maximize the value of the moments that fill each day—to compose, as the cliché goes, the "soundtrack of one's life"—advertisers and data harvesters are encouraged to treat this same soundtrack as a means of tracking users through sound.[78] For instance, a video on the Spotify for Brands site invites prospective advertisers to take "a deep dive into a day in the life of the Spotify for Free listener," so they might discover "the various ways brands can be a part of each moment." Shot from an idealized user's point of view, the video presents an image of daily life that is partitioned into a series of discrete settings and activities: commute, work, lunch, workout, "chillin'," and party. It is no coincidence that each of these segments corresponds to a playlist category found on Spotify. The video's message is clear: just as an appropriate music may be found to accompany every moment, so too may an appropriate advertisement.

Yet the value of streamed music isn't limited to its ability to follow users through their daily routine. That value also resides in the ability of streamed music to multiply the number, variety, and specificity of the moments that compose this routine, including those that music can accompany and that other, rival media cannot. This is the assertion made by Spotify's Danielle Lee during a presentation at New York Advertising Week in 2016. Discussing the different contexts in which individuals can listen to streaming audio, she makes an important distinction: "If you think about those moments when you are connected, such as driving, running, cooking, [for] many of them it's not possible to watch video."[79] She later expands on this point, clarifying what sets music (and streaming) apart from other media: "You can see from the data that audio is a companion through more parts of the day than video. So while you may sing along to your favorite songs in the shower, chances are that you aren't watching the artist's video."[80] Addressed to an audience of marketing professionals, the claim advanced by Lee aimed at differentiating the data and user profiles that Spotify produces from those of rival media outlets—at that time, YouTube—for which music is just another form of audiovisual content.

In addition to granting advertisers access to those moments that lie beyond the reach of video- or text-based media, music streaming allows access to more private moments, including those when individuals are particularly exposed, both figuratively and literally. The example of music listened to while showering is exemplary. Speaking at the Ad Training Summit (ATS) in New York in 2015, one of Lee's erstwhile colleagues at Spotify, Jana Jakovljevic, cited showering playlists to illustrate the degree to which Spotify can monitor individuals' activities via music. "Yes, a user will create a playlist for partying and working out, that makes sense, but they are also creating playlists for more obscure activities. For example showering. We have 39,000 showering playlists on Spotify, 550,000 shower streams per day. So we not only know what our users are listening to, we also know their personal activities as well." After a brief pause, she follows up this comment with what appears to be an impromptu aside: "Maybe a little bit too personal sometimes."[81] The aside, and the nervous laugh she lets slip on uttering it, are perhaps indicative of a guilty conscience, an awareness of the abuse of confidence that is being committed when Spotify and other firms use people's quotidian musical practices as a way of getting them to divulge aspects of their lives that they may not wish to divulge.[82]

If streaming platforms have been quick to exploit the extensive character of individuals' relation to music, they have been equally quick to exploit the intensive character of this relation. One way they have done so is by drawing attention to the strong affective charge that runs through most people's musical preferences and practices. The implication is that users' emotional attachment to music will redound to the benefit of the advertisers whose ads are streamed alongside this music. Thus, in their bid to sell marketers and data aggregators on the virtues of streaming music, platforms habitually stress music's status as a "passion point" whereby attention may be captured, advertising messages imparted, and valuable consumer information harvested. "We connect artists, fans, and brands through the passion point of music," Pandora announces to prospective advertisers.[83] Similarly, Spotify touts its brand-sponsored playlists as a way of "reach[ing] and engag[ing] target audiences through the passion point of music."[84] Tacit in claims such as these is the proposition that music generates a stronger response than other kinds of online content (video, podcasts, video games, and so on). Such claims hearken back to the "hypodermic needle" theory of the media popular in the 1930s and 1940s, according to which radio, cinema, and other mass media were seen to possess an almost magical capacity to directly "inject" ideas and beliefs into audiences. But in contrast to this long-discarded model of media communication, which was developed in order to denounce the dangers of propaganda, Pandora and Spotify's updated version of this discourse is not critical but celebratory. That music might function as the tip of the proverbial needle, that the passions it arouses might serve to open a more direct line of communication with users' psyches, is extolled precisely because it enables streaming platforms to valorize the user attention they garner and the user data they generate.

Yet the relation that individuals have with music and that platforms seek to capitalize on is not just intensive in the sense that it is infused with a high degree of affective force. According to a long-standing and widespread trope, music is intensive in the additional sense of affording access to our innermost lives, to an extent that other media cannot replicate. In this respect, platforms draw on a vein of aesthetic discourse on music that extends back at least as far as the German Romantics, for whom music was nothing less than a sensuous figuration of the modern subject's interiority. Holly Watkins, in charting the progressive elaboration of this "metaphor of depth" in German musical thought, has noted how for writers such as W. H. Wackenroder and E. T. A. Hoffman, the "truth of the self" was not to be discovered through rational self-reflection, as Enlightenment thinkers had maintained; rather, it could be glimpsed only via a medium whose ineffability and ephemerality provided an analog to the boundlessness and elusiveness of the soul. Vestiges of this discursive tradition linger to this day; indeed, streaming platforms' efforts to inflate the unique affordances of music are built on the foundation provided by these earlier efforts. This is implicit in the arguments advanced by streaming platforms and their representatives. "You are what you listen to," proclaims customer analytics start-up Preceptiv, in promoting its ability to generate incisive psychographic profiles of individuals on the basis of their musical preferences.[85] Brian Whitman, formerly of the Echo Nest, goes further in proclaiming that "music preference can predict more about you than anything else. If all I know about you was the last five books you read, I wouldn't know much."[86] It is by means of assertions such as these that data on one's listening habits are qualified as equivalent to—and thus a potential proxy for—data about who one "really" is. At the same time, such claims portray music as an invaluable resource for anticipating other behaviors, other interests, and other desires, beyond strictly musical ones.

As proof of concept for the notion that our musical dispositions have a special power to predict other dispositions, the Echo Nest announced in advance of the 2012 US presidential election that by analyzing the taste profiles of users who self-identified as Democrat or Republican, it was then able to employ machine learning techniques to accurately infer the political orientation of other users, strictly on the basis of their listening behavior.[87] In 2014, Pandora announced that it was going even further, microtargeting political ads based on the partisan affiliations that users' listening habits disclosed.[88] Already problematic when they were announced, such claims seem all the more disturbing in light of revelations in March 2018 concerning Cambridge Analytica's unauthorized exploitation of Facebook user data to microtarget political advertisements for the 2016 Trump presidential campaign. Yet perhaps the most remarkable aspect of Cambridge Analytica's alleged misuse of user information is how entirely unremarkable it is, being standard practice within the largely unregulated market for personal data.[89] Indeed, the fact that such quantities of data are so readily available on the open market makes it all the more imperative for streaming platforms to persuade potential buyers of user data and attention that what we listen to is uniquely revealing of who we really are. In platforms' telling, music's distinctive value derives from the possibility that the information it generates might close the gap separating our profiles from our selves. And it is distinctive insofar as other media lack music's purported capacity to pierce the external facades individuals erect, to confound the artifices of "self-presentation" they engage in, so as to gain admittance to the "backstage" area where their authentic selves are thought to reside.[90] As Danielle Lee notes elsewhere in her pitch to advertisers, "If social media is a filter, streaming is a mirror. So much of social media is about curating your persona. It's a performance of sorts, it's for public consumption." By contrast, Lee argues, "Streaming is all about a reflection of who you really are. It's different, because you are not crafting a public image for others. You're just you, living in the moment."[91] If it is true that music's capacity to both permeate and envelop the listener is no small part of the pleasure or utility it provides, it is no less true that these same qualities cast it as a potent means of knowing the listener, both inside and out. In this way the very qualities of music that people put to work in shaping their everyday lives and regulating their emotional lives are increasingly turned against them. What makes music so powerful a "technology of the self," as Tia DeNora and others have posited, is also what allows streaming platforms to repurpose it as an equally powerful technology of surveillance.[92]

Optimizing Music for Surveillance

More than just a provocative turn of phrase, the characterization of music as a technology of surveillance highlights the performative capacities that music possesses and streaming platforms exploit. But while all music that is streamed will necessarily generate data, not all music is equally well suited for generating the large quantities or the particular kinds of data that platforms prize. Music liable to keep users streaming for longer stretches of time, for instance, will help generate a proportionately larger volume of data, while music that is more readily indexed to identifiable moods, contexts, or activities is more amenable for ad targeting and consumer profiling. Furthermore, by influencing the kinds of music they promote, platforms' commercial priorities may surreptitiously influence the creative choices of musicians, producers, and songwriters in turn. By encouraging them to optimize their music for streaming, platforms by extension encourage them to optimize their music for surveillance.

Much ink has been spilled pondering how streaming's attention economy has already started to influence music production. Perhaps the most basic change identified to date is in the length of tracks; as noted in chapter 1, pop songs listed in the Billboard Hot 100 have grown shorter over the past twenty years, contracting from roughly 4′30″ on average circa 2000 to 3′30″ in 2018.[93] Meanwhile, the number of hit songs clocking in at 2′30″ has increased sixfold over the same period. One consequence of the decreasing length of songs is a commensurate shortening of their constituent elements, in particular intros and outros: in a track that is just 2′30″ long, musicians don't have the luxury of heightening listener anticipation through an extended build-up, or indulging in a coda that seems as if it could go on forever (for example, the "Theme from *Shaft*" or "Hey Jude").[94] Also characteristic is the appearance of hooks, choruses, and drops within the first thirty seconds of a track, in order to grab listener attention long enough to get past the critical thirty-second threshold.[95] Clearly, the overall trend toward shorter songs cannot be interpreted simply as a "streaming effect," since tracks were already shrinking well before the rise of streaming.[96] Even so, it is likely that the peculiar incentive structure of platforms has reinforced this tendency. Viewed in the cold light of economic rationality, any track longer than the industry-standard thirty seconds necessary to qualify for a royalty payment gains nothing from this excess duration, while running the risk that listeners might lose interest and skip ahead in their queue. Shortening tracks has additional benefits as well. As Aisha Hassan and Dan Kopf have noted, shorter songs mean that more listeners are likely to listen to an album in its entirety, since "the next new track is never too long away."[97] The same logic applies equally well to the editorial playlists compiled by platforms. Inasmuch as the overarching aim of services is to keep listeners listening—and thus generating user data—they have just as much of an incentive to promote shorter tracks, since these have been shown to increase user retention.

Also encouraging user retention are changes to the content of songs. Choruses, for instance, not only tend to appear earlier in tracks, at times preceding the first verse (a relatively rare occurrence in the standard verse-chorus form dominant from the 1960s to the 2000s).[98] More important, they may not appear at all—or at least not in their customary guise. Breaking with the convention whereby the chorus is a high point toward which the verse and prechorus build, a notable tendency in recent years has been to minimize the registral, dynamic, or tonal features that set choruses apart. Describing this trend—what they dub the "death of the chorus"— Nate Sloan and Charlie Harding have noted that whereas nine out of ten songs in the end-of-year Billboard Top 100 in 1999 were in a clear verse-chorus form, by 2019 this ratio had dropped to just three out of ten.[99] As with the shortening of track lengths, the diminished salience of the chorus cannot be blamed entirely on streaming services. The chorus's decline, too, was already underway in the prestreaming era, which suggests that multiple factors are at play. Sloan and Harding, for their part, contend that one reason for choruses' decreasing prominence has been the adoption by mainstream pop of loop-based structures drawn from genres less invested in the verse-chorus paradigm, such as hip-hop and EDM.[100] Here, too, streaming, while not wholly responsible for this development, may nevertheless amplify it. The erosion of a strong contrast between verse and chorus, in favor of a more consistent mood or vibe, may help make a song fit more readily into the smooth flow of a mood and activity playlist. And considering how such playlists are used to track the moods and activities of users, this provides services with an added incentive for promoting tracks that remain in a single emotional register throughout.

Also relevant are the machine listening tools platforms routinely employ in organizing their catalogs. Spotify is exemplary. While certain of the platform's audio analysis algorithms are capable of identifying salient transitions within a track, many of the key metrics utilized—for example, danceability, energy, speechiness (to distinguish spoken-word tracks from music), acousticness, instrumentalness, liveness, and valence (that is, affect)—each compute a single, global value for a track, measured along a scale that ranges from zero (when a trait is absent) to one (when it is maximally present).[101] Take, for example, Dua Lipa's neodisco track "Hallucinate" (see figure 3.3). For danceability, it has a score of 0.627 and, for energy, a score of 0.69, reflecting the song's upbeat tempo and four-on-the-floor beat.[102] For instrumentalness and acousticness, it receives the lower scores of 0.033 and 0, which follows from the prominence of Dua Lipa's vocals and of various digitally processed sounds, respectively. Also low is the figure for liveness (0.0742), because this is a studio recording (the faint trace of liveness that the algorithms register is perhaps an artifact of Dua Lipa's vocals and the handclaps interspersed across the song). For speechiness, the score is 0.139—low but not absolutely so, perhaps on account of the half-spoken, half-sung vocals featured in the break preceding the song's final chorus. As for the song's valence, its score sits somewhere near the middle (0.627), comporting with the way the otherwise lively and animated character of the track is tempered by a certain tonal ambivalence, as the bright, major-mode quality of individual chords is undercut by the darker, minor-pentatonic movement between them. Yet the numerical values assigned to different aspects of the track's overall sound matter less than the fact that the only thing Spotify's machine listening tools capture is the track's overall sound. Specific details disappear, absorbed into a single global score. No distinction is made between a song that builds in intensity until discharging in a climactic chorus, versus one that maintains a constant affect throughout. Whether this indifference to internal variations in affect, intensity, and so on is intentional, an oversight, or a limitation of the algorithms involved is unclear. Whatever the case, this prioritization of the general over the particular will also have knock-on effects, both in terms of how Spotify organizes music and, ultimately, how certain artists create music in response to platform incentives.

How might one sum up these different tendencies—the declining salience of the chorus, the rise of the monotonic mood playlist (happy, sad, chill, and so on), and the growing use of global, statistical measures to evaluate tracks? Taken together, what they conjure to mind is not so much a "waning of affect," of the sort Fredric Jameson identified in connection with postmodernity but rather its flattening, with stark contrasts in musical and expressive character smoothed over in favor of a single, consistent mood or vibe.[103] In a trenchant reading of this trend, Paul Rekret likens the "flatter" and "more hushed" sound of the 2010s to a "picturesque

```
{
    "danceability": 0.627,
    "energy": 0.69,
    "key": 10,
    "loudness": -5.396,
    "mode": 0,
    "speechiness": 0.139,
    "acousticness": 0.033,
    "instrumentalness": 0,
    "liveness": 0.0742,
    "valence": 0.627,
    "tempo": 122.053,
    "type": "audio_features",
    "id": "1nYeVF5vIBxMxfPoL0SIWg",
    "uri": "spotify:track:1nYeVF5vIBxMxfPoL0SIWg",
    "track_href": "https://api.spotify.com/v1/tracks/1nYeVF5vIBxMxfPoL0SIWg",
    "analysis_url": "https://api.spotify.com/v1/audio-analysis/1nYeVF5vIBxMxfPoL0SIWg",
    "duration_ms": 208505,
    "time_signature": 4
}
```

3.3 Spotify's audio analysis of Dua Lipa's "Hallucinate"

landscape painting, devoid of discernible figures in the foreground."[104] Pop music, he writes, increasingly presents listeners with "the musical illusion of harmony one obtains from a distant gaze," where "tensions and social strife are lost to the blurring beauty of broad brushstrokes."[105] There is evidence that a leveling out of music's affective curve is becoming something of a convention, at least among a handful of genres that have coevolved alongside streaming services. Paradigmatic is what journalist Liz Pelly has dubbed "streambait pop," or what *New York Times* music critic Joe Caramanica refers to as "Spotifycore."[106] In Pelly's account, *streambait* describes "muted, mid-tempo, melancholy pop." Popularized by figures such as Lana Del Rey, Billie Eilish, and Clairo, in Pelly's reading the genre is best represented by lesser-known yet heavily streamed artists (such as Charlotte Lawrence, Sasha Sloan, and Nina Nesbitt), who have all benefited from repeated placement on Spotify's editorial playlists. For Pelly, this is a music that is designed to evoke rather than provoke, whose rough edges have been sanded off to make it as frictionless as the user interface through which it is streamed.[107] "It has this soft, emo-y, cutesy thing to it," remarks one producer Pelly quotes. Elsewhere in the article the same producer recounts songwriting sessions in which the intention was to "make one of those sad girl Spotify songs," attesting to the fact that the sound has already congealed into a recognizable genre marker (institutionalized in the later creation of an editorial playlist on Spotify devoted to such music, "sad girl starter pack").[108]

At times, the discourse surrounding Spotifycore comes dangerously close to rehashing the long-standing tradition that maps aesthetic oppositions onto a rigid gender binary. Within this heteropatriarchal frame, feminized genres such as pop and mood music (and, more recently, streambait pop) serve as foils against which some valorized—and masculinized—other might shine by comparison. Hence, it is vital to make clear that if there is anything at issue with Spotifycore, it is not the genre per se, nor the artists identified with it, but the way their music is exploited by streaming platforms. If the "chill-hits Spotify sound" has been actively promoted by the service, as Pelly writes, it is because it is seen to mesh well with a "playlist logic requiring that one song flows seamlessly into the next, a formula that guarantees a greater number of passive streams."[109] Such music appeals to Spotify, in short, because it is "music that streams well."[110] And because it is such a good fit for the chill playlists that feature prominently on streaming services, such music also appeals on account of the kind of real-time mood, activity, and behavioral data that it can generate for platforms.

In addition to Spotifycore, other kinds of music seem particularly well adapted to streaming's peculiar commercial logic. A case in point is the sort of instrumental music that is a staple of playlists such as Spotify's "Peaceful Piano" or "Stress Relief." Lacking a single generic frame, the repertoire that makes up the bulk of such playlists might best be described as an updated brand of mood music, mixing new age, ambient, and production musics—what Paul Allen Anderson has referred to as "neo-Muzak."[111] Indeed, many of the tracks populating such playlists originate in production music outfits—a source of controversy, given allegations of the role played by such enterprises in seeding music by so-called fake artists on Spotify (see chapter 4). Arguably the one defining feature that binds these musics together is their shared lack of defining features. Distinguished less by the characteristics they exhibit than by those they abjure, such music satisfies the "un-salience conditions" that, for music theorist Frank Lehman, are what enable successful ambient tracks to be sufficiently ignorable.[112] This is true of the music featured on Spotify's relaxation and sleep playlists, which are characterized mainly by a lack of vocals, of sudden transitions, of clear points of articulation, or of clearly localized sound sources (notably, this "soft focus" sound is one of the clearest points of connection linking neo-Muzak to the "easy listening" era, whose heavy use of reverb helped smooth over the music's sharper edges).[113] The sheer accumulation of absences such as these lends latter-day mood music a peculiar sort of presence—what, following Don Ihde, we might describe as the "absent presence" that characterizes environmental surrounds.[114] It is music that creates a negative space that listeners can fill with other things and other activities. And considering the commercial stake they have in getting listeners to use music rather than listen to it, it is easy to understand why Spotify and other platforms have heavily promoted playlists where this sort of ambient-cum-production music will be found.

Functionally similar though worlds apart aesthetically is another genre embraced by streaming services: lo-fi hip-hop. Though rooted in the experimental work of producers such as J Dilla, Flying Lotus, and Madlib in the 1990s and early 2000s, contemporary iterations of the genre owe as much to the particular distribution channels by which its sound has circulated over the years. One of these was the Cartoon Network's nighttime programming block Adult Swim: in the early 2000s, the channel began using the scratchy, jazz-tinged grooves of J Dilla and others in its bumper music and advertising, bringing the style to the attention of a wider (and younger) audience, many of whom would later grow up to become the core audience for—and in some instances creators of—lo-fi hip-hop.[115] Also critical for the genre's development has been another distribution channel, the YouTube live stream. Introduced to the platform in 2011, within a few years live streams had become lo-fi hip-hop's epicenter, with the accompanying live chat providing fans a forum for interacting with both the music and one another[116] As the popularity of these channels grew, so too did their operators, with curators such as ChilledCow, College Music, and Chillhop attaining a degree of prominence that most of the genre's producers lack.[117] The way these curators have framed their live streams has also helped to solidify many of the genre's iconic features. These include graphics of anime characters studying, sleeping, chilling, and so on, along with paratexts that reinforce such functional uses of the music (for example, "beats to relax/study to").[118]

More recently, the unforgiving economics of YouTube live streaming has led curators to seek out other sources of revenue, with many launching labels and expanding their activities to other streaming platforms. The two tactics go hand in hand: by producing rather than simply curating music, entrepreneurs such as College Music can leverage their renown within the lo-fi hip-hop scene into a claim on the revenue generated by the artists they have signed, while audio-only platforms like Spotify offer a more lucrative way of monetizing playlists, at least compared to the paltry ad revenue generated by the single advertisement that usually precedes a YouTube live stream.[119] While certain characteristics of live streams are lost in translation (for example, live chats), others have been retained, such as the genre's anime-inspired iconography and framing as "music for" (studying, chilling, and so on). Also retained have been the curators' sizable followings. By early 2020, Lofi Fruits' playlist "lofi hiphop to chill, relax, study, sleep" had attracted around a million followers on Spotify. More than a year later, fueled in no small part by pandemic-driven lockdowns, its follower count had grown to 5.8 million, making it a contender for the title of most popular third-party playlist on Spotify. The same goes for other lo-fi playlists (ChilledCow's main playlist has 5.3 million followers at the time of writing, while Spotify's proprietary playlist "Lofi Beats" has just north of 4 million).[120] Commenting on the genre's growing popularity on streaming services, Chaz Jenkins (of music analytics firm Chartmetric) has argued that it reflects "a long-term trend" on Spotify, with "playlists created for a context" steadily increasing in popularity.[121] One upshot of this, according to Jenkins, is an abandonment of the sort of variation in style and mood that characterizes the sequencing of tracks on most album-length releases. Whether this change is due to changes in taste, the molding of consumer preferences by streaming platforms, or broader changes that late neoliberalism has made to music's place in everyday life (see chapter 5), the predilection among users is, according to Jenkins, for a more "consistent experience," one that playlists centering on a single mood or theme are better equipped to provide.[122]

More mainstream pop artists have not been insensible to these transformations. Symptomatic has been experimentation with "mood EPs," short compilations that artists or labels assemble out of tracks culled from some recent (or not-so-recent) release. The short EPs that result are typically centered on a specific theme, activity, or affect.[123] Examples include the short, six-track "chapters" extracted from Taylor Swift's 2020 album *folklore*; or the series of EPs compiled out of excerpts from Lauv's album

~how i'm feeling~ (*workout, driving vibes,* PARTY VIBES, *lonely,* and so on); or Justin Bieber's grasping effort to cash in on the pandemic-induced surge in telecommuting, *Work from Home*. A number of factors are at play in this microtrend. In part, it is one tactic that musicians and rights holders use to obtain preferential placement on services' algorithmic feeds. By repackaging existing tracks, an artist's music can continue to show up in algorithmically curated new release playlists (for example, Spotify's "Release Radar"), even if none of the tracks is actually new. Equally significant is the precise way that labels and artists go about deaggregating and reaggregating music. Not only are the resulting minicompilations shorter, increasing the likelihood of retaining listeners all the way through, but in addition, they provide listeners with the sort of "consistent experience" that Chartmetric's Jenkins forecasts as the future of music consumption. That the source of consistency is located in the specific mood, vibe, or activity that tracks are supposed to evoke, reflect, or accompany is also revealing. What it may signal is a growing willingness among producers to make music designed to "fit [users'] lifestyles" (to cite Jenkins again), instead of the reverse. But it may also signal that artists and record producers have begun to internalize the priorities of platforms, including their interest in music that points beyond itself, to the activities, moods, and environs with which it is associated.

Music Data beyond Music Platforms

Streaming's long-term effects on musical creativity remain to be seen. But this is not the only pressing question that music's use for data extraction raises. Another is what becomes of the information that services collect. Up to this point, the focus of this chapter has been on the most noticeable fate awaiting such data: their translation into targeted advertising, branded playlists, and the like. Less overt—but no less significant—are other uses to which such data are put once they exit the enclosure of the streaming service and circulate in commercial contexts far removed from those of music distribution and consumption. What happens to the data that streaming services share with third parties is murky, in part because the number and identity of these commercial partnerships are themselves murky. But even when deals have been made public, the quantity and kinds of user data that change hands and the conditions under which they do so are also unclear.

In the case of Spotify, the best publicized of these arrangements have been with other consumer-facing companies, such as Facebook, Uber, Tesla, Tinder, and Virgin Airlines. While many of these relationships have been pursued chiefly as a way for the company to draw in new users or to "upsell" freemium users to the premium tier, these arrangements also benefit both Spotify and its corporate partners by providing access to data they would otherwise lack.[124] A vivid illustration can be seen in Spotify's collaboration with genealogy and DNA testing firms Ancestry.com and 23andMe, which provide personalized playlists based on "the unique sound of your ancestry."[125] For Spotify, the arrangement reinforces its commitment to hyperpersonalization, inasmuch as DNA testing frames knowledge of one's genetic code as a way of "reveal[ing] something essential" about oneself (that such framing reproduces racist and eugenicist ideologies equating DNA with destiny seems to be of little concern to Spotify).[126] For Ancestry.com and 23andMe, a similar dynamic is at play. The clearest benefit they reap from the partnership is the prospect of tapping into a younger clientele. Facing waning consumer demand for their core products by the end of the 2010s, both Ancestry.com and 23andMe sought to redefine themselves as business-facing medtech firms, instead of consumer-facing genealogy companies.[127] In this light, partnering with Spotify offers these companies not only a new customer base but a new source of behavioral data, one that might profitably complement the genetic data they already possess.

Less well publicized are the commercial arrangements that platforms forge with digital marketing firms and data brokers. The complexities of the online advertising industry require stand-alone platforms to contract with a host of outside firms to serve ads or successfully monetize user information. These include supply-side platforms, which serve as brokers for digital media outlets auctioning off ad inventory; demand-side platforms, which serve as brokers for advertisers bidding on ad space; ad exchanges, which coordinate the real-time buying and selling of programmatic advertising; data management platforms, which collect, store, and make available data that can track users across different devices, websites, and platforms; data aggregators, which buy and sell consumer information, organized by demographic and psychographic segments; audience measurement companies; and so forth.[128] Certain larger conglomerates, such as Google and Amazon, have constructed their own enclosed ad networks, performing in-house many of the operations that a stand-alone service would have to contract out to third parties. The opposite has been the case with Deezer and, until recently, Spotify. As noted at the beginning of this chapter,

Spotify's drive to claim a growing share of the market for audio advertising (abetted by its move into podcasting) has resulted in the launch of its own proprietary ad network. Unveiled in early 2021, this represents a major step toward the creation of a self-enclosed ad ecosystem for Spotify, one that would rival within the domain of audio advertising Google's dominance of search and Facebook's dominance of banner ads. Whether Spotify will succeed in its goal of effectively monopolizing online audio advertising is an open question. That Amazon has used its digital home assistant, the Amazon Echo, to make inroads into the same market means that Spotify's efforts will not go unchallenged.

Among the varied intermediaries that make up digital ad markets, two merit special attention: data management platforms (DMPs) and data aggregators. Both are notable because both function as clearinghouses where all sorts of data from all sorts of sources—including streaming services—are gathered, ordered, linked, and partitioned in numerous ways. Data aggregators, for instance, enable streaming platforms to acquire information on users that can be used to complement the data the platforms themselves collect. But being buyers as well as sellers of third-party data, aggregators also make it possible for platforms to monetize some part of the user data they collect, which can then be purchased by all sorts of clients. For instance, by mid-2020, the data aggregator BDEX offered information for roughly 60 million users of Apple Music, 100 million users of Pandora, 43 million users of Google Play Music, and 60 million users of Spotify.[129] According to BDEX's website, prices range between one and five dollars per thousand profiles; and while all the information on offer is duly anonymized, clients can nonetheless request a range of unique identifiers (hashed email addresses, browser cookies, mobile phone identifiers, even postal addresses), which can easily be used to specify individuals.[130] As for DMPs, one of their core functions is to harmonize the user profiles created by different companies, making it possible to track the same individual across different websites and devices. Pandora, for instance, credits its ability to seamlessly integrate advertisers' user profiles with its own to its commercial relation with the data management platform Krux: "Data onboarding [for example, transferring data from an external source] can prove extremely valuable for advertisers . . . who seek to leverage Pandora's massive reach and cross-medium messaging to speak directly to their known customers."[131] This is not the only benefit: "Matching [customer] data directly to Pandora's listeners also provides a significant opportunity for marketers looking to glean unique and valuable insights about their customers' musical preferences, listening habits, and technographic attributes that would be hard to find anywhere else."[132]

As this last quote makes clear, DMPs and data aggregators are important channels by which information collected by streaming platforms gets released into the wilds of the digital economy. And while advertising makes up a significant part of this economy, it is just a part. Apart from marketers and adtech firms, there are a wide range of companies with an interest in personal information, including credit rating agencies, banks, healthcare providers, insurers, governmental agencies, and finance companies. "All data is credit data," exclaimed the CEO of fintech firm Zest Finance in 2012.[133] "All our data is healthcare data," declared a pair of digital health researchers some seven years later, in a call for more stringent regulation of the data that tech companies have accrued.[134] Despite the differences in ideology, chronology, and context separating these two statements, their isomorphism ("all data is X data") nevertheless speaks to the underlying fungibility of data. Anything can be connected to anything else, once all and sundry have been reduced to data and organized according to the paratactic logic of the database. The disavowal of causal explanation and the belief in the power of correlation that underpins the big data ideology means that even the most trivial details of a person's life can be pressed into service in drawing inferences about other features. As Paul Ohm and Scott Peppet put it, "because of big data advances in data analytics, we may soon learn that 'everything reveals everything'"—which is to say that "every fact about an individual reveals every other fact about that individual."[135] Indeed, the more esoteric the correlation the better, if for no other reason than it justifies the expansive data collection that tech companies, adtech start-ups, and data brokers all engage in.

Furthermore, anecdotes attesting to the power of the telling detail help enterprises distinguish themselves from competitors. This in turn may help persuade potential clients that the profiles, scores, and classifications they construct are all the more predictive because they are all the more exhaustive. Predicting a loan applicant's credit risk on the basis of their previous credit card payments is unremarkable. It takes a more discerning eye (or algorithm) to tease out the connection between one's creditworthiness and one's handwriting, say, or one's musical behaviors.[136] As Robert Prey asks, "What if a taste for early '90s Nu Metal indicates a higher propensity to default on a debt repayment?"[137] While he acknowledges that this scenario might "seem far-fetched, even ridiculous," he also notes the existence of numerous companies that already "correlate data on a bewildering array of indicators."[138] Prey isn't alone in drawing a line between new forms of credit scoring and what in the banking sector are known as "alternative data" (for example, data from nonfinancial sources, such as social media).[139] In a patent application filed in 2012, the microcredit start-up Lenddo described how nontraditional data might be used to determine prospective clients' risk of default:

> If [a] user applies for a loan in the amount of 10,165 Php [Philippine pesos] for the purpose of text books for a class he is taking, but . . . the system learns through his recent communications that the user wants to accompany his friends [to] an upcoming three day music concert selling tickets for the price of 10,165 Php, this calls into question the credibility of the user and the probability of the loan being approved is negatively impacted.[140]

In this scenario, the musical activity being monitored is concertgoing rather than streaming. But the illustration is suggestive nevertheless, as it plays on the widespread notion that our musical habits are especially revealing about ourselves—and not always in a positive way.

It isn't happenstance that Lenddo's hypothetical scenario involves loans denominated in Philippine pesos. At the time the company filed the patent application in 2012, its operations were confined to just two national markets, the Philippines and Colombia.[141] Nor is it happenstance that the company's operations have been concentrated in emerging markets. The use of alternative data in credit and consumer scoring is particularly pronounced in the Global South, targeting populations on the margins of the formal economy. Most fintech start-ups justify their interest in developing economies by declaring their ethical commitment to "financial inclusion."[142] Their self-appointed mandate is to extend financial services to the "unbanked," those underserved by established financial institutions because they lack the documentation (such as credit history and records of financial transactions) traditionally used to determine creditworthiness. Less euphemistically, fintech companies take advantage of the precarity of local populations in countries such as the Philippines, as well as the relative weakness of local regulatory and enforcement regimes, to prize open new sites of value extraction in a digitally mediated version of neocolonial domination. As Rob Aitken puts it, "forms of precariousness are not only the result of expulsion" but "also emerge out of complex but often adverse forms of 'inclusion' targeted to those at the edges of the global economy."[143] Driving such predatory financial inclusion is the intensive collection of personal information via social media, online activities, and mobile phone usage, as well as third-party data acquired via aggregators and brokers. It is by such means that fintech companies can pass judgment on one's "digital character" (to use Tamara Nopper's term), deciding the terms of one's future indebtedness.[144]

Whether data collected on music streaming are part of the pool of indicators by which digital character is judged is hard to say for sure. But as Martin Daughtry points out, in discussing the difficulties involved in tracking music's environmental impacts, "speculation may be the only way to even begin to address [these impacts]."[145] The same goes for music's far-flung effects within digital ecosystems. Moreover, information disclosed by or about fintech firms offers some suggestive clues. Another especially intensive site of fintech activity since the 2010s has been India, thanks to the sheer size of its population, with a relatively high percentage of Indian citizens only loosely attached to the formal economy and hence the banking sector.[146] As a result, opportunities for growth are enormous. Consider the local start-up CreditVidya. According to its website, the company's mission is to make "financial services accessible at affordable cost to all creditworthy individuals."[147] Clients who download CreditVidya's mobile app are told that its proprietary algorithms will make a series of critical decisions, all within the space of a minute: whether they qualify for credit, in what amount, at what interest rate, and so forth. For users apprehensive about sharing too much data, CreditVidya's website reassuringly states that the consent screen "clearly articulates what data is collected and the purpose for which it will be used."[148] However, an investigative report revealed that the data scraped by CreditVidya's software development kit (SDK) went well beyond what its consent page suggested, with music streaming apps among those subject to covert data gathering. "The CreditVidya SDK," a member of the fintech research group Cashless Consumer observed, "was . . . found in a Sai Baba app, Ilaiyaraaja Hits app, and other music apps," noting that users are most likely "clueless about this background data collection."[149] Given their status as "black boxes," it is unclear how much weight CreditVidya's algorithms accorded music data in determining one's creditworthiness. Also unclear is whether the company shares this data further, with other companies. What is clear, however, is that such information forms some part of the ten thousand data points that the start-up's algorithms allegedly use in assessing prospective borrowers.

In the United States, regulation has hampered the use of alternative data for financial services to some extent. But only to an extent. Laws such as the Equal Credit Opportunity Act of 1974 (expanded in 1976) impose strict limits on the kinds of information that banks and credit unions are able to use in scoring clients. Yet such regulations do not apply to the relatively new sector of "marketplace lending," which, like its homologues in the Global South, seeks to expand credit markets by preaching the gospel of financial inclusion.[150] The proliferation of these novel sources of credit has in turn increased pressure on established banks, credit rating agencies, and regulators to loosen restrictions on the kinds of data used for credit scoring. Nor are credit scores the only metrics for which alternative data may be used. A panoply of other ratings shape people's life chances, across a wide variety of domains. Among the secret consumer scores tallied as part of a 2014 World Privacy Forum report are medication adherence scores, health risk scores, consumer profitability scores, job security scores, collection and recovery scores, youth delinquency scores, casino gaming propensity scores, and many, many others.[151] As is the case with fintech credit ratings, the black-boxed nature of consumer scores such as these makes it difficult to say exactly what kinds of information are taken into account or how they are used.

Compounding this lack of transparency is the fact that the impacts of certain forms of data may be mediated by the various categories they help construct, to which individuals are then assigned. For instance, behavioral data, such as that gleaned from a person's listening habits, may be used to assign individuals to different demographic and psychographic groups. And such categorizations may then serve as data points informing other metrics. Furthermore, points of resemblance within one dimension of a profile often are extrapolated to draw inferences about other, seemingly unrelated dimensions. The term of art for this process is the *identification of look-alikes*, that is, people who exhibit "similarities in certain socio-demographic characteristics" without being "necessarily connected in real life."[152] A study of alternative data's use in credit scoring offers the following illustration:

> Take the example of a person that lives on the other side of the country, who likes the same music groups as you do, and joined the same Facebook groups. Although it is clear that you have some similarities, it is very probable that you will never meet or be friends with that person. However, the information included in these similarities can be an important source of information to predict [credit] default behavior since similar behavior in one domain (e.g. preferences) might imply similarities in other domains.[153]

The complications introduced by the recursive operation of classifications and inferred attributes further underline the difficulties involved in trying to ascertain the exact degree to which any kind of data, including music data, contributes to consumer scores. Absent regulatory oversight that might compel companies to disclose how such scores are constructed, one can only draw inferences on the basis of the clues that are publicly available.

One domain that offers suggestive hints is automotive insurance. Like fintech firms, insurers have taken considerable interest in the commercial possibilities opened up by the reams of data now at their disposal. Not only does this quantity of data allow insurers to market policies to individuals lacking credit histories, but it also makes possible finer-grained risk assessments. Underwriters, according to one industry report, can now assemble for each individual policyholder "a risk pool of one."[154] One benefit of individualized risk assessments for insurers is that they facilitate "price optimization"—that is, price discrimination.[155] Another benefit specific to the United States is that personalized risk assessment provides insurance companies a way of distancing themselves from the industry's sordid history of overcharging residents of predominantly African American neighborhoods for car insurance. While pressure from civil rights activists led insurers to largely abandon the explicit use of racial categories in underwriting in the 1960s (a move later institutionalized by a 1976 Supreme Court ruling), race-based pricing has continued in practice, even as the industry adopted "colorblind" actuarial methods.[156] By basing insurance rates on attributes that function as proxies for race—namely, clients' zip codes—insurers have effectively imposed what Devlin Fergus describes as a "hidden consumer tax" (or "ghetto tax") on inner-city drivers.[157] Echoing fintech efforts to target the unbanked, insurers' construction of "captive racial consumer markets," Fergus explains, "are often about inclusion, though in high-cost terms—a practice often termed 'reverse redlining.'"[158] Given this context, one argument advanced in favor of alternative data's use for risk assessment is that these data offer a way past such color-blind racism, by incorporating into scoring decisions information gleaned about driving behavior via in-car sensors. Yet the use of alternative data also makes possible the introduction of new proxies for the racialized categories the insurance industry has ostensibly renounced.

Music preferences provide one such proxy, especially given the entrenched racialization of music genres within the US popular music industry from the late nineteenth century on. Significant in this regard are the series of studies that insurers, InsurTech, and auto finance companies have commissioned or cited over the years, to examine the effects of music listening on driving behavior.[159] According to these studies, the genres most closely associated with aggressive or risky driving behavior are genres such as hip-hop and heavy metal—which is to say, genres identified as Black in the first instance and as working-class and youth-oriented in both instances. Conversely, safe driving behavior is associated with genres habitually associated with older, white, and middle-class listenerships (for example, classical music or folk). A particularly explicit instance of this metonymic chain linking age, race, and class to music and to driving behavior can be seen in an infographic published by the insurer Allianz in 2012 (see figure 3.4). Above a color-coded bar running from red on one end (labeled "dangerous") to blue on the other (labeled "safe") are images of artists, acting as metonyms for the genres—and the driving behaviors—with which they are associated. On the dangerous side of the spectrum are images of Eminem, Jay-Z, and Dizzee Rascal, while on the safe side are images of Mozart, Andrea Bocelli, and Barbra Streisand. In light of insurers' evident interest in the correlation of music taste and driving behavior, it is not hard to see how classification as a "hip-hop music fan" or an "urban

3.4 The racialized coding of "safe" vs. "dangerous" driving music

music fan" in a consumer database may factor into other classifications—say, as a "risky" driver versus a "safe" one.[160] And, as Ruha Benjamin has observed, "if someone is marked 'risky' in one area, that stigma follows him around much more efficiently, streamlining marginalization."[161] Again, whether the studies cited by insurers on music and driving actually bespeak their use of music data in assessing risk is hard to say. But the industry's own statements suggest this is so. "Driving with the beat of the music," one report cautions, "can lead to higher insurance rates."[162]

Private corporations aren't alone in availing themselves of the vast troves of data circulating on the open market. For governments as well, data brokers function as critical intermediaries to which surveillance can be outsourced, including practices that might otherwise be prohibited by law. In the United States, for instance, strict regulations govern the data collection that the National Security Agency (NSA) is permitted to undertake. On paper, at least, the agency's dragnet of electronic communications applies only to foreign nationals located abroad, with surveillance on US citizens unlawful without a warrant. In practice, however, the NSA has routinely subverted such legal restrictions; for instance, the PRISM program disclosed by Edward Snowden in 2013 notoriously provided a back door the agency used to mine data from leading internet companies in the United States.[163] There are also other, perfectly legal work-arounds that the NSA can exploit to undertake mass surveillance. What it cannot collect directly, the agency can simply purchase from third-party vendors. Though scaled back somewhat by recent court rulings, the "third party" doctrine established by the US Supreme Court in 1976 holds that citizens have "no reasonable expectation of privacy" to any information voluntarily tendered to companies such as internet service providers and wireless carriers, as well as any platform that collects, stores, and processes user data.[164] Coupled with the doctrine of first sale, this legal precedent grants data brokers wide latitude in reselling data to any party, for any purpose—including governmental agencies. "It is a reasonably open secret that US law enforcement and intelligence agencies procure data files from [data brokers] to understand the American population," remarks one industry representative.[165] These data may include credit and consumer scores, as well as information on the various demographic and psychographic categories to which individual profiles have been assigned (for example, "Insecure Debt Dependents," "Uninvolved Conservatives," "Bourgeois Melting Pot," and so forth).[166]

A report published by Amnesty International shortly after Donald Trump's inauguration as president in 2016 details how such third-party classifications could prove useful in creating the kind of registries of Muslims, undocumented immigrants, and other targeted populations that candidate Trump had promised to institute if elected. While the US Census Bureau hasn't collected information on religious affiliation since the 1950s, the authors observe that many data brokers have no compunction in trafficking in such information. "A search on NextMark," they note, "contains several entries for 'Muslim,'" while "the much larger Experian . . . offers '181 detailed ethnicities' in its list catalogue, including the category 'Islamic,' alongside 11 other religions."[167] Nor are brokers constrained to resell only information that has either been directly observed or divulged. As is true of the broader data economy, information begets more information, via the correlations that emerge across linked data sets. To drive this point home, the article's authors cite Michal Kosinski, a professor of organizational behavior at Stanford who helped pioneer the kind of "predictive personality modeling" later employed by Cambridge Analytica: "You can easily train a model that predicts religious affiliation based on status updates, Facebook likes, and other social media information."[168] But even overt markers of identity aren't necessary, as Kosinski explains: "When I talk about digital footprint, people usually think of it like this: if you regularly visit a Muslim website, we might guess that you are a Muslim. But that is not what I am talking about. Nowadays we can go to your Spotify playlist and make a highly accurate prediction that you're a Muslim based on which songs you listen to."[169] The means by which streaming services know their listeners, in other words, are the same means by which other parties—private and public alike—may get to know them as well. By enacting music as a technology of surveillance, platforms make it possible for all sorts of other actors, from corporations to data brokers to intelligence services, to do the same.

• • •

A running theme throughout this chapter concerns how music's use as a means of consumer surveillance is inseparable from its use in extracting the valuable resources that are listener attention and user data—resources that platforms can rent to advertisers or "share" with vaguely defined "partners." Of note is the transformation that music's status undergoes across these various transactions. If platforms tout the special powers of music in their efforts to valorize the user attention and information they harvest, once the data generated by means of music enter into circulation within the wider data economy, music's specificity recedes in importance. Streaming data become just additional data points among the hundreds and thousands of others that are used to construct people's data profiles and to position these within the statistical distributions by which all sorts of ratings and scores are measured. When the powers ascribed to inference are such that "everything reveals everything," then no individual piece of information is itself especially meaningful.[170]

In a way, though, the fate that awaits music data is already inscribed in the way platforms such as Spotify and Pandora tout their data's specific affordances. If these and other services loudly proclaim that there is something special about music, that its ubiquity and intimacy makes it ideal for tracking users, both inside and out, this is only because music is already being cast as a proxy for something else. What is valued isn't music per se. What is valued is its indexicality, its ability to point beyond itself to aspects of the user that are otherwise inaccessible. And while it is impossible to say how this incentive structure might influence music's future development, there is a strong possibility that it will encourage the creation of music that in some way points beyond itself, to a specific mood or context of use. But for this sign value of music to be realized, listening habits would have to undergo a commensurate change, with listeners treating music as a utility, just as platforms already do. Also necessary would be techniques of measurement that could reliably gauge user engagement with musics bearing a particular sign value. Such metrics and the ways they can be manipulated are the subject of the next chapter. As for music's enactment as a utility—or more specifically, as a means of social reproduction—that is a subject taken up in the fifth and final chapter.

Chapter Four

Counterfeiting Attention in the Streaming Economy: Spam, Click Fraud, and Fake Artists

Seldom has an album heard by so few people garnered so much attention as Vulfpeck's *Sleepify*. It has elicited considerable commentary since being uploaded to Spotify in March 2014. And interest only increased once *Sleepify* was pulled from the service seven weeks later. For good reason: the record exemplifies the sort of unintended consequences to which the incentive structure of streaming services gives rise. For media theorist Pelle Snickars, Vulfpeck's album is "illustrative of the fundamental changes the recording and music industry has gone through during the last 15 years."[1] Others have made similar claims about *Sleepify*, seeing it as an example of the kind of "creative crowdsourcing" artists must now undertake to make a living from music or as a funhouse mirror reflecting the "changing face of the music industry."[2]

Why has Vulfpeck's *Sleepify* attracted such attention? Part of what makes the album so noteworthy is that so little occurs that is worthy of note. *Sleepify* consists of ten tracks, all more or less identical, because all consist of nothing but silence. Indeed, according to band member Jack Stratton, it is "the most silent album ever recorded," each track having been produced by setting the tone generator on the sound editing software Audacity to zero.[3] All that distinguishes one track from another are minor variations in timings and titles. Each lasts only thirty-one or thirty-two seconds, and titles consist of multiples of the letter Z (track one is titled "Z," track five "Zzzzz," track ten "Zzzzzzzzzz"). At an audible level, however, successive tracks are indistinguishable, with nothing to mark where one track ends and the next begins.[4]

Such unobtrusiveness is, of course, the point. In a video posted at the time of *Sleepify*'s release, Stratton encouraged the group's fans to play the album on repeat while they slept—whence the album's title and the roughly thirty-second duration of each track.[5] Since streams are eligible for royalty payments only if they play for thirty seconds, the album's tracks were just long enough to cross this threshold but short enough to maximize the number of streams accumulated per listening session. According to one estimate, listeners who streamed the album on repeat overnight would generate roughly 840 streams, translating to $5.88 apiece. If enough listeners were to do this several nights in a row, the result would be a sizable chunk of money.[6] As an incentive for the band's fans, Stratton promised to use the proceeds to fund Vulfpeck's fall 2014 tour, allowing them to play gigs free of charge. In addition, the band would use Spotify's analytics to identify where *Sleepify* was streamed the most and use that information to determine the tour's itinerary.[7]

Two months after *Sleepify* debuted, Spotify notified Vulfpeck that the album violated the platform's terms of service and would be taken down. By this point, however, the album had already racked up some five million streams, earning roughly $20,000 (a payment Spotify honored). Just as important, the album had generated substantial press for Vulfpeck. Stories about the group's exploit circulated across mainstream news outlets, trade publications, blogs, and social media. For certain commentators, there was an element of sweet revenge in Vulfpeck's stunt. The band may have gamed the platform, but given the pittance that artists receive from Spotify, turnabout was fair play. Vulfpeck, wrote one blogger, "highlighted Spotify's pathetic royalty rates while denying them any real new music."[8] For others, *Sleepify* underlined how little music's specificity matters once it is reduced to just another stream of data. This is the position of Snickars, for whom *Sleepify* shows how much "music is . . . deprived of meaning when [it is] treated as data."[9] For still others, the exercise highlighted the changing division of labor between artists and audiences; according to performance theorist T. Nikki Cesare Schotzko, the album was emblematic of a trend whereby "the artist's goal toward doing *nothing*" depends on "the audience's willingness to do *something*."[10]

But what, exactly, did the audience for *Sleepify* do? They may have streamed its tracks millions of times, but that doesn't mean that they listened to them that much, or at all. The discrepancy is important, since the assumption that the playback of a track is a reliable indicator that it has indeed been listened to is a fundamental premise of the streaming economy. It is by means of play counts and other related metrics that streaming services purport to quantify listener attention. And as discussed in chapter 3, it is this attention—how it is directed; toward which artists, tracks, or playlists; and for how long—that is among the most valuable forms of data that platforms collect on users' listening behavior. Bearing this in mind, it is not hard to see why Spotify moved to suppress *Sleepify*. Vulfpeck's album presented a significant danger to the platform, threatening to skew its measures of user attention and corrupt its listening data. And data corrupted are data devalued—not once but twice over. Corrupted data are robbed of some part of their use value, as a means by which playlists may be assembled, similarity relations established, and recommendations targeted—all critical tasks if Spotify is to retain its customer base. But such data are also robbed of some part of their exchange value: as one observer noted, advertisers are unlikely to pay platforms if their "commercials are falling upon unconscious ears."[11] Spotify's decision to remove Vulfpeck's album was thus a way of forestalling the depreciation of the platform's data assets, of safeguarding the validity (and value) of the metrics that translate user engagement into a numerical score. For Vulfpeck, by contrast, the motivations were different. Once the stream is established as a measure of attention, and once measures of attention become the principal means of calculating royalty payments, artists have much to gain by boosting this figure, in whatever way possible. Attracting a mass audience is one way of doing so. Counterfeiting listener engagement is another. Yet these two approaches aren't as easy to disentangle as they might at first appear, for as soon as listening is translated into a numerical measure, any distinguishing mark that would crisply delineate attention from inattention disappears behind the qualitatively undifferentiated number that comes to stand in its place.

By throwing into relief the paradoxes that follow from streaming's quantification of user attention, the *Sleepify* affair highlights a pair of themes explored in this chapter: the centrality of engagement metrics within the streaming economy and their fragility as a basis for this economy. Music streaming services are not alone in the importance they attach to user attention. An oft-remarked feature of digital capitalism is the way the explosive growth in information circulating online challenges people's ability to absorb it, filtering meaningful signals from noise. Under these conditions, attention becomes increasingly prized to the extent it becomes increasingly scarce. I will return to discourses of the "attention economy" and the fantasies underpinning them shortly. But for now, a curious feature of this economy needs to be underlined: namely, that attention's value derives from the very qualities that make it so difficult to capture, to measure, and hence to treat as an object of economic exchange. We already encountered this peculiarity in chapter 3, in connection with the perennial difficulties that audience measurement presents. But Vulfpeck's success in getting people to listen to an album without actually listening to it throws into relief attention's elusive character. This quality makes attention resistant to the measurement necessary for it to be consistently priced. But, by the same token, this quality also inflates the price attention commands. The more attention slips through the meshes of the economy that seeks to pin it down, the more precious it becomes.

Also highlighted by the *Sleepify* controversy is another challenge streaming services face in trying to assign a dollar value to attention. As something that can be assessed only through imperfect proxies (play counts, click-through rates, "time on site," and so on), the attention of users is difficult to authenticate. Granted, this is a problem that haunts all forms of communication. Even in face-to-face encounters, people resort to bodily cues to gauge the engagement of others, lacking direct access to their psyches. Likewise, in live musical performance, audience engagement is signaled indirectly, in some cases by dancing or applause, in other cases by silence. Yet difficulties in measuring engagement are exacerbated for digital platforms, where numerous layers of mediation—including the platform itself—stand between actors. For that reason, such measures are particularly liable to deception, simulation, and misdirection. This discrepancy—between the heightened value attached to attention and its susceptibility to (mis)appropriation—is central to the three case studies explored in this chapter. The first centers on the commandeering of user attention by what many commentators refer to as "musical spam," tracks that stand in a parasitic relation to some popular track, siphoning off some of the streams (and revenue) that track might otherwise accrue. A second case study turns to the simulation of user attention, focusing on the marketplace for fake streams and followers. A third considers music that strives to free ride on user attention, in the form of the so-called fake artists Spotify commissioned to produce tracks for the site's mood-based playlists. In all these cases, the value attached to musical attention is simultaneously underlined and undermined. The more it is diverted or dissimulated, the more its status as something worth diverting or dissimulating is affirmed.

The (In)attention Economy

For some time, a range of commentators—including computer scientists, media theorists, business consultants, and advertisers—have heralded an epochal shift in the economy, claiming that attention has been transformed into a currency of sorts, rivaling money as a medium of exchange.[12] First floated in the 1970s by Herbert Simon, the underlying premise of the attention economy thesis is that a "wealth of information" results in "a scarcity of whatever it is that information consumes"—that something being "the attention of its recipients."[13] Until recently, the story goes, it was information that was relatively scarce and hence valuable. With the rapid expansion of digital media over recent decades, however, such scarcity conditions no longer obtain. Instead, we find ourselves in a putatively novel era of informational abundance. This wouldn't be so consequential but for hard limits in our ability to make sense of all the content we are bombarded with. One limit is psychophysiological—what some, likening humans to computers, refer to as a ceiling on human "processing capacity."[14] Another limit is temporal. As legal scholar Tim Wu observes, "we exist in an environment limited by time—168 hours per week."[15] With demands on attention increasing and the supply constrained, it follows that attention itself would displace information and become itself a scarce (and hence valuable) resource.

Overlooked by claims that we are living in an era of unprecedented media saturation is that similar claims have been made in the past, whenever a new medium of communication has emerged. In the eighteenth century, the expanding book trade in Britain gave rise to concerns about readers "drown[ing] under a tidal wave of print."[16] Also overlooked is that media saturation is scarcely a universal experience. Access to the "wealth of networks" isn't universal, being shaped by race, class, gender, geography, and ability.[17] Even for those suffering from media overload, the problem may reside not in a quantitative increase in content but in a qualitative change in our relation to it. As Matthew Crawford notes, the problem may be a lack of "authoritative guidance of the sort that was once supplied by tradition, religion, or the kind of communities that make deep demands on us."[18] Something like this dynamic can be witnessed in regard to streaming services, whose interest in personalized recommendation has been motivated, among other things, by their very success in displacing traditional gatekeepers (such as radio station programming directors and record store clerks). Absent the orientation provided by figures who had hitherto been instrumental in guiding consumer taste, a mounting concern among platform operators by the mid-2010s was that the overabundance of musical choices confronting users might paralyze them, ultimately resulting in their disengagement from the platform. The result was a good deal of investment and publicity put into recommendation and curation services such as Spotify's Discover Weekly or Deezer's Flow, which were hailed as the means by which the so-called paradox of choice that threatened to overwhelm users might be preempted.[19]

Read in light of the attention economy model, platforms propose a relatively straightforward transaction, inviting users to trade their attention in exchange for various forms of information—most notably music, itself understood as a form of information. At first glance, this transaction appears equitable. Appearances can be deceiving, however, since technologies of mechanical and digital reproduction reduce the costs of copying information goods to the point that such costs approach zero. By contrast, the expenditures in time and effort that attention requires remain stubbornly constant. Even if "the ways in which we intently listen to, look at, or concentrate on anything have a deeply historical character," as Jonathan Crary notes, such historical transformations do not alter the fact that listening to, looking at, or concentrating on anything cannot help but take time.[20] Music may be (re)produced more quickly and efficiently than in the past, but it is not clear how it could be listened to more quickly or efficiently. The result is a "strictly asymmetrical" relation between media and their consumers: as Georg Frank notes, even as the media are able to "disseminate information in the form of technical reproductions," consumers still must "pay with live attention for each copy."[21] In a way, the asymmetry is akin to that described by William Baumol and William Bowen in their analysis of the "cost disease" that affects the performing arts.[22] As Baumol and Bowen note, the rising costs incurred by concerts, theatrical productions, and other labor-intensive forms of cultural production stem from the fact that productivity in the performing arts remains basically static relative to other, more productive sectors of the economy. Whereas the labor time needed to manufacture goods tends to decrease thanks to technological advances, the labor time needed to perform a string quartet or song remains the same today as in the past. As a consequence, the performing arts and other so-called stagnant sectors (education, health care, and so on) become ever more expensive relative to the increasingly inexpensive goods produced in other, more productive sectors. Typically cited to explain the economic peculiarities of live performance, the cost disease has a corollary in cultural consumption, as technical reproduction affords productivity gains that cannot be matched by human attention. As a result, users pay a much higher cost in terms of the attention they expend than platforms do in providing users with the music they attend to.

Also complicating idealized models of the attention economy is the fact that the exchange between platforms and users is seldom a one-to-one trade of information for attention. For premium-tier subscribers, money as well as attention is tendered. Nor does attention run in one direction only. Platforms themselves lavish users with attention, in a variety of ways. One takes the form of recommendation and other forms of personalized address: while these may be algorithmically generated, that doesn't keep people from feeling as if they are being attended to and even recognized, after a fashion.[23] "I'm a huge fan of Spotify, and particularly Discover Weekly," exclaimed one user shortly after the personalized playlist was launched in summer 2015. "Why? It makes me feel *seen*."[24] Another kind of attention is supplied via music itself, to the extent that it seems to address or speak to users; as Nancy Baym notes, "when music . . . affects audiences, it can feel like a direct line of heart-to-heart communication has opened."[25] But a no less significant kind of attention platforms lavish on users takes the form of consumer surveillance, as discussed in chapter 3. Even as users attend to the music platforms provide, platforms attend to the attention of users. And at the same time as platforms provide users with information, in the form of digital music, users provide platforms with information, via their listening practices.

Rather than a simple exchange of attention for information, then, the attention economy as it is realized on streaming services involves a complex, bidirectional flow of attention, information, and money. Much of the attention that services harvest passes into the other circuits they intermediate. Some goes to the music being listened to and, by extension, to the music's creators. Some of it is skimmed off and channeled to advertisers, in the case of freemium tiers. And some of it accrues to the platform itself, building up its brand. For each of the parties concerned, the attention aggregated has both a use value and an exchange value. For musicians, attention is useful in cultivating a fan base, while measures of user attention factor into the formulas that determine the revenue share they are due. For advertisers, attention is useful in alerting targeted audiences to their clients' products, while the size and composition of these audiences determine the prices advertisers are charged to access users' attention. And for platforms, user attention is useful as a resource for fine-tuning the features that attract, retain, and monetize clients, while also serving as one of the core assets that impart value to the platform itself as an asset.

This attentional arbitrage is what allows platforms to position themselves as "obligatory points of passage" on which others depend. But it also creates opportunities for manipulation and deception, for a number of reasons. First, as intermediaries bringing together different parties (users, artists, advertisers, rights holders), platforms also keep them apart. As noted in chapter 1, platforms, like other interfaces, not only connect but also separate. Second, the procedures platforms employ to capture user activity, "datify" it, and prepare it for analysis are all premised on the fantasy that from within the digital enclosures platforms erect they can reliably access what lies beyond. To sustain this fantasy demands that platforms resort to a sleight of hand, replacing something that resists tabulation with something that doesn't, at the same time as they treat the two as equivalent. Consider plays and play counts. The assumption is that for each play that is registered there is some corresponding action (namely, listening) on the far side of the interface. But even if a series of mediations links a user's actions to the signals representing them, once a signal is recorded it acquires an existence independent of the actions that produced it. From this point forward it is a signifier like any other, unable to cross the bar separating it from what it signifies. Yet the belief these signifiers are reliable proxies for such real-world referents is what provides them with whatever validity (and hence value) they are ascribed. In this way, signals generated from within the digital enclosure come to stand in the blank space where user attention is imagined to reside.

Furthermore, to the extent digital traces are taken to unproblematically index an action on the user's part, they necessarily transform the action they represent. When streams, for instance, are treated as proxies for user attention, attention is recast as something as discrete and quantifiable as the number representing it. Driving this process are technical as well as economic demands: not only does quantification make data fit for processing, but it is also the condition of possibility for attention to be assigned a dollar value. And yet such quantification excludes the qualitative features—attention's fluid, flickering, and variable character—that have historically formed the basis of its use value. Writing on the history of attention, Jonathan Crary notes how nineteenth-century models characterized it as something slippery and hard to sustain, its expenditure pushing toward a "threshold at which it breaks down."[26] Within these accounts, attention was less a stable mode of consciousness than an activity that sought to stabilize consciousness, to arrest its ebb and flow. "Attention," Crary writes, "always contained within itself the conditions for its own disintegration, it was haunted by the possibility of its own excess."[27] Balanced precariously between these two poles, attention lacks the fixity it seems to possess when assigned a numerical value.

Where, exactly, attention shades into either inattention or overattention is difficult to pin down. But it is a problem that streaming platforms are obliged to confront, if they are to guarantee the integrity of the listener "impressions" they trade in. Where platforms draw this line can have significant repercussions for artists. Here we might compare *Sleepify* to the fate of another album that Spotify removed from its service. In April 2015, the indie folk duo Smokey and the Mirror released their self-produced album *Thin Black Line*. To publicize its release, the duo notified their roughly 2,500 Facebook followers and sent an announcement to the four thousand subscribers of their email list. Their efforts paid off. Over the next two months, the album's tracks were streamed some 79,000 times.[28] Yet the algorithms Spotify uses to track listening activity deemed the high play count anomalous, leading to its removal from the platform's catalog.[29] As Smokey and the Mirror's distributor, CD Baby, explained, "a handful of users playing an album or track on repeat" constitutes an "abusive" form of streaming activity in Spotify's estimation.[30] For Smokey and the Mirror, excessive fan engagement had the same outcome as disengagement had for Vulfpeck. In both cases, Spotify's statistical analyses flagged patterns of listening activity that fell outside the normal distribution, with the music responsible for such aberrant listening behavior banned from the service. Episodes such as these underline that the data analytics streaming platforms employ are not just descriptive but also disciplinary. Data points located too far from the mean are treated not just as statistical deviations but as potentially ethical ones. Quantitative measures of how user activity is distributed along a curve produce qualitative decisions about whether engagement is attentive or not, valid or not, valuable or not.

Notably, platforms seldom spell out the criteria they use to identify such deviations. Rather, these criteria are defined in negative terms, in opposition to transgressions that are themselves ill-defined. This failure—or inability—to specify what constitutes musical attention bears out a claim made by Thomas Davenport and John Beck in their 2001 book *The Attention Economy*: namely, that while "its absence is surely felt," attention's presence is by contrast "difficult to document."[31] Hard to positively verify, attention can be gauged only through the absence of its absence. A number of implications follow from this. For one thing, the fact that "to attention attention cannot be paid" (as Paul North puts it)[32] suggests one reason why it is so easily dissimulated. For another, this difficulty in pinning down attention calls into question the commonplace that sets it in opposition to distraction. Rather than being antithetical to distraction, attention is a particular form of it, requiring distraction from anything other than the matter at hand. Conversely, distraction is just a particular form of attention, namely attention that is deemed to have been misplaced or misapportioned. As North remarks, "there is no distraction, only an attention to the zero degree."[33]

What counts as attention or distraction varies not just across different sociohistorical contexts but also according to who is paying attention, what they are attending to, and so forth. Writing on eighteenth-century literary culture, Natalie Phillips notes that definitions of attention and distraction were "situational, determined by social and historical context as much as by a specific style of mind." The same activity (reading) could be coded in antithetical terms, depending on one's social rank: "a lady studying a didactic work for the improvement of her mind might be seen as attentive," while "a servant girl sitting on the stairs lost in a novel was more likely to be seen as 'distracted' from her work."[34] Similarly, the privatized musical experience afforded by mobile devices has often been condemned for diverting attention from public space and distracting listeners from their surroundings. A virtuous form of musical engagement viewed from one angle becomes a troubling symptom of social disengagement when viewed from another.[35] Also important is the precise object of (in)attention. Depending on what music is being listened to, focused listening may be deemed either good or bad. Where a given artist or type of music is situated relative to the nebulous line separating art from "mere" entertainment will affect whether or not that artist or music is seen to merit attention. It will also affect whether the act of listening is deemed a diversion from more worthy pursuits or as a worthy pursuit in its own right.

Even within a particular music culture, different aspects of music may be judged to deserve more or less attention. Thus, when Adorno, in his infamous inventory of listening styles, defines the "expert listener" as one who can "name the formal components" of a complex work such as Anton Webern's Trio for Strings, op. 20, "hearing past, present and future moments together so that they crystallize into a meaningful context," he makes structure central to musical attention.[36] This prioritization of form devalues other kinds of listening, focusing on other musical features—whence his charge that those who attend to affect above all else (Adorno's "emotional listener") are guilty of reducing musical experience to "the torpor of vague reveries."[37] Conversely, when Charles Keil defends jazz and other Afrodiasporic musics against accusations that they lack syntactic complexity, he does so by recentering attention away from harmonic-melodic processes and toward metric, rhythmic, and gestural ones. In music that swings, Keil notes, "the focus of attention" is anchored in "the tension generated by a complex relationship between meter and rhythm."[38] Though less concerned than Adorno with defining "adequate listening," Keil's efforts to identify the "technical emphases" of jazz and other improvisation-based genres implicitly endorse a specific way of engaging with such music. Listening for formal processes such as those found in Webern would miss the point. But whether it is form or rhythm and gesture that are prioritized, presupposed in such efforts at hierarchizing musical parameters is the notion that there exist multiple poles of musical attraction to be hierarchized. Musical attention can be misplaced only if it can attend to a range of phenomena. And since music is multiply mediated, it follows that there is a multiplicity of ways attention can be apportioned: not just auditory, musical listening can also be kinesthetic, cognitive, visual, corporeal, and so forth. This excess means attention to music will always be insufficient. Even the most attentive musical listening is inattentive in some respect.

The diversity of ways that attention can be distributed across the multimodal phenomenon that is music has significant implications for the attention economy at work in streaming. First, the aporetic quality of attention sheds light on the negative way in which platforms define "legitimate" listening behavior. For even as services seek to identify "abusive" forms of streaming, there are advantages to leaving the boundary between legitimate and illegitimate listening activity fuzzy. By doing so, streaming services can compass situations in which attention and inattention overlap, accommodating a more variegated range of listening practices. These include the kinds of engagement elicited when music is used for exercise and listening for the beat becomes paramount.[39] These practices also include the more diffuse attunement to affect typical of music's use to set a mood.

And they include as well what historically qualifies as close or attentive modes of listening.

Beyond this, the impossibility of disentangling attention from distraction calls into question attention's surety as "the new currency of business" (as the subtitle of Davenport and Beck's book on the subject characterizes it).[40] Quantitative measures of listener engagement are therefore at perennial risk of being faked, hijacked, misappropriated, or otherwise manipulated. Combine the uncertainty of this currency with the profit to be won by inflating measures of user attention, and what results are conditions propitious to all sorts of deceptive practices: music that passes itself off as something it isn't, streams of doubtful authenticity, artists who produce music under assumed identities, and so forth. The design of platforms facilitates such practices. Even as they mediate the interactions of different actors, such interactions are circumscribed, creating information asymmetries ripe for exploitation. Exchanges are limited to what Kate Crawford and Tarleton Gillespie describe as "thin form[s] of communication, remarkable more for what they cannot express than what they can."[41] Missing from platforms are many cues that might help distinguish the genuine from the fake.[42] The relative paucity of paratexts, for instance, makes it easier to dissimulate a recording's identity. Furthermore, while platforms have enormous amounts of information on music and listeners alike, there are significant limits to how informative such information is. Add to this the fact that the quantity of traffic on their sites makes platforms dependent on algorithms to monitor suspicious activity, and it is easy to see how they can be gamed—or, just as problematically, how they can turn up false positives, as in the case of Smokey and the Mirror.

Spam and Soundalikes

For streaming platforms, few problems have proved as intractable as musical spam. *Spam* isn't the only term used to describe the phenomenon. Nor is it an uncontested one. In the context of digital music, spam has been used to designate a wide range of items: knockoff or soundalike covers, karaoke versions of tracks, cheap sonic filler (such as white noise or, in the case of Vulfpeck, silence), gags, mislabeled or incorrectly tagged music, tracks claiming to feature superstars that they don't, and so on. If these different kinds of music share anything, it is that they are regarded by platforms and certain users as parasites disrupting the frictionless musical experience streaming is supposed to provide. Far from being accidental to streaming, however, so-called musical spam is a by-product of the archival impulse that underwrites platforms' promise to make "every song ever" available.[43]

Concerns about spam have been present in discourse about streaming from its earliest days. In a 2012 blog post, industry analyst Mark Mulligan noted that the ballooning catalogs of digital music distributors had failed to translate into a comparable increase in musical diversity, as many had hoped. "It would be nice to think that [increasing catalog size] was down to labels digitizing vast quantities of back catalogue, or even because of a surge of semi-pro artists. The answer though ... is much less appealing. Digital catalogues are so much bigger now because of filling and fluffing from covers, tributes, and karaoke tracks."[44] A rough survey of Apple's iTunes catalog revealed that, on average, only 10 percent of tracks attributed to top-selling artists were actually by them, with the remainder consisting of "filler drivel, endless cover versions, tribute acts, and karaoke tracks."[45] A search for Rihanna's music, for instance, returned 4,500 tracks, of which 94 percent were covers, duplicates, or karaoke versions. For Mulligan, such figures cast doubt on then-popular discourses about the untapped value residing in the "long tail"—that is, the theory that reduced costs of data storage and transmission had made it profitable to match niche products to niche tastes (more on this in the next section). The trouble was that much of the material constituting the long tail was not alternatives to hits but derivative, secondhand versions of hits. Hence Mulligan's conclusion: "The pseudo long tail is killing the real long tail."[46]

Five years later not much had changed. "Never before has a song title or artist name been more important than the actual songs themselves," journalist Adam Raymond remarked in an article from July 2017. In documenting how different actors had "gamed" streaming platforms—Spotify above all—Raymond decried the "coverbots and ripoff artists who vomit out inferior versions of popular songs every week, flooding [Spotify's] website with dreck."[47] Raymond's criticisms echoed those of streaming users. The Spotify Community Forum includes numerous complaints from over the years about the clones, karaoke tracks, and other false hits returned by the platform's search engine. "The biggest problem in Spotify is those cover bands," wrote one user in 2012. "There is no need [for] cover bands or karaoke versions, just the original one!"[48] A year later, another user chimed in with a similar criticism: "When searching for music, there are too many cover bands returned that are higher up the results than the original. . . .

Why am I paying premium price to listen to amateur cover bands?"[49] Fast forward to 2019, and the issue was still unresolved: "I don't know what algorithm is happening to make me suffer through every obscure or poorly done cover of a song that I may or may not even like, but it's really getting old.... How has this not been addressed yet? At least make a feature where you can shut off that annoying trait that seems to define Spotify nowadays. Stop being so basic! Dear God please."[50]

User complaints about musical spam did not go unheeded. Executives at streaming services were quick to acknowledge the need to address the issue. "We recognize that it's a problem we haven't fully solved yet," one Spotify executive acknowledged in 2013.[51] A similar admission was made by Jon Maples, vice president of product management at Rhapsody. In response to customer complaints, he announced, the service had removed some ten thousand offending tracks from the service. "It just clutters the experience," he remarked.[52] At the Echo Nest, prior to its acquisition by Spotify, tools to help clients root out the music of "spammers, fakers, and cloners" were already being developed by 2013. In a blog post from April of that year, one of the firm's software engineers, Aaron Mandel, provided a taxonomy of spam, as well as the countermeasures each type demanded.[53] Heading up the list of offenders were what Mandel dubbed "cloners," producers of soundalike or copycat covers of popular songs. According to Mandel, such artists try to replicate "the originals as closely as possible with whatever time and talent they have."[54] Identifying soundalikes was relatively straightforward, given that most bore titles or were credited to artists whose names resembled those being copied, or else were included in albums passing as hits compilations (for example, *Top 40 Chart Hits 2013*, by the group Chart Hits Allstars). A second type of spam consisted of pseudopersonalized music. Most commonly tied to some special occasion (weddings, proms, birthdays), spam of this sort consisted of otherwise identical versions of the same track, apart from the minimal customization provided by incorporating a person's name into a song's title or lyrics. To identify this kind of spam, it generally sufficed to look for artists having abnormally large catalogs. "Spammers [like] The Birthday Bunch have a catalog comparable in size to Frank Sinatra or Johnny Cash, which raises a flag," Mandel observed.[55] A third category included various kinds of sonic filler (for example, white noise, silence), which often solicited plays by promising some kind of subliminal self-improvement (to succeed in business, make friends, and so on). Finally, a grab bag fourth category covered among other things the music of "hyperprolific" artists, who release the same recording multiple times under different titles. In this last case, audio fingerprinting could be used to identify duplicate copies of a track.[56]

For Mandel, the motivation for removing spam was self-evident. It was "easy to predict whether a listener wants to hear any of these tracks," the answer being "almost always 'no.'"[57] Musical spam should be limited, in other words, because it represented an abuse of users' attention. Yet despite the efforts of Mandel and others, the kinds of music he qualified as spam have remained a fixture on streaming services. For most platforms, the costs associated with rooting out every offending track outweigh the benefits. Discussing fraud more broadly, Dan Davies observes that the problem is that "we can't check up on everything, and we can't check up on nothing." The critical decision thus becomes "how much effort to spend on checking." Fraud, he writes, is "an equilibrium quantity," with "the optimal level" in any given economy "unlikely to be zero."[58] As with the broader economy, so too for music streaming. Besides, the competitive dynamics peculiar to this sector incentivizes platforms to turn a blind eye to deceptive practices, up to a point. For one thing, as Snickars notes, permissiveness as to what can be uploaded to streaming platforms helps to swell their catalogs—which is significant, given that catalog size has long been an important site of competition between platforms.[59] Furthermore, as Mandel observed, unlike email spam, musical spam presents challenges to algorithmic filtering. Part of the problem is that spam evolves in tandem with music itself ("the process isn't fully computerizable," he remarks, "because new types of spam are always appearing").[60] Changes of style and fashion constantly open up new opportunities for deception. For instance, the trend toward "featured artists" and collaborations in commercial pop in recent decades has encouraged the production of spam that purports to feature a nonexistent collaboration with some celebrity artist to help drive clicks.[61] The rapid pace of technological development and (forced) obsolescence poses similar problems. Filtering techniques developed to work with one interface (such as search bars) may prove less effective on newer interfaces. For instance, as the market has grown for voice-controlled home assistants (for example, Google Home, Amazon Echo), so too have complaints about the music these devices return in response to user commands. One post to Spotify's Community Forum in 2017 noted that Google Home routinely plays back karaoke versions of songs rather than the originals, complaining that it "defeats the purpose of voice control if I have to go to my phone to stop the album then go manually find the one I want."[62]

No doubt the greatest difficulty in addressing musical spam is in defining it. While it may be tempting to regard spam as an empty signifier, given the wide variety of musics the term references, the word itself is significant. Critical discussions of spam in other forms of computer-mediated communication (email, search results, community forums, and so on) shed light on the politics of describing music as such. Particularly important are two qualities of spam—its bulk and its capacity for displacement. Hito Steyerl, for one, has noted that different metaphoric applications of the term *spam*—from its initial *détournement* in a Monty Python sketch, through its adoption in Usenet forums and Multi-User Dungeon environments in the 1980s, to its more recent commercial exploitations—all center on "verbal reiteration" and "uncontrolled replication."[63] In the Monty Python sketch, spam, as both product and word, multiplies so prodigiously that it eventually blots out all else. The image of a world drowned in a rising tide of verbal nonsense inspired its subsequent adoption as an aggressive tactic deployed in early text-based computer networks, where simply repeating the word ("SPAM SPAM SPAM . . .") became a way to clear the screen of rival users' text. Commercial spam operates likewise, overwhelming email and other communication channels with unsolicited messages. As Steyerl notes, these practices all hinge on using words not as bearers of meaning but as "extensive objects," which by materially occupying a communication channel take up the space that might be devoted to meaningful expression.[64]

This brings us to displacement. In his history of spam, Finn Brunton defines the phenomenon as a "project of leveraging information technology to exploit existing gatherings of attention."[65] Wherever attention congregates, spam proliferates, in the hope of diverting some portion of it. For Brunton, it is this expropriation via interception that makes spam "exploitative." Spammers not only "extract some value from attention," but in so doing they "devalue it for everyone else."[66] At this point Brunton's concern with spam's appropriation of user attention intersects with Steyerl's observations about how it transforms signifiers into dumb matter. If information consumes attention, then the proliferation of nonsense passing itself off as meaningful communication further squanders an already precious resource.

Transposed to the domain of digital music, the term *spam* carries much of this conceptual baggage in tow. As such, the term's application to music is not just descriptive but performative. Characterizing music thus highlights certain features while downplaying others. At a basic level, the label transforms musical judgment from a matter of aesthetics into a matter of ethics. Music tagged as spam gets enacted in a specific way: as a problem in need of remedy. In addition, calling something spam foregrounds the iterability characteristic of digital music and how it can metastasize as a form of "uncontrolled replication." Like text-based spam, musical spam would appear to depend on the promiscuity of digital reproduction—on the speed, ease, and cheapness with which digital data may be copied. But in contrast to practices such as file sharing, where the reproducibility of digital data facilitates access to some desired object (such as an MP3), spam exploits this attribute of digitality for a diametrically opposed end, substituting what isn't wanted for what is. Spam depends on digital reproduction because spam, in short, is a numbers game. Or, as Steyerl puts it, "spamming is the pointless repetition of something worthless and annoying, over and over again, to extract a tiny spark of value lying dormant within audiences."[67]

Consider personalized music, such as the innumerable birthday songs found on streaming platforms. The producer Mixtronic, for instance, has released dozens of albums titled *Joyeux Anniversaire*. Each contains a different assortment of names, drawn from seemingly random stretches of the alphabet: volume 21, for example, is subtitled *Prénoms Filles et Garçons de L à Y* ("Girls' and Boys' Names from L to Y"). The albums also vary in how many tracks they include: some feature just eight songs, while others contain more than twenty. What doesn't vary is the duration of the tracks: with few exceptions, each lasts two minutes and fifty-four seconds, give or take. The near-identical duration of the tracks results from the fact that the tracks themselves are nearly identical. Each presents the same pop-inflected, synth-laden arrangement of "Happy Birthday," sung in French, with changes from one track to another minimized in order to minimize the labor of customization.[68] Even the integration of the addressee's name betrays little effort. At the point where a name would traditionally be sung, the phrase "joyeux anniversaire" is simply repeated, while a jarring overdub of a second vocal part intones the addressee's name (see example 4.1). In this instance, the cheapness of digital reproduction functions as a means of filling as many niches within the long tail as possible, in the hope of garnering the odd stream.[69] A song such as "Joyeux Anniversaire Elodie" may not receive many hits on its own. But combined with the plays that Mixtronic's other songs generate, the trivial investment of time and effort made in customizing "Joyeux Anniversaire" can nonetheless translate into a nontrivial return.

If personalized music exploits digital technologies at the level of production, to create minimally differentiated replicas of the same recording,

Example 4.1 Mixtronic arrangement of "Joyeux anniversaire, Elodie!"

other kinds of spam exploit these technologies at the level of distribution. Such is the case with soundalikes, tracks emulating popular songs in the hope of poaching some of the attention (and revenue) they attract. Consider knockoff cover versions of Taylor Swift's "We Are Never Ever Getting Back Together" by the artists Tanya Swing and American Girl. A striking feature of these and other soundalikes is their deviation from the norms that have evolved around cover songs since the 1960s.[70] Part of a longer tradition of "versioning," the cover song in its contemporary form grew out of a commercial strategy popular in the postwar record industry, whereby hit records would be rapidly remade by other labels to capture some of the hits' audience and sales. In the racially segregated industry of the 1940s and 1950s, this method of "hijacking hits" was, as Michael Coyle puts it, "one of the favored means for white capital to exploit black talent."[71] In many instances, R & B records by Black artists that exhibited crossover appeal were quickly covered by white artists, whose access to the mainstream market allowed their versions to overshadow and outearn the originals. It was only toward the end of the 1950s that the practice of covering songs began to assume its present form and meaning. This was due partly to the recording's ascendancy over sheet music as the music industry's core commodity and partly to the nascent rock community's embrace of a romantic ideology of authorial originality.[72] Under these conditions, the term *cover* began to refer to something more than just a new interpretation of an existing song. Rather, it designated a new interpretation of a particular recording of a song, with the latter serving as a point of intertextual reference for the cover.[73] As Gabriel Solis observes, a successful cover is one where "the coverer creates a sense of his or her own authorship in authoring the recording," even as "he or she draws some measure of the original author's creativity to him or herself."[74] Covers, in other words, depend on a particular distribution of attention. Listeners must maintain a kind of dual awareness, if they are to discern what is novel about the cover and what is derivative, apportioning aesthetic value accordingly.

Soundalikes, by contrast, do not seek to create any distance between themselves and the originals they copy. Instead, they seek to collapse this distance as much as possible, so they can stand in for the original. Although soundalikes have been a feature of the record industry since at least the 1960s, the province of budget labels such as Embassy, Tops, Warwick, and Pickwick Records, such copycat recordings occupied a marginal place within the predigital music economy.[75] The costs involved in pressing and distributing physical recordings, the expense of acquiring mechanical licenses, the lowered price point at which knockoff recordings were generally sold to attract unsuspecting customers—all these factors diminished the already narrow profit margins that producers of soundalikes could hope to achieve.[76] With digital reproduction, however, the economic calculus changes. To be sure, soundalike artists still incur a number of fixed production costs: the cost of licensing the song, producing the recording, getting it distributed (via distributors such as DistroKid and TuneCore), and so on.[77] And while distribution costs aren't entirely eliminated, digital reproduction does reduce these enough to make the production of soundalikes more attractive. Like personalized songs, soundalikes play a numbers game: their creators wager that out of the millions of a platform's users, a small but significant enough fraction will listen to the cover rather than the original. And given that there is no additional marginal cost for every additional stream that is streamed, once production costs are recouped any extra revenue generated is pure profit.

Digital reproduction figures into the logic of the soundalike in another way as well: not as a means of production or reproduction but as an ideal. Unlike traditional covers, soundalikes make no effort to put a personal stamp on a song but instead seek to efface themselves before the originals they emulate. By mimicking other songs as closely as humanly possible, they strive to disguise that they are in fact remakes. The key word here is *humanly*. Cover artists cannot employ technologies of mechanical or digital reproduction, because doing so would expose them to legal liability, transforming a track from a cover into a copy. For soundalikes, digital reproduction represents the asymptotic limit of perfect emulation that they aspire to but can never attain. Writing for *Pitchfork*, critic Maura Johnston offers an evocative image of how the ideal of machinic precision and the reality of human performance combine in the soundalike. She likens what separates an original from a soundalike to "the difference between an intricate line drawing and a version of it fed through a malfunctioning photocopier."[78] In this analogy, knockoff cover artists occupy the place of the machine, the malfunctioning photocopier, whose mechanical precision they try but fail to match.[79] Yet as powerful as this analogy is, it would perhaps be more apt to say that soundalikes strive to pass a Turing test in reverse. If in the classic Turing test the goal is to create a machine that can deceive human interlocutors into thinking that it, too, is a human, in the case of a soundalike the goal is the opposite: to create a human performance that can fool listeners into thinking it is the product of a machine.

Even the most faithful cover counts for little, however, unless it is streamed in place of the original. User attention must be attracted before it can be appropriated. Yet the decision to play a soundalike versus an original isn't entirely up to the user, resulting from the joint action of users, algorithms, interfaces, devices, and audio files. At times, the selection of a soundalike is due to a platform's algorithms misreading user input, as when voice-controlled smart speakers return a cover rather than the original that has been requested. It may also come about when listening to or liking a cover has the unintended consequence of training a recommendation engine to populate a user's playlists with other covers. One user on the Spotify Community Forum, for instance, complained that "upwards of 50% of the songs recommended for me are low-quality or poorly executed covers," all because he had "liked several cover songs" in the past.[80] Instead of interpreting the user's action as signaling an interest in one cover in particular, Spotify's algorithms treated it as signaling an interest in cover songs in general.

At other times, the selection of a soundalike is due to users misreading some algorithmic output (for example, search results). As noted in chapter 1, streaming platforms are quite abstemious with the paratexts that accompany individual track listings. On most platforms, a search query will typically generate a list of titles and artists, and little else, leaving informational gaps that creators of soundalikes can exploit. But just as important as the quantity of the information about a track's identity is the kind of information provided. Helpful in this regard is a distinction Judith Donath has drawn in a study of deception within 1990s-era Usenet forums, contrasting "assessment signals" with "conventional signals."[81] In general, assessment signals are more reliable indexes of a person's identity or status: it is relatively easy for a person possessing a particular skill or attribute to demonstrate it, while dissimulation is usually fairly difficult or costly to pull off. On Usenet forums, Donath notes, displays of expertise were effective assessment signals by which users could judge another's knowledge of a subject (for example, aquarium maintenance, motorcycling, hacking).[82] While such displays can be faked, of course, doing so convincingly requires substantial effort. By contrast, conventional signals draw on shared codes to lay claim to some identity, trait, or skill (for example, credentials). As such, they are both less costly to display and less costly to evaluate. But for that very reason, they are more prone to manipulation.

In the case of soundalikes, the fact that the paratexts that frame music on streaming platforms consist primarily of conventional signals facilitates deception. The most common conventional signals are names (of tracks, artists, albums). All serve as identity cues for the audio files to which they are linked, the humanly legible counterpart to the machine-readable metadata attached to files. As is to be expected, the titles of soundalikes tend to hew quite closely to the originals they copy. More important for signaling (or obscuring) a track's identity are other names—in particular those of artists. One evergreen strategy is to have a name incorporate or reference the original in some way. A crude yet effective approach is simply to append words such as *tribute, made famous by,* or *klone* to the name of the artist whose music is being copied (for example, The #1 Garth Brooks Tribute Band). This tactic peaked around 2011 or 2012, at a time when the catalogs for many famous acts still hadn't been licensed to digital music platforms. Following Apple Music's 2015 revision of its terms of service, which prohibited such deceptive naming practices, this tactic fell out of fashion (though the uptick in tracks falsely claiming to feature celebrity artists may be understood as an updated variant of this practice).[83] In response, producers of soundalikes turned to more allusive forms of citation. On occasion, soundalike artists make use of alliteration, a case in point being Tanya Swing's covers of Taylor Swift's music. On other occasions they make use of near-homonyms, such as June Jett (in lieu of Joan Jett). On still other occasions, the original artist's name is dropped in favor of a reiteration of the track's title, perhaps to increase its ranking in search results: examples include Rihanna's "Where Have You Been," performed by the group Where Have You Been All My Life, or No Doubt's "Don't Speak," performed by the group Don't Speak.

In some cases, the title of a track may strategically diverge from the original. Take the song "Human," by British singer-songwriter Rag'n'Bone Man. Released in mid-2016, by December of the same year the song had reached the number-two position on the British charts. Its success led to a slew of knockoffs, though few bore the title "Human." Most opted instead to take their name from the opening of the song's refrain: "I'm only human after all." Such was the case with versions by DJ Shamy, John "The Ragin Cajun" Jones, John C. Simon, and Deep Down, to name just a few (see figure 4.1). Underpinning this change is the wager that most listeners wouldn't know the song's actual title, only the opening of its (oft-repeated) chorus. What it counted on, in other words, was a particular combination of attention and inattention: that listeners had attended to the song's lyrics but not its title.

A similar balance of attention and inattention is at play in assessment signals. By and large the audio file itself provides this kind of signal, by resembling the music it purports to be. Absolute resemblance would be ideal, of course. But exact reproduction would amount to a legally fraught and potentially ruinous infringement of copyright. Near-copies such as soundalikes are also costly, in their own way, in terms of the time and effort

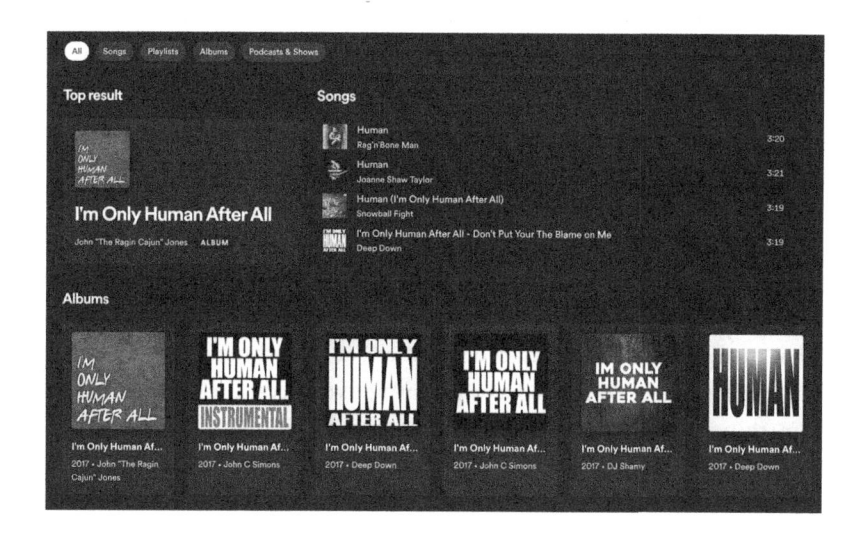

4.1 "Human" soundalikes ("I'm Only Human After All")

required to produce them. But they can reduce this cost by exploiting the margin separating attention from inattention. Vital in this respect is that a song's resemblance to the original matters less than its resemblance to what listeners can recall of the original. For a soundalike to succeed in rerouting attention away from the original and toward itself, it is necessary for users to have paid enough attention to a song to seek it out and to have a vague sense of what it sounds like but not enough of one to tell the difference between the soundalike and the original. "Sometimes it hits me how many people around me don't know that some of the music they listen to are covers," states one user posting to the Spotify Community Forum, noting their own surprise upon learning that "a song I like, actually [is] a cover."[84] Also facilitating the appropriation of user attention are playback conditions discouraging attentive listening—whence the overrepresentation of soundalikes on compilations and playlists intended for use in exercise, at parties, or as part of other activities. In contexts such as these, listener attention may not be wholly focused on the music being played, or may focus only on certain, salient parameters (such as beats per minute). Telling in this regard are reviews of soundalike compilations on digital download sites, where a mistaken click represents a potential loss not just of time or attention for consumers, but also of money. Many reviews complain of the misleading character of such compilations. "Please be aware that the original artists do not sing on this album," wrote one reviewer of Super Fitness Music's album *Top 40 Running Tracks*, adding that the covers were "very amateurish." Others, by contrast, were unbothered by the counterfeit status of the music. "[I] have not used [it] for running but walking. Great tracks and almost 2 hours of music. Great for doing housework too."[85]

Such conflicting responses complicate the uncritical labeling of certain musics as spam. For if spam is defined as a misuse of others' attention, it isn't clear whether this is the case when attention is divided between music and some other activity or when attention is so focused on some aspect of music that it disregards others. This is another way of saying that the "spamminess" of certain musics is not a fixed or objective trait, contrary to what many of the journalists, programmers, and users maintain. As noted earlier, it is better conceived as a performative effect: the designation of something as spam helps to produce it as such. But it is also a situational effect, varying from person to person and from context to context. In a way, this bears out Brunton's observation that debates over what counts as spam often resolve into debates over the values held by the different communities hosted by a platform.[86] This is a problem from which streaming services are not exempt, given their aspiration to contain every sort of music and by extension every sort of music community.[87]

Often, what some users denounce as junk cluttering streaming services is viewed quite differently by others. A vivid example of this tension can be witnessed in connection to karaoke versions of tracks, which, along with soundalikes, are one of the main forms of music frequently criticized as spam. As one Spotify user complained, "I really don't like when there are Karaoke albums thrown in with the Artist's actual albums. . . . It really ruins my listening experience when I click 'Play Shuffle' on an artist I can get songs NOT done by the artist."[88] More pointed was a mock poll posted to the Spotify Community Forum:

> "Do you want your search results cluttered with Kareoke [sic]?" **"Yes/no."**
>
> "Do you want your search results filled with bands that tries to sound like The Beatles or Led Zeppelin—and fails?" **"Yes/no."**
>
> Guess how many "yes" there will be?[89]

Any doubts about this user's answer to these questions were immediately dispelled by a postscript appended to the post: "P.s. The answer is zero." However, the confident assumption that everybody feels likewise is misplaced. Posts to the Spotify Community Forum over the years make it clear that just as many users were eager to see the platform make it easier, not harder, to find things like cover songs and karaoke tracks. "I was thinking that with your big library, adding a karaoke function would be really really cool," wrote one user.[90] Another implored the company to "please add more Karaoke songs to Spotify!"[91] The wishes of users like these were realized to some extent in 2022, when Spotify began rolling out a new karaoke function across the different national markets in which it operates. But what may represent a welcome addition to one fraction of Spotify's user base will likely be viewed differently by another fraction, for whom karaoke is less a boon than a blight.

Disagreements over whether karaoke has too great or small a presence on streaming sites are instructive. What they highlight are the disputes that inevitably arise when transposing the pejorative label *spam* from other contexts to the realm of digital music. A large part of the issue is that music introduces so many confounding variables. One of these is taste. Another is the variety of ways people engage with music: as an object of aesthetic appreciation; as a medium of social bonding (or distinction); as an accompaniment to everyday activities; as a resource in identity formation; and as an occasion for imaginative or, in the case of karaoke, real coparticipation. Taking these variables into account, can one really say with confidence that what is experienced for certain listeners, in certain settings, as an unwanted appropriation of attention will be experienced likewise for others, in other settings?

A further complication arises in the case of soundalikes more specifically. Even though listeners are often unaware of or indifferent to the hijacking of their attention—as user testimonials confirm, not to mention the sheer number of streams that soundalikes receive—the fact that stream counts determine royalty payouts means that it isn't just attention that so-called spam siphons off. It is also income. Granted, the sums in question are negligible, at least relative to the overall economy of streaming platforms. For the superstars whose music is the most frequent target of soundalikes, the number of streams lost to the latter is a drop in the bucket. As of summer 2022, the more than 20 million streams that John "The Ragin' Cajun" Jones's cover of "Human" had received on Spotify was dwarfed by the 700 million-plus streams Rag'n'Bone Man's original had accumulated. And even those soundalikes that manage to capture the attention of listeners don't entirely displace this original. Ideally, people who listen to knockoff covers of "Human" would still believe that they are listening to Rag'n'Bone Man. The perfect soundalike, that is, would act as a window through which the original is still discerned, more or less distinctly depending on the cover artist's skill and the listener's familiarity with the original.

Perhaps a better way of understanding this dynamic is via the bifurcation attention undergoes once it becomes a tradeable commodity. Like all commodities, attention thus acquires a twofold character, as use value and exchange value. Generally speaking, what soundalike artists seek to appropriate is the exchange value of attention, rather than its use value. The main thing they are after is time—the time that might otherwise be spent listening to the original, the time that is tabulated in the form of a play count, and the time whose numerical representation determines royalty payments. The concrete work that attention performs on behalf of its recipients—its role in building reputation, bestowing recognition, and so on—is to be not only relinquished but actively avoided. Drawing attention to the soundalike as such, or to the artist who made it, would defeat the purpose. The point for the soundalike artist is *not* to be recognized. Soundalikes simultaneously appropriate the attention of users and invite their inattention. They seek to capture attention in its quantitative form, as exchange value, but forgo it in its qualitative form, as use value. And they are only able to do this thanks to the division of attention that platforms perform, by making measures of user engagement central to their peculiar economy.

Fake Streams

SEOClerk.com is a microlabor platform. Like other, better-known sites such as Amazon's Mechanical Turk, CrowdFlower, or Fiverr, the platform acts as a virtual labor market, bringing together buyers and sellers of digitally mediated services. Those seeking to have tasks done can publish job descriptions, detailing among other things the prices they are willing to pay for tasks, while those looking for work can advertise the services they offer and the fees they charge, in addition to bidding on jobs posted to the platforms. Where SEOClerks differs from other microlabor platforms is in the precise nature of the services being bought and sold. The site is what is sometimes referred to as a "black-hat marketplace," where individuals pay others to produce counterfeit digital goods: fake reviews for Amazon, ersatz followers for Twitter and Instagram, bogus Facebook likes, as well as fake plays on streaming music platforms.[92] "Are you struggling to make your SPOTIFY Music [sic] more popular?" asks one freelancer advertising on the platform. To remedy this predicament, musicians can purchase a thousand streams from the seller at the cost of just US $2, though wholesale discounts are also available (40,000 streams go for $55, 100,000 for $90, and 500,000 for $420).[93] If this offer isn't attractive, there are plenty of others to choose from. Another seller appeals to economic reason: "Your music is your business, let me help you grow your business. I will gain you 5,000 SPOTIFY Plays. The greatest factors that determine popularity and how tracks are ranked on SPOTIFY are the total number of plays and recent frequency of plays. When you buy SPOTIFY plays you are directly increasing the popularity of your music."[94] Judging from posts by would-be buyers of bulk streams, such arguments do not fall on deaf ears. "I am marketing a new song on Soundcloud, I am looking to ensure it brings in an appropriate amount of traffic," declared one listing posted in 2016.[95] To improve the chances that the song might gain traction, the prospective buyer offered to pay up to $100 for 150,000 plays, provided that they would be delivered within four days. Still other job listings are even more urgent in their pleas:

Counterfeiting Attention → 169

"trying to get my album on Itunes top 100 in the USA . . . will pay whatever just as long as i get in top 100. tired of my album getting no recognition. . . . PLEASE HELP lol."[96]

The buying and selling of bulk streams on SEOClerks isn't anomalous. Since 2010, traffic in the tokens by which reputation, ranking, and above all attention are counted online has grown in tandem with the platforms on which such tokens serve as valuable tender. By 2017, it was estimated that between 9 percent and 15 percent of all Twitter accounts were bots designed to emulate humans—a figure that translated to 29–48 million of the platform's 319 million active users at the time.[97] Twitter is not alone. In May 2018, Facebook announced that it had deactivated 538 million fake user accounts in the first quarter of that year, in advertising its commitment to rooting out fraudulent activity; left unsaid was that this represented just under a quarter of the platform's more than 2.2 billion then-active users.[98] Reports such as these have led one journalist to wonder how much of the internet is fake (roughly 40 percent, by his calculations).[99] Yet platforms where such counterfeit signals circulate are scarcely innocent victims of such fraudulence. Rather, they are its willing accomplices, since successful monetization of user attention and data hinges on the size of their user base. As one cybersecurity expert has noted, platforms "have a perverse incentive to let it happen. . . . They want to police [fake traffic] to the extent it doesn't seem obvious, but they make money off of it."[100]

For many platforms the monetization of user attention is indirect, realized by means of advertising (such is the case with Twitter and Facebook). On music platforms, by contrast, the connection between measures of user attention and financial compensation is more direct, at least for rights holders. After all, how many streams a track accrues in a given reporting period determines artists' revenue share. But in addition to the obvious economic incentive motivating artists to increase streaming numbers, the trade in fake streams is revealing for other reasons as well. Above all, it highlights the failed promise of digital distribution to level the playing field between superstars and the multitude of recording artists who struggle to have their music heard, let alone earn a living from it. One way of conceptualizing this broad category is by analogy to the Marxian notion of the surplus population, a group excluded from the wage relation because they are superfluous to the reproduction of capital (the unemployed, the economically inactive, those working in the informal sector, and so on).[101] Along similar lines, we might imagine the countless musicians whose music goes largely unheard as a surplus artistic population, a group that is in some sense redundant for both audiences and for the attention-extractive industries that monetize them (including streaming platforms). The desperation of the buyer who would "pay whatever just so long as i get in [the] top 100" is the desperation of someone for whom this superfluity is a vivid experience, for whom the diminished role of gatekeepers online has not translated into a substantial improvement in the chances of winning recognition—or income—for their work. On the contrary, the removal of barriers to entry brought about by music's move online since 2000 has had the paradoxical effect of making musicians' work both more accessible and less likely of actually being accessed. From this perspective, demand for fake streams is to be understood less as an ethical lapse than as an entirely rational response to what mainstream economists might describe as a form of market failure. Viewed from a more critical angle, however, the suboptimal allocation of (musical) goods appears less as a deviation from the proper functioning of markets than as a realization of their built-in tendency toward concentration and consolidation.

It was not supposed to be this way. Digital distribution was supposed to attenuate, not exacerbate, the divide separating superstars from the rest. Such was the rhetoric that imbued the recommendation systems that music information retrieval researchers envisaged in the early, heady days of the digital music economy. One of the main benefits claimed for such discovery tools was their ability to match niche artists with niche audiences. The swollen ranks of pre-internet gatekeepers, the story goes, had limited the range of musics available to audiences, at the same time as they narrowed the audiences available to most musicians. It was this unsatisfactory arrangement, in which idiosyncratic styles and idiosyncratic tastes were both ill-served, that motivated many MIR researchers to seek out a technical fix in the form of personalized recommendations. Brian Whitman, erstwhile head of the Echo Nest, recounted how his experience toiling in obscurity as a composer of IDM (intelligent dance music) in the 1990s informed his subsequent work in music recommendation. At a TEDx presentation in 2012, he recalled how predigital distribution channels made it difficult for a niche musician such as himself to make a living:

> You're working hard on your art and you really believe in it and you work all the time on it. . . . And the problem with it is that once you make this amazing thing, you try to get it out there. . . . And for me you know the world of music was just shut off. You know, the kind of music I was making . . . I was not a teen boy pop star, I was making very weird,

complicated music that had a very small niche market. And I saw this, and you know the only way to get anywhere was to know somebody or to make more popular music or whatever.[102]

Whitman was not the only MIR researcher whose work was motivated by a frustration with older distribution models. Many involved in designing recommendation systems assumed the idealistic (or paternalistic) stance that it was their duty to use "non-obvious recommendations" to push audiences toward novel, unknown, or obscure musics. Such was the case with Òscar Celma, head of research at Pandora, who declared in 2010 that "one of the goals of a recommender should be to promote the tail of the [distribution] curve by providing relevant, personalised novel recommendations to its users."[103] In their efforts to redirect music consumption away from the head of the distribution curve, where hits clustered, toward the tail, where neglected musics were confined, designers of music recommendation systems assumed a quasi-ethical mandate: not only would recommenders diversify consumers' tastes, but they would also lessen the disparities in the music industry.

As Celma's remark makes clear, his stance—like that of many other MIR developers—was informed by the model of "long tail economics" that Chris Anderson popularized in the mid-aughts.[104] According to Anderson, the market dominance of hit songs, blockbuster movies, and the like in the past was not inevitable but resulted from the physical constraints of predigital distribution channels. "Lockstep culture is the exception, not the rule," he posits.[105] In the analog era, limits to the amount of shelf space in brick-and-mortar stores, in the number of screens per movie theater, or in the page counts of publications meant that space was at a premium. To occupy such valuable real estate, an item had to be worth the cost, which incentivized distributors to stock only those that generated a sufficient return. With the development of online distribution, however, search, storage, and transaction costs fell precipitously, eroding the material conditions that previously ensured blockbusters' dominance. Not only were niche products more accessible, but they had become more profitable to boot. "If you combine enough of the non-hits," he observes, "you've established a market that rivals the hits."[106] This calculus underpins Anderson's prediction that supply and demand would steadily drift away from the fat head, where hits reigned, toward the ever-lengthening tail, where niche goods and audiences were dispersed. "If the twentieth-century was about *hits*," he declares, "the twenty-first will be equally about *niches*."[107]

With the passage of time, many of Anderson's Pollyannaish predictions about the impending democratization of cultural production and consumption have proved themselves to be exactly that: Pollyannaish, being hard to square with empirical evidence. Studies conducted since 2010 point to the continued dominance of hits. Even before streaming had displaced digital downloads, there were clear signs that a superstar economy remained in force within the online music market. Examining statistics for the iTunes store, Anita Elberse noted that for the year 2011 just over a hundred of the site's roughly eight million tracks—which is to say 0.001 percent—accounted for 15 percent of total downloads. By contrast, 94 percent of the tracks on the site had sold fewer than a hundred units, and a third had been downloaded just once.[108] This dynamic endured once streaming overtook downloads. In a 2013 report, Mark Mulligan indicated that the top 1 percent of artists were responsible for generating 77 percent of recorded music revenue, a ratio that was more or less unchanged according to a study published some eight years later, in 2021.[109] While these figures are specific to the UK market, there is no reason to suspect that the skewed distribution of attention (or income) is substantially different elsewhere. In Mulligan's account, the persistence of winner-take-all tendencies on streaming platforms resulted from the fact that platforms are not entirely exempt from the sort of physical and spatial constraints that dogged predigital distribution channels. Paradoxically, the layout of platform interfaces offers less "'front end' display" than the average record store window display. This is particularly true on mobile devices: while a streaming app only "has a few square inches of smartphone screen" at its disposal, a brick-and-mortar store would typically enjoy "dozens of square feet of window space."[110]

These aren't the only constraints that continue to funnel both attention and revenue to a small number of top earners. In addition to physical limits, there are also cognitive and temporal ones. The scarcity of shelf space in brick-and-mortar record stores may no longer be an issue, but the scarcity of what economists Robert Frank and Philip Cook term "mental shelf space" remains. "In many product markets," they observe, "we are either unable to, or we simply choose not to, keep track of a host of similar competing products."[111] Time constraints also play a role in sustaining music's superstar economy, seeing as how most listeners do not have the luxury of plumbing the depths of streaming platforms' catalogs. For Elberse, such time constraints mean that most listeners are "light consumers," who opt for the most readily accessible—and hence

Counterfeiting Attention → 173

most popular—items. Conversely, more obscure artists and titles tend to be the province of "heavy consumers," the narrow slice of the population that has invested sufficient time and effort to be "familiar with many alternatives."[112] Meanwhile, lowered barriers to entry and the democratization of access to distribution have increased the pool of musicians vying for the attention of audiences—which in turn reduces each individual artist's or group's chances of actually capturing such attention. For Frank and Cook, this represents an unaccounted-for negative externality of winner-take-all markets, as each entrant diminishes the probability of success for all others.[113] Compounding this problem is the fact that most streaming platforms operate on a global scale. While one might think that an increase in the absolute number of both producers and consumers of music connected through the intermediary of a streaming platform would come out as a wash, the winner-take-all dynamics of the digital music economy are such that they tend to focus a greater amount of user attention toward a relatively smaller proportion of artists.

Taken together, the forces that continue to push listeners in the direction of hit tracks on digital platforms would appear to cancel out if not override those that might instead impel listeners in the direction of more obscure titles. But it is not just data on listening behavior that suggest this is so. The burgeoning market for fake streams seen on sites such as SEOClerks also attests to this fact. To be sure, demand for such counterfeit tokens of listener engagement is not restricted to just those unheard musicians who make up the surplus artistic population on streaming platforms. Major labels and certain high-profile artists signed to them have been credibly accused of artificially boosting play and follower counts. A case in point is the allegation that Tidal surreptitiously inflated the play counts of Kanye West's *Life of Pablo* and Beyoncé's *Lemonade* albums on the platform, a ruse that would have benefited not only the two artists in question but also the platform itself, making it appear more popular than it actually was.[114] Such endeavors are continuous with other tactics that artists, labels, and media companies use to improve the sales figures and chart position of recordings, such as the widespread "bundling" of albums with tickets, merch, and other seemingly unrelated commodities.[115] And the use of misleading promotional practices is hardly a new phenomenon. Antecedents include the claques paid to loudly applaud performers in nineteenth-century French grand opera, as well as the recourse publishers (and, later, record labels) have had to payola as a way of securing exposure for their products.[116]

That these and other tactics for manufacturing the appearance of popularity have proved so durable over the years suggests that they are not individual lapses but instead have a systemic basis.[117] Even if established artists and major labels also have incentives to game streaming metrics, however, disparities in economic and symbolic capital mean that the stakes are very different for them compared with less well-known artists. For the latter, purchasing streams is a way of overcoming the catch-22 according to which success in attracting attention often hinges on having attracted it already. This bears out one of Yves Citton's theses about the "ecology of attention": namely, that people tend to pay heed to what others pay heed to. Because individuals "are attentive to one another," Citton writes, "the direction taken by the attention of one of them pushes the attention of the other in the same direction."[118] The difference with streaming is that platforms take this informal principle of everyday social interaction and formalize it, transforming it into an engine of accumulation.

This institutionalization of the principle that it takes attention to get attention is underlined by the tips that platforms offer aspiring musicians wishing to promote their music. Consider Spotify's FAQ for artists. Prior to 2018, when the Spotify for Artists service was redesigned to get more independent musicians to directly upload their recordings to the platform, the advice given to artists was fairly limited. Beyond some pointers on how to improve a track's visibility, the page addressed a few specific questions: how to boost a track's position in search results, how to get a song placed on an editorial playlist, how to get one's music featured on the browse page, and so on. Yet for all these problems, basically the same solution was suggested. As regards search results, the FAQ page noted that the ranking of items returned by a query is determined by a combination of factors, the most important being the taste profile of the individual user and an item's popularity on the platform. Having little control over listener taste, artists are nominally in a position to influence their music's popularity—whence Spotify's declaration that "the more streams and followers you have, the higher up you'll appear in searches."[119] Similar guidance was offered to artists wishing to have their music featured on Spotify's browse page. After listing the factors that determine what appears on users' browse pages (listening history, location, and so on), the site again emphasized that "the more people listen to your music, the more likely your music will show up in Browse."[120]

Even following the 2018 relaunch of Spotify for Artists, most of the advice remained unchanged. Superficially, artists now had more tools at their disposal for promoting their music on Spotify. Most notably, they could now submit previously unreleased tracks for consideration on one of Spotify's curated playlists (those already released would continue to be selected on the basis of curator taste, the company's proprietary data, and other unspecified factors). Still unclear, however, were the criteria by which new releases would be chosen for a playlist. Moreover, the freedom granted to artists—the freedom to submit one's music for consideration—was more formal than effective. Considering the number of tracks uploaded to the platform each day (as of 2022, estimates place the figure around 100,000), the chances that any given one might actually be chosen for promotion remain exceedingly low.[121] The closest thing to a concrete suggestion for improving a track's chances for selection is, again, to increase its "visibility": "Our playlist editors are always looking out for the hottest and freshest talent. You can make sure you stay on their radar by building your fanbase and engaging with your audience on Spotify."[122] The common refrain in all of these tips, past and present, is that the best way to bring one's music to the attention of curators and algorithms is for it to have already accrued a certain baseline level of attention to begin with.

Conditions such as these help explain why a gray market trade in services promising to boost play counts and other indices of user engagement has emerged. But such services don't just respond to demand; they also help to manufacture the demand they promise to satisfy. The site Mass Media+, for instance, offers clients seeking to "gain influence on social media" a variety of options for doing so. Packages that can be purchased on the site include likes and retweets on Twitter, repins on Pinterest, and channel subscribers on YouTube. In connection with streaming platforms more specifically (Spotify, SoundCloud, and JioSaavn), the company cites a number of reasons prospective customers should pay for the company's services. Foremost is increased "visibility and engagement." Observing that "many artists on [JioSaavn] are passed over and ignored because their songs have very few plays," the company claims that by purchasing streams a musician can foster "the impression your music is worth checking out and should not be ignored!"[123] Likewise, Mass Media+ notes that purchasing plays can attract "new listeners to your music who [will] hopefully start following you and become fans."[124] A notable feature of such appeals is the way they invoke the self-reinforcing processes streaming platforms like Spotify allude to in suggesting that attention begets more attention. By purchasing plays from Mass Media+, the site suggests, clients may kick-start a positive feedback loop, the attention economy's version of the "Matthew effect" that Robert Merton christened in reference to a passage from Scripture ("For unto everyone that hath shall be given, and he shall hath in abundance"). But it is another group—those ensnared in a negative feedback loop—to whom the company's pitch is addressed. "There are so many great artists out there struggling to gain traction," the website remarks elsewhere, with the prospect of gaining such "traction" held forth as one of the company's main selling-points.[125]

As an object of desire, "traction" is a slippery thing. It points to an indiscernible threshold, one that cannot be figured in a precise number of plays or listeners. But even as Mass Media+ plays on such desires for real or symbolic recognition—as well as anxieties about its absence—the company makes other, more direct inducements to potential clients. Among the reasons given for making use of the company's services are two short words: "Earn More." The web page elaborates: "Not only do our Saavn plays increase your popularity, but these royalty eligible plays can put money in your pocket as well. Buying Saavn plays is a win-win all around!"[126] Other outlets selling streams are even more forthright about the financial benefits. Take Streamify, a service active in the late 2010s that has since ceased operations. A page on its website (titled "Why Streamify") features an image of a disembodied hand holding a wad of twenty-dollar bills. A caption elaborates: "Sales are necessary. Streamify increases your play count and gets you more royalties. The plays you receive from Streamify are absolutely 100% real and eligible for royalties."[127]

The different pitches that Streamify, Mass Media+, and other streaming promotion sites make anticipate the different ends to which these streams, once purchased, might be put. At one end of the spectrum are situations in which counterfeit streams are a means to an end, a way of kick-starting a virtuous cycle whereby (artificial) attention attracts (real) attention. This may be understood as just the latest development in a long history of music promotion, using new technologies to do what older, "analog" methods such as song plugging did in the past: hype a musical product. This development may also be understood as a form of online impression management, on a par with other forms of identity play and deception that take place on the internet: the fluffing of profiles on dating sites, the padding of résumés on LinkedIn, the careful curating of selfies on Instagram feeds, and so on. Encouraging such play are the internet's affordances as a communication medium. As Whitney Phillips and Ryan Milner note, "people engage in various forms of identity construction and deception in digitally mediated spaces because they are able to."[128] The same is true for streaming platforms, where play counts and follower counts don't just reflect listener activity but also help to fashion the public image of individual tracks or artists. In the case of streams bought in bulk, the aim of such manipulation is to create an impression of popularity in the hope of actually making it a reality. Royalty payments may increase as a result of boosting play counts, but in many cases this appears to be a secondary concern, at least in the short run.

At the other end of the spectrum are practices that treat ersatz streams not as a means to an end but as an end in itself. Here the aim is to inflate play counts in order to boost income. The cultivation of an audience over the long run, or the conversion of "fake" streams into "real" ones, is beside the point. Exemplary in this regard is what the music press dubbed the "Bulgarian Spotify Scam."[129] The affair centered around two playlists—"Soulful Music" and "Music from the Heart"—that generated enough streams in late 2017 to propel them to the upper reaches of Spotify's charts.[130] Both playlists were unusual on a number of counts. Both featured a larger-than-average number of tracks ("Soulful Music," for instance, included 467); all the tracks bore ISRC codes identifying their country of origin as Bulgaria (though this too was likely faked); the duration of each track was unusually short, lasting just over thirty seconds apiece, recalling Vulfpeck's *Sleepify* album; and the playlists attracted a small number of listeners—roughly 1,200—who were responsible for a large number of streams. Taking these peculiarities into account, it would appear that some individual or group created these playlists, populated them with cheap, perhaps algorithmically generated production music, and then set up 1,200 paid user accounts to play them at random. The last two points are key: by using paid subscriptions instead of freemium accounts, the scam's perpetrators ensured they would receive a higher payout rate, while the shuffle function helped disguise anomalies in listening activity. To set up the accounts would have cost only $12,000—perhaps even less, if the accounts were acquired using one of Spotify's promotional discounts. Yet the returns reaped by this investment were substantial. According to calculations made by *Music Business Worldwide*, within a single month the two playlists grossed somewhere between $288,000 and $415,000.[131]

Notably, this exploit was perfectly legal.[132] Spotify presumably received payment for the subscriptions the scam's perpetrators used. If the company suffered any loss, it was to its reputation. It was other artists on the platform who were the scam's principal victims. In effect, the playlists skimmed money from the revenue pool out of which Spotify pays rights holders, money which might have otherwise gone to other musicians. Here it is important to recall that Spotify, like other streaming platforms, has to date employed a pro rata (or service-centric) approach to allocating royalty payments. According to this model, the revenue generated by users is aggregated. Labels receive a cut of this total, corresponding to the percentage of the total number of tracks streamed on the platform for which their catalog was responsible. They then distribute the revenue to artists in their rosters, proportionate to the number of streams generated by each (the amount of money actually paid out may be significantly reduced by deductions claimed by labels, as well as by the sort of dubious accounting methods for which the record industry has long been notorious).

Key to the scam is that the pro rata model funnels revenue into a single royalty pool, severing the payments made by listeners from those received by rights holders. Hence if certain listeners stream more tracks per month on a service than others do on average, then they can effectively skew payouts toward their favored artists. It was thanks to this quirk of the pro rata model that the perpetrators of the scam were able to receive more from Spotify's revenue pool than they had put into it. Had the company allocated revenue according to a user-centric distribution model (UCD)—touted by many artists and artist-advocates as more equitable than pro rata payment—the scam wouldn't have worked, since UCD distributes revenue only to those artists that a user happens to stream during a given month, and to no others.[133] What a user listens to, and how much they listen to it, should in principle have no impact beyond determining how the proceeds of their individual monthly payment is divvied up. As a result, users wouldn't be able to skew payouts by streaming certain musics more intensively than others. By way of illustration, consider a scenario where a user streams nothing but a single artist's music during an entire month. Under UCD, it wouldn't matter if they streamed it just once, a hundred times, or a thousand times: either way, the effects of their listening behavior would be contained, with the artist in question receiving the user's monthly fee, minus the cut taken by the platform, and nothing more. Had such a model been in place, it would have ruled out the kind of wealth transfer that the pro rata approach enables and that the perpetrators of the Bulgarian Spotify Scam exploited. In theory, at least, a user-centric model would have ended up *costing* the scammers money, since they would have received only about 70 percent back from their up-front investment (the aggregate cost of the subscription fees, minus the roughly 30 percent taken by the platform). As it was, the small investment the scammers fronted returned a far larger payout, a surplus that was financed by other rights holders.

Breaching norms of conduct without breaking laws, this affair may be understood as instantiating a failure in platform governance. Following Tarleton Gillespie, this amounts to a twofold failure: a failure not just in the governance of platforms but also in the governance exercised by platforms.[134] In terms of the governance of platforms (by external regulators and public agencies, for example), there is little regulation preventing or punishing such questionable transfers of wealth from one user group to another. At least this is true at present, particularly in the United States, where the technology sector has long enjoyed substantial protections and minimal oversight. In terms of their self-governance—that is, the regulation of platforms by platforms themselves—in principle this offers greater latitude in rooting out fraudulent activity. Complicating matters in practice are the competing pressures and incentives to which streaming platforms are subject. As Gillespie notes, platforms across the board have increasingly assumed the responsibility of "policing the activity of their users" not only in order "to meet legal requirements, or to avoid having additional policies imposed," but also in order "to avoid losing offended or harassed users, to placate advertisers eager to associate their brands with a healthy online community, to protect their corporate image, and to honor their own personal and institutional ethics."[135] But given their interest in appealing to the widest possible user base, and in keeping with the libertarian ideology regnant within the tech sector, most services exercise only minimal (self-)regulation. That these contradictory forces lead a company such as Spotify to overlook or tolerate a certain degree of fraudulent activity bears out Davies's claim that fraud is an "equilibrium quantity."

Where this equilibrium settles depends on the economic costs involved in monitoring the vast catalog of recordings and equally massive user base platforms host. As profit-seeking enterprises, streaming services strive to reduce labor costs as much as possible. For that reason, they rely almost exclusively on algorithmic methods for identifying artificially inflated play counts and follower counts. A cheap method for detecting anomalous activity, such automated tools are most effective at combating equally cheap methods of generating fake streams—that is, those that likewise rely on automation. Conversely, individuals wishing to increase their play counts and follower counts also have an interest in containing costs, especially those, like the perpetrators of the Bulgarian Spotify Scam, whose primary motivation is financial. The least expensive and most straightforward way of boosting streams is provided by platforms themselves, in the form of the auto-repeat button included in most user interfaces. This was the tool that Vulfpeck encouraged fans to use in upping the play count of *Sleepify*. But precisely because of its simplicity, playing the same songs on repeat results in statistical patterns that are easy for platforms to detect.

More sophisticated are bots that can play back specific tracks, albums, and playlists on loops of variable duration, across a range of (simulated) locations, using a number of (fake) user accounts. Many such tools are available for purchase online. A case in point is the now-defunct application Spotviewbot, which for $97 promised to "easily add thousands of plays on Spotify songs."[136] The initial version of the program, released in 2016, had a straightforward interface. It included fields where users could enter the URL of the playlist(s) to be streamed, set the duration a song is to play before skipping to the next, and specify the number of plays to be cycled through before logging out. A particularly important setting gave users the choice of how many different threads (that is, accounts) to run simultaneously, justifying Spotviewbot's promise that users could generate a "potentially unlimited" number of streams. The more threads running concurrently, the more plays one could rack up.[137]

An updated version of Spotviewbot released in 2018 added a number of new features (see figure 4.2). Where previously only a fixed value could be entered for the duration a track was to play before skipping forward, the updated version allowed this value to vary within a specified range. Likewise, where previously only a fixed number of streams could be played per session, now this number could be made to fluctuate. The through line connecting these and other new features was to generate unpredictable patterns of activity that would confound Spotviewbot's algorithmic adversaries, the automated systems platforms use to root out fake plays. It isn't hard to imagine this dynamic evolving in a manner akin to the "arms race" Brunton has described in the escalating competition pitting spam bots against spam filters.[138] But such a state of affairs has already come to pass, after a fashion: methods of statistical analysis used by platforms to stem the tide of counterfeit streams have already improved to the point that listening behavior evincing too much regularity, or the wrong kinds of regularity, risks sanction.[139] Not only can the offending user accounts be banned; also at risk are tracks and artists streamed through (allegedly) illegitimate means. Under these conditions, dissimulating attention through automated means isn't enough. What is necessary is to dissimulate the haphazard fashion in which human attention moves across different objects, at different moments in time.

For artists using fake streams as a means of gaining visibility, the prospect of having their music removed due to the failings of a computer script is a significant deterrent. But what is deterred might not be the purchase of fake streams per se so much as the purchase of streams fabricated through automated technologies. For this reason, it is common for services purveying bulk streams and followers to advertise the "authenticity" (and hence the safety) of their wares. A post on fiverup.com is representative: "Buy plays and make your music work as a secondary income stream for you and your career! * No bots, real plays! Stop buying FAKE plays that's why your not getting PAID!! * Our plays are 100% SAFE * Earn revenue from real plays * Increase your play count and get more royalties * These plays are REAL."[140] A similar announcement on SEOClerks proclaims "**NO BOTS USED**—We work with a distribution center that gives your track(s) real plays by real people. (Service might take longer than others but it is guaranteed to be real people listening to your music)."[141] Worth underlining in this listing is its reference to a "distribution center" in explaining how client orders are fulfilled. The term is suggestive, precisely because it is so slippery. A term such as *distribution center* evokes the flat, colorless language of supply-chain logistics to lend the listing an air of legitimacy. But at the same time it is vague enough to compass less legitimate methods of accruing streams. Other, equally vague formulations appear in other offers

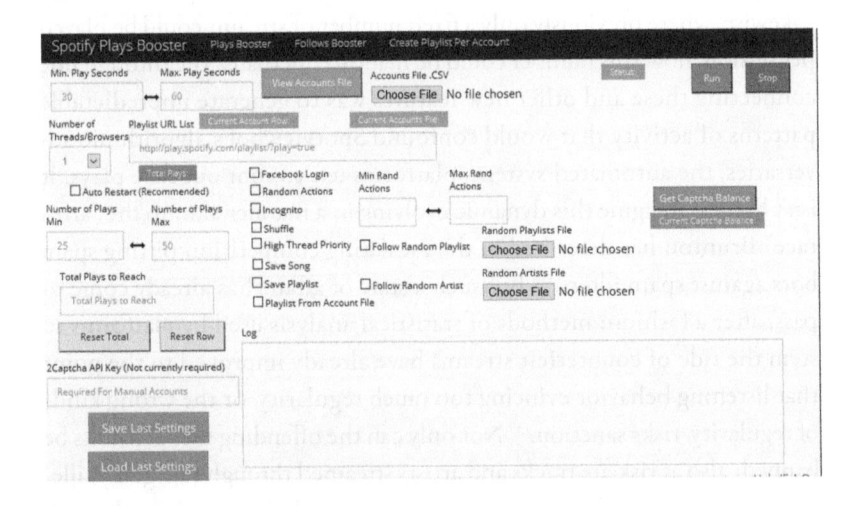

4.2 Spotviewbot interface

boasting of the authenticity of the streams the services furnish. The service Wbix alludes to the "expert teams" it mobilizes on behalf of clients, while Streamify makes reference to a "partner list" it draws on, which includes "music promoters, DJs, online radio stations, playlists, and various other parties."[142] Who, exactly, are these "various other parties"? It is impossible to say. Indeed, it is hard to imagine an emptier signifier than this, broad enough to cover all sorts of personnel, none of whom need to be affiliated with the music industry, even as the rest of the actors cited by Streamify (music promoters, DJs, and so on) would lead unsuspecting clients to believe so.

Given the opacity of the market for counterfeit streams, it is difficult to say with certainty what terms such as *distribution centers*, *expert teams*, and *partner lists* actually designate. But the contours of the global division of digital labor, coupled with hints embedded in posts at SEOClerks, fiverup.com, and other microlabor platforms, suggest a likely candidate: clickworkers, whether working as individual contractors or (less commonly) as wage workers employed by click farms. Concentrated in the developing economies of South and Southeast Asia, such clickwork is mainly performed by low-paid, precarious workers, who carry out the kind of rote, repetitive tasks that keep the flows of digital capitalism moving: creating social media accounts, moderating content for platforms, clicking online ads, labeling data sets, liking or rating items, training AI systems, and, of course, generating plays on streaming services.[143] In keeping with the logic of offshoring more generally, click farms profit from a form of labor arbitrage, one facilitated by the free flow of data across platforms whose operations span international borders. In addition, the low levels of formal employment in countries such as Bangladesh or the Philippines—major centers for clickwork—ensure the existence of significant surplus populations, from whose ranks a seemingly inexhaustible supply of fresh recruits for the transnational digital proletariat can be drawn.[144]

Like other forms of digital labor, the actual work performed by clickworkers remains largely hidden; the same platforms that connect buyers and sellers of streams, clicks, and retweets also make possible their separation, both physical and psychological. But in contrast to the kinds of labor often researched in digital media scholarship, which are disappeared through their disavowal as labor—that is, through the belief that the work of watching, listening, or generating content does not really count as work—in the case of clickwork this labor is made invisible in a more direct way, by being placed at a geographic remove from consumers. This physical divide maps onto other fault lines in the global economy, as counterfeit digital goods produced in countries of the Global South (India, Indonesia, Pakistan, Bangladesh, and the Philippines) tend to flow to purchasers concentrated in the wealthier countries of the Global North (the United States, the United Kingdom, and so on).[145] As Antonio Casilli observes, "in the present context of global connectivity, these reserve laborers are spatially hidden and consigned to remote places," a marginalization exacerbated by "gender, class, and race disparities" in the extraction of "unpaid/underpaid digital labor."[146] Further compounding such distancing is the widespread use of subcontracting. This may take the form of "local lengthening," as online sellers of digital services act as brokers, bridging the gap between their international customer base and a local labor force.[147] At other times, the supply chain for fake streams is extended via the microlabor platforms through which they are purchased. Standard practice is for an individual or firm selling streams to then buy them from another vendor operating on the same or different platform, who may in turn buy them from still another vendor, and so forth.[148] The results of these practices are reseller networks whose reticulations are so complex that it is difficult to tell where they begin and where they end.

One effect of such ramified supply chains is to obscure the origins of the goods and services that flow downstream through them—which, for the buyers and sellers of artificial streams, has the advantage of making it harder for streaming platforms to distinguish "real" plays from those bought and paid for. But another effect is to further depress the wages of those located at the far side of the supply chain, the clickworkers responsible for repeatedly pressing play, letting a track run for a specified length of time, and then skipping to the next. The money flowing from paying customers diminishes as it moves upstream through the supply chain, with each intermediary claiming a portion for themselves, leaving little at the end for those doing the clicking. And while much clickwork takes the form of freelance labor, performed by self-employed contractors having some degree of control over their working conditions, in other instances it takes the form of piecework, carried out by wage laborers in what may justly be described as digital sweatshops.

Consider the testimonial of Alberto, a former click farm worker from the Philippines.[149] Working shifts that could last up to twelve hours, Alberto and his fellow employees were given targets they had to attain before being paid for any of their work on a given day. Failure to reach these targets frequently led to punitive actions: "If we're below where we're supposed to be, we'll get a verbal warning, and if we're still behind in a few hours... they'll turn off our personal fan for half an hour. Not the lower fans on the computer, but the fan on us."[150] To avoid such disciplinary measures, Alberto and his coworkers were compelled to multitask, as they struggled to fulfill orders being processed simultaneously: "A song will be going while you go to different sites liking things. You need to sign in and out of different accounts, and one tab will be the Facebook tab. Another will be the Twitter tab. The Instagram tab. The YouTube tab."[151] But if the SoundCloud plays that Alberto and others produced were in any sense "real"—as opposed, say, to those produced by bots—it was only because a human was performing this otherwise mechanical task. It certainly wasn't because Alberto and his coworkers were attending to the tracks they had been tasked with promoting. On the contrary: listening to music was prohibited on-site, as was the use of any device (such as noise-canceling headphones) that might distract employees from their work. As a result, the one sound Alberto retained from his time as a clickworker was not that of music. It was the endlessly repeated sound of the clicks themselves. "In the company, it was a giant room. It was in a warehouse. Few people talked, so all you would hear is the clicks. Hundreds and hundreds of clicks. When I went home at the end of the day, sometimes it would echo."[152] He was not the only one to suffer from this sort of auditory trauma: "Numerous people at my company had it. Some would hear clicking hours after work. Most, like me, can't stand key clicks anymore."[153]

There is a bitter irony in the fact that these digital wage laborers, charged with promoting music on SoundCloud, were themselves unable to listen to music. But this is not the only irony, nor the most bitter. Another is the perverse form of mutual dependency that links a clickworker such as Alberto to artists who pay for bulk streams on the other side of the globe. Despite stark differences in terms of geography, culture, economic status, and life chances, what binds the two together is a shared desire to stave off consignment to the category of human surplus. One group sells the labor of clicking in an effort to avoid absorption into the local surplus population, the very size of which ensures their remuneration remains as low as the cost of the plays, likes, retweets, and clicks they manufacture. The other group buys the clicks thus produced, in an effort to avoid being absorbed into a different sort of surplus population, a specifically artistic one, whose marginalization within the attention economy of online streaming ensures their marginalization within its money economy as well.

"Fake" Artists

In August 2016, *Music Business Worldwide* (MBW) reported that Spotify had quietly branched out into largely uncharted territory for the platform: the commissioning of original content.[154] While the shift from content distribution to content creation was by then already well underway among video streaming services, with Netflix leading the way, the economics of music licensing had made such initiatives too risky for most digital music platforms to undertake. Not wishing to upset the labels whose massive stockpile of IP they depended on, there was little upside for services to pursue music production directly. These risks made Spotify's alleged turn to commissioning new music hard to explain, even as it clarified why the platform was doing it on the sly. According to MBW, Spotify had paid a handful of producers a flat fee to produce tracks conforming to specifications spelled out in advance. In general, tracks were to be instrumentals and had to "fit certain genres and themes, including jazz, chill, and peaceful piano playing."[155] The music, the article asserted, was then placed within certain of Spotify's proprietary playlists, where they appeared under assumed artist names rather than those of their creators. The same pseudonyms also purported to identify who owned the tracks' master rights. But, the report noted, those identified as rights holders weren't the actual rights holders. The reason was that "they're made-up people."[156]

Given the fraught history concerning questions of authenticity and inauthenticity in commercial popular music, one might have expected MBW's report to have caused a stir.[157] Yet outside a relatively small circle of digital music professionals, the exposé received little attention at the time. Matters changed almost a year later, when MBW's report was cited in Adam Raymond's *New York* magazine article on the various forms of fakery plaguing streaming platforms (discussed earlier).[158] The renewed attention directed at Spotify's alleged incursions into music production prompted a strident response from the company: "We do not and have never created 'fake' artists and put them on Spotify playlists." MBW felt compelled to respond in turn.[159] A few days later it published a new post, which named the artists and songs alleged to be "fake." Of the fifty tracks the report highlighted, all had been featured prominently on one of Spotify's popular mood- or context-based playlists ("Peaceful Piano," "Deep Focus," "Sleep," "Ambient Chill," and so on), where they had cumulatively racked up 520 million streams (equivalent to approximately $3 million in royalty payments). In addition, all the tracks in question could not be found on any platform but Spotify.[160] As for the artists to whom the tracks were credited, none had much of an online or social media presence. Nor did any of them have a discernible relation to industry personnel or institutions: no agents, no management, nothing.

That these artists were featured prominently on Spotify and nowhere else was curious but not dispositive. To corroborate its reporting, MBW reached out to senior figures in the music industry, who backed up its allegations: "We've been very aware of these artists," one insider confided. "Some of the acoustic covers playlists contain 'artists' owned by a third-party indie production company that's been doing cheap covers for years. We're confident that the acoustic piano stuff is owned by Spotify under assumed names."[161] Another added: "We've been told that third-parties are involved, and at least some of the people behind the fake artists agree to insanely low margins, which obviously has a financial benefit to Spotify."[162] Remarks like these threw into a different light Spotify's insistence that it had never "created fake artists," as well as its flat denial of owning the rights to the tracks in question (according to Spotify, "We do not own rights, we're not a label, all our music is licensed from rights-holders and we pay them—we don't pay ourselves").[163] While it may have been true that Spotify wasn't directly responsible for making the music in question, this didn't rule out the platform's having outsourced its production to third parties. Furthermore, even if licensing fees had been paid to rights holders, this didn't mean that the same rates were being applied across the board. Indeed, if MBW's sources are to be believed, the rates for the recordings in question were "insanely low" relative to industry standards.

Spotify wasn't alone in issuing strategically vague disclaimers. So too did Epidemic Sound, the production music company accused of having created much of the music in question. Having established a lucrative business providing royalty-free music beds for television and digital video producers, by 2016 the Stockholm-based firm had decided that the kind of background music that was its forte might attract additional listeners (and revenue) on streaming platforms. Epidemic's CEO, Oscar Höglund, denied that Spotify had contracted the company to supply bespoke music for its mood playlists. "I can tell you that they've never, ever commissioned a track from us," Höglund asserted.[164] Also brushed aside were accusations that Epidemic Sound had sold the underlying rights for its tracks to Spotify, a common practice in the world of production music, where content creators wishing to avoid the messy entanglements of licensing can often pay a one-time, flat fee instead.[165] But as with Spotify's carefully crafted denials, those made by Epidemic Sound are notable less for what they said than for what they omitted. Unspecified was the rate at which Spotify paid royalties to Epidemic Sound, with Höglund remaining mum on the question.[166] As for why so many of Epidemic Sound's tracks ended up on Spotify's heavily promoted playlists, Höglund suggested it was a mix of artistic merit and good fortune. Epidemic's music, he asserted, went through the same selection process: "You can send up music centrally to Spotify and put it out there on a regular basis, but you never know whether or not any track is going to get picked up."[167] But if Epidemic Sound didn't benefit from preferential treatment, then its success in placing tracks was nothing short of extraordinary. At one point in 2017, 65 percent of the fifty-two tracks on the playlist "Ambient Chill" came from its roster of artists.[168] On another occasion, twenty-eight of its tracks were placed on a mood playlist the same week that sixteen tracks by more famous artists (such as Brian Eno and Bibio) were dropped from it.[169]

Lacking access to company records, it is impossible to say what arrangement Spotify had with Epidemic Sound or with any of the other producers of music by so-called fake artists. Even so, many journalists and industry personnel surmised that the aim was to reduce the amount of revenue Spotify was obliged to share with rights holders—above all the three major labels—and to thereby fortify its position in upcoming licensing renegotiations. "It's one of a number of internal initiatives to lower the royalties they're paying to the major labels," a former Spotify employee acknowledged.[170] The strategy was not without risks, as it threatened to aggravate rights holders whose intellectual property remains the platform's lifeblood.[171] But the strategy also put the platform in an apparently contradictory position. Even as it was in open conflict with spammers, scammers, and listening bots, Spotify appeared to be gaming its own system. Like buyers of fake streams, Spotify was diluting the revenue pool it was obliged to share with rights holders. It was simply doing so on a much grander scale.

Curiously, around the same time the "fake artist" affair was erupting, Spotify was making news for another reason. On 12 July 2017, the company announced the creation of a new research lab in Paris, to be headed by François Pachet.[172] An important figure in the development of MIR, Pachet was poached from Sony Paris due to his expertise in music artificial intelligence (AI). According to the post announcing his hire, Pachet had "been working on assisting artists in music composition for over a decade," making him uniquely qualified to run a center whose focus was "on making tools to help artists in their creative process."[173] Similar rhetoric runs through the press release, with Spotify taking care to present the new initiative as a means of assisting, not displacing, musicians. Others looked on this move with a more jaundiced eye, connecting Pachet's hire with the still unfolding controversy around "fake artists." Taking note of the financial benefit that would accrue to Spotify were it to increase the amount of reduced-rate or royalty-free music being streamed, journalist Tim Ingham wondered aloud whether Spotify's "next obvious step" might be to "begin upstreaming AI-created music onto its hugely popular mood, genre and activity-based playlists."[174] MBW was not alone in posing the question. Even before Pachet's arrival at Spotify had been announced, another outlet, *Music Ally*, had already speculated that AI-generated music would be even more cost-effective than production music for filling up the platform's mood and activity playlists.[175] According to journalist Stuart Dredge, it was a matter of time before one of the growing number of music AI start-ups was acquired for this purpose:

> IF mood-based playlists for sleep, focusing and chilling out are popular (which they most-certainly are) and IF the AI-music startups' algorithms can start to produce music good enough for these kinds of uses (and let's be honest, this is a "WHEN" not an "IF") then why wouldn't production-music firms or even major labels be in the market for acquiring [AI music] startups like Jukedeck, Amper Music and the rest to capitalise? But that said, why wouldn't Spotify also be mulling that strategy?[176]

The announcement of Pachet's hiring a few days after these words were posted on the *Music Ally* website only seemed to strengthen Dredge's case.

Others were less confident about the likelihood of AI-generated music finding its way onto mood playlists. "It's a little hard to imagine Spotify so blatantly building a pipeline of computer-generated music solely for its own financial benefit," mused an article in the tech magazine *Fast Company*.[177] Others noted that the Flow Composer application Pachet had designed at Sony wasn't fully automated, "requir[ing] a human being ... to arrange and produce the material after Sony's tech had written it."[178] But perhaps the most common source of skepticism had to do with the quality of AI-generated music. Referring to music certain artists had made using Flow Composer, one commentator dismissed the threat of an imminent AI takeover by posing a simple question: "What about the fact that these songs are dogshit?"[179] Taste is of course subjective; one person's dogshit may be another's favorite jam. But then again, taste may not be the main criterion for evaluating AI-generated music. Commenting on the current state of AI-produced music, industry consultant Mark Mulligan observed that "AI music is nowhere near being good enough to be a 'hit,' but that's not the point. It is creating 21st-century muzak."[180] Many leaders of music AI start-ups appeared to be of the same mind. Whether algorithms can compose interesting music was an open question; less so was whether they can "compose music that puts you to sleep." "Absolutely" was the answer given by Ed Newton-Rex in a 2017 interview. The CEO of AI production music firm Jukedeck (later acquired by TikTok), Newton-Rex added that this kind of application represented "exactly the kind of field in which AI can be useful."[181] But this is of course also the kind of field that Spotify's mood and activity playlists cater to, where success may be more a question of utility than aesthetics.

Whatever the long-term prospects of commercial music AI, discussions of its suitability for mood and activity playlists have some bearing on the music of so-called fake artists. Perhaps their compositions, too, should be assessed less on aesthetic than on functional grounds—less, that is, in terms of whether they sound "good" than whether they "work." Significantly, one defense of the music by "fake artists" was that if it were any worse than music produced by name artists, then surely users would have signaled their displeasure, whether by skipping tracks, selecting a different playlist, or quitting the application. "If Spotify is able to produce music that is better than what's being made by artists/producers out there, then I don't see a problem with it": such was the opinion of one Redditor commenting on the controversy.[182] Another observed that "Spotify users have an unlimited 'skip' button; nobody is being forced to listen to music."[183] Besides overlooking the influence platforms exert on user responses, by determining what does or doesn't appear on the interface, the problem with this appeal to consumer sovereignty is that it assumes the sort of engaged listening that a playlist such as "Deep Sleep" discourages. Indeed, Spotify's experiment in replacing music by "name artists" with that of "no-name artists" was premised on precisely this sort of listener disengagement. It was premised, that is, on listeners' attention being dispersed across playlists rather than directed at individual tracks. Listeners' focus, presumably, would be less on this or that piece of music than on the general atmosphere, vibe, or affect such music engendered. By enabling the particular to free ride on the general in this way, the cheaper content that had been interspersed across a mood or activity playlist could pass by without drawing undue attention to itself. Indeed, Spotify seems to have counted on users paying little heed to this music *as* music, lest they be tempted to seek out more information about its composers, their backgrounds, and other music by them, among other things. On this front, Spotify appears to have guessed correctly. After all, it was only after industry insiders alerted the press that the practice was brought to public attention. If not for this disclosure, how long might the platform have continued to plant such music on its mood playlists, unbeknownst to listeners?

• • •

That a company such as Spotify has seen fit to game its own system suggests that the sort of fakery examined in this chapter is not a contingent feature of streaming platforms but systemic. Nor is Spotify an outlier. Revelations made in early 2018 regarding Tidal's inflation of its subscriber numbers only lend credence to the claim that "[m]usic streaming numbers are meaningless" (as one article on the incident declared).[184] There is a simple explanation for this. If imposture is rampant within the streaming economy, it is because this economy rests on a more fundamental imposture: the unwarranted claim that streaming services are able to authenticate the data that they generate, circulate, and set to work in allocating resources, whether these resources are music, money, attention, or data. If any fraud is being committed, it is in platforms' efforts to make quantitative metrics pass for qualitative judgments, or in passing off digital traces for the attention they allegedly index. The algorithms used to detect fraudulent listening activity know nothing of truth and deception, of what is "real" or "fake." Even if they could approximate human judgment, they would still reveal little about the actions or motivations that led to one track being streamed over another. All they can do is log user activity, compare its patterns to those previously classed as suspect, and calculate their degree of similarity or divergence. Likewise, the techniques used to classify certain tracks as spam do not—indeed, cannot—distinguish originals from knockoffs, or "real" music from sonic filler. Computer code may be shaped by ideologies that endow these distinctions with meaning, but the code itself is ignorant of such ideologies. All it can do is compare certain configurations of data and metadata to others and indicate where anomalies occur—as, for instance, when otherwise identical audio files possess different metadata or when a play count is disproportionately high compared to other measures of artist popularity.

And yet platforms are obliged to maintain the useful fiction that holds data about listening to be commensurate with listening, data about music with music, data about users with users. Otherwise the authority vested in these data would collapse. Were they to be seen as lacking a purchase on the real-world phenomena they ostensibly track, measures of user activity such as play counts would be deprived of their performative force. Streaming platforms, in short, need to assert that with enough data and sufficiently sophisticated data analytics, they can lay hold of a truth that exists beyond data and that would authorize such data, but that would nonetheless do so strictly by means of data. This may be understood as a version of the big data ideology discussed in chapter 3, according to which statistical analysis, if performed with a large enough data set, is able to pass beyond the plane of statistical models, substituting the map for the territory it represents. The difference is that while advocates of the big data ideology proclaim that "correlation is enough," dismissing the need for any sort of grounding in causal explanation, streaming platforms do not seek to displace causation by correlation so much as blur the line between the two. What they seek, in other words, is to instill the belief that the digital, datafied versions of music, listeners, and listening they construct are able to achieve a form of self-transcendence, approximating their extradigital counterparts to the point the two effectively converge. It isn't that the map is to take the place of the territory; rather, the distinction between map and territory is to be dissolved.

Both the efficacy of streaming platforms and their foundational imposture hinges on the "as if" character of this relation. On the one hand, it is the presumption of their functional equivalence that allows data objects to appropriate the authority that resides within the things they claim to represent: the musical actors, objects, and phenomena to which the data are said to correspond. On the other hand, acting as if data about phenomena were functionally equivalent to these phenomena involves a disavowal, a denial of what John Cheney-Lippold describes as the "incollapsible distinction" separating the two.[185] It is this denial that forms the basis of the systemic (self-)deception that underpins streaming platforms and that in turn makes possible the other, more workaday deceptions that take place within the digital regimes they govern. By treating patterns in a series of data points as if they were equivalent to patterns in musical behavior, the door is opened to all sorts of other false equivalences: tracks that pose as something they aren't; clicks that simulate the irregularities of human listening activity; and (meta)data that refer not to the actual creator of a track but to some fabricated identity instead.

Chapter Five

Streaming, Cheap Music, and the Crises of Social Reproduction

Sleep

In July 2014 Spotify introduced a new category to its Browse page: Sleep. Clicking on the tab called up an array of playlists, promising to induce states ranging from calm relaxation to blissful oblivion. A press release announcing the launch of this and another new playlist category, Dinner, described Sleep as "your new home for synapse-stroking, non-invasive, care-banishing, pillow-smoothing, muscle-relaxing playlists."[1] The update was consistent with a broader reorientation underway at the platform. Spotify's pursuit of a mass audience in the early 2010s had led it to adopt features that aimed to accommodate and promote a more passive, "lean back" listener experience.[2] One of these was the Browse page itself, which debuted in 2013. So too was the growing importance attached to the playlist, which soon became the dominant medium of music's organization on this and other platforms. Still another was Spotify's growing emphasis on "moments," on providing users with music to accompany their daily routines (which, as we've seen in chapter 3, generates valuable information on what people are doing or feeling as part of these routines). From this standpoint, Sleep's inclusion on the Browse page was a logical extension of Spotify's new approach to listener engagement. Sleep rounded out the list of activities that make up people's everyday lives, which Spotify's playlists now addressed (Workout, Party, Focus, and so on). Yet Sleep also marks a limit, being the point beyond which users can lean back no further. No longer content with providing music for (and collecting data on) all our waking moments, Spotify was now taking aim at a part of users' lives that had previously eluded its grasp.

There is some irony in the fact that Spotify introduced this playlist category to its Browse page in the wake of the *Sleepify* affair, discussed in chapter 4. The same kind of listener nonengagement that had led to the removal of Vulfpeck's album from Spotify's catalog was now being actively promoted by the platform. Yet this quirk of history was more than just ironic; it was also symptomatic. The coincidence of these two events brought into focus the growing prominence of music for sleep, both within and beyond streaming platforms. A celebrated example is Max Richter's eight-hour composition *Sleep*, described by the composer as "my personal lullaby for a frenetic world."[3] Similar initiatives abound: sleep concerts organized by musicians such as William Basinski, Robert Rich, Christoph Heemann, and Adam Basanta; records such as *Sleep Better* by EDM producer and accredited sleep science coach Tom Middleton, *Liminal Sleep* by Icelandic postrock band Sigur Rós, and *Weightless* (billed as "the world's most relaxing song") by ambient group Marconi Union in collaboration with a sleep therapist; and the many smartphone apps that use music to lead listeners from a state of wakefulness to the land of Nod.[4]

Technological innovations have had a hand in this proliferation of somnogenic musics. Although musical sleep aids such as lullabies have existed since time immemorial, the development of recording technologies have made it possible to induce sleep using the dead musical labor stored on a record or CD. And with advances in digitization, audio compression, and broadband connectivity, it is easier than ever to let music play without interruption for the duration of one's slumber. Technology is only part of the story, however. A more significant factor driving the growth in music for sleeping has to do with broader concerns centering on sleep's parlous status at present. As sociologist Simon Williams observes, sleep has become "a contested matter in . . . the 'wired awake' era of go-faster or turbo-capitalism."[5] For Williams, the quickening pace of economic life is largely responsible for the widespread sleep deprivation (or "sleep debt") that is a hallmark of the present. Reinforcing such systemic tendencies are ideological discourses that not only justify sleep loss but celebrate it. Representative is an article in *Entrepreneur* magazine, which exhorts readers to "Sleep Less, Feel Better, and Get More Done."[6] Sleep, the article contends, is a luxury that neoliberal subjects in good standing should renounce, given the precious hours of entrepreneurial activity it squanders. At the same time, however, the mounting strains on this physiological and psychic necessity have transformed sleep from a matter of personal well-being into a public concern. While this has made the "politics of sleep" more salient, it has also encouraged the development of new forms of expertise and biopolitical regulation. Increasingly sleep is subject to "the ministrations of medical science," Megan Brown remarks, as a host of "sleep-related symptoms are identified and categorized, creating new disorders and syndromes, which are then remedied or relieved through treatment regimens."[7] This in turn has fueled a sleep industry which, by 2017, was already valued at $30–40 billion worldwide.[8]

Perhaps the most trenchant response to the troubled state of sleep is Jonathan Crary's 2013 book *24/7: Late Capitalism and the Ends of Sleep*.[9] According to Crary, subjects of contemporary capitalism find themselves caught between two incompatible temporalities. One is the inflexible, nonstop, and machinic time of capital accumulation, which has created a 24-7 world that dissolves "distinctions between day and night, between light and dark, between action and repose."[10] The other is the cyclic time of human life, with its oscillation between periods of wakefulness and repose. The clash of these conflicting temporalities has endowed sleep with a significance both symbolic and practical. Sleep marks a limit that capital seeks to overcome, an intractable impediment to its drive to construct a world where production, circulation, or consumption would never cease. Sleep's "profound uselessness and intrinsic passivity" mark it as a rare moment when human bodies cannot be enlisted to either create surplus value (through productive labor) or realize it (through the purchase of commodities).[11] Crary, for this reason, regards sleep as a form of silent protest. "Sleep," he remarks, "is an uncompromising interruption of the theft of time from us by capitalism."[12] What makes sleep a site of resistance, in other words, is "the stunning, inconceivable reality . . . that nothing of value can be extracted from it."[13]

And yet. The limits that sleep's "profound uselessness" would seem to impose are precisely what Spotify's Sleep page seeks to obviate. Where once a lack of consciousness might have impeded consumption, Spotify's Sleep page presents the two activities as entirely compatible. Music is cast as something that listeners may consume not just to bring on sleep but can continue to consume, even once they have lost all consciousness of doing so. By furnishing playlists that can play for hours on end, racking up streams (and royalty payments) regardless of whether users are awake or not, Spotify ensures that music's consumption is no longer constrained by human physiology (the same goes for other platforms offering sleep-centered playlists—which, thanks to product convergence, is virtually all of them). Furthermore, the limits that sleep playlists aim to surmount aren't just those affecting consumption. After all, on streaming platforms every act of consumption is also an act of production, generating not just a response *in* listeners but data *about* listeners. And it isn't just user activity that generates user data and data assets. These can also be produced by user inactivity. Simply by letting a sleep playlist run without skipping a track or disrupting its flow, users generate implicit feedback, perhaps indicating that they are indeed asleep. And even if platforms cannot actually know whether or not this is the case—an argument advanced in chapter 4 with respect to the various forms of imposture platforms facilitate or engage in themselves—accuracy is beside the point. What matters is that data and data assets are being produced regardless, with sleep playlists transforming what had been a momentary reprieve from production and consumption into their continuation by other means.

But there is still another sense in which sleep is productive. Well before streaming platforms reintegrated this seeming respite from economic activity back into its fold, sleep already participated in producing the peculiar commodity that is labor power. In this regard, Crary and others who treat sleep as an escape from capitalism fall victim to the same blind spot that has long afflicted classic Marxist theorizations of the capitalist mode of production. Namely, they minimize the contribution of reproductive work in producing individuals capable of performing productive labor. They fail to formulate the key question that socialist feminists and other thinkers of social reproduction have raised: "Who produces the worker?"[14] Historically, a disproportionate share of reproductive work (caregiving, child-rearing, socialization, education, and so on) has been performed by women or has been coded as "women's work." This gendering is both a cause and an effect of the neglect of this work, its under- or unwaged status, and its disavowal as labor. I will expand on these points in what follows. But for now, what is to be highlighted is how streaming services automate such reproductive work, by transferring the living labor of caregivers to the dead labor of algorithmic procedures. Within this paradigm, digital media in general and streaming platforms in particular assume some of the work of social reproduction that once, by necessity, fell to humans; and music, for its part, is cast as a resource or a technology by means of which such work can be performed.

This chapter examines the causes and consequences of streaming's transformation of music into a resource for social reproduction. From a certain perspective, this transformation is no transformation at all, seeing as how music has long served as a resource or technology of care. If it has appeared otherwise, this is thanks to the elevation of music's purposelessness into a guiding principle within post-Kantian aesthetics. What the aestheticization of music has tried (and failed) to repress are its functional and utilitarian affordances. Viewed in this light, streaming doesn't endow music with a utility it previously lacked; rather, it is one of many forces encouraging a return of music's repressed efficacy. Indeed, streaming services have a strong incentive to promote music's everyday affordances, since doing so allows them to capture more data on people's everyday lives by means of music (see chapter 3).

What is more, music's enactment as a means of social reproduction is a development that extends well beyond the streaming industry, part of a broader tendency under neoliberal capitalism that prizes music, the arts, and culture not on account of their aesthetic worth but on account of their "expediency" for other social, political, and economic ends.[15] But if streaming's enactment of music as a technology of care doesn't mark a decisive break, it does signal a shift in what counts as useful or necessary for social reproduction. The sociohistorical contingency of what counts as a necessity is a fact broadly acknowledged; as Louis Althusser once quipped, "the quantity of value (wages) required to reproduce labour-power is not determined by the needs of a 'biological' minimum wage alone, but by those of a historical minimum. (English workers need beer, Marx says, while French proletarians need wine)."[16] And a key factor driving changes in the resources necessary for social reproduction are changes in the labor power it is tasked with reproducing. While music has often functioned as a way of synchronizing and pacing various forms of manual labor, the growing reliance within contemporary capitalism on cognitive, affective, and communicative labor makes music's capacity to regulate moods, physiological states, and social interactions all the more important—not just for listeners but for capital as well.

This chapter unfolds in four parts. After providing a brief overview of social reproduction theory, I consider the historical forces responsible for making music as streamed attractive as a resource for reproductive work. The specific affordances of music are of course important, but so too is its cheapness relative to other sources of care. I then examine some of the ways streaming platforms have framed music as a resource for living and encouraged its users to treat it likewise. Finally, the last section of this chapter considers how digital music's capacity not only to work for and on listeners but to do so *cheaply* has become particularly important against the backdrop of the inexorable rise in the costs of social reproduction and the concomitant drive under neoliberalism to shift the burden of these costs on to private individuals and households. As music's utility as a cheap resource makes it an increasingly attractive resource for health-care providers, policy makers, insurance companies, wellness programs, and other actors in the care economy, its use as an inexpensive resource shifts the costs thus saved elsewhere—above all, onto the musicians and musical communities who find themselves increasingly deprived of the capacity to reproduce themselves as musicians.

Music, Streaming, Social Reproduction

As discussed in chapter 2, a notable feature of streaming platforms is the way they decouple music's use value(s) from its exchange value. Services pay for music, while users pay for the service. But what users don't pay for is music, at least not directly. This fact—that streams carry no price, even as subscriptions do—subtends the analogy between streamed music and water. But many other things are subject to a similar delinking of use value and exchange value. One is nature, understood as a domain categorically distinct from society, whose "fruits" are therefore treated as free for the taking. Another is the art world, inasmuch as post-Romantic aesthetics defines it in opposition to the world of commerce. And still another is the work of social reproduction.

Any definition of social reproduction will necessarily be partial, given the diversity of the activities involved.[17] It ranges from everyday, material obligations, such as housework; forms of immaterial labor, such as providing emotional support and fostering social ties; and, in the longer run, intergenerational processes of child- and eldercare. This sampling of the kinds of work that fall under the banner of social reproduction underlines its indispensability for the maintenance of life. At the same time, this work is also indispensable for the maintenance of capital, by providing the latter with a steady supply of labor power at little or no direct cost. But despite its necessity for keeping the gears of the economy moving, reproductive work is routinely discounted. Neither classical political economy nor more orthodox strands of Marxist thought have paid much heed to such work, given their shared concern with the formal economy. When processes of social reproduction are acknowledged, they are routinely reduced to the purchase of the goods and services necessary for the subsistence of workers. Representative are Althusser's comments on the matter. The "reproduction of labour-power [is] ensured," he explains, "by giving labour-power the material means of reproducing itself: *wages*." And with these wages, the worker has "what he needs to procure food, clothing, and shelter; in short, what he needs to present himself at the factory gate again *the next day*, and every further day God grants him."[18] Yet, as Marxist feminists such as Silvia Federici, Lise Vogel, and Tithi Bhattacharya have all underlined, the mere purchase of consumer goods doesn't suffice. Like other means of production, means of reproduction demand work for their use value to be realized. Just because one has bought soap doesn't mean the dishes wash themselves.

One reason for this systematic neglect of social reproduction stems from the entrenched notion that the activities involved are *not* work. This is partly a failure of the imagination—but not just that. It also reflects a material reality, the outcome of the historical process by which economic activity was progressively disembedded from other social institutions, including those charged with social reproduction (most notably the family, as it has evolved under capitalism). That is, if economists left and right have paid little heed to such work in theory, it is in no small part because capitalism had already done so in practice. "However necessary these [reproductive] activities are for the production and reproduction of labor power, *they are structurally made non-labor*," writes the Endnotes Collective.[19] As a consequence, the work of reproduction is often cast as a biological necessity, rather than as a socially mediated labor process. Such appeals to nature go hand in glove with the historic gendering of social reproduction as an activity proper to those identified as women. The upshot is that the figure of the mother or housewife comes to be seen as one for whom the provision of care is a matter of instinct, not as a subject produced via a historical process of abjection (which suggests that eliminating the gendered division of labor isn't simply a matter of revalorizing what has historically been cast as "women's work," as a certain reading of the "wages for housework" demand might suggest, but would require a broader dismantling of the gender binary).

This qualitative discounting of social reproduction has a corollary in its quantitative discounting. Placed outside the sphere of formal work, reproductive work tends to be un- or undervalued. Even when its status as work is acknowledged, care is nonetheless regarded as a gift freely given, a token of love or some genetically hard-wired propensity.[20] The rift that opens between the use values such work produces and its systemic devaluation has significant repercussions for the gendered and racialized subjects to whom it is routinely delegated, a major factor in the historic and ongoing subjugation of women and of women of color especially, given their overrepresentation in care professions. For the devaluation of care work continues unabated, even when it gets formalized or marketized as services administered by public institutions, private philanthropies, or commercial enterprises. Childcare, for instance, can be done by a nanny, the employees of a cooperative or a state-run day care center, or by (unwaged) private caregivers. The same goes for food preparation, education, processes of acculturation, gestation—you name it.[21] How care work gets distributed across these different spheres changes from one sociohistoric conjuncture to another, with the neoliberal era notably defined by a massive (re)privatization of reproductive activities. Yet a constant of care-based employment has been its low remuneration, when it is remunerated at all.[22] As Evelyn Nakano Glenn notes, "paid carework has long been treated as though it was an extension of women's unpaid domestic labor rather than as a legitimate form of wage labor with its own standards, training requirements, and pay scales."[23] The result is a persistent downward pressure on the wages of care workers, regardless of whether they are employed by commercial enterprises or public agencies.

At this point an initial approach can be made to how music is implicated in reproductive work. While a tradition in critical sociology has examined music's role in the intergenerational reproduction of class—the main point of reference being Bourdieu's work on taste and social distinction—less attention has been paid to the way music participates in social reproduction at a more material, quotidian level.[24] And yet there is nothing more banal than the way individuals use music as a tool by which they regulate themselves and others not just affectively but also physiologically, cognitively, interpersonally, and so forth. Spotify's Sleep page and other wellness-oriented playlists are recent examples of this practice. But the use of music to care for oneself and for others long predates the advent of streaming. Indeed, histories of domestic musicking are inextricably bound up with histories of social reproduction and with the changing status and functions of reproductive work across history. For instance, the relegation of music making in the home to women during the latter half of the nineteenth century, with daughters being "chained to the piano," socially mandated to "provide leisure listening for male family members," is symptomatic of the way capitalism has isolated reproduction from production, gendering the one as feminine and the other as masculine, coding the one as nonwork and the other as work.[25] Likewise, gendered assessments of mood music as feminized and aesthetically deficient in the mid-twentieth-century United States are equally symptomatic of this tendency.[26] And more recently, Tia DeNora's research into music's use in everyday life has highlighted the increasingly important role music has assumed as a "technology of the self," a development that is impossible to disentangle from an ambient neoliberal ethos that privileges self-care at the expense of collective care.[27]

If the rise of streaming marks a turning point within this longer history, it is in part because it substantially increases the number and variety of occasions when music may be engaged in reproductive activities. Furthermore, streaming platforms do not simply afford such use of music; they actively encourage it. Spotify's Sleep page is exemplary without being exceptional. Most rival services also promote context-, activity-, and mood-based playlists, promising to facilitate or improve a wide range of activities. YouTube Music's "Music for Cooking" playlist promises to get users "dancing in the kitchen," while Amazon Music's "Cleaning the House" playlist tells users to "get out your cleaning products and get pumped up to clean with these pop favorites."[28] For its part, Apple offers a variety of voice-activated playlists to accompany all sorts of daily activities and chores, from "Waking Up" to "School Dropoff" to "Grocery Shopping." Other examples are easy to find. Data underscore the appeal that playlists like these have for listeners. A 2018 study of user activity on Spotify, conducted by music analytics firm Chartmetric, reported that although playlists oriented around artists or genres were still dominant, playlists based on mood, activity, or context enjoyed a higher median follower count (160,000 followers on average, compared to 103,000 for "conventional" artist- or genre-based playlists).[29] In addition, context-based playlists at the time were adding followers at a faster rate than content-based playlists had been. What such figures indicate, the report posited, is a reorientation of listening practices, one that involves "adjusting music to the user's life" instead of "the user adjusting to the music."[30]

Yet the idea that activity-based playlists do not simply respond to user demand but also reflect a broader recentering of music around the lives of listeners should be taken with a grain of salt. Among other things, this idea simultaneously reflects and reinforces a (neo)liberal belief in the autonomy of the individual, a belief that disregards not only the degree to which structural forces constrain individual action but also how individual action can unwittingly help to sustain the very structures that constrain it. Here, again, social reproduction theory offers a crucial corrective by stressing how the work involved in replenishing labor power cannot help but help sustain capital at one and the same time. Using music to sleep more soundly ensures not only individual well-being but also one's readiness to go back to work the following morning. The same holds true for music that helps improve one's exercise routine, study habits, interpersonal relations, or mood. In short, music is not simply a technology of the self, as DeNora has claimed, nor a technology of surveillance, as argued in chapter 3. Rather, music can and often does serve as a technology of social reproduction as well.

To what extent music enters into processes of social reproduction depends on a range of factors, some technological, some ideological, some economic. With respect to the last of these, the importance of social reproduction stems not just from the necessary tasks it performs but from the fact that it performs them so cheaply. This imperative to reap the greatest benefit at the lowest cost gives rise to one of the many structural contradictions that characterizes social reproduction under capitalism. On the one hand, the fact that capital can tap resources at little or no expense means that it can keep its own costs below what they might otherwise be. Being un- or underwaged, care work provides a subsidy that holds down the price of labor power.[31] The same goes for other inputs to economic activity, such as natural resources; as Jason Moore notes, "the cheaper the raw materials and energy, the higher the rate of profit."[32] On the other hand, by obtaining energy, raw materials, labor power, and other inputs at lower than replacement cost, capital tends to erode the resources on which it depends. In the case of natural resources, the tendency is for a continuous drawing down of the "ecological surplus"—that is, the accumulated mass of resources yielded by various environmental and geophysical processes over time (such as fisheries and freshwater supplies).[33] In the case of reproductive work, one can witness a similar tendency toward depletion (of time, energy, emotional resources, physical well-being, and so on), as "resource outflows exceed resource inflows ... over a threshold of sustainability."[34] And the same can be said of cultural resources of various stripes, including music.

Exacerbating these pressures on people's abilities to care for themselves and for others has been capital's success since the 1970s in hollowing out public services. By shifting the burden of reproduction away from the state and onto private households, capital has managed to simultaneously lower its tax obligations and open up new markets for all sorts of commodified reproductive goods and services. Together, these tendencies have produced a generalized crisis of social reproduction that has been a hallmark of the neoliberal era.[35] But while this crisis and its effects are global, they are not evenly distributed. Insulating wealthier individuals and households is their capacity to purchase on the market many of the reproductive services that might otherwise be publicly funded (say, by hiring a private nanny, sending one's children to private schools, buying bottled water instead of drinking from the tap, and so on). Yet the more elites buffer themselves from the crisis of care, the more they off-load the effects of this crisis onto others. Outsourcing child- or eldercare to paid labor, for instance, relieves this burden only by displacing it elsewhere, to those relegated to the lower rungs of the global division of care work (as can be seen in the expansion of international care chains in recent decades, as immigrant women have assumed an increasing share of caregiving responsibilities in the wealthier nations of the Global North).[36]

Underpinning both the expropriation of cheap resources (natural, social, cultural) and the resulting degradation of these resources is capital's blindness to its own dependence on them. "Capitalism's economy," Nancy Fraser explains, "stands in a relation of *denial* vis-à-vis its background conditions. It disavows its dependence on them by treating nature, social reproduction, and public power as 'free gifts,' which are inexhaustible, possess no (monetized) value, and can be appropriated ad infinitum without any concern for replenishment."[37] For this disavowal to be effective, reproductive processes, the work/energy of nature, and other cheap resources must all be understood as other to the capitalist economy. That is, prior to the sorts of distributive struggles that take place within the formal economy, there is a more basic struggle over the boundaries of the formal economy. These struggles determine which kinds of spheres get included within the economy and which are expelled: nature and reproductive work, as well as certain forms of art and culture. These are struggles over what gets counted as work and what doesn't, who gets counted as a worker and who doesn't, and which kinds of activities and objects are valued and which aren't.

One result of this dissociation is for spaces and activities seen to lie outside the economy to develop their own value systems, distinct from and often opposed to the capitalist law of value. Yet the same act of separation that affords extraeconomic spheres a degree of autonomy also leaves them vulnerable. Lacking value according to the sole metric that counts for capital (namely, exchange value), activities and processes that take place within the extraeconomic domains of nature, culture, and social reproduction, among others, are just as likely to be defined as valueless, making the fruits of their activities all the more susceptible to expropriation. Here it is important to clarify how expropriation differs from the more familiar mechanisms of exploitation. Significantly, exploitation adheres to a principle of formal equality, even as it creates and reinforces material inequality. Like other transactions in a nominally free and fair market, the sale of labor power for wages is premised on an exchange of equivalents: a day's work for a day's wages.[38] Yet this formal equality masks the real inequality of the situation. Workers may receive compensation sufficient to buy the resources necessary to replenish themselves, yet the value their labor power creates exceeds the value necessary for its replenishment. The resulting differential—between the wages paid for a day's work and the value created during that same day—is the surplus value that accrues to property owners. By contrast, expropriation makes no effort to conceal the inequality on which it depends behind a facade of formal or legal equality. Rather, it trades on precisely the sort of ontologized division that separates work from housework, society from nature, economic activity from its extraeconomic others. And it is on the basis of such divisions and the incommensurability established between these separate(d) spheres that the uneven and nonreciprocal character of the transactions that take place across their frontiers is legitimized: justifying asymmetries in exchange between economic subjects and their extraeconomic others is a putative asymmetry in their being. Enacted as radically other, lacking the semblance of equality that workers as owners of labor power are accorded, the work of reproduction, nature, and culture is thereby rendered free for the taking.[39]

How Music Got Cheap

Key to music's treatment as a resource for social reproduction has been its historic ambivalence vis-à-vis capitalism. As is true of the arts more generally, music's oft-cited "economic exceptionalism" aligns it with nature and social reproduction as a domain that sits uneasily within capitalist modes of value production.[40] Often, this very fact justifies the unpaid or underpaid nature of the work music performs—work that capital benefits from, along with the rest of society. While accounts of music's and the arts' exceptionalism vary, broadly speaking what they all tend to highlight is the way artistic labor's subsumption by capital is only partial, seldom being reorganized to maximize efficiency (what in Marxian terms is referred to as "real subsumption"). What Dave Beech says of visual art—that it "has not been fully transformed by the capitalist mode of production"—applies equally to music.[41] This is true even for its most thoroughly commercialized variants; as Bill Ryan observes in relation to the culture industries, musicians like other artists represent a particularly "recalcitrant form of labor," one that is "structurally incompatible with yet fundamental to the process which creates cultural commodities."[42] This can be seen in the considerable autonomy that most recording contracts grant artists over the production process: as a rule, they are allowed to use whatever advance they receive from a label to make an album however they see fit, provided that they deliver a "commercially" and "technically satisfactory" product on schedule (which means that labels are equally free not to release records they deem unsatisfactory).[43]

This exceptionalism has contradictory effects. In many instances, indifference or resistance to market logics has the effect of depressing the dollar value of both music and musical labor. As Beech notes, artists often "forego sales for values internal to their practice," since "market demand is not the principal source of incentives for art practice."[44] Willingness to forgo monetary rewards—perhaps because of an overriding commitment to art, perhaps because one is paid in other kinds of currency ("psychic income")—is common among musicians. Describing "the deeply discounted compensation" that artists habitually receive, arts administrator John Kreidler notes that

> in comparison with most occupations, artists and arts workers ... tend to accept a higher measure of nonmonetary rewards—that is, the gratification of producing art—as compensation for their work. By accepting such nonmonetary rewards, artistic workers in effect discount the cash price of their labor.[45]

Empirical evidence reveals the extent of this discount. One study, using US Census data from a sixty-year period spanning the 1940s to the 2000s, indicates that artists' earnings during this period were on average 30 percent less than those of other professionals having comparable levels of education and training.[46] Even among artists, musicians are exceptional in how great a discount they give. A 2005 survey by the National Endowment of the Arts, for instance, found that the median annual income for musicians ($22,600) was not only half of other professionals ($43,200) but also a third lower than other professional artists ($34,800).[47] While in many instances the discounting of musicians' labor is imposed on them by other, more powerful actors (such as major labels and streaming platforms), often it is a condition that musicians accept voluntarily. As research in artistic labor markets underlines, many creative workers are willing to cede the extra income that might be earned working longer hours at a day job, provided they gain more time for their artistic practice.[48] But just as important as the fact that musicians discount their labor is the broader expectation that they should do so—that it is only natural that musicians should forsake material rewards out of devotion to their art. Under these conditions, musicians who are hard-nosed in ensuring they receive fair pay for their work run up against the broader societal belief that such an attitude represents a betrayal (of their audience, of their art, and so on).

Music's perceived distance from routine forms of work may contribute to the discounting of musical labor in another way. The fact that music represents an attractive alternative to the drudgery of nine-to-five jobs, as well as offering potential recourse for those shut out of ordinary labor markets, helps fuel what certain cultural economists describe as a chronic "oversupply" of aspiring artists, or what I referred to in chapter 4 as a substantial surplus population within the arts.[49] While the development of the modern music industries in the nineteenth century established a (fuzzy) distinction between professional and amateur, official barriers to entry to musical employment have been rare, at least in countries where free market orthodoxy reigns. Though musicians' unions have used exams and other credentialing systems as a way of controlling membership—and hence the market price for musicians' skills—most advanced capitalist economies have largely left the labor market for music unregulated.[50] At the same time, technological developments (such as drum machines and sequencers) and changing aesthetic norms (for example, the valorization of amateurism in genres such as punk and indie music) have also lowered barriers to entry. Since 2000, these trends have accelerated: the ready availability of low-cost digital audio workstations (DAWs) and other music production tools has enabled amateur musicians to create increasingly professional-quality recordings, while the advent of digital music distributors such as DistroKid allows independent musicians to bypass gatekeepers and self-release recordings. Developments such as these have further blurred the line separating amateurs from professionals. They have also contributed to the massive increase in the amount of music entering circulation each year.

While its self-reported figures shouldn't be taken at face value, Spotify claims that the number of tracks uploaded to its service rose from 20,000 a day in 2018 to 100,000 a day in 2022.[51] In both cases, quantitative growth in both music and musicians intensifies competition on streaming platforms for both user attention and the revenue indexed to this attention. The symbolic and affective qualities that make music such an appealing line of work also make it harder to win meaningful remuneration for this work.

As noted, however, music's economic exceptionalism is contradictory, with downward pressure on the price of musical labor being just one potential effect. The same values that might lead artists to renounce material gain for the less tangible rewards of artistic practice may also militate against altering this work in response to economic pressures.[52] Resistance to economic rationality, in other words, need not lead to music's cheapening; it may just as well make the production of music more costly, by ensuring its relative labor intensivity. This latter possibility is borne out by the "cost disease" diagnosed by Baumol and Bowen. As discussed in chapter 4, this describes the tendency of labor costs in the performing arts to rise over time, thanks to an inability or unwillingness to achieve the sorts of productivity gains available to other sectors of the economy. Increasing efficiencies in the production of manufactured goods, coupled with the largely stagnant productivity within the performing arts, causes the costs associated with these two sectors to inexorably diverge: the more the per-unit labor costs of standard commodities decrease, the more the per-unit labor costs of the performing arts increase relative to the latter. The result is a dilemma. If musicians' income is to keep pace with the wage gains that often (though not always) follow from productivity gains, then the price of performances will necessarily skyrocket. If, however, their income is held in check to keep ticket prices affordable, then the standard of living of musicians will deteriorate relative to other workers.[53] In the case of classical music and other traditional performing arts, a standard way out of this dilemma is to fill the widening gap between production costs and earned income via public or private patronage (though perhaps the most important subsidy comes from artists themselves, via the day jobs that many hold down in order to support themselves and their artistic work).

Significantly, the performing arts aren't the only sector subject to stagnant productivity. It can also be seen in many service professions, including a large number of those involved in social reproduction: education, health care, childcare, eldercare, and so on. Whether mediated by the market or provided as a public service, care work has likewise exhibited a similar tendency toward price inflation, wage deflation, or some combination of the two.[54] I will come back to this issue later. For now, what needs to be underlined is that in the performing arts, the main obstacle in making such work more efficient is the fact that what is being put on display is the act of working itself. "The work of the performer is an end in itself," remark Baumol and Bowen, "not the means for the production of some good."[55] By contrast, the principal obstacle to increased efficiency in reproductive work is to be found in the high quotient of affective labor such activities demand.

Despite these parallelisms linking musical work to care work, there is an important discrepancy separating the two, which shapes the relation of both to each other and to capital. Unlike care, the work of musicking can be automated, after a fashion. Isn't this, after all, what technologies of mechanical and digital reproduction achieve? As Aaron Benanav and John Clegg point out, a surefire means of increasing the productivity of service work is to turn it into something other than service work: "The only known way to drastically improve the efficiency of services is to turn them into goods and then to produce those goods with industrial processes that become more efficient over time."[56] Such is the case with the appliances that populate many modern households. Items such as coffee machines, lawn mowers, and vacuum cleaners transform reproductive work that would otherwise be performed by living labor into forms of dead labor, objectified means of social reproduction. Likewise, technologies of sound reproduction convert what was by necessity a service prior to its advent (musical performance) into a good (a recording). However, while many of the efficiencies provided by household appliances have long been offset by changing norms regarding cleanliness, nutrition, parenting, and so on, as Ruth Schwartz Cowan has documented, the same dynamic doesn't apply to music.[57] True, recorded music isn't a perfect substitute for live musical performance. But in many cases it is a sufficiently adequate one. Indeed, much of the marketing of recorded music, from the "tone tests" of the early twentieth century to the present, has centered on persuading consumers that recordings are just as good as if not better than live performance (describing an early advertising campaign of Victor, for instance, Richard Leppert notes how it played on the fantasy that "[Enrico] Caruso is singing for you alone in your home").[58] Hence, even as live music remains socially, economically, and aesthetically significant, many of the spaces and occasions where the performance of music would have been necessary in the past—in the home, in restaurants and bars, in movie theaters to accompany films, and so on—can now be animated by the dead labor inscribed in the grooves of a record or in the binary digits of an audio file.

As with other manufactured goods, the productivity increases afforded by sound recording stem from its potential for mass (re)production, a possibility largely ruled out for live music (amplification, simulcasts, and live streaming can go some way in increasing the reach of a live performance but are limited by capacity restrictions, the ephemerality of the event, or some combination of the two). While sound reproduction doesn't make the process of writing a song or producing a record any more efficient—though other technologies might, such as notation software, auto-tune, DAWs, or generative AI—it does make it possible for the work embodied in a song or recording to continue to *do work* long after the fact, via mass reproduction. Furthermore, the stubbornly high fixed costs of producing originals provides a strong incentive for record companies to pursue hits, since each additional copy of a record produced and sold decreases the per-unit cost of musical labor proportionately.[59] This logic is clear in physical recordings such as CDs. But it is also operative in digital music, the main difference being that the marginal costs of (re)production are smaller still—without, however, reaching zero.[60] If there is a difference in kind and not just degree between mechanical and digital reproduction, it is that the rivalry and excludability of the physical objects produced by the former make them well suited to act as private rather than public goods. Even if creative production stands in an ambivalent relation to capitalism, expressed in its resistance to real as opposed to formal subsumption, its industrial reproduction resolves this ambivalence enough to allow certain of music's embodiments (recordings, sheet music) to don the commodity form. By contrast, digital reproduction, by driving down the cost of making individual copies to the point that it resembles a rounding error, makes it possible for recorded music to shed the integument of the private good.

While the threat digitization posed to recording industry profits initially led labels to engage in rearguard actions that sought to uphold recorded music's rivalry and excludability (strengthening copyright enforcement, cracking down on file-sharing sites, imposing DRM technologies), streaming adopts a different approach. Platforms may have little choice but to respect the property claims of rights holders. In relation to users, as we have seen, platforms are able to treat music otherwise. Once licenses are secured from labels and other rights holders, services are able to make as many cheap copies of music as users might demand, on demand. The private good users pay for is the right to treat music as if it were a public good—provided, of course, that it only behaves as such within the confines of the platform. As a consequence, streaming not only reconciles itself to but institutionalizes music's exceptionalism, using it to make money otherwise, via the rents paid to access the service, the attention and data of users, and so on. The genius of the platform model, in other words, is that it doesn't seek to overcome or neutralize the qualities that make music resistant to subsumption. Instead, the model preserves and even fortifies music's eccentricity vis-à-vis capital, even as it fences this resource off, charging a toll for access.

How Cheap Nature/Energy/ Labor/Money Subsidize Cheap Music

Facilitating platforms' treatment of music as a privatized public good— and hence as a cheap source of work that can work for and on users—are the subsidies provided by a number of the other "cheaps," which, for Jason Moore, constitute the unacknowledged conditions of capital accumulation: cheap labor, nature, energy, and money, among other things. "Capital must not only ceaselessly accumulate and revolutionize commodity production," Moore remarks. "It must ceaselessly search for, and find ways to produce, . . . a rising stream of low-cost food, labor-power, energy, and raw materials."[61] Recorded music's enactment as a low-cost resource likewise rests on a foundation provided by other low-cost resources. Foremost among these is cheap energy. A major factor responsible for making the costs of digital reproduction so negligible are the minimal expenditures of raw materials and energy required to copy an audio file. But as Kyle Devine, Sean Cubitt, and others have argued (and as already noted in chapter 1), the digital doesn't transcend music's material conditions so much as redistribute them. And while the amount of energy required to copy and transmit an individual file across a network may be relatively small, once one adds up the billions of streams that platforms traffic in each day, the carbon footprint of streaming is anything but. A 2019 report by the Shift Project estimated that digital technologies were responsible for 3.7 percent of worldwide greenhouse gas emissions, a percentage set to double by 2025.[62] Driving this growth has been "the explosion of data traffic," to which streaming and other forms of "consumption on demand" are major contributors.[63] Nor is the problem simply that the environment has become a sink for the emissions generated by digital media use. Despite platforms' self-proclaimed commitment to draw as much of their energy needs as possible from renewables, their continued reliance on fossil fuels amounts to a reliance on the free work that biochemical processes have performed across vast stretches of geological time. If digital reproduction appears to cost next to nothing, it is because it is so heavily subsidized by the ecological surplus it at once draws on and draws down. It is by expropriating the dead labor of nature that the dead labor of musicians can be copied so quickly, so prolifically, and at such low cost.

Another subsidy to streaming comes from the raw materials used to manufacture playback devices. Smartphones, noise-canceling headphones, smart speakers, and the like are all built using an array of rare earth metals, ranging from the indium used for touchscreens to the lithium that fuels batteries. As with other, more commonplace inputs, mining companies and the transnational corporations they supply treat such rare earth metals as "free gifts" of nature, taking for granted the slow work of nucleosynthesis and geological sedimentation that have produced them. "Looking from the perspective of deep time," write Kate Crawford and Vladan Joler, "we are extracting Earth's history to serve a split second of technological time, in order to build devices that are often designed to be used for no more than a few years."[64] But if mineral deposits yield themselves to mining companies free of charge, the same cannot be said of the costs involved in locating, extracting, and processing these resources. To keep these as low as possible, suppliers routinely make use of child and forced labor, taking advantage of the fact that rare earth mining is concentrated in countries with weak administrative states, often due to the corruption rampant in economies built around resource extraction.[65] But suppliers employ more widespread and less controversial methods of wage suppression as well. Principal among these are the entwined threats of unemployment and immiseration, with widespread un- and underemployment in countries where many mining companies operate giving them free rein to suppress worker pay.

Further up the global commodity chain, at the point of production, it is another feature of the international division of labor that keeps the cost of digital music low. This is the abundant supply of cheap labor in places such as China, where a large percentage of digital devices are manufactured. Not just an effect of absolute population size, the massive reserve army that feeds factories in export zones such as Shenzhen and the Pearl River Delta is also a product of the post-Mao decollectivization of agriculture, a policy that has compelled millions of newly proletarianized subjects to migrate from the countryside to the city to seek work.[66] As neoclassical economists are wont to remind us, excess supply in the face of constant demand tends to drive down prices, for labor as for any other commodity—which is simply a bloodless way of saying that the more people lack the means of subsistence, the fiercer the competition is among them for whatever work there is to be had, at whatever wage. Small wonder, then, that the devices on which music is streamed are so inexpensive. According to one estimate, an iPhone manufactured entirely in the United States would cost in the vicinity of $30,000.[67] That new models can be acquired for a fraction of that price points to yet another subsidy that streaming enjoys, provided by systems of transnational labor arbitrage and unequal exchange.

Last but hardly least is the subsidy provided by cheap money. To hold down the monthly fees that premium users pay, services rely on the significant infusions of capital they receive from investors and their own parent corporations. Recall, in this connection, that streaming services integrated into larger conglomerates—such as those offered by Apple, Google, or Amazon—aren't obliged to turn a profit. The superprofits that companies such as these generate in the markets where they enjoy a monopoly position (search advertising for Google, e-commerce for Amazon, and so on) enables them to price subscriptions below cost. Stand-alone platforms such as Spotify and Deezer, by contrast, have benefited from a historical moment when the price of money itself was kept exceptionally low (a window that may now be closing, with postpandemic inflationary pressures leading central banks to raise interest rates, lest the value of assets get depreciated away). As Robert Brenner and others have noted, one of the main responses to the global economy's steady decline in profitability since the 1970s has come in the form of monetary stimulus.[68] Spearheaded by the US Federal Reserve, interest rates were repeatedly slashed beginning in the mid-1990s, making access to credit easier and less costly for corporations and private households alike. A knock-on effect of this loose-credit, cheap-money regime was to massively inflate asset prices, ranging from real estate to stock prices to song catalogs. The rising value of assets gave rise in turn to a series of speculative bubbles, as more and more money was pumped into the global financial system even as the number of profitable sites of investment has dwindled, with the tech sector being seen as one of the few exceptions to the rule.[69] It was in large part thanks to this regime of "privatized" or "asset-price Keynesianism" that many digital platforms were able to not only gain seed funding but to subsequently stay afloat. With plenty of cheap money at their disposal, investors have long been happy to underwrite the day-to-day operations of a company such as Spotify, despite its repeated failure to turn a profit, in the expectation of massive returns once it obtained the monopoly position it perennially promises but has yet to deliver (see chapter 3).[70] Lacking such financing, Spotify would either have gone under some time ago or else been obliged to raise user fees to cover operating costs—two eventualities that may yet come to pass if postpandemic economic dislocations represent more than a temporary hiccup and instead herald the end of the cheap-money regime of the past thirty years.

Whether it results from artistic labor's incomplete subsumption by capital; the labor discount freely provided by artists; an influx of musicians into the labor market; technologies of digital reproduction; the massive appropriations of energy, nature, and labor that feed digital media; or some combination of all of the above, the cheapening to which digital music is subject effectively cheapens the work that music may itself perform, both for listeners and on listeners. The more its use value stands in stark contrast to its negligible exchange value, the more music comes to resemble a "free gift," comparable to those that nature or the work of social reproduction are seen to provide. As Nancy Fraser remarks, "capitalist economies constantly siphon value from [non-economic] realms while simultaneously denying that those realms have any value."[71] Separation from the formal economy may shield certain populations, objects, and activities from workaday forms of exploitation. But it does so by exposing them to the risk of expropriation, of being treated as "free gifts" that can be taken without being replenished. Such is the risk that nature, care, and not least of all music increasingly face, as economic stagnation and declining levels of growth since the 1970s have driven the search for new forms of unpaid work and energy outside capitalism that can be harnessed to sustain the accumulation process within it. Dependent on the use values provided by "social reproduction, public power, and natural inputs"— the three extraeconomic domains addressed by Fraser—capital disavows the work these perform, refusing for better or worse their expression in terms of exchange value. To the three extraeconomic realms that Fraser identifies, a fourth should be added: that of culture and, more specifically, music. Its diminished exchange value in an era of digital reproduction makes the various use values it affords all the more susceptible to expropriation, making cheap music an attractive resource for the provision of cheap care.

Surplus Use Values

Streaming services don't just rely on music's enactment as a cheap resource. They also accelerate this tendency, by enjoining listeners to treat it as such. Consider, once more, Spotify's Sleep page. In the press release announcing its launch, the platform cajoled individuals into using the new feature by appealing to the gratifications that sleep alone affords: "Sleep is the ultimate release from pressure, the ultimate retreat from the cares of the day."[72] The pleasure invoked here is provided not by music but by the physical condition music brings about. And if appeals to the satisfaction provided by a good night's sleep weren't enough, the press release offered a more pressing reason why users should avail themselves of this new genre of playlist. Sleep, we are reminded, is a necessity for good health, indeed for life itself: "You've got eight hours to save your life—why not get started right now?"[73]

While not always presented in such stark terms, appeals that go beyond the pleasures of music to the needs it might address—physiological, affective, social, or otherwise—are a recurrent feature of the rhetoric surrounding contextual playlists. Take the Dinner category, introduced to Spotify's Browse page alongside Sleep. "Everybody has to eat," the same press release declares.[74] But while music may not possess the same power to induce eating as it does to induce sleeping, it can nonetheless help transform this necessity of life into something more than a mere necessity: "Even if you burn the sauce or overcook the potatoes, everything will taste a little bit better with great music."[75] Here as elsewhere, Spotify mobilizes a familiar neoliberal discourse of self-improvement in marketing its contextual playlists to users. This is a discourse that Spotify assumes users will have absorbed and to which they will therefore be receptive, even as its recourse to ideologies of unending self-amelioration helps reproduce the image of the good life they promulgate. As Maria Eriksson and Anna Johansson put it, "Spotify's promotion of music as functional primarily privilege[s] a subject determined to strive for well-being," with music cast as a device that "contributes to personal enhancement."[76] Unstated but implicit in this framing is the notion that subjects are somehow in need of enhancement, or that they are somehow deficient in regard to well-being. Implicit as well is the notion that subjects will suffer a loss by not taking advantage of these ameliorative properties of music. If sleep playlists can "save your life," then it is no longer Spotify's responsibility to justify why users should listen to them. Rather, the onus is on users to justify why they shouldn't, don't, or won't.

A common thread that runs through the framing of these and other contextual playlists is the notion that streaming services offer a means of tapping into certain supplementary benefits that music might have, above and beyond whatever "purely" aesthetic gratifications it might afford. One might describe such benefits as surplus use values latent in music, which streaming brings forth. Or, to use the language of mainstream economics, one might describe it as a form of "consumer surplus" that users of streaming services enjoy. The more streaming platforms succeed in persuading users that their mediation of music helps elicit these supplemental benefits, the more likely the platforms are to succeed in persuading users that they are the beneficiaries of this surplus—that they are receiving two (or more) services for the price of one. A user pays for entertainment or distraction and gets a technology of social reproduction at the same time. A user pays for a luxury good and gets a necessity at the same time. The reverse is also true, say for a user (such as a business) that subscribes to a streaming service for functional purposes. In this case, whatever nonutilitarian enjoyment music provides is a bonus. One pays for a necessity and gets a luxury good at the same time. Either way, the user enjoys this surplus at no extra charge.

As a particular kind of equipment for living, activity- and mood-based playlists represent a key site where music's surplus use values are performatively realized. As such, these playlists are critical to streaming platforms' enactment of music as what Marie Thompson has termed a reproductive sound technology.[77] In line with DeNora's observations about music's uses in everyday life, such playlists tend to be structured less around music's symbolic or representational qualities than around its pragmatic and nonrepresentational ones. It is not that the semiotic aspects of music are entirely absent. Like music's strictly aesthetic qualities, these too are still operative; they are just reframed as auxiliary to the utilitarian functions that music is tasked with discharging. Chartmetric's 2018 study of contextual playlists underlines this point, drawing attention to the increasingly common tendency for playlists to combine these two dimensions, the musical and the extramusical, the symbolic and the pragmatic.[78] Representative are running playlists defined by genre as well as tempo, or beats per minute (BPM). Spotify's "Run This Town 150–165 BPM" invites users to "run to the world of R & B and HipHop," while its "Indie Kicks 150–155 BPM" does the same, albeit to "indie and alternative hits." Likewise for "Just Get Going! 155 BPM," which instead consists of "boosting pop tracks" that promise to "keep you motivated along the way!" If these three playlists differ little in terms of intended effect—all three aim to get users running at a cadence around 155

BPM or so—where they do differ is in terms of the music used to produce this effect, along with the entire network of associations, meanings, and identities that the different genres in question mobilize. That these playlists operate at the symbolic level of identification as well as the pragmatic level of bodily entrainment is punctuated by the stock photos that accompany them. Each reflects—and performatively enacts—the gendered and racialized logics that have long undergirded the modern system of musical genre. The runner shown in the image accompanying "Indie Kicks," for instance, is a young white man; in "Run This Town," it is a young black man instead; and in "Just Get Going!" it is a young white woman. Helping users to stay fit, such playlists also help to reproduce them as labor power. But the playlists also help to reproduce users as racialized and gendered subjects, by perpetuating the racialization and gendering of different musics.

Despite the continued importance of genre- and artist-based forms of musical categorization, within contextual or activity-based playlists these features are usually cast in a subordinate position relative to music's affective and nonrepresentational qualities. Tellingly, the three running playlists just cited all appear on Spotify's workout page, not on the pages dedicated to hip-hop, pop, and indie music, respectively. It is genre and identity that inflects activity, not the other way around. Likewise, the grammatical structure of the titles that adorn many context- and activity-oriented playlists treats attributes such as genre, geography, gender, or ethnicity as modifiers, which inflect mood and activity, rather than the reverse (for example, "Classical Sleep," "Soul Coffee," "Indie Sunshine," "Jazzy Morning," "Country Heartache"). What playlists such as these foreground is less music's capacity for signification than for action: its ability to entrain users to its rhythms, to alter and regulate mood, to coordinate action, to mask other sounds, to structure the flow of time, to induce movement, and so forth. And to realize this capacity for action, the different tracks that make up contextual playlists need to exhibit a narrow set of musical traits: regular rhythms and fast tempos in the case of running playlists, a particular modal and timbral palette in mood playlists, a soft dynamic level and slow-to-moderate tempos in chill playlists, and so on.[79] Or, in the case of sleep playlists, what is decisive is not the presence but the absence of certain attributes: vocals, sudden transitions, loud dynamics, fast tempos, and the like.[80] In all these cases, the same cluster of features that binds tracks together within a playlist is presumably what also provides the music with whatever restorative, transformative, and affective powers it is said to possess.

If playlist descriptions are quite specific about the effects that listening to them will supposedly engender, they remain remarkably open-ended in other respects.[81] Qualitatively determinate, these playlists are at the same time quantitatively indeterminate, the main promise they extend being one of *more*: more concentration, more wellness, more restful sleep, and so on. The enhancement music brings to activities or to users themselves is in principle boundless. Recall, in this regard, the claim made in the press release announcing Spotify's Dinner playlists, that everything "taste[s] a little bit better with great music." Assertions such as these, which testify to music's capacity to enhance any situation, abound on streaming platforms. Such appeals to improvement without end are most clearly manifest in playlist categories such as "Focus," which promise to augment users' productivity; Amazon's "Classical Focus," for example, claims to "boost your brainpower with Bach, Vivaldi, and more."[82] The same goes for playlists meant to accompany other kinds of work, most notably housework: Pandora's "Country Cleaning," for instance, guarantees to "make those household chores just a little more enjoyable!"[83] But even among playlists intended to accompany leisure activities, the implication is that music can help wring more fun, relaxation, or pleasure out of every passing moment. "Elevate your evening and unwind with the lush sound of these ethereal tracks": such is the promise (or command) that the Spotify playlist "Evening Chill" extends to users.[84]

One way of interpreting the language of productivity that infuses playlists addressed to nominally unproductive moments of free time is to read it as an index of how neoliberalism has blurred the line separating labor from leisure. But if social reproduction theory has made anything clear, it is that leisure time has always been "productive," being necessary for the regeneration of life as well as labor power. And where there is productivity, there is production—and by extension producers. Leisure for some entails work for others. This reality was apparent in the middle-class household of the Victorian era: its constitution as a "haven in a heartless world" was largely thanks to the labors of women, including the archetypal "piano girl," whose domestic production of music was simultaneously the musical production of domesticity.[85] Yet the same gendered dynamic held even after recording technology had transformed music making from a service produced in the home into a good purchased on the market. While recording technologies like the phonograph and player piano were often depicted as labor-saving devices at the turn of the twentieth century, on a par with other household appliances, they did not entirely do away with domestic musical labor. As Marie Thompson observes, the phonograph functioned as a tool by which women's "affective management of the household" could be accomplished. And just as "women's music in the Victorian home served to establish appropriate moods and help secure the emotional wellbeing of the family," so too did reproduced music serve as a means by which wives and mothers could perform the work of "regulat[ing] the emotional resonances of domestic space."[86]

Furthermore, to the extent recordings did relieve women of some of the work required in regulating the household's affective soundscape, they did so only by displacing this work elsewhere. The dead labor of recording artists was perhaps the most apparent of these surrogates. But other, less immediately discernible actors, objects, and processes also found themselves enrolled to perform the labor required for others to enjoy leisure. These included geochemical forces, responsible for producing the raw materials out of which records and playback devices were fashioned; industrial manufacture, and especially the labor of record plant workers, whose work transformed these raw materials into consumer goods; and the predominantly carbon-based sources of energy that drove the entire commodity chain, from the production of recordings to their eventual playback. More than a hundred years on, the same dynamic holds, even as music's function as a labor-saving device has been eclipsed by its potential as a labor-enhancing one. As ecological economist Giorgis Kallis notes, if "tools make us more 'productive,'" this gain "does not come out of thin air." Some of it may be due to increases in efficiency. But more typically gains in productivity are due to the "additional sources of work"—provided, say, by fossil fuels— that tools can mobilize "on top of our own."[87] The same is true for music recast as a tool or technology. The music that makes up "focus" playlists can channel one's energies only thanks to the energy that went into its making and that course through it when it is played back. Likewise, if "chill" playlists can provide a release from work, it is because of the work that has been embodied in the recording and set to work by means of it.

Curation as Care

Another way that streaming services cast music as a resource for care is through the intermediation they perform in filtering, promoting, and recommending music on behalf of users—a suite of practices that falls under the catchall term curation. The word carries significant historical baggage.

Derived from the Latin word for care (*cura*), adopted by the Church to designate those "entrusted with the care of souls" (curates), the word's subsequent transposition from the sacred to the secular realm was accompanied by a transformation in the entities toward which care was directed.[88] With the rise of museum culture in seventeenth- and eighteenth-century Europe, the task of the curator no longer concerned the welfare of animate beings; rather, it became one of selecting, preserving, and presenting physical items judged worthy of solicitude. Once removed from everyday life and divested of use value, curated objects were able to serve as "autonomous objects of pure contemplation."[89]

With the more recent demotic extension of curation to denote virtually any act of selection, the meaning of the term has shifted yet again, with some of its older, previously repressed connotations returning in force. At one level, the curation of music on streaming platforms is still routinely framed as an expression of care or concern for music. Here one might consider how companies such as Pandora and Beats Music (both prior to and following its acquisition by Apple) played up the intense affective investment that the musicologists and curators they employ have in music, as a way of differentiating their services from rivals.[90] At another level, however, the care that curators are supposed to embody is just as often directed toward the users on whose behalf music is selected and ordered. If mood-based playlists are not exactly charged with the care of souls, they are nonetheless charged with ministering to the spirits of listeners. Nor is this the only transformation the term has undergone. Whereas the rise of museum culture under modernity required that curation defunctionalize the objects in its care, the kind of curation that takes place on streaming platforms tends to refunctionalize music, presenting it as something that is good for activities beyond that of "pure contemplation." But arguably the most important way that curation evinces care for users is by affording them the experience of being seen. Testimonials indicate that for certain users, at least, personalized recommendations elicit a sense of being the object of another's solicitudes. Recall in this connection a user comment cited in the previous chapter, which extolled Spotify's Discover Weekly because "it makes me feel *seen*."[91] For listeners such as this one, personalized recommendations are a sign that someone—or something—has taken note of one's tastes, desires, and personality.

It isn't just individuals who are the objects of platforms' ministrations. While personalization is central to how streaming is marketed, other services that platforms promote focus instead on interpersonal relations and music's role in fostering these. The social features that platforms have integrated into their interfaces—such as the "Friend Feed" that Spotify introduced in 2011, in partnership with Facebook—are one expression of this phenomenon. More notable for present purposes are the various family plans that services have rolled out over the years, especially those that allow content to be tailored or filtered specifically for children. Such plans merit close consideration, given the family's continued importance as a key site of capitalist reproduction.[92] It is not merely that this durable social form provides the fantasmatic basis on which the social order is erected, naturalized, and maintained. In addition, the family represents a key locus of unpaid reproductive work, with the calcification of the private-public divide in the nineteenth century being an important turning point in both the gendering of reproductive work as "women's work" and its institutionalized isolation from the sphere of (masculinized) productive labor. The more recent reprivatization of care work brought on by neoliberal disinvestment in public services since the 1970s has further consolidated the family's nodal position within circuits of capitalist reproduction, even as increasing precarity and market dependency have made the kinship relations on which people rely increasingly "fragmented, extended, and heterogeneous."[93] Under these conditions, it isn't hard to fathom how cheap digital technologies such as streaming might come to be seen—and used—as a cheap technological fix, alleviating some of the strains brought on by social reproduction's reprivatization.

Streaming services offer a handful of ways to mitigate the burdens of family care. One is by taking charge of tasks for users overwhelmed by caregiving responsibilities. The Apple Music Kids and Family Music page, for instance, presents itself as a solution to the time scarcity afflicting the parents of infants: "Feedings. Burpings. Changes. Repeat. Repeat. Repeat. We can't blame you if music isn't at the top of your to-do list."[94] More significantly, many platforms frame their curated playlists as either directly assisting caregivers or performing certain kinds of work for them. While music may not be able to feed, burp, or change soiled diapers, it can nonetheless help calm, distract, or keep children busy. It can also help to put them to sleep. On Spotify's Kids and Family page, for instance, lullaby playlists abound. Examples include "Lullaby Baby," "Baby Sleep," "Music Box Lullabies," "Sweet Lullabies," and "Disney Lullabies," the latter being the product of a cross-promotional partnership Spotify entered into with the media conglomerate in summer 2019, just as the platform was ramping up its kid- and family-centered fare.

Another important—and controversial—task that platforms perform for caregivers is to shield children from musics deemed inappropriate. Virtually every platform labels explicit tracks, following industry practices established in the wake of 1980s-era crusades against obscenity in popular music.[95] Beyond the application of crude and often inaccurate labels such as these, there are other, more sophisticated methods for restricting what kinds of music children can hear. These include parental controls, which can automatically block any content tagged as explicit; customizable user accounts for family plan members; specially designated kids' playlists; and separate apps intended for children (such as Spotify Kids).

The importance certain users attach to these and other forms of curation as care emerge most clearly in the criticisms that their perceived shortcomings elicit on user forums, message boards, and chat rooms. A complaint on the Deezer community forum, for instance, flagged the children's playlist "Happy Roadtrip" for containing sexually explicit material. Singling out the DNCE song "Cake by the Ocean," the user in question reminded Deezer of its "moral obligation" to ensure that music addressed to children be age-appropriate.[96] On another forum, operated by the website Commonsense Media, Spotify comes in for especially harsh criticism in light of its general lack of parental controls prior to 2019. "There is very little editing of the songs like on the radio," remarked one reviewer. "You get the full curse word versions. I let my kids sign on using my login and they pulled up the songs they've heard many times safely in the car and BAM out blare the curse words. They won't be using it until there is a kid-friendly version."[97] Another user acknowledged that the "app/service is great for music exploration." The problem, however, is that "there are . . . Penthouse porn sounds as well as Porn soundtracks. If you know where and how to search" (according to the commenter, he became aware of this issue only after "search[ing] my 15-year old's phone").[98]

Heightening concerns about the kinds of inappropriate material circulating on digital platforms have been highly publicized reports about the disturbing and often violent videos that can be readily found on certain children's apps, above all YouTube Kids. In late 2017, a series of pieces came out that described the nightmarish images unsuspecting children might stumble on while using the app: videos in which popular cartoon characters drink bleach, undergo painful dental procedures, wield (and sometimes use) knives and guns on one another, and have body parts swapped seemingly at random, among other things.[99] Occasionally acted out by human performers but more often than not crudely animated (perhaps using some form of algorithmic automation), such videos insinuated themselves into users' feeds via a primitive yet effective form of search engine optimization, stringing together popular keywords to form often nonsensical phrases (for example, "Drowned Head Spiderman and Elsa Under pool sponges" or "Wrong Ears Wrong Heads Cartoon Finger Family").[100] Driving the controversy was the fact that YouTube Kids, like most social media platforms, doesn't screen content in advance but only responds after the fact to videos that have been flagged by users as objectionable. By outsourcing a portion of the work of content moderation to users, YouTube may save itself some money; but the result, as Tarleton Gillespie observes, is that "even the most heinous content gets published, at least briefly, . . . before anything that might be done in response."[101] As a result of the negative publicity, a number of advertisers pulled their ads from YouTube Kids in late 2017.[102] And enough revenue was lost for Alphabet, YouTube's parent company, to announce that it would institute more stringent restrictions on site uploads (subsequent reports indicate that these measures fell short of purging YouTube Kids of disturbing content).[103]

While the uproar surrounding such cheap, exploitative, and often violent videos is understandable, a close reading of complaints leveled at music platforms suggests that what is often at stake isn't necessarily the harm that inappropriate or explicit music might actually inflict on children. Often, the problem would seem to be the threat that such music poses to an idealized and ideologically freighted image of childhood. Coursing through the repeated charge that platforms have somehow lapsed in their "moral obligation" to children—and hence to the adults who have placed children in the algorithmic care of streaming services—is a latent commitment to "reproductive futurism," what queer theorist Lee Edelman defines as a hegemonic ideology that imagines the future strictly through the prism of the Child.[104] Within this heteronormative belief system, the desires, needs, and claims of the present are subordinated in the name of the Child to come, with this figure coming to stand as "the fantasmatic beneficiary of every political intervention."[105] While Edelman sees reproductive futurism as a stable and quasi-universal feature of US politics, it is perhaps more accurate to say that investment in the figure of the Child has been mainly driven by white, middle-class, and heteropatriarchal families increasingly anxious about their ability to reproduce themselves into the future. That not all children are allowed to occupy the valorized position of the Child underscores its classed and racialized character, with poor, Black, queer, trans, and immigrant children routinely denied this privilege (as José

Esteban Muñoz notes in an important rejoinder to Edelman's work, it would be a grave error to conflate actually existing children with "the privileged white babies to whom contemporary society caters").[106] This clarifies why the decline of the Fordist-era male breadwinner family—coded as white and middle-class—has been accompanied by an intensified drive to safeguard this fantasmatic construct, as a way of buttressing the ideal for which it is both the organizing principle and overriding telos. The result has been a steady stream of moral panics surrounding threats to children and childhood innocence since the 1980s (over, for example, satanism, strangers bearing candy, video games, and heavy metal and hip-hop, to name just a few).[107] And with the passing of years, these panics have only become more extreme, the latest and most notable example being QAnon's fever dreams of a global child trafficking network. The more the heteronormative and racialized ideology of reproductive futurism comes under pressure, the more extreme the efforts to prop it up.

The ability of the figure of the Child to embody a future whose realization promises to retroactively confer meaning on the present ultimately hinges on its categorical separation from the adult. The various children-oriented features and playlists on streaming services are one set of technologies that helps to maintain this ideological division. A case in point is the Spotify Kids app, which provides the children of Spotify subscribers with a digital enclosure of their own (see figure 5.1). First introduced in Ireland in late 2019 and subsequently expanded to other markets, the app was a belated effort by the platform to catch up with rivals that had been quicker to address parental concerns. "We know the importance of understanding parents' needs and making sure they would have peace of mind about the content their kids are consuming," explained Spotify business officer Alex Norström in announcing the app's rollout.[108] The needs of parents are not the only ones that Spotify Kids serves, however. Spotify also benefits from separating out the listening activity of adults from children. Even though the company publicizes its commitment to safeguarding the privacy of children (vouching not to share their data with advertisers, for instance), Spotify, by siloing their listening data, also ensures that children's musical preferences won't sully the profiles of adult users. This is presented by Spotify—and perceived by certain users—as a boon, with recommendations and personalized playlists no longer at risk of being wrecked by the "horrors of kids music."[109] But it is a boon to Spotify as well, since the "cleaner" the data on individual users, the greater the value of these data. Even if Spotify doesn't monetize children's data, this doesn't rule out the

5.1 Spotify Kids as "safe" enclosure for children

possibility that by ceding this particular terrain Spotify is able to more effectively exploit the data of adult family members.

Furthermore, just because Spotify Kids is free of targeted ads doesn't mean advertising is absent from the app. On the contrary: one of the most striking aspects of the Kids app, compared with the standard Spotify app, is the number and prominence of branded playlists. Disney-themed playlists are the most conspicuous: alongside "Disney Lullabies" are playlists devoted to specific franchises (*The Lion King, Toy Story, Frozen*, and so on), as well as more general compilations (for example, "Disney Hits").[110] Also well represented are other popular children's brands (Pokémon,

224 ← Chapter Five

Barbie, the Muppets, Thomas the Train Engine, Cocomelon, and so on). The financial arrangements that underwrite the prominence of such brand-oriented playlists aren't public knowledge. What is clear, however, is that these playlists perform important promotional work for the owners of the IP in question. Every time a track on a Pokémon playlist is streamed, not only does it generate a royalty payment for its corporate owners; it also serves as a thinly veiled commercial for all the off-platform games, films, manga, and other products that form part of the wider Pokémon franchise.

Considered from a broader and longer-term perspective, however, the entire Spotify Kids app may justly be read as one giant advertisement, for nothing other than Spotify itself. To the extent the app's kid-friendly curation appeals not solely to adults concerned about the dangers posed by mature or inappropriate content but to actually existing children, Spotify Kids acts as a training ground that prepares its preadolescent users for their eventual graduation to the "grown-up" version of the service. A different kind of reproduction is at work here: the intergenerational reproduction of Spotify's user base. A key part of this project is the reproduction of the particular modes of listening that the platform encourages. Tellingly, the large number of branded playlists on Spotify Kids are complemented by an equally large number of context- and activity-oriented playlists: "Back to School," "Wash Your Hands," "Arts and Crafts Time," "Let's Eat," "Mind Your Manners," "Weekend Playdate," and so forth. And while the app's

5.2 "Your Daily Routine" playlist

cartoonish icons and vibrant colors depart from the stock photos and black-and-green color scheme of the standard Spotify interface, the overall way that music is framed and users are interpellated does not. The playlist "Your Daily Routine," for instance, is described as "songs to help your kids establish a productive daily routine, from waking up and brushing their teeth to potty training, taking a bath, and getting to sleep at night!"[111] (See figure 5.2.) If at one level Spotify Kids reinforces the segregation of Adult and Child, necessary for the ideology of reproductive futurism to do its work, at another level the app troubles this distinction, by teaching children to treat music in the same way as it enjoins adults to—as a resource that can help organize the "productive daily routine" that Spotify assumes to be an unalloyed good, for the child no less than for the adult.

Crises of Social and Musical Reproduction

However much streaming services encourage music's use as a cheap resource, perhaps the strongest incentive for listeners to use music in this way comes not from within but from beyond the platform, from larger-scale and longer-term socioeconomic trends. Recorded music may have been cheapened as a result of decreasing marginal costs of reproduction and music's partial decommodification on platforms, while the rhetoric attributing surplus use values to music may make it seem as if users of digital music services are getting something more than "just" music, at no extra cost. Cheapness, however, is not an absolute but a relative term. Set against the backdrop of care work's rising cost in the United States and elsewhere since the 1980s, digital music and digital media more broadly appear very inexpensive indeed. As noted earlier, rising prices within this sector are driven by the same dynamic afflicting the performing arts: the cost disease. If in live performance an impediment to increased productivity is the fact that the "work of the performer is an end in itself," in social reproduction means and ends are impossible to disentangle.[112] The quality and effectiveness of care hinges on how and by whom it is provided. The importance of the relationship between caregiver and care receiver, Susan Donath observes, means that "reducing the labor content of caring work ... will always affect the final 'product.'"[113] Even were it possible to speed up or scale certain kinds of reproductive work, doing so would diminish the interaction involved and hence the quality of the care. At best, reproductive work would be taken *care of* without exhibiting the same degree of *care for* others—whence the insuperable limit that confronts attempts to accelerate or automate care work.[114] What such initiatives run up against is that the temporalities of capital and care are opposed, a point Judy Wajcman underscores: "giving and receiving care involves *slowness*: 'being there,' as well as the emotional, affective dimensions of time" (emphasis mine).[115] Given the need to take one's time, any effort to speed up or make more efficient the work of social reproduction will degrade the very "output" it is supposed to produce.

As with the performing arts, the cost disease that afflicts social reproduction can be mitigated in a number of ways. One is to suppress either the individual or social wage paid for care. This is the solution with the longest pedigree, given the tremendous amount of reproductive work that has historically been relegated to the unpaid sphere of the private household. But even when reproductive services take the form of waged work, underpayment isn't the exception but the rule. Research conducted by Paula England, Nancy Folbre, and others over the years has highlighted the wage penalty that care workers typically suffer.[116] Like artists, people whose jobs involve attending to the well-being of others—nurses, childcare providers, teachers, nursing home assistants, and social workers, among others—tend to be paid less on average than others having comparable levels of training and experience. Working in tandem with this systemic devaluation of care work is the segregation of the labor market along the lines of race, gender, and immigration status, with women, people of color, and immigrants overrepresented within the care sector.

Yet the labor discount foisted on care workers has done little to contain the rising costs of care. This can be seen clearly in figure 5.3, which plots the rates of inflation for medical, hospital, and childcare services relative to the general rate of inflation in the United States. As the chart indicates, the costs for health- and childcare services remained roughly in line with the overall consumer price index up until the mid-1980s, at which point their trajectories began to inexorably diverge. In the decades since, inflation in these sectors has outpaced its rise in the rest of the US economy, the result being a conspicuous increase in these services' real (and not just nominal) costs. On average, medical care by the end of the 2010s was two times as expensive in real terms than it was prior to this divergence, education and childcare roughly three times as expensive, and hospital care almost four times as expensive. Offsetting this upward trend to a degree are decreasing real prices for other items, in particular manufactured goods such as

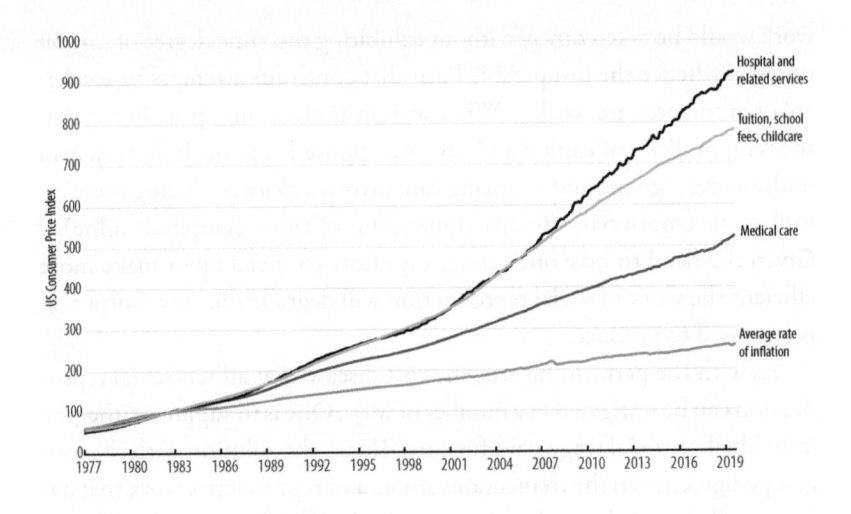

5.3 Inflationary trends in the US care sector, 1977–2020

consumer electronics. Indeed, as the cost disease thesis predicts, one factor pushing prices up in the relatively stagnant care sector is the fact they are going down in more productive sectors.[117] But even if these countervailing tendencies cancel each other out on paper, they don't necessarily do so in the everyday lives of most people, given that the consumption of manufactured goods and personal services—especially care services—unfolds at very different tempos. On account of their relative durability, many manufactured goods—computers, cars, home appliances, and so on—are acquired intermittently. By contrast, not only is the need for care of one sort or another a near constant for most people, but because care is "consumed" at the same moment it is produced, it must be procured on a regular basis. Cheap consumer goods may be a boon for households suffering from the effects of persistent wage stagnation (keeping in mind, however, that the offshoring of production responsible for the abundance of low-cost goods is itself a major factor in wage stagnation). Yet whatever savings are offered by inexpensive manufactured goods offset the rising costs of care only at the aggregate level, not at the level of the individual person or household.

Under circumstances such as these, streaming's enactment of music as a potential source of cheap care is a boon to those whose budgets are strained by the rising costs of social reproduction, especially as the neoliberal retrenchment of public services has compelled households to shoulder an increasing share of these costs. Nor is it just individuals or households who might find this bargain attractive. Critically, institutions engaged in the provision of care services—whether public agencies, nonprofits, or commercial enterprises—are no less sensitive to the budgetary pressures caused by the rising costs of social reproduction. That so many of them seek to contain these costs by paying care workers so little makes this clear. The implacable logic of the cost disease, coupled with the neoliberal imperative to reduce all manner of social spending, means that anything promising to do some of the work of social reproduction at no or low cost will inevitably be recruited to do so.

Commercial enterprises and nonprofits have been among those seeking to recast music as a form of surrogate care. Their success in doing so depends not just on touting music's specific benefits but on convincing governmental agencies, health-care providers, insurance companies, and other third-party payers of its cost-effectiveness, at least relative to other forms of intervention. A case in point is the Sync Project, a subsidiary that biotechnology company PureTech Health launched in 2015.[118] Before being sold to audio equipment manufacturer Bose in 2018, the Sync Project's self-proclaimed mission was to develop music "as a precision medicine."[119] To that end, the company developed apps that combined listening data and biometric data (gathered from smartphones and wearable devices) to create personalized, algorithmically generated music having therapeutic value for pain management, memory support (for individuals with dementia), dyslexia rehabilitation, improved immune response, and sleep therapy, among other things.[120] Posts to the company blog routinely cited research attesting to music's health benefits. Yet press releases, blog posts, and other promotional media issued by the company advertised another advantage of music: its cheapness. "Sync Project aims to commercialize the clinical applications of [its] platform and deliver a personalized, *low-cost*, non-invasive therapy, across a range of conditions," announced one press release (emphasis mine).[121] Another communiqué described how using music in rehabilitation settings would be comparatively "easy and inexpensive," potentially decreasing the pain medication physicians would need to prescribe.[122] Music's negligible exchange value, it would appear, is just as important as its health-related use values.

Equally illustrative is the nonprofit Music and Memory. Incorporated in 2010, the organization's mission is "to bring the therapeutic benefits of personalized music to elderly residents in long term care to improve quality of life."[123] Underpinning the organization's work is music's extraordinary capacity to lodge in people's memories, making it ideal for creating "cognitive connections" in those suffering from dementia. At a practical level, what has made music's use in memory retrieval and mood management feasible at scale has been the development of affordable technologies such as MP3s, iPods, and (later) on-demand streaming, which enable nursing home workers with little experience in music therapy to conduct targeted interventions with patients.[124] Among the benefits Music and Memory cites is music's ability to give individuals suffering from diminished cognitive functions a "means of communication and self-expression," as well as rendering patients "more cooperative, attentive, and willing to accept care" by curtailing "reactive behaviors." But most important of all, music-based interventions can "reduce reliance on anti-psychotic, anti-anxiety, and anti-depressant medications," providing an alternative that avoids not only the side effects that accompany many psychotropic drugs but also the considerable expense they incur.[125] "Despite the enormous sums of money spent on mood- and behavior-altering medications that are often not particularly effective, nothing compares to [music] when it comes to improving quality of life," declares one nursing home executive in a testimonial posted to Music and Memory's website.[126]

Reducing the medication administered to nursing home residents isn't the only source of savings. Consider the state of Wisconsin, whose Department of Health Services started funding Music and Memory programs in eldercare facilities beginning in 2013. The agency cited several reasons for initiating the program, including improved quality of life, improved cognitive function, and increased interpersonal engagement. Yet the department's mandate to promote "efficiencies" in long-term care,[127] driven by the austerity politics being pursued by then-governor Scott Walker, made budgetary considerations key to its support for the program. Recourse to music "decreased staffing costs due to decrease in behaviors, medications, alarms, etc."; "decreased worker's compensation"; "decreased liability"; and helped "delay in enrollment into public long-term care funding program (Medicaid)."[128] What music does appears to be less important than what it doesn't do, which is cost much. A glowing assessment of Music and Memory in the *Economist* spelled out the cost-benefit calculus at work. "Tailoring music therapy to the individual is cheap but can reap great rewards," the article announced.[129] Noting that "streaming services now offer range and affordability to healthcare professionals," the article celebrated Music and Memory largely because its treatments were "cheap to run."[130]

The same calculus can be discerned in public initiatives seeking to enroll music and the arts to offset the costs of social reproduction. Representative is a report issued by the UK's All-Party Parliamentary Group on Arts, Health, and Well-Being in 2017. Titled *Creative Health: The Arts for Health and Well-Being*, the report is a creature of the conjuncture out of which it was born.[131] On the one hand, the UK's publicly funded health-care system, the National Health Service (NHS), continues to enjoy broad support in the country. Even if public opinion polls point to mounting concerns with the deteriorating quality of the service, largely unchanged is support for the ideal that the NHS embodies—that health care is a right guaranteed to all, paid for collectively via general taxation.[132] On the other hand, the decades-long effort by Conservative- and Labor-led governments alike to introduce market-based reforms, coupled with the austerity measures imposed following the financial crisis of 2008–2009, have done much to hollow out the NHS. While funding has risen since 2010, allocations have not kept up with price increases in the health-care sector, leading to declining standards of care.[133] It was against this backdrop, one defined by decreasing real expenditures in the face of rising costs, that *Creative Health* was issued. And this context helps to explain the report's fixation on the economies that can be achieved by means of music and the arts more generally. Acknowledging that cost-benefit analyses have "serious shortcomings" when it comes to economically exceptional activities such as music and the provision of care, the document nevertheless devotes many pages to exactly this sort of exercise.[134] A through line running across the report's roughly two hundred pages is "the cost effectiveness of the arts in health and social care, through savings and avoided costs."[135] To take one example, the "Arts on Prescription" project is extolled for bringing about a "37% drop in GP consultations and a 27% reduction in hospital admissions," which, when extrapolated, translates into a "saving of £216 per patient."[136] Also lauded are certain music therapies, which, by "enhanc[ing] neural plasticity" and "bolstering resistance to dementia," may help delay patients' placement in residential care; and "if five percent of admissions could be delayed by a year," the report observes, "£55m would be saved."[137]

In the United States, where health-care coverage for working-age adults and their dependents has historically been tied to private employment, a similar interest in music's utility for healthy living can be seen in initiatives backed by employer-sponsored wellness plans. Writing on the corporate arrogation of the term *wellness*, John Patrick Leary notes that "employees' health isn't valuable [to employers] because workers' lives outside the workplace are important," but because "employees' health and happiness will minimize their cost to the company and maximize their productivity *at work*."[138] Corroboration for Leary's claim can be found in the pages of *Corporate Wellness Magazine*, the official journal of the Corporate Health and Wellness Association. A 2014 article, for instance, observes that "medical costs associated with treating stress, depression, and anxiety exceed $300 billion annually," with a major challenge facing companies being how to "reduc[e] these costs."[139] Noting that "only recently has music started to take the lead in major wellness campaigns," the article singles out managed-care conglomerate Kaiser Permanente for the way it has integrated music into its "healthy living" programs. Elsewhere, the article advises that workers should be steered away from "music that keeps them trapped in stress, anxiety, frustration, or disappointment" and redirected instead toward music that "increase[s] productivity, happiness, and/or positive attitudes."[140] Implementing such music-based interventions, the article claims, will help employers to "decrease turnover," "reduce sick days," "shrink worker compensation claims," "improve employee moods," "increase customer satisfaction," and "boost sales."[141]

Forming the backdrop of initiatives such as these has been a proliferation of apps, devices, and services specializing in "wellness music" since the mid-2010s. A 2020 article written for the Global Wellness Summit, for instance, highlighted the growth of musics promoting healthy living as one of the most notable wellness industry trends in recent years.[142] In addition to the increasing number of mood and activity playlists on streaming services, the article also cites a surge in music-based wellness apps such as Headspace, myndstream, and Calm; "audio wellness" festivals; personalized AI-generated music created by services such as Endel, Weav, and Mubert; and wearable devices, such as DropLabs' EP 01 sneaker, which transmits vibrations to runners' feet in time with the beat detected in a given track. "Change is here," the article announces, predicting that "music created (and listened to) as intentional medicine will be a big trend in 2020 and beyond."[143] The article's timing was propitious, published just as COVID-19 was beginning to spread across the globe. The pandemic seemed to accelerate music's use as a technology of care.[144] If only for a brief period of time, videos of people singing from apartment balconies and news reports of musicians performing via video links for patients in hospital wards captured the public imagination.[145] Seeing an opportunity, a number of corporations, start-ups, and charitable groups seized on the occasion to bolster the use of streaming services, digital assistants, and other audio technologies for care work. Amazon and Bose, for instance, partnered with the nonprofit Musicians on Call to provide patients with headphones, Amazon

Fire tablets, and free subscriptions to Amazon Music to help them get by while quarantined in hospitals. "We're honored to work with Musicians on Call," announced one Bose representative, remarking that "our headphones can help provide patients with access to music, entertainment, and even a little quiet, during a time when they need it most."[146]

At the same time, platforms such as Deezer and Spotify quickly moved to unveil new "at home" pages, with playlists organized around the various household activities, hobbies, and chores that now made up a much greater proportion of people's lives while in confinement (cooking, bathing, home exercise, childcare, sex, cleaning, and so on). For those living on their own during lockdown, Deezer's "Stay at Home" channel offered a form of surrogate companionship, promising "to keep you company while you spend your days at home." The playlist "Dancing with Myself," for instance, suggested that enforced solitude should be seen as an opportunity rather than as a hardship, encouraging users to "stay home & dance like no one is watching!"[147] Playing on music's much-vaunted capacity to connect people across distances, Spotify for its part unveiled a new "Listening Together" campaign. To publicize the initiative Spotify launched a "visualization-based microsite," where individuals could both see and listen to music that users located all over the globe happened to be streaming at the same time.[148] Meanwhile, celebrity-curated playlists gave users the chance to engage in an ersatz form of collective participation: one could listen to music while "gaming together" with Polo G, "cooking together" with Migos, or "working out" together with Ellie Goulding. "Spotify believes in the limitless power of audio," the press release remarked. "Our hope is that these playlists will allow listeners to forge a common bond with people around the world who are also using audio to stay connected."[149]

• • •

To the extent music's use as an inexpensive fix actually does help in mitigating the ongoing crisis of social reproduction, it does so by displacing this crisis elsewhere—onto the ecosystems from which cheap energy is drawn; onto the workers whose labor is exploited to manufacture digital devices; and not least of all onto musicians and musical communities, whose conditions of existence have been significantly diminished by the changes streaming has brought about in both the amount and the structure of the payments they receive for their work. The more that cheap music is framed not as a luxury but as a necessity, the more the cheapness of music likewise becomes a necessity—which is to say that recourse to music as a means of

The Crises of Social Reproduction → 233

staving off the general crisis of social reproduction will likely exacerbate the more specific crisis of reproduction that confronts both musicians and musical communities. Making this all the more likely is the fact that one of the chief agents driving music's transformation into a plentiful and inexpensive resource for care work is the partial decommodification it undergoes as a result of the combined effects of digital reproduction and the platform business model. And, as noted in chapter 2, music's partial decommodification on streaming platforms amounts for most musicians to a wholesale decommodification of their labor, a reality reinforced by the intensified winner-take-all tendencies that platforms exacerbate. Denied meaningful income from recordings, at perpetual risk of relegation to the swelling ranks of the artistic surplus population, musicians no less than anyone else also find themselves beset by the rising costs of social reproduction that the reprivatization of care has increasingly shifted onto private individuals and households. That this situation may not be new—that musicians' livelihoods have long been precarious—is undoubtedly true, as David Hesmondhalgh and others have pointed out.[150] But it is also true that many of the support systems and economic conditions that once helped musicians get by in spite of their precarity (for example, cheap housing, more generous unemployment benefits) have eroded significantly.[151] The result is the ironic situation in which even as their work is called on to shore up increasingly strained systems of social reproduction, many musicians face mounting difficulties in reproducing themselves as *musicians*. And not just as musicians: for every time their music is placed on a chill or workout playlist, music workers are being enlisted to act as care workers at the same time. They are being enlisted, that is, to perform the invisible and uncompensated work of social reproduction, above and beyond their more visible yet still largely un(der)compensated work of musical production. Which raises the question: What obligation do we, as a society, have to care for the musicians who are increasingly being called on to care for us?

Epilogue

Hardly any aspect of social life was left untouched by the coronavirus pandemic that swept the globe in 2020. And few areas were as profoundly or adversely affected as music. The most immediate impact was the near-complete cessation of live performance, as social distancing measures made in-person concerts untenable. Less direct but no less important were the effects that followed from the sudden loss of what over the past twenty years has been musicians' main source of income. Recall in this connection David Bowie's prediction, discussed in chapter 2: that with the rise of online music distribution, live performance would henceforth become the "only unique situation that's going to be left"—and thus the only scarce commodity that most musicians would have left to sell. The pandemic threw the prescience of this observation into relief. Yet in revealing how much musicians had come to depend on live performance, the pandemic also revealed how little they earned from other sources, above all streaming services. To be sure, dissatisfaction with the paltry revenue generated by streaming was nothing new.[1] But the loss of earnings that had long offset (and thus helped to mask) the meagerness of streaming payments intensified long-simmering grievances about how little platforms pay artists. Thanks to the acute crisis brought on by the global pandemic, a chronic and longer-standing one—the crisis of musicians' ability to reproduce themselves as musicians—came to a head.

As a result, the year 2020 marked a pivot in the brief history of music streaming, as grassroots mobilization and public pressure mounted for a thorough overhaul of the digital music economy. Already by March of that year a petition had begun circulating online pressuring Spotify to triple the amount they paid per stream. Not only would this increase provide musicians with immediate relief in the face of the pandemic-related lockdowns but also, by making this change permanent, artists would henceforth be able to "make a living wage and not be left vulnerable to living gig to gig."[2]

In the United States, the following month, April 2020, saw the formation of the Union of Musicians and Allied Workers (UMAW). While the proximate cause for the group's founding was the loss of income brought on by the pandemic, its roots reached further back, to political actions undertaken by its founding members in years prior (including a successful protest in 2017 against the South by Southwest festival for the "deportation clause" included in artist contracts, which authorized festival organizers to notify immigration officials about acts from abroad participating in off-festival shows).[3] Initially focused on lobbying the US Congress to provide assistance to musicians and music venues as part of its COVID-19 relief legislation, UMAW soon turned its energies to the dysfunctions of the streaming economy. In October 2020 it launched its "Justice at Spotify" campaign, which, among other things, called on the platform to double the per-stream payouts to artists, change its revenue distribution model, make public all closed-door contracts (especially those with major labels), and provide more extensive credits for recordings.

Elsewhere similar initiatives were underway. In the United Kingdom, the #BrokenRecord campaign was launched in April 2020 thanks to a viral Twitter thread by Tom Gray, member of the band Gomez, who was then serving on the council of PRS for Music, a UK-based copyright collection agency.[4] Gray decried not just the role of streaming platforms in suppressing artist income but also the disproportionate share of streaming revenue that major labels claimed, little of which made its way back to the artists on their rosters. If there was to be any hope of "rebuild[ing] the lost middle class of music," Gray argued, it was imperative to "start the pressure now."[5] His call did not go unheeded. A few weeks later, the British Musicians' Union, in partnership with the Ivors Academy, initiated the "Keep Music Alive" campaign, whose overarching goal was to "fix streaming now."[6] Significantly, the Keep Music Alive campaign petitioned the UK government to launch an inquiry into the streaming economy—a demand that would be satisfied in late 2020, when the Department of Digital, Culture, Media and Sport formed a parliamentary committee to investigate the sector.[7]

Thanks to these and other pressure campaigns, a raft of proposals were brought to wider public attention as the 2020s got underway. Some were old, some new, and all aimed at rebuilding the digital music ecosystem along more equitable lines. My purpose in this epilogue is to survey some of these proposed reforms, as well as some alternatives already under construction, in order to limn their potential, as well as their potential shortcomings. What follows is a sketch of some of the possible futures that music might have, once its subjection to platform capitalism is either brought under tighter regulation or superseded altogether. And yet it is necessary to recognize that this sketch is just that—a sketch—and as such provisional. Its rough contours are liable to change as economic conditions shift, which is another way of saying that the possible futures mapped here will evolve as the balance of power between contending forces does: between capital on the one hand, labor on the other, and all those who, despite being ejected or discounted by the formal economy, nonetheless help produce the conditions necessary for the ongoing reproduction of both.

Reforms and Alternatives

Among the proposals that gained traction in 2020, one of the most popular called for the industry-wide adoption of a user-centric distribution model (UCD) to replace the pro rata system that has dominated the streaming economy since its inception (this, for example, is one of the demands that UMAW made as part of its Justice at Spotify campaign). As will be recalled, the pro rata method aggregates user income by subscription tier. These revenue pools are then apportioned to rights holders in proportion to the share of streams their music garnered out of the total registered across the entire platform during a given reporting period. A basic criticism of this approach to revenue distribution is that it delinks the music that individual users listen to from the music that their payments support. One upshot is that the revenue generated by less active users ends up flowing to rights holders favored by more active users, whose consumption is effectively subsidized by the latter (this in turn creates the opportunity for the sort of click fraud discussed in chapter 4). UCD, by contrast, maintains the principle that a user's payments should go only to those musicians whose music they listen to. If a premium-tier user listened to only one artist over the course of the month, then that artist and none other should receive the entirety of the user's monthly payment (minus administrative costs). In addition to providing greater transparency about how money flows from users to artists, a more significant advantage of UCD according to its advocates is that it promises to mitigate the inegalitarian winner-take-all dynamics that benefit superstar artists at the expense of rank-and-file musicians.

Complementing calls to change how revenue is shared have been calls to change how much of it ought to be shared. This is the key demand made by UMAW and other activists: that artists across the board be paid more. Sometimes this demand is couched in relative terms, as with the petition that pressed Spotify to triple royalty payments in response to the pandemic. At other times it is cast in absolute terms, as with UMAW's call for Spotify to pay artists a penny per stream. Either way, the strength of the demand is tied to both its directness and its appeal to a basic sense of economic fairness. If debates pitting UCD against pro rata distribution methods can seem arcane to the wider public, calls to pay artists more have the advantage of being simple and straightforward. And if pressuring platforms to adopt UCD seeks to alter how the streaming pie is divided, pushing for musicians to be paid more seeks instead to increase each slice by increasing the overall size of the pie.

Running parallel to proposals that would change how (or how much) platforms pay musicians has been growing interest in abandoning commercial streaming altogether, developing alternative musical economies instead. One model for moving forward looks backward, to an older tradition of worker-owned cooperatives. In particular, growing awareness of the economic, social, and political harms of platform capitalism has fueled efforts to replace it with a more just, equitable, and democratic system of platform cooperativism.[8] In the domain of digital music, the most significant initiative to date has been the platform Resonate. Founded in 2015, Resonate was conceived in response to widening inequalities within and beyond the music industry.[9] A hybrid producer/consumer (or multi-stakeholder) co-op, Resonate aims to give "everyone involved (fans, musicians, indie labels, and our workers) . . . a say in how the company runs."[10] Among its innovations are its "stream2own" payment model, according to which listeners pay an increasing amount for each successive play of a track, up to the point where they have paid enough to have purchased a copy of the track outright.[11] For listeners, the model combines the benefits of both the streaming and the digital download models: the low cost of the first few plays of a track enables the sort of casual browsing and discovery associated with streaming, while the possibility of purchasing tracks played repeatedly restores to users some of the rights of ownership that streaming has abrogated. For artists, the main benefit of stream2own is that it promises a higher payout rate than is typical of most commercial platforms. But more significant than the particulars of Resonate's payment model is its broader commitment to economic democracy and collective decision-making. Each member—whether artist, listener, or developer—is accorded both a share in the company and a right to participate in its governance, having a say on what features are to be developed, how data are to be managed, and who will serve on the co-op's advisory board, among other things.[12]

Related to yet distinct from the development of platform co-ops have been experiments with the possibilities opened up by blockchain technologies and their offshoots. Resonate, for instance, initially looked to blockchain to undergird its backend operations, receiving a fair amount of its financing early on from Reflective Ventures, a crypto-based investment fund (the cooperative ultimately retreated from these forays into blockchain after suffering losses in the crypto crash of 2018). More recently, the Audius project—an open-source protocol using blockchain—launched a streaming service in 2019 that gives artists the ability to set the conditions for accessing their music. The most straightforward way this feature can be applied is through variable pricing schemes: an artist, for instance, might choose to offer access to their back catalog for a relatively low price while charging more for new releases. Or they might offer fans the opportunity to help finance future projects in exchange for certain rewards (for example, advance access, merch, limited editions, concert tickets).[13] The ability to encode the terms under which content circulates on the platform is central to Audius's claim of empowering artists. It also contrasts with established streaming services, whose pro rata payment method imposes the same price on every stream within a given price tier, with differences in payouts at any moment in time being solely a function of differences in market share. Powering Audius's architecture is a network of node operators. Like other stakeholders, the latter are incentivized to perform critical services (for example, hosting content, indexing metadata) through the issuance of tokens ($AUDIO), which function as a medium of exchange and store of value within the network. Beyond being redeemable for "exclusive features and services," Audius tokens also grant their holders governance rights. And as is the case with other blockchain-based, distributed-ledger systems, the dispersal of information and governance across the network is seen as key to the creation of a more just music economy—though notably justice as defined by Audius is a question of equal opportunity, not egalitarian outcomes. As the project's white paper notes, the "community owned streaming protocol" Audius has established is one in which "participants . . . must continually contribute in value-added ways" to the maintenance and development of the service, lest their "governance power" (and ownership stake) be "diluted and replaced" over time by others.[14] In this, the governing philosophy of Audius recalls nothing so much as the Soviet constitution's garbled rewriting of Marx: "From each according to his abilities, to each according to his work."[15]

Challenges

Increased interest in either reforming or constructing alternatives to commercial streaming has also increased scrutiny of not just the promise but the risks associated with each of these proposals. Consider UCD. Calls to overhaul the allocation of streaming revenue have been around for as long as streaming has, giving rise to a series of studies examining the potential benefits and costs of shifting from a pro rata to a user-centric model. The findings of these studies vary considerably. While a handful suggest that the redistributive effects of adopting UCD would be marginal, others have pointed to a more substantial reallocation of earnings, with international superstars losing some income to middle-tier artists, especially those popular in smaller national markets.[16] A real-world experiment that might help settle these debates is SoundCloud's adoption of "fan-powered royalties" (the platform's branded term for UCD) in April 2021.[17] A year on, the platform touted the new system as a success, noting that some 135,000 independent artists had opted into the new payment structure and as a result were earning 60 percent more than under a pro rata system.[18] Obviously such self-reported success stories should be taken with a grain of salt. Whether they are representative of the changes in income that participating artists will experience over the long run is still to be determined. But even assuming that UCD has the benefits that SoundCloud and other, more impartial proponents claim for it, a more significant obstacle to its widespread adoption across the streaming economy remains the three major labels, each of which has reaped significant rewards from the current model's bias toward global superstars. By mid-2022, the only major to have signed on to SoundCloud's version of UCD is Warner Music Group, though as this book goes to press, Universal Music Group Chairman and CEO Lucian Grange has begun making noises about the need to reform the "economic model" of streaming services to make it more "artist-centric."[19] Whether these tentative gestures in the direction of UCD will bear fruit remains to be seen.[20] But should the major label cartel use the enormous leverage it has over platforms to fundamentally change the way streaming revenue is distributed, it is likely that they will only do so if the new system can be made to advance their interests.

If the redistributive effects of UCD are less than certain, what of the demand that artists be paid more? As noted, a major appeal of this demand is its simplicity. Another is that, if instituted, an across-the-board increase in payout rates would benefit all artists, instead of simply redistributing the existing revenue pool, as UCD does. Yet precisely because this reform would require a significant expansion in platforms' outlays, some commentators have cast doubts on its feasibility. It may be morally and politically desirable to pay artists more, the argument goes, but doing so might deal a potentially fatal blow to the fragile streaming economy. One of the more thoughtful expositions of this argument was advanced by industry analyst Mark Mulligan at the beginning of the pandemic in 2020. Using Spotify as a point of reference, he noted that even a relatively modest increase in payouts would have a number of negative side effects. For instance, a 25 percent increase in payouts (paid for by a 25 percent increase in subscription prices) would cause the losses that Spotify already posts year in year out to balloon. "Spotify lost $184 million in 2019," writes Mulligan. But with this new royalty model, "it would have lost more than $1 billion."[21] This in turn would likely result in cutbacks in both product development and audience growth, which might depress artist royalties in the longer run. Such a change would also leave open the possibility of Spotify ceding market share to larger tech platforms better equipped to absorb such costs. "In the midterm this [change] may benefit artists," Mulligan notes, "but in the longer term (i.e., when Spotify is sufficiently squeezed) these tech majors are likely to follow their MO of 'reducing inefficiencies in the supply chain.' So be careful what you wish for."[22]

To such appeals to economic reason, critics of Spotify have formulated a number of responses. Representatives of UMAW, for instance, have argued that it is not their responsibility to figure out how Spotify and other services should go about ensuring artists receive a fair wage; that is the platforms' responsibility. And if the only way for streaming to make money is by suppressing artist pay, then it would be better for the streaming economy to collapse under the weight of such "unreasonable" calls for reform. "If Spotify's model can't pay artists fairly," UMAW's list of demands reads, "it shouldn't exist."[23] One might go further still. If there is a weakness with UMAW's call for musicians to be paid a penny per stream, it isn't that it goes too far; it is that it doesn't go far enough. As journalist Andy Cush has observed, multiplying the very low payouts artists receive by two, three, or even ten times in many cases wouldn't meaningfully improve their financial situation. By way of example, he cites the case of British violinist Tasmin

Little, whose 3.5 million streams over a six-month period in 2019–2020 resulted in a payment of just £12.34 (it is important to note that Little's exceptionally low payment is almost certainly due as much to the peculiarities of classical recording contracts as it is to Spotify's revenue-sharing model). Cush comments that even were Spotify to increase by tenfold the payments it makes to musicians such as Little, the resulting sum "would still be paltry," amounting to roughly £20 a month.[24] Part of the problem is that increasing the size of payments to rights holders does nothing to change the existing contractual relations between artists and labels. If the terms of these contracts disproportionately benefit labels to the detriment of artists, then increasing payouts will do nothing to alter this inequitable relationship. Another part of the problem is that increased payouts do not alter how payments are structured. As noted in chapter 1, a key way streaming differs from sales is that in the case of the latter, payment is made just once, and is made up front: a buyer pays a larger dollar amount in the present in exchange for the right to play a recording as much (or as little) as they may wish in the future. In the case of streaming, this front-loading of payments—and royalties—no longer obtains, with remuneration being spread out across present and future. So long as artists continue to be compensated in this fashion, according to their music's actual rather than potential use, payouts will continue to be piecemeal, disaggregated into fractional amounts that are dispersed over months, years, decades. And this will continue to be the case even if a platform roughly triples its payout rate, as UMAW demands of Spotify. Three times almost nothing may amount to more, but not by much.

Efforts to work outside the dominant streaming paradigm—whether via cooperatives or blockchain-based decentralized networks—face different challenges. Some of these have less to do with the specificities of the musical economy and more with the perennial problems involved in constructing alternatives to capitalism from within capitalism. In the case of co-ops, left critics from the nineteenth century to the present have highlighted one dilemma in particular: that because worker-owned businesses are still businesses, they have to compete within the same market as capitalist firms.[25] As a result, the "degeneration thesis" sketches two possible fates that cooperatives face: either they fail, as their fidelity to cooperative principles makes them uncompetitive, or they succeed, but only by eroding their principles to the point they become capitalist enterprises in all but name. This is the theory, at least. In practice, many co-ops have managed to carve out a small yet sustainable niche for themselves in the face of these impediments (proponents of cooperatives often point to the Mondragon Corporation in Spain and the network of cooperatives in the Emilio Romagna region of Italy as examples of the movement's successes). Whether a platform co-op such as Resonate will be able to do likewise remains an open question.

Standing in its way is an additional challenge that both Resonate and blockchain-backed networks such as Audius face, relating to the especially brutal competitive dynamics at play in the platform economy. Not only do commercial services enjoy greater access to capital, enabling them to operate at a loss for extended periods of time.[26] In addition, network effects and the monopolistic concentration they encourage strongly favor incumbent firms such as Spotify or Apple, their utility increasing in tandem with the number of users they are able to attract to various sides of the platform. As Thomas Hanna, Mathew Lawrence, and Nils Peters observe, the self-reinforcing feedback loop fostered by network effects can thereby act as "a 'moat'—a way of entrenching and defending platform businesses."[27] The flip side of this positive feedback loop is a negative one: the fewer artists and labels a platform is able to attract, the fewer the users, and vice versa. This would appear to be a bind that Resonate has confronted throughout its short existence. Five years after its founding in 2015, it had managed to draw only roughly two thousand artists to the site, translating to "tens of thousands of tracks." Compared with commercial platforms, this is a minuscule figure—a fact that might explain why Resonate has encountered some trouble in recruiting an active user base to the site. According to a member of the co-op's board of directors, while nearly ten thousand people have "shown interest" in becoming members, this has yet to translate into a durable community of fans. "Active listener levels are still pretty low," he acknowledged, which is a major problem since Resonate "need[s] large numbers to yield a decent living wage for artists."[28]

Lurking behind these difficulties is the fact that cooperatives and decentralized networks, by seeking to circumvent the dominant platform economy, do little to directly confront this economy. Unchallenged is platforms' massive accumulation of economic, political, and cultural power, which gives them outsize influence over the broader environment in which any alternative will have to operate. Indeed, this is a weakness that can be found in virtually all of the proposals discussed thus far. Almost without exception, their focus lies with the unequal distribution of wealth for which streaming is held responsible. As a result, less attention is paid to what is arguably the more decisive factor promoting inequality: the unequal distribution of power, economic and otherwise, that streaming both benefits from and perpetuates. Nor do these proposals address one of the key sources of this power: ownership (of data, patents, copyrights, and so on). Not only does title to these valuable assets entitle their owners to whatever profits they generate; also, and more critically, it grants them the right to determine how these assets will or won't be exploited ("decision rights"). Calls for platforms to pay artists more or to reformulate the revenue-sharing model they use leave this concentration of decision-making power intact. Meanwhile, co-ops and decentralized networks may seek to build rival sites of power by distributing not just wealth but ownership more broadly. But unless there is a significant scaling back of commercial platforms' market dominance, to say nothing of the major labels they serve, smaller, noncommercial entities will most likely be left to fight over scraps. Community or worker ownership is certainly a goal worth striving for. But as Marisol Sandoval incisively points out, "ownership does not necessarily mean security," given the very real possibility that "workers might end up owning very little or nothing."[29]

Music beyond Platform Capitalism

These are not the only areas in which proposed reforms fall short. One upshot of the justified focus on the welfare of artists is a neglect of other harms associated with streaming, as well as other benefits it may have. Of the harms, one of the most consequential is the rampant consumer surveillance and profiling that commercial streaming services engage in. Not only do these practices covertly shape what kind of music users are steered toward and what modes of listening they are encouraged to adopt. In addition to such distorting effects *within* the digital enclosure, there are the cascading impacts that this surveillance has *beyond* its confines, on account of the obscure data-sharing agreements and monetization schemes that platforms enter into with third parties. Apart from UMAW's call for greater transparency as part of its Justice at Spotify campaign, little of the musician-led agitation targeting streaming has focused on platforms' data collection practices, presumably because this is understood to be a problem affecting consumers rather than workers (despite the fact that surveillance is as much if not more of a problem for workers, to say nothing of how these two identities overlap in people's everyday lives). A similar dynamic can be witnessed with regard to streaming's negative environmental impacts. As we have seen, these follow from streaming's treatment of recorded music as a cheap, disposable good—which entails that nature in turn be treated as a cheap, disposable resource. But as the unfolding climate catastrophe makes clear, an economy whose benefits are built on the back of cheap nature will end up costing dearly in the long run. This, too, is an issue left unaddressed by redistributive reforms or attempts to construct worker- or community-owned platforms. Indeed, certain alternatives—in particular those, such as Audius, that rely on blockchain technologies—may actually exacerbate the problem of environmental degradation. The significant carbon emissions generated by blockchain technologies means that however empowering a service like Audius may be for creators, the gains it promises for musicians' welfare may be offset by the harms done to the ecosystem on which musicians depend, along with everyone else.[30]

At the same time, many proposed reforms and alternatives either do not address or would actively work against the real or potential benefits of streaming. For artists, these include the lowered barriers to entry that digital music services afford, especially compared to the pre-internet recording and radio industries, and the potentially global audience they allow artists to reach. For listeners, they include the access that platforms provide to a massive archive of recorded music. Key to these and other advantages is the large-scale aggregation that streaming services have brought about across a number of domains—of listeners, data, musics, and musicians. Lurking within such practices of aggregation is a utopian potential, one that might be realized if it were harnessed to serve the public good, instead of the private interests of platform operators, copyright rentiers, advertisers, shareholders, and even individual(ized) end users. Consider first the aggregation of data. One can—and should—decry the particular forms of data collection that platforms pursue. Yet data collection per se isn't a bad thing. What is problematic is the kinds of data being gathered, the purposes for which they are being accumulated, and the lack of transparency and democratic control over how such information is exploited. Yet there is no reason why gathering together the collective data of a music community could not be put to work in advancing the collective interests of this community—all the more so, inasmuch as data are useful only to the extent they form part of a larger group. Meaningless on its own, any individual data point gains significance and utility in relation to all the other data points that compose a data set.[31] One could thus envisage all sorts of beneficial uses that might flow from the large-scale collection and analysis of music data, once they were harnessed for the common good: tracking racial and gender inequities within the music profession, creating more democratic forms of curation, fashioning new tools for music creation, and so forth. Concomitantly, one could envisage all sorts of alternative models for aggregating, maintaining, and regulating data not as private property but as a public resource (data commons, data trusts, and so on).

Likewise, by gathering together on a single site so much of the world's recorded music, both past and present, streaming platforms have brought us tantalizingly close to realizing the long-standing dream of creating a universal library of recorded music. Yet a wide gulf still separates this utopian possibility from the skewed, dystopian reality that streaming services embody. Criticizing YouTube for having arrogated the term *library* to describe itself, digital media scholar Sarah Roberts scathingly remarks that "YouTube is a library in the same way a pile of unsorted crap thrown on the floor is an 'archive.'"[32] Similar objections might be raised as regards music platforms, for which the term library is equally inapt, albeit for different reasons. What separates Spotify or Amazon Music, say, from a traditional library or archive isn't so much an absence of order. Rather, the difference lies in the fact that the order streaming services impose on their catalogs is one whose principal goal is not to serve either music or a platform's patrons but to ensure a certain return on investment. This might take the form of promoting some musics over others, in exchange for payment in money or in kind ("playlist payola"), or of trying to induce users to consume more music and, by increasing their "dwell time" on the platform, increase the amount of data that can be captured as a result. Serving the individual listener, let alone the broader interests of a community, is an afterthought.

Yet if the analogy between streaming services and libraries holds in any respect, it is because digital media, as we have seen, fall more comfortably within the domain of public as opposed to private goods. All that commercial streaming does is to place a fence around the public good that is digital music and charge a toll for access. But there is no reason why this need be the case. Liz Pelly, for one, has noted that although "physical copies of music have long been available at public libraries," this practice hasn't been extended to the digital domain, a state of affairs that activists should work to rectify: "We don't currently conceptualize universal access to music as a public good, to be managed in the public interest with public funding. We should."[33] Drawing inspiration from music lawyer Henderson Cole's proposal to create an "American Music Library," Pelly argues that "perhaps the problem isn't *streaming* per se but the predatory industry norms that surround it." To pick up the thread of Pelly's argument, while such a transformation in streaming's status and social function may be difficult to achieve politically, it wouldn't present much of a challenge technically. As I argued in chapter 2, commercial streaming has gone some way toward ratifying music's status as a public good, doing little more than circumscribing the space in which it can behave as such. Viewed from this angle, not only would it be more equitable to dismantle this enclosure and treat digital music as a universal public service, it would also be more efficient. After all, the rents that platforms charge users and pass on (disproportionately) to major labels are little more than a species of tax, to the extent that all rents obtained by the exercise of property rights stem from the state's prior constitution of private property as a social form.[34] Hence, rather than outsource what are effectively public functions to private actors, streaming would be better managed if taken in hand by some public or community-run agency. Or, alternatively, one might imagine a share levy being imposed on platforms, by means of which ownership could be slowly but steadily transferred to workers, including musicians, as well as other community stakeholders (a model in this regard may be found in Sweden's Meidner plan, which notably sought to transfer ownership of companies over time from the hands of capital to those of labor, by means of a levy on ownership shares).

The large-scale aggregation of users, data, and audio files that platforms realize is no doubt significant. But perhaps most consequential is streaming services' aggregation of musicians. Exact figures are hard to come by, but most platforms host millions of artists—and in some cases, tens of millions.[35] Of course, just because a large number of musicians are gathered on platforms doesn't necessarily mean that they will feel as if they are part of some broader collective. On the contrary: the design of services militates against such collective identification, being as individuated for artists as they are for listeners. Musician-facing portals (such as Spotify for Artists) hail musicians not as members of some larger community or body but as discrete particulars. Furthermore, the revenue-sharing model employed by most platforms means that, at a practical level, artists find themselves competing against one another within a zero-sum market, where success at winning a greater percentage of streams (and hence revenue) hinges on others receiving a smaller percentage. These conditions are scarcely conducive to the development of a sense of common interest or solidarity.

And yet for all their efforts to interpellate artists as individuals, to isolate them from one another, music platforms cannot help but subject all alike to a single, shared condition. Along with the sheer scale of streaming platforms, the gathering together of musicians within a shared, virtual space creates conditions ripe for the development of new forms of collective consciousness and hence new forms of collective action. Much as the concentration of workers in factories and other sites of employment has often been a key factor in labor mobilization, the same would appear to be the case with the concentration of musicians from across the globe within the virtual space constructed by streaming platforms. A comment by one of the founding members of UMAW, Joey La Neve DeFrancesco, drives this point home. In the course of explaining why the union is so focused on Spotify to the exclusion of other music platforms, DeFrancesco remarks that Spotify "is the workplace people see themselves as being part of." And, like all good organizers, he explains that "you organize in your workplace."[36] Later in the same interview he expands on this point: "Spotify is the reality of our workplace right now. It's where all musicians are. And I think we need to target it. We need to target where the capital is, and target where the power is, in order to build our own collective power to . . . extract more resources from Spotify and these sorts of platforms."[37] It is but a small step from viewing Spotify and other platforms as workplaces to musicians viewing themselves not as artists or "creatives" but as workers. And this is precisely what has transpired, at least among a substantial fraction of musicians, thanks to the combined effects of a global pandemic, the campaigns undertaken by groups such as UMAW and #BrokenRecord, and the longer-standing systemic upheavals that the streaming economy has wrought on musicians' livelihoods. The aggregation of musicians on streaming platforms is so consequential because this development has laid the groundwork for their recomposition as a class not just in itself but for itself.

This is not to downplay the challenges music workers face in mobilizing against Spotify and other platforms. These are multiple. Even if the sudden loss of income caused by the pandemic led a growing number of musicians to see music platforms as their shared workplace, this remains true only in a metaphoric and not in a strictly legal sense. Platforms, of course, don't directly employ musicians. Nor, for the most part, do labels. Rather, the vast majority of musicians are formally classified as independent contractors—a status that, within certain legal regimes, can place significant hurdles in the way of labor organizing. Such is the case in the United States, where existing labor law restricts membership in formally recognized unions to the employees of a private-sector business or public-sector agency. By contrast, collective action jointly undertaken by independent contractors such as musicians would run afoul of antitrust law, counting as a form of horizontal coordination—and hence as a form of unlawful collusion.[38] Compounding these difficulties is the fact that, outside the platform enclosure, the musical workforce is highly dispersed, fissured, and heterogeneous. The direct employment of large numbers of musicians by a single institution or business (for example, as members of a pit band or state-run orchestra) is the exception rather than the rule. Also important at an ideological level is the historic valorization of independence within many music communities. As a "marketplace for symbolic goods" (to borrow Bourdieu's formulation), the musical field is one in which the distinctive artistic identities of musicians are defined through their difference from others, a centrifugal force that is only partly counteracted by the centripetal forces fostered by music scenes, artistic movements, and the like.

The foregoing points to some of the potential obstacles that stand in the way of musicians identifying as workers. So too does the increased militancy of a certain fraction of artists since 2020, which, if nothing else, shows that this identification can't be simply assumed. If it could be, if musicians were constitutionally predisposed to see themselves as workers, then something like UMAW or the #BrokenRecord campaign would likely have taken root much sooner and would have a much broader constituency than either has succeeded in mustering (which isn't to minimize their very real accomplishments on this front). Rather, the *prise de conscience* whereby musicians reimagine themselves as music workers is something to be achieved rather than assumed—and not just once and for all, as a result of a clarifying event like the coronavirus pandemic, but over and over. As such, this self-understanding is always tenuous, never entirely fixed or secure. Important in this regard is that most musicians occupy an ambivalent socioeconomic position, what the sociologist Erik Olin Wright would refer to as a "contradictory class position"[39]—notwithstanding efforts to lump them together with other groups under the crude (and crudely ideological) rubric of the "creative class." True, most musicians have to work for a living, whether by touring, recording, teaching, or performing relational labor, to say nothing of holding down a day job unrelated to their musical pursuits. In this very practical sense, their lived experience is that of a worker. Yet in many instances musicians remain their own bosses—and this remains true even if their agency is highly constrained by more powerful actors or economic forces. Also complicating their position is the important role that assets of various stripes play in determining their economic situation. Despite the fact that many artists transfer rights to their music when signing with labels or publishers, a number of factors encourage a continued sense of ownership, psychological if not legal, over these assets. These include the promise of receiving a percentage of future royalties, as well as the strong symbolic identification many musicians have with their work as an expression or extension of themselves; and this in turn explains the significant investment most creators have in the performance of these assets, even after ownership of them has been ceded to others. In short, even if the grind of everyday creative labor may encourage musicians to see themselves as part of a broadly defined working class, other, countervailing pressures may lead them to view themselves otherwise—perhaps as entrepreneurs or as *petits rentiers*.[40] Whether the balance tips in one direction or another depends on the political-economic conjuncture, of course. But it also depends on the hard work of organizing.

There are still other, more significant obstacles to musicians coming to see themselves as music workers, beyond the contradictory class position they occupy. That for so long music has been regarded by so many as a form of leisure, rather than as a form of labor, is perhaps the most consequential. From this perspective, the work of musicians appears as something other than work. Or, if it is recognized as work, it appears as an attractive alternative to more humdrum forms of employment. It isn't just nonmusicians who hold this attitude. So too do many professional musicians, with music seen as offering an escape route from a life subjected to the alienating and degrading conditions of wage labor.[41] One resurgent line of critique sees this opposition of music making (and creative practice more broadly) to ordinary labor as an ideological construct to be resisted or at a minimum tempered. Not only might this ideology cause us to disregard the hard work it takes for artists to both acquire and exercise their skills; in addition, it might justify the low pay they routinely receive in exchange for their services. Bolstering such critiques in recent years is the way the image of unalienated creative work has been harnessed under neoliberalism.[42] Stripped of much of its emancipatory potential, this image has been wielded as an ideological cudgel, either as a means of getting people to love the labor by which they are exploited, or as a means of getting people to exploit themselves. But to say that popular discourses of the creative worker or creative class may subvert the utopian character of artistic practice isn't to say that these discourses have entirely nullified this utopian character. On the contrary: paeans to the psychic rewards of musical and other kinds of creative work are effective as ideology only because of the real experiences of liberation, of a life beyond alienated labor, that they draw on. For this reason, it is vital not to peremptorily dismiss the utopian horizon embedded in music. After all, few other activities rival musicking's capacity to trouble the real and symbolic boundary capitalism has erected between work and nonwork, labor and leisure. While music's resistance to subsumption by capital might make it harder for musicians to identify as workers, this cost is offset by a potentially greater benefit: namely music's capacity to serve as a beacon, one that points us in the direction of a post-work society.[43]

Nor is it just musicians who need to view themselves otherwise, if any meaningful change to the existing musical economy is to be made. The same is true of listeners. They too need to see themselves in a different light—not primarily as consumers of music or users of a platform but as members of a broader cultural and political community. Or perhaps this formulation isn't quite right. Perhaps it's a question not of getting people to shed one identity (consumer) in favor of another (citizen), but of seeing how the two are mutually imbricated. The social reproduction perspective can be of assistance in this respect, given the stress it has consistently placed on the interconnection of domains routinely viewed as disconnected. What we do as part of a family or household or community conditions what we do as workers, as sources of labor power—and vice versa. And what we do when we consume music has repercussions for other aspects of our selves, just as it has repercussions for the livelihoods of the music workers who are responsible for creating the music we consume. In many ways, this perspective chimes with recent calls to move beyond a libertarian politics of personal autonomy and independence and to turn instead toward a politics of interdependence. For the Care Collective, abandoning the reigning ethos of carelessness and constructing a "caring world" in its place would require that we avow "our interdependences and cultivating a far-reaching ethics of care and solidarity in all our relationships."[44] In the music world more specifically, music producer Mat Dryhurst has likewise urged artists to abandon their long-standing fetishization of independence, recognizing instead that "individual freedoms thrive in the presence of resilient networks and institutions."[45] For Dryhurst, it is only because of the relation of interdependence they have with "a resilient international network of small labels, promoters, publications, and production services" that artists "creating challenging work" are able to do so.

There is much to recommend such appeals to our mutual interdependence. But there is also reason to wonder whether they are sufficient.

Beyond interdependence, there is a need to acknowledge our various *extradependences*, our reliance on actors and forces that extend well beyond the recognized members of a given community, musical or otherwise. Necessitating this intervention is the fact that interdependence, with its emphasis on the relations within a community, neglects the degree to which a community's delineation necessarily entails a constitutive exclusion. Simply extolling interdependence leaves uninterrogated the critical question of who or what gets counted as part of a community and who or what gets left out. Furthermore, just because some actors or activities have been externalized in this way doesn't mean they are inconsequential. Indeed, as we have seen in connection with social reproduction, its utility for the formal economy hinges on its being excluded from this economy. And the more a given community depends on such externalized, abjected others for its ongoing reproduction, the more likely it is that the latter will recede from view, disappearing into the background of people's unreflected assumptions about how the world operates.

What are some of the extradependences of digital music? As a start, one might cite the workers at manufacturing facilities such as Foxconn, whose superexploitation provides the material basis for the relatively inexpensive devices across which much music is streamed. If Apple Music pays on average a higher per-stream rate to musicians than Spotify does, this isn't due to Apple's altruism or some deep-seated affinity the company has with so-called creatives. It is because Apple makes its money from the exploitation of other workers, at the far end of its globe-spanning supply chain, rendering the expropriation of value produced by music workers less important for the company's bottom line.[46] Or one might cite music's extradependence on what classical economists would call the free gifts of nature, or what neoclassical economists would call "ecosystem services," but which might be more aptly described as the massively discounted work of nonhuman nature. This is work whose fruits are readily and unthinkingly expropriated, precisely because their production lies beyond the ken of the economy as it is conventionally understood. Or, to turn the question on its head, one might cite the relation of extradependence that defines how many people interact with music in the course of their everyday lives, in its capacity as a resource for living. In all these cases, social reproduction theory provides a helpful perspective. It aids us in thinking through not just our numerous interdependences but also our equally numerous extradependences (on human labor, on nonhuman nature, on the work music does for and to us, and so on). What the social reproduction perspective points to is the need to pursue struggles that don't just take place within the limits demarcated by capitalism but that intervene at its boundaries, in an effort to redefine these boundaries and thus the space within which capital accumulation is allowed to take place—if it is allowed to take place at all. What it points to as well is the need to forge alliances across otherwise disconnected domains: of work and nonwork, of production and reproduction, of the formal economy and its others. A better future for music cannot be achieved without achieving at the same time a better future for other workers, other systems of care, and the larger environment in which all of them are embedded. To paraphrase UMAW, if commercial streaming services can't exist without the ongoing expropriation of not just musical work but all sorts of other work as well, then perhaps they shouldn't exist in the first place.

Regardless of whether commercial streaming should be better regulated, reformed, or abolished altogether, it is clear that any change to the digital music economy will come about only as a result of collective action. This is the condition of possibility for even the most modest of reforms, such as UCD; for more ambitious projects, such as the creation of platform co-ops; and for still more radical changes, such as the transformation of existing platforms into publicly owned and operated utilities. If the last of these prospects seems far-fetched, utopian even, it is necessary to bear in mind that what is politically possible at any given moment is not fixed but contingent. And the act of making claims, even seemingly impractical ones, is a time-honored method for expanding the horizon of political possibility. Besides, as I have argued throughout this book, streaming services have already laid some of the groundwork for digital music's transformation into a public service. Accepting rather than combating digital music's status as a public good, streaming platforms have simply claimed exclusive title to the space where it is allowed to behave as such. In doing so, they have brought about a partial and incomplete decommodification of music. For many musicians, however, this amounts to a palpable decommodification of their labor—a catastrophic development in a society where the sale of one's labor power is necessary to secure a living. One response to this dilemma would be to try to turn back the clock, to transform recorded music back from a public into a private good, shoring up its commodity status in the process. Examples of this strategy can be seen in the vinyl revival, in the development of alternative platforms devoted to digital music sales (for example, Bandcamp), and most extravagantly in the bubble that formed around nonfungible tokens circa 2021. But as noted in chapter 2, there is another, more radical, and yet ultimately more sustainable solution: not to reverse decommodification but to extend it further, to those goods, services, and resources necessary not just for life but for the good life, including housing, health care, education, and food, as well as music and culture more broadly. Given the multiple and converging crises that confront us at present, as social, natural, and musical ecosystems are increasingly robbed of their capacity to reproduce themselves, the most pragmatic path forward may very well be the most utopian. "Be realistic, demand the impossible." So went a popular slogan of the May '68 uprising in France. More than fifty years on, its imperative remains as urgent as ever.

Notes

Introduction

1. Will Page, "Peak Streaming: Are We There Yet?," *Billboard*, 23 May 2020, 15–16.
2. Amy X. Wang, "For the First Time in Decades, Music Sales Are Growing Again. Guess Why?," *Quartz*, 12 April 2016, https://qz.com/660141/yes-music-sales-are-growing-again-but-they-are-still-half-of-what-they-were-in-1999/.
3. While streaming revenue was the major contributor to industry revenue, licensing deals with social media platforms like TikTok and Facebook also swelled record company coffers. See Mark Mulligan, "Recorded Music Market Shares 2021—Red Letter Year," Midia Research, 18 March 2022, https://www.midiaresearch.com/blog/recorded-music-market-shares-2021-red-letter-year.
4. Per Sundin, cited in Sam Wolfson, "'We've Got More Money Swirling Around': How Streaming Saved the Music Industry," *Guardian*, 24 April 2018, https://www.theguardian.com/music/2018/apr/24/weve-got-more-money-swirling-around-how-streaming-saved-the-music-industry.
5. On the "ideology of plenitude" in the history of music's commodification, see Taylor, "Commodification of Music," 289–90.
6. Rosen, "Economics of Superstars"; Frank and Cook, *Winner-Take-All Society*; Caves, *Creative Industries*, ch. 4 ("Artists, Starving and Well-Fed").
7. On the role of guaranteed revenue minimums for major labels, see the discussion of the 2011 Sony-Spotify contract in chapter 2. See also the testimony given by major label representatives during the United Kingdom's Digital, Culture, Media and Sport (DCMS) Committee's hearings on the economics of music streaming: Digital, Culture, Media and Sport Committee, House of Commons, "Oral Evidence: Economics of Music Streaming, HC 868," 19 January 2021, https://committees.parliament.uk/oralevidence/1534/pdf/. Figures for worldwide streaming revenue in 2021 are from International Federation of Phonographic Industries, *Global Music Report*, 11. Estimates of major label revenue for streaming for the same year are from Mark Mulligan, "2021 Major Label Revenue Surged, but What Does It Mean," *Hypebot*, 10 January 2022, https://www.hypebot.com/hypebot/2022/01/2021-major-label-revenue-surged-but-what-does-it-mean-mark-mulligan.html.

8   See Cooke, *Dissecting the Digital Dollar*, 84.

9   Major label representatives have denied engaging in this practice, most recently during the United Kingdom's DCMS Committee hearings on the economics of streaming (see note 7). Lacking public access to record companies' books, it is impossible to verify their claims (historical precedent suggests their claims shouldn't be taken at face value).

10 "8 out of 10 Music Creators Earn Less than £200 a Year from Streaming," *News*, Ivors Academy, 7 December 2020, https://ivorsacademy.com/news/8-out-of-10-music-creators-earn-less-than-200-a-year-from-streaming-finds-survey-ahead-of-songwriters-and-artists-giving-evidence-to-a-select-committee-of-mps/.

11 Quoted in Tchernova, *Case for a Job Guarantee*, 51. A caustic footnote to Hopkins's remark is provided by the producer Thinnen in November 2020, in a tweet responding to Spotify's recently unveiled plan that would give artists preferential ranking on the platform's interface in exchange for a reduced royalty rate. You might get "more plays on Spotify," Thinnen (@SoThinn) quipped, "but you can still only afford a medium sized meal deal for your bi-monthly dinner." Twitter, 2 November 2020, 2:02 p.m., https://twitter.com/SoThinn/status/1323339662556102656.

12 On this point, see Drott, "Why the Next Song Matters."

13 Christophers, *Rentier Capitalism*, xvi.

14 Bellamy Foster, McChesney, and Jonna, "Monopoly and Competition."

15 Wallerstein, "The Bourgeois(ie) in Concept and Reality," 103.

16 On this point, see Bellamy Foster, McChesney, and Jonna, "Monopoly and Competition," 26–31. See also Davies, "Economics and the 'Nonsense' of Law."

17 Christine Jurzenski, "Live Nation Stock Can More than Double in Three Years," *Barrons*, 8 April 2020, https://www.barrons.com/articles/live-nation-stock-can-more-than-double-in-three-years-analyst-51586380765.

18 Ed Christman, "Publisher's Quarterly: Sony/ATV Reigns Again as Concord Breaks into Top Ten," *Billboard*, 9 May 2019, https://www.billboard.com/articles/business/8510805/music-publishers-quarterly-q1-sonyatv-hot-100-radio.

19 Dimitrakaki and Lloyd, "Social Reproduction Struggles," 2.

20 See, for instance, Gibson-Graham, *End of Capitalism*; Fraser, "Behind Marx's Hidden Abode"; Fraser and Jaeggi, *Capitalism*; Moore, *Capitalism in the Web of Life*; DeAngelis, *Omnia Communis Sunt*.

21 Gibson-Graham, *End of Capitalism*, 6. See also Gibson-Graham, *Postcapitalist Politics*, 54–59.

22 Fraser, in Fraser and Jaeggi, *Capitalism*, 29.

23 Fraser and Jaeggi, *Capitalism*, 72.

24 The key text is Bourdieu, *Distinction*. See also Green, "Musical Meaning and Social Reproduction."

25 See Beech, *Art and Value*; Abbing, *Why Are Artists Poor?*
26 On this point, see Sinnreich, "Music Cartels."
27 Benjamin, *Work of Art*.
28 For an incisive treatment that relates the development of certain of these industries and concepts of pitch, tone, and note, see Parkhurst and Hammel, "Pitch, Tone, and Note."
29 Stahl and Meier, "Firm Foundation"; Klein, "'New Radio'"; Gopinath, *Ringtone Dialectic*; Sinnreich, *Piracy Crusade*, 126–130.
30 On the environmental impacts of streaming, see Devine, *Decomposed*.
31 This literature is too expansive to be fully cataloged here. Much of it will be cited in due course, but some key texts include Anderson, *Popular Music*; Burkart, "Music in the Cloud"; Morris and Powers, "Control, Curation, and Musical Experience"; Marshall, "'Let's Keep Music Special'"; Morris, *Selling Digital Music*; Prey, "Music Analytica"; Johansson et al., *Streaming Music*; Eriksson et al., *Spotify Teardown*; Negus, "From Creator to Data"; Scherzinger, "Political Economy of Streaming"; Goldschmitt and Seaver, "Shaping the Stream"; Arditi, *ITake-Over*; Durham, "Circulatory Maintenance." Also important are the insightful critiques of the streaming economy advanced by musicians, journalists, and cultural critics working outside academia: in particular Liz Pelly's articles for the *Baffler* and other magazines, David Turner's newsletter *Penny Fractions*, and Cherie Hu's *Water and Music*.
32 Dolan, "Musicology in the Garden," 88.
33 Daughtry, "Did Music Cause?"
34 Fleischer, "If the Song Has No Price," 154.

One. Streaming Music

1 JioSaavn, home page, accessed 30 November 2022, https://www.jiosaavn.com/corporate; Tidal, home page, accessed 16 April 2021, https://tidal.com.
2 Amazon Music, "Amazon Music FAQs," accessed 30 November 2022, https://www.amazon.com/b?node=15730321011; Apple Music, home page, accessed 30 November 2022, https://www.apple.com/apple-music/; JioSaavn, home page.
3 Apple, "Introducing Apple Music—All the Ways You Love Music. All in One Place," 8 June 2015, https://www.apple.com/newsroom/2015/06/08Introducing-Apple-Music-All-The-Ways-You-Love-Music-All-in-One-Place-/.
4 See, for instance, Napster, home page, accessed 17 June 2019, https://us.napster.com/home.html; Idagio, home page, accessed 17 June 2019, https://www.idagio.com/us/; Pandora, home page, accessed 17

June 2019, https://www.pandora.com. On this trope, see Gopinath and Stanyek, "Anytime, Anywhere?"

5   Pandora, home page.
6   Deezer, home page.
7   Boomplay, home page, accessed 26 January 2020, https://www.boomplaymusic.com/.
8   On this point, see Steingo, "Sound and Circulation."
9   McGowan, *Capitalism and Desire*, 149.
10 Born, "On Musical Mediation," 7.
11 On the stream as a "single-use product," see Anderson, "Stream Capture."
12 Frith, "Copyright and the Music Business," 57.
13 On Deezer, see Fanen, *Boulevard du stream*, 228. On Grooveshark, see Eliot van Buskirk, "EMI Drops Suit against Grooveshark Music Service, Licenses It Instead," *Wired*, 13 October 2009, https://www.wired.com/2009/10/emi-drops-suit-against-grooveshark-music-service-licenses-it-instead/. On Baidu, see Haseeb Ali, "Baidu Inks Distribution Deal with Major Record Labels," *SNL Kagan and Communications Report*, 21 July 2011. On Spotify, see Maria Eriksson et al., *Spotify Teardown*, 42–43.
14 Rogers, *Death and Life*, 85–86.
15 David Pakman, quoted in Kim Hart, "Breaking the Law to Get a Break: Social Site Partners with Music Label That Sued It," *Washington Post*, 21 March 2008, D1.
16 Stephen Carlisle, "The Music Modernization Act: What's in It, Why Is It in There, and Is It a Good Thing?," 16 November 2018, http://copyright.nova.edu/music-modernization-act/. See also Sam Backer, "Streamlining the Streaming Regime," *Baffler*, 19 January 2021, https://thebaffler.com/latest/streamlining-the-streaming-regime-backer.
17 Eight Mile Style, LLC, et al. v. Spotify USA, Inc., No. 3:19-cv-00736 (M.D. Tenn. Aug. 21, 2019).
18 Jem Aswad and Chris Williams, "Spotify, Google, Pandora, Amazon Go to U.S. Appeals Court to Overturn Royalty Increase," *Variety*, 7 March 2019, https://variety.com/2019/music/news/spotify-google-and-pandora-go-to-u-s-appeals-court-to-overturn-royalty-increase-exclusive-1203157697/; Jem Aswad, "Hit Songwriters Slam Spotify's Attempt to Lower Royalties: 'You Used Us,'" *Variety*, 9 April 2019, https://variety.com/2019/biz/news/spotify-secret-genius-songwriters-lower-royalties-1203184870/.
19 Justin Tranter (@tranterjustin), Instagram, 7 March 2019, https://www.instagram.com/p/Buu6JEXlleB/.
20 For more on the importance of EULAS to digital music platforms, see Anderson, *Popular Music*, 26–27.
21 Rossiter, *Software, Infrastructure, Labor*, 5.
22 Morris, *Selling Digital Music*, 2.

23 Morris, *Selling Digital Music*, 34–35.
24 Sterne, "What's Digital in Digital Music?," 99; Sinnreich, *Mashed Up*.
25 Powers, "Lost in the Shuffle"; See also Morris, *Selling Digital Music*, 63.
26 Micah Singleton, "Tidal Will Make 'Master' Quality Recordings Available to Its HiFi Subscribers," *The Verge*, 5 January 2017, https://www.theverge.com/2017/1/5/14171748/tidal-master-level-recordings-high-res-audio-hifi.
27 Yanggratoke et al., "Predicting Response Times"; Eriksson et al., *Spotify Teardown*, 89–90.
28 On this point see Hu, *Prehistory of the Cloud*, 4.
29 Bob Keaveney, "Why Pandora Is Moving Its Data to the Cloud," *Biz Tech*, April 2019, https://biztechmagazine.com/article/2019/04/why-pandora-moving-its-data-cloud-1.
30 Xavier Biseul, "Les coulisses techniques de Deezer," *Journal du Net*, 25 January 2016, https://www.journaldunet.com/solutions/cloud-computing/1171716-les-coulisses-techniques-de-deezer/.
31 On Pandora, see Keaveney, "Why Pandora Is Moving Its Data"; on Spotify, see Jordan Novet, "Spotify Said It's Relying More on Google's Cloud Even as the Companies Compete in Music Streaming," *CNBC*, 28 February 2018, https://www.cnbc.com/2018/02/28/spotify-is-relying-googles-cloud-according-to-ipo-filing.html.
32 Jamie Carter, "A Tale of Two Internets: How Content Delivery Networks Are Guzzling Up the Web," *Tech Radar*, 1 July 2017, https://www.techradar.com/news/a-tale-of-two-internets-how-content-delivery-networks-are-guzzling-up-the-web.
33 "Cisco Visual Networking Index: Forecast and Trends, 2017–2022," 27 February 2019, https://www.cisco.com/c/en/us/solutions/collateral/service-provider/visual-networking-index-vni/white-paper-c11-741490.html.
34 Devine, *Decomposed*, 28.
35 Devine, *Decomposed*, 29; see also Eriksson, "Online Music Distribution," 26.
36 Spotify, *Sustainability and Social Impact Report 2018*, 28 February 2019, https://s29.q4cdn.com/175625835/files/doc_downloads/gov-docs/2018-Spotify-Sustainability-Report-FINAL.pdf; Spotify, *Equity and Impact Report 2021*, 31 March 2022, https://www.lifeatspotify.com/reports/Spotify-Equity-Impact-Report-2021.pdf.
37 Also excluded from Spotify's calculations is the energy required to run user devices.
38 Spotify, "Energy," artist page, accessed 14 January 2020, https://open.spotify.com/artist/7r1iWhA4kNyYvnBgEcAMfO?si=MYIzsejJSYKtb5J236Qodw. Since 2020, Energy's artist page has been disambiguated, which is good news for the band and its

fans. See Spotify, "Energy," artist page, accessed 30 April 2023, https://open.spotify.com/artist/1rmfnfmeR6oZoZdb7YmTOp?si=FAffUhyMRW2wg3SDpE28hg. The older artist page still exists, however, with its eclectic mix of energy-related song titles or artist names. See Spotify, "Energy," artist page, accessed 30 April 2023, https://open.spotify.com/artist/7r1iWhA4kNyYvnBgEcAMfO?si=gtbeSis-Qgejfdsdtxx9Uw. Nevertheless, the broader phenomenon that Energy's artist page previously embodied persists elsewhere on Spotify and other platforms. Consider Spotify's artist page for the Réunionnais séga group Progression, two of whose top tracks (as of early 2023) are songs by the EDM producer Tiësto, and two of whose top releases are by a 1990s breakbeat group by the same name. See Spotify, "Progression," artist page, accessed 30 April 2023, https://open.spotify.com/artist/4PGVD4TtOm5BqcAnumBqPH.

39   Bagley, *Extensions of Programming Language Concepts*, 26.
40   Eriksson, "Close Reading Big Data."
41   ISWC Network, home page, accessed 2 January 2020, http://www.iswc.org/.
42   Morris, *Selling Digital Music*, 86.
43   Muikku, *Metadata of Digital Music Files*, 9.
44   Dani Deahl, "Metadata Is the Biggest Little Problem Plaguing the Music Industry," *The Verge*, 29 May 2019, https://www.theverge.com/2019/5/29/18531476/music-industry-song-royalties-metadata-credit-problems.
45   See Morris, *Selling Digital Music*, 74.
46   In the case of CDDB, the metadata fields filled out by users were uploaded to a central database. CDs would then be compared to the listings in the database, and if a recording's timings matched, it was identified as this CD and no other, on the assumption that no two discs would have identical track timings. See Morris, *Selling Digital Music*, 71–72.
47   On the MSN Music Search Engine, see Christopher Weare, in Dannenberg et al., "Panel: New Directions," 3–4. On Pandora's Music Genome Project, see Tim Westergren, "Music Genome Project," 26 November 2005, https://web.archive.org/web/20051126033548/http://www.pandora.com/mgp.shtml.
48   For labels, music analytics promise to rationalize the vagaries of artist and repertoire (A&R) development, potentially reducing labor costs. See Cherie Hu, "A&R Moneyball Is Hotter than Ever. But Will It Actually Improve the Music Business?," *Music Business Worldwide*, 25 October 2018, https://www.musicbusinessworldwide.com/ar-moneyball-is-hotter-than-ever-but-will-it-actually-improve-the-music-business/.
49   Darrell Etherington, "Spotify Acquires the Echo Nest, Gaining Control of the Music DNA Company That Powers its Rivals," *TechCrunch*, 6 March 2014, https://techcrunch.com/2014/03/06/spotify-acquires-the-echo-nest/.

50   Niclas Molinder, "Why Building More Rights Databases Won't Solve the Music Industry Metadata Problem," *Hypebot*, 30 January 2018, https://www.hypebot.com/hypebot/2018/01/why-building-more-rights-databases-wont-solve-the-music-industry-metadata-problem.html; https://auddly.com/about/, accessed 9 January 2020.
51   Molinder, "Why Building More Rights Databases."
52   Molinder, "Why Building More Rights Databases."
53   DDEX, "Frequently Asked Questions," accessed 9 January 2020, https://ddex.net/implementation/frequently-asked-questions/.
54   DDEX, home page, accessed 9 January 2020, https://ddex.net/.
55   Wikipedia, s.v. "Porn groove," accessed 9 January 2020, https://en.wikipedia.org/wiki/Porn_groove.
56   DDEX, "Frequently Asked Questions," https://ddex.net/implementation/frequently-asked-questions/.
57   "How Broken Metadata Affects the Music Industry (and What We Can Do about It)?," *Soundcharts*, 15 July 2019, https://soundcharts.com/blog/music-metadata.
58   These figures are cited in Muikku, *Metadata of Digital Music Files*, 9.
59   On project-based employment in the arts, see Faulkner and Anderson, "Short-Term Projects," 87. See also Menger, *Le travail créateur*, 338 and passim.
60   See McKelvey and Hunt, "Discoverability."
61   Johnson, "Analyzing Genre," 130–31.
62   Peterson and Simkus, "How Musical Taste."
63   See, in this regard, Johnson's comparison of the paths charted by "related artists" for Nicki Minaj versus groups such as the Talking Heads or Tame Impala. Johnson, "Analyzing Genre," 139.
64   For a related discussion of how music metadata reproduce racialized, gendered, and classed categories via Spotify's annual Valentine's Day playlists, see van Bohemen, Schaap, and Berkers, "Sex Playlist." See also Werner, "Organizing Music, Organizing Gender"; and Seaver, "Seeing Like an Infrastructure."
65   Victoria Young, "Strategic UX: The Art of Reducing Friction," *Telepathy*, 10 February 2015, https://web.archive.org/web/20160306220513/http://www.dtelepathy.com/blog/business/strategic-ux-the-art-of-reducing-friction. Young's claim is cited approvingly in Hartson and Pyla, *UX Book*, 814.
66   Mat Budelman and Mark Kizelshteyn, "Three Principles for Designing ML-Powered Products," *Spotify Design*, October 2019, https://spotify.design/article/three-principles-for-designing-ml-powered-products.
67   Budelman and Kizelshteyn, "Three Principles."
68   Budelman and Kizelshteyn, "Three Principles."

69 Linda Tischler, "Spotify Unveils a Bold New Brand Identity," *Fast Company*, 12 March 2015, https://www.fastcompany.com/3043547/spotifys-new-look-signals-its-identity-shift.

70 Stanley Wood, "Design Doesn't Scale," *Medium*, 26 July 2016, https://medium.com/@hellostanley/design-doesnt-scale-4d81e12cbc3e.

71 Michelle Kadir, quoted in Rebecca Greenfield, "Inside the Redesign: Why Spotify Went Black," *Fast Company*, 2 April 2014, https://www.fastcompany.com/3028603/inside-the-redesign-why-spotify-went-black.

72 Kadir, quoted in Greenfield, "Inside the Redesign."

73 Kadir, quoted in Greenfield, "Inside the Redesign."

74 On this point, see Baade, "Lean Back."

75 Khamis, "The Aestheticization of Restraint."

76 Amazon Music, "Spa Day," playlist, accessed 30 April 2023, https://music.amazon.com/playlists/B01LWLW14O.

77 See, for instance, Scott Timberg, "It's Not Just David Byrne and Radiohead: Spotify, Pandora, and How Streaming Music Kills Classical and Jazz," *Salon*, 21 July 2014, https://www.salon.com/test/2014/07/20/its_not_just_david_byrne_and_radiohead_spotify_pandora_and_how_streaming_music_kills_jazz_and_classical; and Becky Roberts, "How Streaming Saved the Music Industry but Left Some Genres Behind," *What Hi-Fi?*, 13 June 2019, https://www.whathifi.com/us/features/rip-classical-music-how-spotify-saved-the-music-industry-but-left-some-genres-behind.

78 Jean Cook, "Invisible Genres and Metadata: How Digital Services Fail Classical and Jazz Musicians, Composers, and Fans," *Future of Music Coalition*, 13 October 2013, http://futureofmusic.org/article/article/invisible-genres-metadata.

79 Cook, "Invisible Genres and Metadata."

80 Anonymous, "Musician Credits Specifically for Jazz Music," Spotify Community Forum, accessed 31 January 2020, https://community.spotify.com/t5/Live-Ideas/Musician-credits-specifically-for-jazz-music/idi-p/4669959.

81 Craig Havighurst, "The Devaluation of Music: It's Worse Than You Think," *Medium*, 11 October 2015, https://medium.com/cuepoint/the-devaluation-of-music-it-s-worse-than-you-think-f4cf5f26a888.

82 Christian Harper, "Adding Album Credits and Liner Notes to Streaming Music Services," accessed 31 January 2020, https://www.change.org/p/spotify-adding-album-credits-and-liner-note-to-streaming-music-services.

83 Morris, *Selling Digital Music*, 17.

84 Such Kleinian splitting of technologies into good and bad objects is commonplace, with digital media routinely placed in the latter category. See Prior, *Popular Music*, 82.

85 Zielinski, "Art and Apparatus."
86 Zielinski, "Art and Apparatus."
87 Galloway, *Interface Effect*.
88 This drive is not a new one. In the late 1990s, media theorists Jay Bolter and Richard Grusin already described the quest among designers to develop "interfaceless" interfaces. See Bolter and Grusin, *Remediation*, 3.
89 A case in point is the fantasy of the "zero button music player" envisaged by Paul Lamere (formerly of the Echo Nest), which would minimize "the interactions necessary to get good music to play." See Paul Lamere, "The Zero Button Music Player," *Music Machinery*, 14 January 2014, https://musicmachinery.com/2014/01/14/the-zero-button-music-player-2/.
90 One might think of this as a consumption-side version of Baumol and Bowen's "cost disease," the difference being that it involves limits not on the productivity of labor but of leisure (i.e., how much can be consumed in a certain period of time). The cost disease is discussed at greater length in chapters 4 and 5. See Baumol and Bowen, *Performing Arts*; Baumol, *The Cost Disease*.
91 Dan Kopf, "The Economics of Streaming Is Making Songs Shorter," *Quartz*, 17 January 2019, https://qz.com/1519823/is-spotify-making-songs-shorter/. A study of German musicians indicates that some have consciously adapted to this demand for brevity: "I produce songs … so that they are ideally short. And that you, of course, need to try and catch the listener with something in the first five seconds." Quoted in Mühlbach and Arora, "Behind the Music."
92 Robinson, *Content Delivery Networks*, 13.
93 Robinson, *Content Delivery Networks*, 14.
94 Robinson, *Content Delivery Networks*, 10–12.
95 Robinson, *Content Delivery Networks*, 14
96 Robinson, *Content Delivery Networks*, 14.
97 Robinson, *Content Delivery Networks*, 14.
98 Austerberry, *Technology of Video and Audio Streaming*, 7.
99 Austerberry, *Technology of Video and Audio Streaming*, 8.
100 On the anachronism of treating older broadcast media as streaming media, see Morris and Powers, "Control, Curation, and Musical Experience," 2.
101 Sony Music, "Digital Audio/Video Distribution Agreement." The leaked contract was first published by *The Verge*, before Sony issued a takedown notice. Nonetheless, copies can still be found online. See Micah Singleton, "This Was Sony Music's Contract with Spotify," *The Verge*, 19 May 2015, https://www.theverge.com/2015/5/19/8621581/sony-music-spotify-contract.
102 Sony Music, "Digital Audio/Video Distribution Agreement," 14.
103 Sony Music, "Digital Audio/Video Distribution Agreement," 14.

104 Sterne, *MP3*, 9.
105 Williams, *Television*, 86.
106 Morris and Powers, "Control, Curation, and Musical Experience," 2.
107 Morris and Powers, "Control, Curation, and Musical Experience," 2.
108 Fisher, *Nature of Capital and Income*, 51.
109 European Commission et al., *System of National Accounts 2008*, ch. 3 ("Stocks, Flows, and Accounting Rules").
110 Hill, "On Goods and Services," 318.
111 Hill, "On Goods and Services," 318.
112 Hill, "Tangibles, Intangibles, and Services," 437.
113 Hill, "On Goods and Services," 319.
114 Tsing, "Supply Chains and the Human Condition." On special economic zones, see Easterling, *Extrastatecraft*, ch. 1.
115 For instance, the subtitle to Tim Anderson's *Popular Music in a Digital Music Economy* describes the contemporary record industry as an "emerging service industry"; Anderson, *Popular Music*. See also Dörr et al., "Music as a Service"; Arditi, "Digital Subscriptions"; Wikström, *Music Industry*, ch. 3; and Mueller, *Media Piracy*, 72–73.
116 Mueller, *Media Piracy*, 72.
117 Mueller, *Media Piracy*, 73.
118 Sony Music, "Digital Audio/Video Distribution Agreement."
119 Spotify AB, System and method for early media buffering using detection of user behavior, US Patent 2017/0048563, filed 27 October 2016, and issued 16 February 2017.
120 Haßlinger, "Efficiency of Caching," 74.
121 See Meinel and Sack, *Internetworking*, 783.
122 Aegidius, "Music Streaming Metaphor," 53.
123 See Anderson, *Popular Music*, 68–69.
124 As David Arditi puts it, possession of a recording means that "we can listen to it for as long as the recording will continue to play." Arditi, "Digital Subscriptions," 305.
125 This isn't a novel point. See, for instance, Eisenberg, *Recording Angel*, ch. 2 ("Music becomes a thing").
126 According to Attali, "People buy more records than they can listen to. They stockpile what they want to find the time to hear." Attali, *Noise*, 101. Historical and ethnographic studies of record collecting paint a less pathologizing portrait of the practice. See, for instance, Straw, "Sizing Up Record Collections"; and Shuker, *Wax Trash and Vinyl Treasures*.
127 See, in this connection, Anderson's gloss on Attali's treatment of stockpiling, which extends the concept beyond individual listeners (Attali's focus) to analyze its utility for media companies as a hedge against risk. Anderson, *Making Easy Listening*, 20–23.
128 Dymski and Elliott, "Taxonomy of Primary Exploitation," 344.

129   See, for instance, Graeber, *Debt*; Lazzarato, *Governing by Debt*; Soederberg, *Debtfare States*.
130   Lazzarato, *Governing by Debt*, 87.
131   Harvey, *Marx, Capital and the Madness of Economic Reason*, 40.
132   See Guyer, "Obligation, Binding, Debt and Responsibility." For an account that complicates received notions of debt's temporality, see Adkins, *Time of Money*, ch. 3 ("The Speculative Time of Debt").
133   Lazzarato, *Making of Indebted Man*, 30.
134   Other inducements include the bundling of subscriptions with cell phone plans; see Arditi, "Digital Subscriptions," 313.
135   Srnicek, *Platform Capitalism*, 72.
136   Alexandra Schwartz, "Rent the Runway Wants to Lend You Your Look," *New Yorker*, 22 October 2018, 44–49; Tatyana Bellamy-Walker, "You Already Have Subscriptions for Movies and Diapers. Why Not the Couch?," *Inc.*, 19 February 2020, https://www.inc.com/tatyana-bellamy-walker/jay-reno-feather-disrupting-ownership-furniture-rental.html.
137   See, for instance, Warrillow, *Automatic Customer*; Tzuo, *Subscribed*.
138   Ashley Lutz, "Millennials Don't Care about Owning Anything and It's Destroying Traditional Retail," *Business Insider*, 28 May 2015, https://www.businessinsider.com/millennials-are-renting-instead-of-buying-2015-5/.
139   Srnicek, *Platform Capitalism*, 72
140   This list is derived from Warrillow, *Automatic Customer*, ch. 2 ("Why You Need Automatic Customers").
141   Warrillow, *Automatic Customer*.
142   Marx, *Capital*, 1:719.
143   Marx, *Capital*, 1:719.
144   On the relative value of platform data and promotion versus royalty payments to artists, see Mühlbach and Arora, "Behind the Music."
145   Mark Mulligan, "What's the Value of Exposure When Exposure Is All There Is?," Midia Research, 6 May 2020, https://www.midiaresearch.com/blog/what-is-the-value-of-exposure-when-exposure-is-all-there-is.
146   Mulligan, "What's the Value of Exposure."
147   Aegidius, "Music Streaming Metaphor," 42.

Two. Streaming Capital

1   David Bowie, quoted in Jon Pareles, "David Bowie, 21st-Century Entrepreneur," *New York Times*, 9 June 2002.
2   On Chopin, see Eideldinger, *Chopin*, xxvi. A modern pop song using the metaphor is Michel Polnareff's 1981 record "Radio" ("Ça chante et ça prose / Ça coule comme de l'eau / Jour et nuit /Radio"). For contemporary musicology, see Kramer, *Why Classical Music Still Matters*, 27.

3. Bowie, in Pareles, "David Bowie, 21st-Century Entrepreneur."
4. Gavin Castleton, "The Fallacy of Music Like Water," *Hypebot*, 29 February 2012, https://www.hypebot.com/hypebot/2012/02/the-music-like-water-fallacy.html. See also Andrew Dubber, "Music Like Water Revisited," *New Music Strategies*, 26 October 2007, https://newmusicstrategies.com/?s=water.
5. Mark Mulligan, "The Rise of New Streaming Markets: Midem 2019," Midia Research, 4 June 2019, YouTube video, https://www.youtube.com/watch?v=7GqLcHiHjvY.
6. Kusek and Leonhard, *Future of Music*.
7. Daniel Ek, quoted in Stephanie Busari, "Spotify Founder: I'm Not Music Industry's Savior," CNN, 8 December 2011, https://www.cnn.com/2011/12/08/tech/web/spotify-daniel-ek/index.html.
8. Historically, this process has been understood in terms of the commodification of audiences (or audience attention), though as argued later it is better understood in terms of assetization and rent extraction. The foundational texts are Smythe, "Communications," and Smythe, *Dependency Road*, ch. 2. For extensions of this process to digital media, see Fuchs, "Dallas Smythe and Digital Labor." For a corrective to audience commodification theories, which conceptualizes the relation in terms of rent, see Prey, "'Now Playing. You.'"
9. Kopytoff, "The Cultural Biography of Things," 64.
10. On this point, see Hammel, "Music, the Realist Conception," 48–49.
11. See Adorno, "Fetish-Character in Music" and "On Popular Music," in *Essays on Music*; and Horkheimer and Adorno, *Dialectic of Enlightenment*.
12. Kusek and Leonhard, *Future of Music*, 7 and 6.
13. Heidegger, *Question concerning Technology*, 3–35.
14. Kusek and Leonhard, *Future of Music*, 9.
15. Kusek and Leonhard, *Future of Music*, 9.
16. See Midnight Notes Collective, "Introduction to the New Enclosures."
17. Kusek and Leonhard, *Future of Music*, 11.
18. Kusek and Leonhard, *Future of Music*, 9.
19. Kusek and Leonhard, *Future of Music*, 18.
20. See Bogost and Montfort, "Platform Studies"; Helmond, "Platformization of the Web"; Langley and Leyshon, "Platform Capitalism"; Srnicek, *Platform Capitalism*; van Dijck, Poell, and de Waal, *Platform Society*.
21. Gillespie, "Politics of 'Platforms.'"
22. Rochet and Tirole, "Platform Competition"; Eisenmann, Parker, and Van Alstyne, "Strategies for Two-Sided Markets"; and Gawer, *Platforms, Markets, and Innovation*.
23. On "network effects," see Parker, Van Alstyne, and Choudary, *Platform Revolution*, 16–34; Evans and Schmalensee, *Matchmakers*, ch. 2; and Moazed and Johnson, *Modern Monopolies*, ch. 7. For critical perspec-

tives, see McChesney, *Digital Disconnect*, 132–33; Srnicek, *Platform Capitalism*, 45–46; Langley and Leyshon, "Platform Capitalism"; Khan, "Amazon's Antitrust Paradox," 785–86; and Larson, *Bit Tyrants*, ch. 1.

24 Eriksson et al., *Spotify Teardown*, 14 and 156.
25 Eriksson et al., *Spotify Teardown*, 156.
26 As, for instance, in Rochet and Tirole, "Platform Competition"; and Eisenmann, Parker, and Van Alstyne, "Strategies for Two-Sided Markets."
27 See, for instance, Rosa, *Social Acceleration*, 162–63.
28 Adkins, Cooper, and Konings, *Asset Economy*, 13.
29 Adkins, Cooper, and Konings, *Asset Economy*, 15.
30 Alex Webb, "Bob Dylan's Latest Tune Is 'Hey Mr. Cash Machine Man,'" *Washington Post*, 8 December 2020, https://www.washingtonpost.com/business/bob-dylans-latest-tune-is-hey-mr-cash-machine-man/2020/12/07/09cfdefa-38b4-11eb-aad9-8959227280c4_story.html.
31 Hipgnosis, home page, accessed 14 June 2022, https://www.hipgnosissongs.com/; Andy Lewis, "Song Catalogs Are Selling for Big Bucks, but Will the Trend End on a Bum Note?," *LA Magazine*, 14 June 2021, https://www.lamag.com/culturefiles/song-catalogs-sales/; Brian Croce, "Michigan Retirement Likes the Sound of Its Concord Music Stake," *Pensions and Investments*, 29 April 2019, https://www.pionline.com/article/20190429/PRINT/190429867/michigan-retirement-likes-the-sound-of-its-concord-music-stake.
32 Moulier Boutang, *Cognitive Capitalism*, 140–41.
33 See Doganova, "Discounting the Future."
34 Perelman, "Rise of Guard Labor."
35 Cohen, "Commodifying Free Labor Online," 179. See also Mosco, *Political Economy of Communication*, 150–51.
36 The traditional split between major labels and artists for album sales is 85/15, whereas for licensing it is closer to 50/50. See Cooke, *Dissecting the Digital Dollar*, 84. This is part of a longer history of record labels' dubious (and exploitative) accounting practices. See Passman, *All You Need to Know*, 77–94.
37 Data for the market share of major labels are derived from Ed Christman, "2019 Nielsen Music Report," *Billboard*, 11 January 2020, 16. Data for the market share of streaming platforms are derived from Mark Mulligan, "Music Subscriber Market Shares H1 2019," Midia Research, 5 December 2019, https://www.midiaresearch.com/blog/music-subscriber-market-shares-h1-2019/.
38 For independent labels, the Merlin network offers similar leverage. See https://merlinnetwork.org/, accessed 3 May 2023.
39 Tim Ingham, "Spotify Is on a Collision Course with the Major Record Companies. Here's Why," *Music Business Worldwide*, 14 August 2018, https://www.musicbusinessworldwide.com/spotify-is-on-a-road-to

-collision-with-the-record-industry-heres-why/; Daniel Peters, "Spotify, Amazon, and Pandora Reportedly Proposing Lower Streaming Royalty Rates to US Copyright Royalty Board," *NME*, 25 October 2021, https://www.nme.com/news/music/spotify-amazon-and-pandora-reportedly-proposing-lower-streaming-royalty-rates-to-us-copyright-royalty-board-3078300.

40 See DeWaard, "Derivative Media," 108–15; DeWaard, "Wall Street's Content Wars"; and David Turner, "How Private Finance Drained the Record Industry," *Penny Fractions* 127, 13 May 2020, https://pennyfractions.ghost.io/how-private-equity-drained-the-record-industry/.

41 For a useful overview, see Cooke, *Dissecting the Digital Dollar*, 65–68.

42 Beer, *Metric Power*.

43 Micah Singleton, "This was Sony Music's contract with Spotify," *The Verge*, 19 May 2015, https://www.theverge.com/2015/5/19/8621581/sony-music-spotify-contract.

44 András Ronái makes a similar point in noting that platforms base their appeals to consumers on "a *general idea of music*." Ronái, "Frictionless Platforms, Frictionless Music," 109. While platforms have occasionally used artist exclusives to lure users to their services—a tactic that has the added bonus of "generat[ing] a torrent of data" in the process, as Leslie Meier and Vincent Manzerolle point out—these are the exceptions that prove the rule. See Meier and Manzerolle, "Rising Tides?," 544. On the role of aggregators, see Galuszka, "Music Aggregators and Intermediation"; and Eriksson et al., *Spotify Teardown*, 91–99.

45 Spotify, "Amplifying Artist Input in Your Personalized Recommendations," 2 November 2020, https://newsroom.spotify.com/2020-11-02/amplifying-artist-input-in-your-personalized-recommendations/.

46 Charleton Lamb, cited in Stuart Dredge, "Spotify's New Artist Tool Could Boost Streams (with a Discounted Royalty Rate)," *MusicAlly*, 2 November 2020, https://musically.com/2020/11/02/spotify-artist-tool-boost-streams-discounted-royalty-rate/.

47 Eriksson et al., *Spotify Teardown*, 164.

48 Spotify, "Our Business Model" (video), Investor Day, March 2018, https://investors.spotify.com/events/investor-day-march-2018/default.aspx.

49 Spotify, "The Big Picture" (video), Investor Day, March 2018, https://investors.spotify.com/events/investor-day-march-2018/default.aspx.

50 Spotify, "The Big Picture."

51 McChesney, *Digital Disconnect*, 132.

52 Prey, "Locating Power in Platformization," 4.

53 Such was the case with Rdio, which filed for bankruptcy in 2015. See Janko Roettgers, "Fight Songs," *Variety* 330, no. 4 (2015): 72, 74.

54 Jodi Dean, "Neofeudalism: The End of Capitalism?," *Los Angeles Review of Books*, 12 May 2020, https://lareviewofbooks.org/article/neofeudalism

-the-end-of-capitalism/; Graeber, *Debt*, 95–98; Schrift, *Logic of the Gift*; Satyal, *Rethinking Capitalist Development*; DeAngelis, *Omnia Communis Sunt*. On "accumulation by dispossession," see Harvey, "'New' Imperialism." On capital's dependence on expropriation as well as exploitation, see Fraser and Jaeggi, *Capitalism*, 30 ff. On the "diverse economies" hidden by capitalist hegemony, see Gibson-Graham, *Postcapitalist Politics*.

55 See DeAngelis, "Does Capital Need a Commons Fix?"
56 Perzanowski and Schultz, *End of Ownership*, 25–26.
57 Chuck Philips, "Used CD Sales Put Industry in a Spin," *Los Angeles Times*, 24 December 1992.
58 See Demers, *Steal This Music*; Macleod, *Freedom of Expression®*.
59 This distinction derives from Hubbs, "Digital Music and Public Goods," 141.
60 On this point, see Gillespie, *Wired Shut*; Burkart, *Music and Cyberliberties*; Perzanowski and Schultz, *End of Ownership*; and Scherzinger, "Towards a History," 51–57.
61 On tethering, see Scherzinger, "From Torrent to Stream."
62 On digitization's collapse of different moments of economic activity, see Kjøsen, "Accident of Value," 53.
63 Gillespie, *Wired Shut*, 51.
64 IFPI, *Connecting with Music: Music Consumer Insight Report*, September 2017, 19, accessed 23 July 2019, https://www.ifpi.org/downloads/Music-Consumer-Insight-Report-2017.pdf.
65 Bruce Naughton, "YouTubNow Offline as Music Industry Scores Two Wins vs Stream Rippers," *Hypebot*, 16 May 2019, https://www.hypebot.com/hypebot/2019/05/youtubnow-offline-as-music-industry-scores-two-wins-vs-stream-rippers.html.
66 Office of the United States Trade Representative, "2018 Out-of-Cycle Review of Notorious Markets," https://ustr.gov/sites/default/files/2018_Notorious_Markets_List.pdf.
67 See Sicker, Ohm, and Gunaji, "Analog Hole."
68 Fleischer, "If the Song Has No Price," 154. For the first ten-plus years of Spotify's existence the fee was stable at a fixed monthly price of 9.99 USD/EUR/GBP for an individual subscription. However, postpandemic inflationary pressures have led Spotify executives to hint that a price hike is inevitable. But at the time of writing, such an increase in the subscription fee has yet to be implemented.
69 Fleischer, "If the Song Has No Price," 154.
70 Fleischer, "If the Song Has No Price," 158.
71 Sterne, *MP3*, 208–18.
72 See, in this connection, Leyshon, *Reformatted*, ch. 3.
73 Sterne, *MP3*, 214.
74 Hagen, "Playlist Experience," 643.

75 Krueger, *Rockonomics*, 189.
76 Hardin, "Tragedy of the Commons."
77 For a complementary account, see Hubbs, "Digital Music and Public Goods," 146.
78 A similar argument is made in David Turner, "Streaming Saved the Record Biz, Not Artists," *Penny Fractions* 126, 29 April 2020, https://pennyfractions.ghost.io/streaming-saved-the-record-biz-not-artists/.
79 Moore, *Capitalism in the Web of Life*, 64.
80 See for instance Stahl, *Unfree Masters*.
81 Smith, *Inquiry*, 34.
82 Smith, *Inquiry*, 34.
83 Ricardo, *On the Principles*, 56.
84 Say, *Treatise on Political Economy*, 9.
85 On water as an "uncooperative commodity," see Bakker, *Uncooperative Commodity*.
86 DeAngelis, *Omnia Communis Sunt*, 39.
87 Kusek and Leonhard, *Future of Music*, 12.
88 Linton, *What Is Water?*, 3.
89 Linton, *What Is Water?*, 3.
90 Helfrich, "Common Goods Don't Simply Exist," 62.
91 Kusek and Leonhard, *Future of Music*, 8. To their credit, Kusek and Leonhard acknowledge the reality of water scarcity. To their discredit, they consign this problem to the past and to other parts of the world: "If we zoom back to the days before water was ubiquitously available (and ubiquitously paid for), some people *did* have to pay right then and there to obtain their water.... Fights broke out over access to water, and in Africa and the Middle East, many wars were fought over access to water." Kusek and Leonhard, *Future of Music*, 9–10. Leaving aside the implication that struggles over water rights concern only nonwhite, non-Western populations, Kusek and Leonhard also err in consigning water scarcity to the past. On the contrary: it is a future that capitalism all but guarantees for us, given the depletion of freshwater reserves and transgression of other ecological limits. See Bellamy Foster, Clark, and York, *Ecological Rift*, 17.
92 Marx, *Capital*, 1:1044.
93 For a defense of this distinction's utility in understanding artistic production, see Beech, *Art and Value*, 252–55. For an interpretation that rejects not just the productive/unproductive distinction but also Marx's thought as a resource for "understanding cultural commodities as commodities," see Taylor, *Music and Capitalism*, 21.
94 If certain kinds of work are difficult to render as abstract labor, however, this is largely due to their sociohistorical definition and not to some fixed attribute. For instance, the importance attached to individual expression in post-Romantic ideologies of art is what makes artistic

work premised on this ideology hard to square with abstract labor qua "undifferentiated human labor" (Marx, *Capital*, 1:150).

95 See, in this connection, Kassabian's remarks on the "sourcelessness" of ubiquitous music. Kassabian, *Ubiquitous Listening*, 9–10.

96 Morris and Powers, "Control, Curation, and Musical Experience," 108.

97 On music's affordances for social reproduction, see my "Music in the Work"; Thompson, "Your Womb"; and Thompson, "Sounding the Arcane."

98 According to Mühlbach and Arora, the contributions musicians make to streaming platforms resemble the "free labor" of users, given that "payment to the producer tends towards zero." Mühlbach and Arora, "Behind the Music."

99 La Berge, "Decommodified Labor."

100 Alexander Billet, "A New Union of Musicians Is Taking on Spotify," *Jacobin*, 12 April 2021, https://www.jacobinmag.com/2021/04/union-musicians-allied-workers-spotify-streaming; Nile Rodgers, "Music Makers to Congress: We Are Family," *The Hill*, 9 June 2016, https://thehill.com/blogs/congress-blog/labor/282716-music-makers-to-congress-we-are-family; Bruce Houghton, "Songwriters Urge Users to #CancelSpotify," *Hypebot*, 10 April 2019, https://www.hypebot.com/hypebot/2019/04/songwriters-urge-users-to-cancelspotify.html; Shawn Reynaldo, "Pull Your Music off Spotify," *First Floor*, 5 May 2020, https://firstfloor.substack.com/p/first-floor-36-pull-your-music-off.

101 Taylor Swift, "For Taylor Swift, the Future of Music Is a Love Story," *Wall Street Journal*, 7 July 2014. See also Jack Dickey, "Taylor Swift on 1989, Spotify, Her Next Tour, and Female Role Models," *Time*, 13 November 2014, https://time.com/3578249/taylor-swift-interview/.

102 See, for instance, the Fair Trade Music advocacy group: Fair Trade Music International, "In Today's Music Economy, What's Missing?," accessed 9 August 2019, https://www.fairtrademusicinternational.org/.

103 Alex Young, "Artist-Owned Streaming Service Tidal Promises to 'Re-establish the Value of Music,'" *Consequence of Sound*, 30 March 2015, https://consequenceofsound.net/2015/03/artist-owned-streaming-service-tidal-promises-to-to-re-establish-the-value-of-music/.

104 Fridell, "Fair-Trade Coffee," 100; Carrington, Zwick, and Neville, "Ideology of the Ethical Consumption Gap"; Gunderson, "Problems with the Defetishization Thesis," 116.

105 Swift, "For Taylor Swift, the Future of Music Is a Love Story."

106 Marshall, "Do People Value Recorded Music?," 148. Looking back at the pre-internet market for physical recordings, Marshall observes that beyond "the ability to play . . . music," the value consumers attached to physical recording stemmed as much from its material qualities, as well as its utility for self-presentation and identity construction. Marshall, "Do People Value Recorded Music?," 150.

107 Damon Krukowski, in Sasha Frere-Jones, "If You Care about Music, Should You Ditch Spotify?," *New Yorker*, 19 July 2013, https://www.newyorker.com/culture/sasha-frere-jones/if-you-care-about-music-should-you-ditch-spotify.

108 Damon Krukowski, "How to Be a Responsible Fan in the Age of Streaming," *Pitchfork*, 30 January 2018, https://pitchfork.com/features/oped/how-to-be-a-responsible-music-fan-in-the-age-of-streaming/.

109 One might think of this last possibility as a musical Meidner plan, after the (unsuccessful) Swedish policy that sought to transfer ownership of firms from capital to labor. See Guinan, "Socialising Capital." See also my discussion of this possibility in connection with AI-generated music, in "Copyright, Compensation, and Commons."

110 On this point, see Jappe, *Les aventures de la marchandise*, 127.

Three. Music as a Technology of Surveillance

Portions of this chapter were previously published as "Music as a Technology of Surveillance," *Journal of the Society for American Music* 12, no. 3 (2018): 233–67. © Cambridge University Press.

1 Daniel Ek, "SORRY," *Spotify News*, 21 August 2015, https://news.spotify.com/us/2015/08/21/sorry-2/.

2 A copy of the August 2015 privacy policy can be found at the Internet Archive. "Spotify Privacy Policy (Effective as of 19 August 2015)," https://web.archive.org/web/20150822032627/https://www.spotify.com/uk/legal/privacy-policy/.

3 Thomas Fox-Brewster, "Location, Sensors, Voice, Photos?! Spotify Just Got Real Creepy with the Data It Collects on You," *Forbes*, 20 August 2015, http://www.forbes.com/sites/thomasbrewster/2015/08/20/spotify-creepy-privacy-policy/; Gordon Gottsegen, "You Can't Do Squat about Spotify's Eerie New Privacy Policy," *Wired*, 20 August 2015, https://www.wired.com/2015/08/cant-squat-spotifys-eerie-new-privacy-policy/.

4 "Spotify Privacy Policy (Effective as of 19 August 2015)."

5 Amir Efrati, Scott Thurm, and Dionne Searcey, "Mobile App Makers Face U.S. Privacy Investigation," *Wall Street Journal*, 5 April 2011. An analysis of the Pandora mobile app from 2011 reported that it gathered information on the device's location, altitude, device brand, model, and IP address. Tyler Shields, "Mobile Apps Invading Your Privacy," *Veracode*, 5 April 2011, http://www.veracode.com/blog/2011/04/mobile-apps-invading-your-privacy/.

6 "Kanye West, Tidal Sued over Flip-Flopping on Exclusivity of 'Pablo,'" *Billboard*, 18 April 2016, http://www.billboard.com/articles/business/7334196/kanye-west-tidal-sued-exclusivity-the-life-of-pablo.

7 Gottsegen, "You Can't Do Squat."
8 Spotify press release cited in Green, "Is Spotify Crossing the Line with Its Creepy New Privacy Policy?," *Information Age*, 20 August 2015, https://www.information-age.com/spotify-crossing-line-its-creepy-new-privacy-policy-32644/.
9 "Spotify Privacy Policy (Effective as of 19 August 2015)."
10 Anderson, *Popular Music*, 27.
11 The concept of "surveillance capitalism" is a contested one. An influential approach regards this as a corruption of capitalism, with companies preying on rather than serving their customers; see Zuboff, *Age of Surveillance Capitalism*. For critiques of Zuboff, see Lauer, "Plastic Surveillance"; and Evgeny Morozov, "Capitalism's New Clothes," *Baffler*, 4 February 2019, https://thebaffler.com/latest/capitalisms-new-clothes-morozov. An alternative tradition, rooted in Marxism, regards surveillance as a long-standing feature of capital's relation to both consumers and workers. See Bellamy Foster and McChesney, "Surveillance Capitalism."
12 On the exploitation of user data by digital media companies more broadly, see Cohen, "Valorization of Surveillance"; Andrejevic, "Surveillance and Alienation." Work addressing music's participation in such processes is less extensive; important interventions include Anderson, *Popular Music*; Gopinath and Stanyek, "Tuning the Human Race"; Morris, *Selling Digital Music*; Prey, "'Now Playing. You,'"; Liz Pelly, "Big Mood Machine," *Baffler*, 10 June 2019, https://thebaffler.com/downstream/big-mood-machine-pelly.
13 Kayla Tausche, "Spotify Raises $350m at $8b Valuation" CNBC, 1 May 2015, http://www.cnbc.com/2015/05/01/spotify-raises-350-million-at-8-billion-valuation-sources.html; Andrew Flanagan, "Spotify Reportedly Secures Goldman Sachs Funding Amidst Rumors of Apple Offensive," *Billboard*, 4 May 2015, http://www.billboard.com/articles/business/6553850/spotify-reportedly-secures-goldman-sachs-funding-amidst-rumors-of-apple.
14 On this point, see Eriksson et al., *Spotify Teardown*, 164.
15 YCharts, "Spotify Technology SA (SPOT): Spotify Technology Market Cap," accessed 9 September 2022, https://ycharts.com/companies/SPOT/market_cap.
16 Cited in Robert Cookson, "Spotify's Revenues Double but Losses Widen," *Financial Times*, 23 May 2016, https://www.ft.com/content/b34cb170-2107-11e6-9d4d-c11776a5124d.
17 Stan Schroeder, "Spotify Lost $26.7 Million in 2009," *Mashable*, 22 November 2010, https://mashable.com/2010/11/22/spotify-loss-2009/.
18 Tim Ingham, "How Can Spotify Become Profitable?," *Music Business Worldwide*, 11 May 2015, http://www.musicbusinessworldwide.com/how-can-spotify-become-profitable/.

19 Spotify Technology S.A., "2019 Annual Report," https://s22.q4cdn.com/540910603/files/doc_financials/2019/ar/Spotify-2020-AGM-Annual-Report-on-Form-20-F.pdf.

20 Ingham, "Spotify Is on a Collision Course with the Major Record Companies. Here's Why," *Music Business Worldwide*, 14 August 2018, https://www.musicbusinessworldwide.com/spotify-is-on-a-road-to-collision-with-the-record-industry-heres-why/.

21 See Hwang, *Subprime Attention Crisis*, 89.

22 IAB Europe, "The Buyer's Guide to Digital Audio," November 2020, https://iabeurope.eu/knowledge-hub/iab-europe-buyers-guide-to-digital-audio/.

23 Alison Schiff, "Spotify Is Launching an Audience Network for Audio Ads," *AdExchanger*, 22 February 2021, https://www.adexchanger.com/audio/spotify-is-launching-an-audience-network-for-audio-ads/.

24 Chris Bryant, "Spotify's $26 Billion Value Is Hard to Put Your Finger On," *Bloomberg*, 9 April 2018, https://www.bloomberg.com/opinion/articles/2018-04-09/spotify-s-26-billion-value-is-hard-to-put-your-finger-on. On the role of intangible assets in the valuation of firms, see Moulier Boutang, *Cognitive Capitalism*, 32–33.

25 Joshua Brustein, "Spotify Hits 10 Million Paid Users. Now Can It Make Money?," *Bloomberg*, 22 May 2014, http://www.bloomberg.com/news/articles/2014-05-21/why-spotify-and-the-streaming-music-industry-cant-make-money.

26 See Anderson, *Popular Music*; Prey, "'Now Playing. You'"; Eriksson et al., *Spotify Teardown*; and Pelly, "Big Mood Machine."

27 Music's use as a technology of surveillance is hardly new; and as is more generally the case, the surveillance of consumers by businesses lags behind the surveillance of labor by capital. Significant in this regard has been the use of music not just as a means to manage the conduct of workers—say, by setting the tempo of labor—but also as a means of monitoring the labor being performed. Particularly under chattel slavery in the United States, work songs functioned as a way for overseers to gauge the pace, intensity, and quality of forced labor. On this point, see Cruz, *Culture on the Margins*, ch. 2. On the continuities between past efforts at monitoring and controlling African Americans and modern regimes of mass surveillance, see Browne, *Dark Matters*.

28 A more pronounced break can be seen with regard to record labels. When their main source of revenue came from the record sales, their interest in consumer behavior seldom extended beyond the point of purchase; see Anderson, *Popular Music*, 22; and Arditi, "Disciplining the Consumer," 174.

29 See, for instance, Parker, Van Alstyne, and Choudary, *Platform Revolution*.

30 Smythe, "Communications"; Smythe, *Dependency Road*, esp. ch. 2.

31 In an earlier article on which this chapter is based, I followed Smythe's position in many key respects, most important among them his treatment of audience attention as a commodity that is sold, rather than as an asset to which access is rented. This is a mischaracterization that the present chapter seeks to rectify.
32 Smythe, *Dependency Road*, 37–38.
33 Warner, *Publics and Counterpublics*, 88. See also Ang, *Desperately Seeking the Audience*, 5.
34 Warner, *Publics and Counterpublics*, 70.
35 See Brackett, *Categorizing Sound*.
36 Simpson, *Early 70s Radio*. See also Weisbard, *Top 40 Democracy*.
37 Meehan, "Ratings and the Institutional Approach." On efforts to measure web traffic and their role in Napster's failed attempt to transform itself into a viable enterprise, see Morris, *Selling Digital Music*, ch. 3.
38 Ang, *Desperately Seeking the Audience*, 34.
39 On telephone polling in early radio research, see Taylor, *Sounds of Capitalism*, 48–51; on audimeters, see Buzzard, *Tracking the Audience*, ch. 1; on Broadcast Data Systems, see McCourt and Rothenbuhler, "SoundScan and the Consolidation of Control"; and on "portable people meters," see Buzzard, *Tracking the Audience*, ch. 5.
40 Anderson, *Popular Music*, 28.
41 An extensive literature exists on the role of "free labor" in digital media. See Terranova, "Free Labor"; Andrejevic, "Exploiting YouTube"; Fuchs, *Social Media*. However, critics have observed that the equation of user activity with labor is misleading: the relation between platform and user doesn't feature the same degree of coercion as that between boss and worker, nor is there a systemic imperative to rationalize the "labor" of users; hence there is no real sense in which platforms exploit users. This doesn't mean, however, that users don't provide, gratis, use values that platforms benefit from. Users' labor may not be exploited, but the fruits of their activities are instead being expropriated (I explore the exploitation/expropriation distinction further in chapter 5).
42 Andrejevic, "Surveillance and Alienation," 284.
43 See Anderson, *Popular Music*, 18.
44 Crain, "Limits of Transparency."
45 Smythe, *Dependency Road*, 39. This distinction is important, since the gap between "audience power" and "audience labor" provides an opening where individuals can exercise agency. Much as the conversion of "labor power" into actual labor can be disrupted by forms of resistance (slowdowns, sabotage, work stoppages), so too can the conversion of "audience power" into "audience labor" (by muting ads, using ad-blocking software, zoning out, and so on).
46 Crain, "Limits of Transparency," 7.

47 See Gitelman and Jackson, "Introduction"; van Dijck, "Datafication, Dataism and Dataveillance."
48 Deleuze, "Postscript on the Societies of Control."
49 Ajay Kalia, cited in Alex Heath, "Spotify Is Getting Unbelievably Good at Picking Music—Here's an Inside Look at How," *Business Insider*, 3 September 2015, https://www.businessinsider.com/inside-spotify-and-the-future-of-music-streaming; see also my article "Why the Next Song Matters."
50 Coalition for Innovative Media Measurement, *Enriching Media Data: Quality is Key Requisite for Maximizing ROI*, June 2015, http://cimm-us.org/wp-content/uploads/2012/07/CIMM_Enriching-Media-Data-Quality-is-Key-for-ROI_June-2015I.pdf.
51 On this point, see Callon, Méadel, and Rabeharisoa, "Economy of Qualities."
52 Pandora's advertising web portal, for instance, announced that it had amassed more than a decade's worth of "listener signals," thereby enabling advertisers to "reach highly engaged and qualified audiences with relevant brand messaging." See Pandora for Brands, "Over 300 Audience Segments Means Greater Customization for Advertisers," 29 June 2015, http://pandoraforbrands.com/insight/300-audience-segments/, accessed 18 December 2016.
53 Amazon launched its streaming service in large part because music "is such a valuable creator of frequent customer interactions." Laura Sydell, "Amazon Prepares to Launch Cheaper Music Streaming Service," *All Things Considered*, 12 October 2016, http://www.npr.org/2016/10/12/497715207/amazon-prepares-to-launch-cheaper-music-streaming-service. A Pandora executive has argued that it is getting "harder to capture attention," but that "audio is one of the most effective ways to break through." See Pandora for Brands, "The Power of Audio: Q&A with Erik Radle," 29 November 2016, http://pandoraforbrands.com/insight/the-power-of-audio-qa-with-erik-radle/, accessed 18 December 2016.
54 Morris, "Curation by Code," 450.
55 Pandora for Brands, "Music Genome Project: Pioneering Personalization," accessed 17 December 2016, http://pandoraforbrands.com/music-genome-project/.
56 One method is "user splitting," which correlates changes in listening correlated with changes in context to subdivide a user profile into several different, context-specific profiles. Adomavicius et al., "Context-Aware Recommendation Systems," 73.
57 Spotify, *Brand Identity Guidelines*, 2013, 4 and 14.
58 Though the video has since been taken down, the accompanying web page is still accessible via the Internet Archive: Pandora for Brands, "Pandora's Premium Programmatic Solution Offers Brands a Quality En-

59 vironment," 16 June, 2015, https://web.archive.org/web/20170121083741/http://pandoraforbrands.com/insight/premium-programmatic/.
59 Pandora for Brands, "Pandora's Premium Programmatic Solution."
60 Spotify for Brands, Twitter, 15 September 2016, 10:00 a.m., https://twitter.com/SpotifyBrands.
61 Eric Hoppe, quoted in Alison Weissbrot, "Pandora Uses Listener Data for More Robust Segments," *Ad Exchange*, 7 June 2016, https://www.adexchanger.com/digital-audio-radio/pandora-uses-listener-data-robust-segments/.
62 Mayer-Schönberger and Cukier, *Big Data*, 61.
63 Chris Anderson, "The End of Theory: The Data Deluge Makes the Scientific Method Obsolete," *Wired*, 23 June 2008, https://www.wired.com/2008/06/pb-theory/.
64 Hariri, Mobasher, and Burke, "Context-Aware Music Recommendation."
65 Tim Peterson, "Spotify to Use Playlists as Proxies for Targeting Ads to Activities, Moods," *Advertising Age*, 16 April 2015, http://adage.com/article/digital/spotify-playlists-gauge-moods-ad-targeting/298066/.
66 "Spotify Launches Playlist Targeting for Brands," *Spotify Press*, 16 April 2015, https://press.spotify.com/us/2015/04/16/spotify-launches-playlist-targeting-for-brands/.
67 In 2016, Spotify, for instance, boasted that it was adding one hundred new segments, including "Moviegoers, Car Buyers, Luxury Shoppers, and Sports Fans." Spotify for Brands, "Introducing: Overlay and Audience Segments," 21 March 2016, https://brandsnews.spotify.com/us/2016/03/21/introducing-overlay-and-audience-segments/, accessed 19 December 2016. Pandora claimed to have over more than three hundred categories for advertisers to choose from, including "Horror TV Enthusiasts" and "Dry Dog Food Shoppers" ("Over 300 Audience Segments").
68 "Spotify Taps Rubicon Project to Automate Audio Inventory," *Business Wire*, 20 July 2016, http://www.businesswire.com/news/home/20160720005442/en/Spotify-Taps-Rubicon-Project-Automate-Audio-Inventory; see also Tim Ingham, "Spotify Is Asking Brands to Bid for Ads Based on Your Individual Tastes," *Music Business Worldwide*, 20 July 2016; Allison Schiff, "For Spotify 2016 Is All about Programmatic," *Ad Exchanger*, 11 February 2016, https://adexchanger.com/publishers/spotify-2016-programmatic/.
69 Amazon Staff, "Amazon Music Offers Free Streaming without a Prime Membership," 18 November 2019, https://blog.aboutamazon.com/entertainment/free-streaming-now-available-on-amazon-music.
70 Amazon Ads, "Audio Ads: Your Brand. Turned Up," accessed 25 June 2020, https://advertising.amazon.com/solutions/products/audio-ads?ref_=a20m_us_gw_aa.
71 Peterson, "Spotify to Use Playlists as Proxies."

72 Kassabian, *Ubiquitous Listening*, 9.
73 See, for instance, Johnson, *Listening in Paris*, ch. 1, and Weber, "Did People Listen?"
74 Goodman, "Distracted Listening."
75 Manabe, "Tale of Two Countries," 478.
76 Gopinath and Stanyek, "Anytime, Anywhere?"
77 Spotify, *Spotify for Brands Global Media Kit*, 2015, n.p.
78 To take one example, Deezer's "Features" page invites potential users to "composez la bande son de votre vie," accessed 23 December 2016, https://www.deezer.com/features.
79 Danielle Lee, "Man vs. Machine: Putting Humanity Back into the Marketing Mix" (presentation at New York Advertising Week, 27 September 2016), http://newyork.advertisingweek.com/replay/#date=2016-09-27~video-id=80~venue=6.
80 Lee, "Man vs. Machine."
81 Jana Jakovljevic, "Jana Jakovljevic, Head of Programmatica Solutions at Spotify, Discusses Cross-Platform Advertising" (presentation at ATS, New York, 2015), YouTube video, https://www.youtube.com/watch?v=xDFDg-oQ1eI.
82 Such aspects include romantic encounters. On this possibility, see van Bohemen, Schaap, and Berkers, "Sex Playlist."
83 Pandora for Brands, "When Pandora Plays, Your Message Works," accessed 28 December 2016, http://pandoraforbrands.com.
84 Spotify for Brands, "Introducing Sponsored Playlists," 26 May 2016, https://brandsnews.spotify.com/us/2016/05/26/introducing-sponsored-playlist/.
85 "Linking Music to Personality," *Preceptiv*, 20 January 2015, https://preceptiv.wordpress.com/2015/01/20/linking-music-to-personality/.
86 Brian Whitman, cited in Tom Vanderbilt, "Echo Nest Knows Your Music, Your Voting Choice," *Wired UK*, 17 February 2014, http://www.wired.co.uk/article/echo-nest.
87 Brian Whitman, "How Well Does Music Predict Your Politics?," accessed 6 January 2017, http://notes.variogr.am/post/26869688460/how-well-does-music-predict-your-politics.
88 Elizabeth Dwoskin, "Pandora Thinks It Knows If You Are a Republican," *Wall Street Journal*, 13 February 2014.
89 Yasha Levine, "The Cambridge Analytica Con," *Baffler*, 21 March 2018, https://thebaffler.com/latest/cambridge-analytica-con-levine.
90 Goffman, *Presentation of Self*.
91 Lee, "Man vs. Machine."
92 DeNora, "Music as a Technology of the Self."
93 Aisha Hassan and Dan Kopf, "The Reason Why Your Favorite Pop Songs Are Getting Shorter," *Quartz*, 27 October 2018, https://qz.com

/quartzy/1438412/the-reason-why-your-favorite-pop-songs-are-getting-shorter/. See also Dan Kopf, "The Economics of Streaming Is Making Songs Shorter," *Quartz*, 17 January 2019, https://qz.com/1519823/is-spotify-making-songs-shorter/.

94 Samarotto, "Trope of Expectancy/Infinity."

95 See Marc Hogan, "Uncovering How Streaming Is Changing the Sound of Pop," *Pitchfork*, 25 September 2017, https://pitchfork.com/features/article/uncovering-how-streaming-is-changing-the-sound-of-pop/; Mark Mulligan, "How Streaming Is Changing the Shape of Music Itself," *Music Industry Blog*, 6 September 2018, https://musicindustryblog.wordpress.com/2018/09/06/how-streaming-is-changing-the-shape-of-music-itself-part-i/; Deana Sumanac-Johnson, "Don't Bore Us, Get to the Chorus? How Streaming Is Changing Songs," *CBC News*, 9 February 2019, https://www.cbc.ca/news/entertainment/streaming-songs-changes-1.5002748. See also Leveillé Gauvin, "Drawing Listener Attention."

96 This is a riff on Katz's "phonograph effect," which designates "any change in musical behavior . . . that has arisen in response to sound-recording technology." Katz, *Capturing Sound*, 2.

97 Hassan and Kopf, "The Reason Why Your Favorite Pop Songs Are Getting Shorter."

98 As Jay Summach notes, the chorus is "typically held in reserve as the final core module—the culmination—of the formal cycle." In other words, the chorus tends to follow the verse, not the other way around. See Summach, "Form in Top-20 Rock Music," 106.

99 "D.O.C. (Death of the Chorus) with Emily Warren," 12 January 2021, *Switched on Pop*, podcast, https://switchedonpop.com/episodes/doc-death-of-the-chorus-with-emily-warren.

100 While hip-hop brought a number of formal innovations to pop, one index of its progressive mainstreaming has been its adoption of a modified verse-chorus paradigm, what Ben Duinker has dubbed the verse-hook form. See Duinker, "Song Form and the Mainstreaming of Hip Hop."

101 See the description of the AudioFeaturesObject, Spotify for Developers, "Web API," accessed 2 May 2021, https://developer.spotify.com/documentation/web-api/reference/#category-tracks.

102 Spotify for Developers, "Get Track's Audio Features," accessed 2 May 2021, https://developer.spotify.com/console/get-audio-features-track/?id=2MUKw7zEirXqdZZ3xC4hOf.

103 Jameson, *Postmodernism*, 10.

104 Rekret, "'Melodies Wander Around as Ghosts,'" 58.

105 Rekret, "'Melodies Wander Around as Ghosts,'" 58.

106 Liz Pelly, "Streambait Pop," *Baffler*, 11 December 2018, https://thebaffler.com/downstream/streambait-pop-pelly; Joe Caramanica, Caryn Ganz,

and Giovanni Russonello, "The Playlist: Pink Returns, Asking Questions with No Real Answers," *New York Times*, 12 August 2017.

107 As András Rónái puts it, "what seems a natural fit for platforms that are increasingly frictionless is *frictionless music*." Rónái, "Frictionless Platforms," 109.

108 Pelly, "Streambait Pop."

109 Pelly, "Streambait Pop."

110 Pelly, "Streambait Pop."

111 Anderson, "Neo-Muzak."

112 Lehman, "Form and Ignorability."

113 Leydon, "Soft-Focus Sound"; Keightley, "Music for Middlebrows."

114 Ihde, *Technology and the Lifeworld*, 111.

115 On nostalgia in lo-fi hip-hop, see Winston and Saywood, "Beats to Relax/Study To."

116 Cherie Hu, "The Economics of 24/7 Lo-Fi Hip Hop YouTube Livestreams," *Hot Pod News*, 28 January 2020, https://hotpodnews.com/the-economics-of-24-7-lo-fi-hip-hop-youtube-livestreams/.

117 Hu, "The Economics of 24/7 Lo-Fi Hip Hop."

118 Lofi Girl, "Lofi Hip Hop Radio: Beats to Relax/Study To," YouTube video, accessed 9 May 2021, https://www.youtube.com/watch?v=5qap5aO4i9A.

119 Hu, "The Economics of 24/7 Lo-Fi Hip Hop."

120 "Lo-fi, High Impact," *Sandbox* 264, 11 November 2020, https://musically.com/2020/11/12/sandbox-issue-264-lo-fi-hi-impact-how-lo-fi-hip-hop-brands-are-chilling-out-millions-of-devoted-listeners/.

121 Jenkins, quoted in "Lo-fi, High Impact."

122 "Lo-fi, High Impact."

123 Eli Ennis, "Why Artists Are Releasing 'Mood EPs' to Game Spotify's Algorithm," *Water and Music*, 5 February 2021, https://www.patreon.com/posts/47173077.

124 For a discussion of this tendency in connection with Spotify's partnership with Facebook, see Eriksson et al., *Spotify Teardown*, 86.

125 See, for instance, Spotify, "The Unique Sound of Your Ancestry," playlist, accessed 16 July 2020, https://open.spotify.com/playlist/3mDsntpXc1JIkfWSiWBEIp.

126 Sarah Zhang, "Your DNA Is Not Your Culture," *Atlantic*, 25 September 2018.

127 Christina Farr, "Consumer DNA Testing Hits a Rough Patch: Here's How Companies Like Ancestry and 23andMe Can Survive," *CNBC*, 9 February 2020, https://www.cnbc.com/2020/02/07/how-dna-testing-companies-like-ancestry-and-23andme-can-survive.html.

128 For a guide to the digital advertising ecosystem, see Clearcode, *AdTech Book*, ch. 4, https://adtechbook.clearcode.cc/adtech-platforms-and

129 -intermediaries/. For an overview of this ecosystem as it relates to Spotify specifically, see Vonderau, "The Spotify Effect."
129 BDEX, "Better Analytics. Deeper Connections," accessed 8 July 2020, https://www.bdex.com/explore-our-data/.
130 See Christl, *Corporate Surveillance*, 69–70.
131 Pandora for Brands, "Choice Matters: Over 1,300 Available Audiences," 4 October 2016, https://www.pandoraforbrands.com/article/choice-matters-over-1300-available-audiences.
132 Pandora for Brands, "Choice Matters."
133 Cited in Quentin Hardy, "Just the Facts: Yes, All of Them," *New York Times*, 25 March 2012, https://archive.nytimes.com/query.nytimes.com/gst/fullpage-9A0CE7DD153CF936A15750C0A9649D8B63.html.
134 Mona Sobhani and Leslie Saxon, "All Our Data Is Health Data," *Medium*, 14 August 2019, https://medium.com/@usccbc/all-our-data-is-health-data-57d3cf0f336d.
135 Ohm and Peppet, "What If Everything Reveals Everything?," 45.
136 See Hurley and Adebayo, "Credit Scoring," 202.
137 Prey, "Musica Analytica," 42.
138 Prey, "Musica Analytica," 42.
139 See Yamini Kona, "The Alternative Data Revolution in Banking," *Fintech News*, 9 July 2020, https://www.fintechnews.org/the-alternative-data-revolution-in-banking/.
140 Jeffrey Stewart, Systems and methods for using online social footprint for affecting lending performance and credit scoring, US Patent 8,694,401, filed January 12, 2012, and issued April 8, 2014.
141 Wikipedia, s.v. "Lenddo," accessed 9 July 2020, https://en.wikipedia.org/wiki/Lenddo.
142 Nick Bernards has noted how fintech narratives of financial inclusion have been presented as a fix for the shortcomings of earlier efforts at formalizing informal economies in the Global South (for example, structural adjustment in the 1980s and 1990s, microcredit programs in the 2000s and 2010s). See Bernards, "'Fintech' and Financial Inclusion," 318.
143 Aitken, "'All Data Is Credit Data,'" 280.
144 Nopper, "Digital Character."
145 Daughtry, "Did Music Cause the End of the World?," 7.
146 Jutla and Sundararajan, "India's FinTech Ecosystem," 56.
147 CreditVidya, "Accelerating Financial Inclusion in India," accessed 10 July 2020, https://creditvidya.com/how-it-works.
148 CreditVidya, "Accelerating Financial Inclusion."
149 Quoted in Gopal Sathe, "How Sai Baba Was Made to Spy on Your Phone for Credit Ratings," *Huffpost India*, 4 July 2019, https://www.huffingtonpost.in/entry/fintech-apps-privacy-snooping-credit-vidya

_in_5d1cbc34e4b082e55373370a. Sai Baba (1838–1918) was an Indian spiritual leader.

150   On the false dichotomy of bank lending using traditional credit scores versus marketplace lending, see Nopper, "Digital Character."

151   Dixon and Gellman, *Scoring of America*, 9.

152   De Cnudde et al., "Who Cares about Your Facebook Friends?"

153   De Cnudde et al., "Who Cares about Your Facebook Friends?"

154   Michael Elliott, "Big Data Analytics: Changing the Calculus of Insurance," *CIPR Newsletter*, 2017, 21, https://www.naic.org/cipr_newsletter_archive/vol23_big_data.pdf.

155   Ed Leefeldt, "How 'Big Data' Gives Insurers a Giant Edge over Consumers," *CBS News*, 12 March 2019, https://www.cbsnews.com/news/how-big-data-gives-insurers-a-giant-edge-over-consumers/.

156   Heen, "Ending Jim Crow Life Insurance Rates," 361.

157   Fergus, "Ghetto Tax," 277. See also Angwin et al., "Minority Households Pay Higher Car Insurance than White Areas with the Same Risk," *ProPublica*, 5 April 2017, https://www.propublica.org/article/minority-neighborhoods-higher-car-insurance-premiums-white-areas-same-risk.

158   Fergus, "Ghetto Tax," 279.

159   See, for instance, Kanetix, "Driving to the Beat of the Music Can Lead to Higher Insurance Rates," *Cision*, 1 August 2013, https://www.newswire.ca/fr/news-releases/driving-to-the-beat-of-the-music-can-lead-to-higher-insurance-rates-512766501.html; "Survey Finds Music Adds to Distracted Driving," *Claims Journal*, 31 August 2012, https://www.claimsjournal.com/news/international/2012/08/31/212934.htm; Direct Auto Insurance, "3 Interesting Ways Music May Affect Your Driving, According to Research," *Driving*, 11 February 2019, https://blog.directauto.com/safe-driving/music-and-driving/; and Insurify Insights, "Speeders Are WAY More Likely to Listen to This in the Car," 2 August 2021, https://insurify.com/insights/speeders-are-way-more-likely-to-listen-to-this-in-the-car/. For an overview of these and other studies, see Brodsky, Olivieri, and Chekaluk, "Music Genre Induced Driver Aggression."

160   These categories are drawn from the Exact Data database. See Exact Data, "Urban Music Fans," accessed 15 July 2020, https://www.exactdata.com/mailing-lists/urban-music-fans-mailing-list.html; and Exact Data, "Hip Hop Music Fans," accessed 15 July 2020, https://www.exactdata.com/mailing-lists/hip-hop-music-fans-mailing-list.html.

161   Benjamin, *Race after Technology*, 13.

162   Kanetix, "Driving to the Beat of the Music."

163   Barton Gellman and Laura Poitras, "U.S., British Intelligence Mining Data from Nine U.S. Internet Companies in Broad Secret Program," *Washington Post*, 7 June 2013, https://www.washingtonpost.com

/investigations/us-intelligence-mining-data-from-nine-us-internet-companies-in-broad-secret-program/2013/06/06/3a0c0da8-cebf-11e2-8845-d970ccb04497_story.html.

164 Steven Arango, "The Third Party Doctrine in the Wake of a 'Seismic Shift,'" *Practice Points*, American Bar Association, 13 June 2019, https://www.americanbar.org/groups/litigation/committees/privacy-data-security/practice/2019/third-party-doctrine-wake-of-seismic-shift/.

165 Tanya O'Carroll and Joshua Franco, "'Muslim Registries,' Big Data, and Human Rights," *Research*, Amnesty International, 27 February 2017, https://www.amnesty.org/en/latest/research/2017/02/muslim-registries-big-data-and-human-rights/.

166 These lifestyle categories are drawn from the *Experian Audience Lookbook*, accessed 14 July 2020, https://www.experian.com/content/dam/marketing/na/assets/ems/marketing-services/documents/product-sheets/audience-lookbook.pdf.

167 O'Carroll and Franco, "'Muslim Registries,' Big Data, and Human Rights."

168 Cited in O'Carroll and Franco, "'Muslim Registries,' Big Data, and Human Rights."

169 Cited in O'Carroll and Franco, "'Muslim Registries,' Big Data, and Human Rights."

170 Ohm and Peppet, "What If Everything Reveals Everything?," 45.

Four. Counterfeiting Attention in the Streaming Economy

Portions of this chapter were previously published as "Fake Streams, Listening Bots, and Click Farms: Counterfeiting Attention in the Streaming Music Economy," *American Music* 38, no. 2 (2020): 153–75. © Board of Trustees of the University of Illinois.

1 Snickars, "More Music," 191.

2 Jared Skoff, "Does the Market Reward Musical Talent? Vulfpeck, Spotify, and the Changing Face of the Music Industry," *Washington University Political Review*, 7 May 2014, https://www.wupr.org/2014/05/07/does-the-market-reward-musical-talent-vulfpeck-spotify-and-the-changing-face-of-the-music-industry/.

3 Stratton, cited in Schotzko, "Sufficiently Advanced Racket," 52.

4 Rauly Ramirez, "Inside Vulfpeck's Brilliant Spotify Stunt," *Billboard*, 17 March 2014, https://www.billboard.com/biz/articles/news/touring/5937612/inside-vulfpecks-brilliant-spotify-stunt.

5 "SLEEPIFY /// The Spotify Funded Vulfpeck Tour," 11 March 2014, YouTube video, https://www.youtube.com/watch?v=KXvncV79LXk.

6 Tim Jonze, "How to Make Money from Spotify by Streaming Silence," *Guardian*, 19 March 2014, https://www.theguardian.com/music

/musicblog/2014/mar/19/spotify-streaming-silence-vulpeck-make-money.

7 Ramirez, "Inside Vulfpeck's Brilliant Spotify Stunt."
8 kidsleepy, "Vulfpeck releases silent album, mocks Spotify's pathetic royalties," *Adland*, 21 March 2014, https://adland.tv/adnews/vulfpeck-releases-silent-album-mocks-spotifys-pathetic-royalties/1418230993. See also Skoff, "Does the Market Reward Musical Talent?"; and Gillian Branstetter, "How Silence Started a Political Revolution on Spotify," *Daily Dot*, 27 March 2014, https://www.dailydot.com/via/spotify-vulfpeck-silence-revolution/.
9 Snickars, "More Music," 195.
10 Schotzko, "Sufficiently Advanced Racket," 55.
11 Cited in Snickars, "More Music," 199.
12 Notably, many foundational texts on the attention economy were published during the dot-com boom of the late 1990s, which persuaded their authors that continued growth in the money economy would provide a material basis for value's migration to the attention economy. As Goldhaber argues, "it is precisely because material needs at the creature comfort level are fairly well satisfied . . . that the need for attention . . . takes on increasing importance" (Goldhaber, "Attention Economy"). Suffice it to say that such predictions of universal material affluence have not been borne out in the decades since.
13 Simon, "Designing Organizations," 40.
14 Or, as Davenport and Beck put it, "telecommunications bandwidth is [no longer] a problem, but human bandwidth is." Davenport and Beck, *Attention Economy*, 2.
15 Wu, "Blind Spot," 781.
16 Phillips, *Distraction*, 2.
17 See, for instance, Chris Gilliard's discussion of "digital redlining" (Gilliard, "Digital Redlining").
18 Crawford, *World beyond Your Head*, 5.
19 On this, see my article "Why the Next Song Matters."
20 Crary, *Suspensions of Perception*, 1.
21 Frank, "Economy of Attention."
22 Baumol and Bowen, *Performing Arts*, ch. 7.
23 This may be understood as a form of what Goldhaber calls "illusory attention," a simulation of personalized attention that papers over asymmetries between those giving and those receiving attention. Goldhaber, "Attention Economy."
24 Cited in Ciocca, "How Does Spotify Know You So Well?," *Medium*, 10 October 2017, https://medium.com/s/story/spotifys-discover-weekly-how-machine-learning-finds-your-new-music-19a41ab76efe.
25 Baym, *Playing to the Crowd*, 10.

26 Crary, *Suspensions of Perception*, 47.
27 Crary, *Suspensions of Perception*, 47.
28 Paul Resnikoff, "Indie Band Gets 79,000 Streams in a Month, Spotify Bans Them for Life," *Digital Music News*, 15 November 2017, https://www.digitalmusicnews.com/2017/11/15/indie-band-spotify-ban/.
29 windshieldman, "Indy Band Album Removed Because of a Too Loyal Fan Base," *Spotify Community*, 24 June 2015, https://community.spotify.com/t5/Content-Questions/Indy-band-album-removed-because-of-a-too-loyal-fan-base/td-p/1157659.
30 windshieldman, "Indy Band Album Removed."
31 Davenport and Beck, *Attention Economy*, 3.
32 North, *Problem of Distraction*, 4.
33 North, *Problem of Distraction*, 4.
34 Phillips, *Distraction*, 18.
35 See, for instance, Michael Bull's remarks about the dialectic of connection and disconnection in iPod culture. Bull, *Sound Moves*, 13.
36 Adorno, *Introduction to the Sociology of Music*, 4.
37 Adorno, *Introduction to the Sociology of Music*, 9.
38 Keil, "Motion and Feeling," 341.
39 See, in this connection, Gopinath and Stanyek, "Tuning the Human Race," 141–42.
40 Davenport and Beck, *Attention Economy*.
41 Crawford and Gillespie, "What Is a Flag For?," 413.
42 See Donath, "Identity and Deception," 29.
43 The phrase is Ben Ratliff's. See his book *Every Song Ever*.
44 Mark Mulligan, "The Long Tail Will Eat Itself: Covers and Tributes Make Up 90% of Digital Music Service Catalogues," *Music Industry Blog*, 14 May 2012, https://musicindustryblog.wordpress.com/2012/05/14/the-long-tail-will-east-itself-covers-and-tributes-make-up-90-of-digital-music-service-catalogues/.
45 Mulligan, "The Long Tail Will Eat Itself."
46 Mulligan, "The Long Tail Will Eat Itself."
47 Adam Raymond, "The Streaming Problem: How Spammers, Superstars, and Tech Giants Gamed the Music Industry," *Vulture*, 5 July 2017, http://www.vulture.com/2017/07/streaming-music-cheat-codes.html.
48 User-removed, "Show Cover / Karaoke Bands after Originals," *Spotify Community*, 12 October 2012, https://community.spotify.com/t5/Implemented-Ideas/Show-cover-karaoke-bands-after-originals/idi-p/170368.
49 hkphooey, "Too Many Cover Bands," *Spotify Community*, 17 August 2013, https://community.spotify.com/t5/Music-Chat/Too-many-cover-bands/td-p/506536.

50 jennifermasami, "Stop. With the Cover Songs," *Spotify Community*, 1 November 2019, https://community.spotify.com/t5/Content-Questions/Stop-With-the-Cover-Songs/m-p/4850903.

51 Ryan Nakashima, "When Did Cover Songs Become Annoying Marketing Ploys?," *Salon*, 30 May 2013, https://www.salon.com/2013/05/30/are_cover_songs_shameless_marketing_ploys_ap/.

52 Nakashima, "When Did Cover Songs."

53 Aaron Mandel, "How We Cope with Spammers, Fakers, and Cloners," *Echo Nest Blog*, 26 April 2013, http://blog.echonest.com/post/48943428838/how-we-cope-with-spammers-fakers-and-cloners.

54 Mandel, "How We Cope with Spammers."

55 Mandel, "How We Cope with Spammers."

56 Mandel, "How We Cope with Spammers."

57 Mandel, "How We Cope with Spammers."

58 Davies, *Lying for Money*, 16.

59 Snickars, "More Music," 196.

60 Mandel, "How We Cope with Spammers."

61 Peter Slattery, "Scammers Are Gaming Spotify by Faking Collaborations with Famous Artists," *One Zero*, 1 June 2020, https://onezero.medium.com/scammers-are-gaming-spotify-by-faking-collaborations-with-famous-artists-42d127e370dc. On the growth of collaborations in pop music, see Philip Kaplan, "The Rise of 'Feat.' in Today's Music," *DistroKid News*, 9 March 2017, https://news.distrokid.com/the-rise-of-collaborations-in-todays-music-8a8bcd386ea.

62 JGard18, "Asking to Play Some Songs/Albums through Google Home Is Bringing Up Karaoke Versions," 25 July 2017, https://community.spotify.com/t5/Ongoing-Issues/Asking-to-play-some-songs-albums-through-Google-Home-is-bringing/idi-p/1768744.

63 Steyerl, "Digital Debris," 73.

64 Steyerl, "Digital Debris," 73.

65 Brunton, *Spam*, xvi.

66 Brunton, *Spam*, 201.

67 Steyerl, "Digital Debris," 74.

68 One prodigious cover artist, Jonathan Young, notes that the high degree of repetition in pop songs helps speed his production of covers: "I can usually record the guitar parts and the chorus once, and then copy and paste that three times." Cited in Lizzie Plaugic, "Sounds Like a Hit: The Numbers Game Behind Spotify Cover Songs," *The Verge*, 8 September 2015, https://www.theverge.com/2015/9/8/9260675/spotify-cover-songs-taylor-swift-adele.

69 Matt Farley exemplifies this approach. Over the years he has uploaded some twenty thousand songs on Spotify, on topics including wind chill, Worcestershire sauce, fertilizer, and himself ("Matt Farley Is a Musical

Spammer Con Man"). See Thomas Smith, "How Matt Farley Built a $65k Per Year Music Empire from His Basement," *Better Marketing*, 28 March 2020, https://medium.com/better-marketing/how-matt-farley-built-a-65k-per-year-music-empire-from-his-basement-99b1192e762a/.

70 On the history of covers and the aesthetic questions they pose, see Weinstein, "History of Rock's Pasts"; Coyle, "Hijacked Hits"; Solis, "I Did It My Way"; and Gracyk, "Covers and Communicative Intentions."

71 Coyle, "Hijacked Hits," 139.

72 On the importance of these two conditions for the development of covering post-1960, see Solis, "I Did It My Way," 298.

73 Gracyk, "Covers and Communicative Intentions," 24.

74 Solis, "I Did It My Way," 315–16.

75 For a helpful overview of soundalikes, see Shawn Setaro, "Soundalike Songs Are a Two-Faced Business," *Medium*, 5 March 2015, https://medium.com/cuepoint/soundalike-songs-are-a-two-faced-business-f44ca9678bef. See also Inglis, "Embassy Records."

76 A 1948 advertisement for the label Tops Records—a pioneer in the production of soundalikes—boasted that its 29¢ discs were "The Lowest Price Record in America." *Billboard* 60, no. 47, 20 November 1948, 42. In the United Kingdom, Embassy Records typically sold its budget discs for little less than half of what mainstream labels such as HMV and Decca charged. See Inglis, "Embassy Records," 164.

77 Platforms make it easier to obtain mechanical licenses by assuming responsibility for calculating the share of revenue to be paid to composers, songwriters, and publishers; in this way, they incentivize the production of covers. Certain platforms (for example, Spotify) have been criticized, however, for failing to pay royalties for all the mechanical licenses they exploit. See Erin Jacobson, "Spotify May Have to Pay Songwriters $345 Million," *Forbes*, 19 July 2017, https://www.forbes.com/sites/legalentertainment/2017/07/19/spotify-may-have-to-pay-songwriters-345-million/#11586f40193d. See also Stephen Carlisle, "How Spotify Pays (or Doesn't Pay) Songwriters," 18 December 2015, http://copyright.nova.edu/spotify/.

78 Maura Johnston, "Why Cover Songs and Tribute Bands Are Big Business," *Pitchfork*, 11 February 2015, https://pitchfork.com/thepitch/665-why-cover-songs-and-tribute-bands-are-big-business/.

79 See, for instance, Johnston's comparison of the Fall Out Boy song "American Beauty/American Psycho" to a knockoff version by the "shadowy outfit" Music Mayhem. Johnston, "Why Cover Songs."

80 AdamStriegel, "Opt Out of Cover Music," *Spotify Community*, 18 October 2017, https://community.spotify.com/t5/Live-Ideas/All-Platforms-Discover-Opt-Out-of-Cover-Music/idi-p/2717398.

81 Donath, "Identity and Deception."

82   Donath, "Identity and Deception," 22. In Donath's example, a poster to a bodybuilding forum affirmed his expertise on the subject by posting a photo of himself.

83   Slattery, "Scammers Are Gaming Spotify."

84   Nyaker, "Put a Link on the Songs That Are Covers of Other Songs!," *Spotify Community*, 24 November 2012, https://community.spotify.com/t5/Closed-Ideas/Put-a-link-on-the-songs-that-are-covers-of-other-songs/idi-p/208410.

85   Amazon Music, *Top 40 Running Tracks*, Power Fitness Music, 2013, https://www.amazon.co.uk/Top-40-Running-Tracks-BodyToning/dp/B00AY8AYHC/.

86   Brunton, *Spam*, 48.

87   Though, as Gillespie points out, when a service's user base is counted in the hundreds of millions, talk of community becomes meaningless; see Gillespie, *Custodians of the Internet*, 88.

88   seawolf1492, "No Karaoke under Aritst's Album or Artist," *Spotify Community*, 1 June 2017, https://community.spotify.com/t5/Closed-Ideas/No-Karaoke-under-Aritst-s-Album-or-Artist/idi-p/1546911.

89   AndreasH, "Karaoke- and cover-filter," *Spotify Community*, 11 April 2011, https://community.spotify.com/t5/Closed-Ideas/Karaoke-and-cover-filter/idi-p/40329.

90   User, "Karaoke function," accessed 10 February 2019, https://community.spotify.com/t5/Closed-Ideas/All-Platforms-Other-Karaoke-function/idi-p/1230745.

91   User, "Please Add Karaoke Songs to Spotify," accessed 10 February 2019, https://community.spotify.com/t5/Closed-Ideas/Please-add-Karaoke-songs-to-Spotify/idi-p/3006734.

92   Farooqi et al., "Characterizing Key Stakeholders."

93   SEOClerks, "1000 Spotify Plays: The Best and Cheapest Service," accessed 3 March 2019, https://www.seoclerk.com/Audio-Music/588533/1-000-Spotify-Play-The-Best-amp-Cheapest-Service.

94   SEOClerks, "5000 Spotify Plays: The Cheapest and BEST Service for Spotify Music," accessed 3 March 2019, https://www.seoclerk.com/Audio-Music/586223/5-000-Spotify-Plays-Cheapest-amp-HQ-Spotify-Plays-BEST-service-for-spotify-music.

95   SEOClerks, "150k REAL Soundcloud Plays w/Likes and Reposts in 4 Days," accessed 3 March 2019, https://www.seoclerk.com/job/Social-Networks/35620/150k-REAL-Soundcloud-Plays-w-Likes-amp-Reposts-in-4-Days.

96   SEOClerks, "Top 100 on Itunes in USA," accessed 3 March 2019, https://www.seoclerk.com/job/Audio-Music/58691/Top-100-on-Itunes-in-USA.

97   Varol et al., "Online Human-Bot Interactions," 288.

98 "Facebook Publishes Enforcement Numbers for the First Time," *Facebook Newsroom*, 15 May 2018, https://newsroom.fb.com/news/2018/05/enforcement-numbers/. In the same press release, Facebook acknowledged that even following this purge, approximately 3 to 4 percent of remaining accounts on the service were likely fake.

99 Max Read, "How Much of the Internet Is Fake? Turns Out, a Lot of It, Actually," *New York Magazine*, 26 December 2018, http://nymag.com/intelligencer/2018/12/how-much-of-the-internet-is-fake.html.

100 Rami Essaid, cited in Nicholas Confessore, "The Follower Factory," *New York Times*, 27 January 2018.

101 By producing technologies that increase labor productivity (namely, machinery, technology, other capital goods), "the working population therefore produces both the accumulation of capital and the means by which it is itself made relatively superfluous." Marx, *Capital*, 1:783.

102 "Changing Music One Listener at a Time: Brian Whitman at TEDxSomerville," 29 April 2012, YouTube video, http://youtu.be/R-DTFaLcRmw.

103 Celma, *Music Recommendation and Discovery*, 105.

104 Chris Anderson, "The Long Tail," *Wired*, 1 October 2004, https://www.wired.com/2004/10/tail/; Anderson, *Long Tail*.

105 Anderson, *Long Tail*, 27.

106 Anderson, *Long Tail*, 22–23.

107 Anderson, *Long Tail*, 16.

108 Elberse, *Blockbusters*, 160.

109 Mark Mulligan, *The Death of the Long Tail: The Superstar Music Economy*, Midia Research, 14 July 2014; Hesmondhalgh et al., *Music Creators' Earnings*, 198. According to Hesmondhalgh et al., 78–80 percent of all streams in the United Kingdom go to the top 1 percent of artists, while 98 percent of streams go to the top 10 percent.

110 Mulligan, *Death of the Long Tail*, 12.

111 Frank and Cook, *Winner-Take-All Economy*, 38.

112 Elberse, *Blockbusters*, 164.

113 Frank and Cook, *Winner-Take-All Economy*, 9.

114 Tim Ingham, "Tidal Accused of Deliberately Faking Kanye West and Beyoncé Streaming Numbers," *Music Business Worldwide*, 9 May 2018, https://www.musicbusinessworldwide.com/did-tidal-falsify-streams-to-bulk-up-kanye-west-and-beyonce-numbers/.

115 Dave Brooks, "As Ticket Bundles Become a Go-To Chart Boost, Not Everyone Is Celebrating," *Billboard*, 10 November 2017, https://www.billboard.com/articles/business/8030253/concert-ticket-bundles-chart-boost-metallica-taylor-swift-kenny-chesney.

116 For a discussion of the claque, see Till, "Operatic Event," 81–82. On payola, see Segrave, *Payola in the Music Industry*.

117 Such deceptive practices can be understood as resulting from the interplay of what Caves dubs the "infinite variety" and "nobody knows" principles underpinning creative economies. Because creative works are qualitatively unique, it is impossible to predict demand for any given one. This uncertainty incentivizes efforts (licit or illicit) to reduce such uncertainty and improve chances for success. See Caves, *Creative Industries*, 146.

118 Citton, *Ecology of Attention*, 84.

119 Spotify for Artists, "Spotify for Artists FAQ," accessed 17 February 2019, https://web.archive.org/web/20170707135829/https://artists.spotify.com/faq/promotion.

120 "Spotify for Artists FAQ."

121 Ingham, "It's Happened: 100,000 Tracks Are Now Being Uploaded to Streaming Services Like Spotify Each Day," *Music Business Worldwide*, 6 October 2022, https://www.musicbusinessworldwide.com/its-happened-100000-tracks-are-now-being-uploaded/.

122 Spotify for Artists, "Spotify for Artists FAQ: How Can I Promote My Music on Spotify?," accessed 28 February 2019, https://artists.spotify.com/faq/promotion#how-can-i-promote-my-music-on-spotify.

123 Mass Media+, "Saavn Packages," accessed 14 June 2018, https://massmediaplus.com/services/saavn/.

124 Mass Media+, "Saavn Packages."

125 Mass Media+, "Saavn Packages."

126 Mass Media+, "Saavn Packages."

127 Streamify, "Why Streamify?," accessed 31 January 2019, https://www.streamify.me/streamify-increase-plays.html.

128 Phillips and Milner, *Ambivalent Internet*, 77.

129 Alan Cross, "What, Exactly, Is the 'Bulgarian Spotify Scam' That the Industry Is Talking About?," *Journal of Musical Things*, 23 February 2018, http://ajournalofmusicalthings.com/exactly-bulgarian-spotify-scam-industry-talking/.

130 Tim Ingham, "The Great Big Spotify Scam: Did a Bulgarian Playlister Swindle Their Way to a Fortune on Streaming Service?," 20 February 2018, https://www.musicbusinessworldwide.com/great-big-spotify-scam-bulgarian-playlister-swindle-way-fortune-streaming-service/.

131 Ingham, "The Great Big Spotify Scam."

132 Amy X. Wang, "A Bulgarian Scheme Scammed Spotify for $1 Million—without Breaking a Single Law," *Quartz*, 22 February 2018, https://qz.com/1212330/a-bulgarian-scheme-scammed-spotify-for-1-million-without-breaking-a-single-law/.

133 For helpful descriptions of the two methods, see Muikku, *Pro Rata and User Centric*, 5–6. While the pro rata method of allocating revenue remains dominant within the industry, a handful of platforms have begun

experimenting with user-centric approaches, most notably SoundCloud and Tidal. I discuss this further in the epilogue.

134 Gillespie, "Regulation of and by Platforms."
135 Gillespie, "Regulation of and by Platforms," 255.
136 Spotviewbot home page, accessed 16 June 2018, http://spotviewbot.com.
137 In a how-to video that has since been taken off of YouTube, one of the program's creators explains that "basically the amount of views you get is how many threads you have, and then what you set the timer to." Elsewhere he notes that a thread set to run all day and to skip every forty seconds will generate approximately two thousand plays per day. YouTube video, accessed 16 June 2018, https://www.youtube.com/watch?v=ayfzi9n9AxI.
138 Brunton, *Spam*, 170.
139 In January 2021, for instance, Spotify purged its catalog of approximately 750,000 tracks alleged to have artificially inflated their play counts. Wallace Collins, "Did Spotify Purge Indie Artist Music on January 1, 2021?!?," *Music Think Tank*, 5 January 2021, http://www.musicthinktank.com/blog/did-spotify-purge-indie-artist-music-january-1-2021.html.
140 Fiverup, "Buy plays and make your music work," accessed 16 June 2018, https://www.fiverup.com/user/floking.
141 SEOClerks, "1,000+ / 1000+ / 1k+ SpotifyPlays REAL PLAYS—NO BOTS for $5," accessed 16 June 2018, https://www.seoclerk.com/Audio-Music/557284/1-000-1000-1k-SpotifyPlays-REAL-PLAYS-NO-BOTS.
142 Wbix, "Buy Spotify Plays," accessed 20 June 2018, https://wbix.com/buy-spotify-plays/; Streamify, "FAQ," accessed 20 June 2018, https://www.streamify.me/faq.html.
143 Jones, *Work without the Worker*.
144 Casilli, "Digital Labor Studies Go Global," 3940–41.
145 Farooqi et al., "Characterizing Key Stakeholders," 6. Similarly, most buyers of services on freelancer.com live in the United States and United Kingdom, while most sellers are located in Southeast Asia or Eastern Europe; see Pongratz, "Of Crowds and Talents," 60.
146 Casilli, "Digital Labor Studies Go Global," 3940.
147 Lehdonvirta et al., "Online Labour Markets."
148 See Farooqi et al., "Characterizing Key Stakeholders," 8. Insight into this practice is offered by a dispute between two parties on the website blackhatworld.com, a forum for the buying and selling of digital services. One of the disputants describes himself as the owner of "a very large social media network." At issue were fake streams he subcontracted to another forum member, in order to get "better plays and more diversity" by dispersing plays globally. See KaisGuy,

Notes to Chapter Four → 291

"Scammed by Spotifymarketer (Fameify.me) for $1000," *Black Hat World*, 14 June 2017, https://www.blackhatworld.com/seo/scammed-by-spotifymarketer-fameify-me-for-1000.947592/.

149 Evan V. Symon, "The Hellish Reality of Working at an Overseas 'Click Farm,'" *Cracked*, 11 December 2017, http://www.cracked.com/personal-experiences-2550-the-hellish-reality-working-at-overseas-click-farm.html.

150 Symon, "The Hellish Reality."

151 Symon, "The Hellish Reality."

152 Symon, "The Hellish Reality."

153 Symon, "The Hellish Reality."

154 Tim Ingham, "Spotify Is Making Its Own Records . . . and Putting Them on Playlists," *Music Business Worldwide*, 31 August 2016, https://www.musicbusinessworldwide.com/spotify-is-creating-its-own-recordings-and-putting-them-on-playlists/. The move toward original content wasn't entirely new: for instance, the platform had previously engaged EDM producer Tiestö to produce tracks for exercise playlists, with tempo adapting to one's pace. But this was an exception that proves the rule.

155 Ingham, "Spotify Is Making Its Own Records."

156 Ingham, "Spotify Is Making Its Own Records."

157 This is a theme that Goldschmitt takes up in an incisive reading of the "fake music" scandal, which complements my own. See Goldschmitt, "Long History."

158 Raymond, "Streaming Problem."

159 Tim Ingham, "Spotify Denies It's Playlisting Fake Artists. So Why Are All of These Fake Artists on Its Playlists?," *Music Business World*, 9 July 2017, https://www.musicbusinessworldwide.com/spotify-denies-its-playlisting-fake-artists-so-why-are-all-these-fake-artists-on-its-playlists/.

160 Another commonality noted by Goldschmitt is that the pseudonyms adopted by artists largely conformed to the naming conventions operative in the genres featured on such playlists. See Goldschmitt, "Long History."

161 Ingham, "Spotify Denies It's Playlisting Fake Artists."

162 Ingham, "Spotify Denies It's Playlisting Fake Artists."

163 Andy Gensler, "Spotify on Non-Existent Artist Allegations: We Do Not and Have Never Created Fake Artists," *Billboard*, 7 July 2017, https://www.billboard.com/music/music-news/spotify-fake-artist-allegations-response-7858015/.

164 Oscar Höglund, quoted in Stuart Dredge, "Epidemic Sound Gives Its Side of the Spotify 'Fake Artists' Controversy," *Music Ally*, 20 November 2017, http://musically.com/2017/11/20/epidemic-sound-spotify-fake-artists/.

165 For instance, on its website, Epidemic Sound offers, for single productions, episodes, or advertisements, the option of paying a "single global license fee," thus avoiding any "additional royalty costs." Epidemic Sound, "Our Subscriptions," accessed 27 June 2018, https://player.epidemicsound.com/pricing/.

166 Andy Gensler and Ed Christman, "How Spotify's 'Fake Artist' Controversy Has Increased Tensions with Label Partners, Could Hurt Its Bottom Line," *Billboard*, 19 July 2017, https://www.billboard.com/articles/business/7872889/spotify-fake-artist-playlist-controversy-record-label-tensions-ipo.

167 Höglund, in Dredge, "Epidemic Sound Gives Its Side."

168 David Turner, "Yes, Spotify Fills Mood Playlists with Fake Artists," *Track Record*, 21 November 2017, https://trackrecord.net/spotify-does-in-fact-fill-mood-playlists-with-fake-ar-1820642310?rev=1511284011158.

169 Cherie Hu, "Those 'Fake Artists' on Spotify? Epidemic Sound CEO Oscar Höglund Says There Was 'No Special Deal,'" *Billboard*, 21 November 2017, https://www.billboard.com/articles/business/8046158/epidemic-sound-spotify-fake-artists-controversy-oscar-hoglund.

170 Quoted in Roy Trakin and Jem Aswad, "Spotify Denies Creating Fake Artists, Although Many Sources Claim the Practice Is Real," *Variety*, 11 July 2017, https://variety.com/2017/biz/news/spotify-denies-creating-fake-artists-although-multiple-sources-claim-the-practice-is-real-1202492307/#!.

171 Gensler and Christman, "How Spotify's 'Fake Artist' Controversy Has Increased Tensions."

172 Spotify for Artists, "Innovating for Writers and Artists," 12 July 2017, https://artists.spotify.com/blog/innovating-for-writers-and-artists.

173 "Innovating for Writers and Artists."

174 Tim Ingham, "Welcome to the Future: Spotify Poaches AI Music Expert from Sony," *Music Business Worldwide*, 11 July 2017, https://www.musicbusinessworldwide.com/welcome-future-spotify-poaches-ai-music-expert-sony/.

175 Stuart Dredge, "Spotify May Have 'Fake Artists' but Wait until AI Music Startups Hit Their Stride," *Music Ally*, 10 July 2017, http://musically.com/2017/07/10/spotify-fake-artists-ai-music/. In a less serious vein, the website Popjustice published a three-month plan for "how robots could replace all pop starts" the day before Pachet's hiring was made public. In an update to the post, added after news of Pachet's appointment was announced, Popjustice noted "maybe this idea isn't totally ludicrous." "Here's How Robots Could Replace All Popstars by October 11," *The Briefing*, Popjustice, 11 July 2017, https://www.popjustice.com/briefing/heres-how-robots-could-replace-all-popstars-by-october-11/.

176   Dredge, "Spotify May Have 'Fake Artists.'"
177   John Paul Titlow, "Why Did Spotify Hire This Expert in Music-Making AI?," *Fast Company*, 13 July 2017, https://www.fastcompany.com/40439000/why-did-spotify-hire-this-expert-in-music-making-ai.
178   Ingham, "Welcome to the Future."
179   Josh Rosenthal, blog comment, in Ingham, "Welcome to the Future."
180   Quoted in Stuart Dredge, "AI and Music: Will We Be Slaves to the Algorithm?," *Guardian*, 6 August 2017, https://www.theguardian.com/technology/2017/aug/06/artificial-intelligence-and-will-we-be-slaves-to-the-algorithm.
181   Dredge, "AI and Music."
182   Harmy Does Reddit, "What do you guys think about the recent hubbub of Spotify allegedly filling up their major instrumental playlists with fake artists to cut royalty costs?," Reddit post, 11 July 2017, https://www.reddit.com/r/WeAreTheMusicMakers/comments/6mjysp/what_do_you_guys_think_about_the_recent_hubbub_of/.
183   Mojo Bone, blog comment, in Tim Ingham, "Why Spotify's Fake Artists Problem Is an Epidemic. Literally," *Music Business Worldwide*, 12 July 2017, www.musicbusinessworldwide.com/why-spotifys-fake-artists-problem-is-an-epidemic-literally/.
184   Ann-Derrick Gaillot, "Music Streaming Numbers Are Meaningless," *Outline*, 9 May 2018, https://theoutline.com/post/4488/tidal-inflated-numbers-report.
185   Cheney-Lippold, *We Are Data*, 73.

Five. Streaming, Cheap Music, and the Crises of Social Reproduction

1   Diego Planas Rego, "Fill Your Evenings with Music: Introducing Dinner and Sleep Categories to Browse," *Spotify Blog*, 2 July 2014, https://web.archive.org/web/20140715154542/http://news.spotify.com:80/us.
2   Eriksson et al., *Spotify Teardown*, ch. 1.
3   Max Richter, liner notes, *Sleep*, Deutsche Grammophon DG 479 5682, 2015.
4   Gabe Meline, "Who Wants to Fall Asleep to 'The Disintegration Loops'?," *KQED*, 27 March 2018, https://www.kqed.org/arts/13828138/who-wants-to-fall-asleep-to-the-disintegration-loops; Joseph Morpurgo, "Dreamcatching: The Remarkable Story of Robert Rich and the Sleep Concerts," *Fact*, 10 October 2014, https://www.factmag.com/2014/10/10/dreamcatching-the-remarkable-story-of-robert-rich-and-the-sleep-concerts/; "Porto in Pyjamas: Sleep Concert to Be Held in Portuguese Villa," *Wire*, 14 August 2014, https://www.thewire.co.uk

/news/32307/sleep-concert-to-be-held-in-portuguese-villa; Philip Sherburne, "The History of Sleep Music: Songs in the Key of Zzz," *Pitchfork*, 20 October 2015, https://pitchfork.com/features/article/9738-songs-in-the-key-of-zzz-the-history-of-sleep-music/; "Introducing Liminal Sleep by Sigur Rós," *Calm Blog*, 15 July 2019, https://blog.calm.com/blog/introducing-liminal-sleep-by-sigur-ros; Alex D., "Music, Health, and AI: Making Unwind.ai with Marconi Union," *Sync Project*, 4 July 2017, http://syncproject.co/blog/2017/7/4/music-health-ai-making-unwindai-with-marconi-union; Andrew Chow, "How Music Could Become a Crucial Part of Your Sleep Hygiene," *Time*, 6 August 2020, https://time.com/5844980/sleep-music/; Kassabian, "Music for Sleeping."

5 Williams, *Politics of Sleep*, 19.
6 Shawn McIntyre, "Sleep Less, Feel Better, and Get More Done with These 3 Tips," *Entrepreneur*, 23 February 2015, https://www.entrepreneur.com/article/241974.
7 Brown, "Taking Care of Business," 174.
8 Dan Goldman, "Investing in the Growing Sleep-Health Economy," McKinsey and Company (August 2017), 4.
9 Crary, *24/7*.
10 Crary, *24/7*, 17.
11 Crary, *24/7*, 10.
12 Crary, *24/7*, 10.
13 Crary, *24/7*, 11.
14 Bhattacharya, *Social Reproduction Theory*, 1.
15 See Yúdice, *Expediency of Culture*.
16 Althusser, *Reproduction of Capitalism*, 50.
17 The literature on social reproduction is extensive. Some key texts include Vogel, *Marxism and the Oppression of Women*; Fortunati, *Arcane of Reproduction*; Federici, *Revolution at Point Zero*; Bhattacharya, *Social Reproduction Theory*.
18 Althusser, *Reproduction of Capitalism*, 149–50.
19 Endnotes Collective, "Logic of Gender," 61.
20 The latter perspective is typical of a certain reactionary strand of evolutionary psychology. See, for instance, Kay, Yuan Ting, and Yang Tan, "Sex and Care," 3.
21 On gestational labor, see Lewis, *Full Surrogacy Now*.
22 On the wage penalty care work incurs, see England, Budig, and Folbre, "Wages of Virtue."
23 Glenn, *Forced to Care*, 9.
24 Bourdieu, *Distinction*; Green, "Musical Meaning and Social Reproduction."

25   Miller, "Working Musicians," 431. See also Solie, *Music in Other Words*, ch. 3.

26   See Keightley, "'Turn It Down!'"; Baade, "Lean Back."

27   For more on how DeNora's work might be read through a historical-materialist lens, see my "Music in the Work of Social Reproduction."

28   Vevo, "Music for Cooking—Upbeat Cooking Playlist," YouTube video playlist, last updated 8 August 2022, https://www.youtube.com/playlist?list=PLkqz3S84Tw-RN9QGNCzKC4CtFqmVExUmo; Amazon's Music Experts, "Cleaning the House," Amazon Music playlist, https://music.amazon.com/playlists/B07MM35ZG1?ref=dm_wcp_bp_pp_link.

29   Jason Joven, "Spotify: The Rise of the Contextual Playlist," *Chartmetric*, https://blog.chartmetric.io/spotify-the-rise-of-the-contextual-playlist-c6f2c26900f4.

30   Joven, "Spotify."

31   As Harvey notes, it is "possible to accumulate in the face of stagnant effective demand if the costs of inputs (land, raw materials, intermediate inputs, labour power) decline significantly," a fact that makes "access to cheaper inputs . . . just as important as access to widening markets in keeping profitable opportunities open." Harvey, *New Imperialism*, 139.

32   Moore, *Capitalism in the Web of Life*, 93.

33   Moore, *Capitalism in the Web of Life*, 95.

34   Rai, Hoskyns, and Thomas, "Depletion," 88–89.

35   See, for instance, Fraser, "Capitalism's Crisis of Care"; Hester and Srnicek, "Crisis of Social Reproduction"; and Care Collective, *Care Manifesto*.

36   Hochschild, "Global Care Chains."

37   Fraser, in Fraser and Jaeggi, *Capitalism*, 72.

38   According to Marx, both worker and employer "meet in the market, and enter into relations with each other on a footing of equality as owners of commodities, with the sole difference that one is a buyer, the other a seller; both are therefore equal in the eyes of the law." Marx, *Capital*, 1:271.

39   In contrast to orthodox Marxian accounts, which identify expropriation with the moment of primitive accumulation in the sixteenth and seventeenth centuries, when commons were forcibly enclosed, Fraser among others has contended that it is rather "an ongoing, albeit unofficial, mechanism of accumulation, which continues alongside the official mechanism of exploitation." Fraser, "Behind Marx's Hidden Abode," 60.

40   For the economist-artist Hans Abbing, *economic exceptionalism* generally refers to the fact that art's self-distancing from the standard economy leads to a greater reliance on gifts and gift giving; see Abbing, *Why Are Artists Poor?* For Marxist art historian Dave Beech, it instead refers to art's resistance to capitalist subsumption; see Beech, *Art and Value*.

41   Beech, *Art and Value*, 23.

42   Ryan, *Making Capital from Culture*, 46, 48.

43   See Passman, *All You Need to Know*, 117.

44   Beech, *Art and Value*, 356.

45   Kreidler, "Leverage Lost," 80.

46   Alper and Wassall, "Artists' Careers," 836.

47   Gaquin, *Artists in the Workforce*, 21.

48   See Throsby, *Economics and Culture*, ch. 6; Robinson and Montgomery, "Time Allocation and Earnings of Artists."

49   See Menger, "Artistic Labor Markets and Careers."

50   On the use of music reading exams to control membership in the American Federation of Musicians, see Roberts, *Tell Tchaikovsky the News*, 5–6. On the failure of French musicians' unions to have the government regulate the musical labor market, see my *Music and the Elusive Revolution*, 58–60, 68.

51   Ingham, "It's Happened: 100,000 Tracks Are Now Being Uploaded to Streaming Services Like Spotify Each Day," *Music Business Worldwide*, 6 October 2022, https://www.musicbusinessworldwide.com/its-happened-100000-tracks-are-now-being-uploaded/.

52   Pertinent here are Bryan Parkhurst's remarks on what he calls "production-tracking" and "unsubsumable" use values. In the former, a thing's use value is tied to how it is produced (for example, handicraft). In the latter, this use value further requires that its production somehow rejects real subsumption. Parkhurst, "Music, Art, and Kinds of Use Values."

53   See Baumol and Bowen, *Performing Arts*, 168–69.

54   On this point, see England, Budig, and Folbre, "Wages of Virtue"; Duffy, Albelda, and Hammonds, "Counting Care Work," 150; and Benanav, "Automation and the Future," 126–28.

55   Baumol and Bowen, *Performing Arts*, 164.

56   Benanav and Clegg, "Misery and Debt"; see also Jason Smith, "Nowhere to Go: Automation, Then and Now, Part Two," *Brooklyn Rail*, April 2017, https://brooklynrail.org/2017/04/field-notes/Nowhere-to-Go-Automation-Then-and-Now-Part-Two.

57   Cowan, *More Work for Mother*.

58   Leppert, *Aesthetic Technologies*, 112. See also Thompson, "Machines, Music, and the Quest for Fidelity."

59   See Hesmondhalgh, *Cultural Industries*, 21.

60   See, in this connection, Parkhurst's critique of "the claim that the value of a unit of information 'tends to zero,'" which, as he notes, "is importantly different from the claim that 'the value of the sold information is zero.'" Parkhurst, "Digital Information and Value," 78.

61   Moore, *Capitalism in the Web of Life*, 53.

62. Ferreboeuf and Lean ICT Working Group, *Lean ICT*, 60.
63. Ferreboeuf and Lean ICT Working Group, *Lean ICT*, 23.
64. Kate Crawford and Vladan Joler, "Anatomy of an AI System: The Amazon Echo As an Anatomical Map of Human Labor, Data and Planetary Resources," AI Now Institute and Share Lab, 7 September, 2018, https://anatomyof.ai.
65. Abraham, *Elements of Power*, 48.
66. Sargeson, "Demise of China's Peasantry," 8.
67. "Rate of Exploitation."
68. See Brenner, *Boom and the Bubble*; Crouch, "Privatised Keynesianism."
69. On this point, see Srnicek, *Platform Capitalism*, 20–21.
70. See Langley and Leyshon, "Platform Capitalism."
71. Fraser and Jaeggi, *Capitalism*, 154.
72. Rego, "Fill Your Evenings with Music."
73. Rego, "Fill Your Evenings with Music."
74. Rego, "Fill Your Evenings with Music."
75. Rego, "Fill Your Evenings with Music."
76. Eriksson and Johansson, "'Keep Smiling!'" 75.
77. Thompson, "Music in the Post-Mom Economy."
78. Joven, "Spotify."
79. Data accessible via Spotify's developer API confirms these claims. A cursory survey of the audio data for the tracks on different activity playlists indicates, for instance, that running playlists tend to feature high scores in terms of "danceability" (that is, metric salience) and "energy" (that is, loudness and spectral presence), whereas chill playlists tend to feature lower "energy" and "valence."
80. To use Lehman's term, music on sleep playlists generally satisfies the "un-salience conditions" characteristic of ambient music; see Lehman, "Form and Ignorability."
81. A parallel reading is offered by Birenbaum Quintero, who, drawing on affect theory, notes how the descriptions accompanying playlists transmute the indeterminacy of musical affect into the determinacy of emotion; see Birenbaum Quintero, "Late Capitalism."
82. Amazon's Music Experts, "Classical Focus," Amazon Music playlist, https://music.amazon.com/playlists/B08FXVJQFP?ref=dm_wcp_bp_pp_link.
83. Pandora Country, "Country Cleaning," Pandora playlist, https://www.pandora.com/genre/country-cleaning.
84. Spotify, "Evening Chill," playlist, accessed 22 April 2023, https://web.archive.org/web/20161226055253/https://open.spotify.com/user/spotify/playlist/0eDq2STmk8tKcD7qWCwrze.
85. See Solie, *Music in Other Words*, ch. 3.
86. Thompson, "Music in the Post-Mom Economy."

87 Kallis, *Degrowth*, 30.
88 Leary, *Keywords*, 59
89 Groys, *Art Power*, 43.
90 On this point, see my article "Why the Next Song Matters."
91 Cited in Sophia Ciocca, "How Does Spotify Know You So Well?," *Medium*, 10 October 2017, https://medium.com/s/story/spotifys-discover-weekly-how-machine-learning-finds-your-new-music-19a41ab76efe.
92 See Cooper, *Family Values*.
93 O'Brien, "To Abolish the Family," 410.
94 Apple Music Kids and Family, accessed 22 April 2023, https://web.archive.org/web/20200408121820/https://music.apple.com/us/curator/apple-music-kids-family/976439538.
95 See, for instance, Chastagner, "Parents' Music Resource Center."
96 "Child-Friendly Content," *Deezer Community Forum*, accessed 10 August 2020, https://en.deezercommunity.com/your-account-and-subscription-5/child-friendly-content-288.
97 Samantha D., "Great App, Not for Kids," *Common Sense Media*, accessed 2 August 2020, https://www.commonsensemedia.org/website-reviews/spotify/user-reviews/adult.
98 "Parent Reviews for Spotify," *Common Sense Media*, accessed 2 August 2020, https://www.commonsensemedia.org/website-reviews/spotify/user-reviews/adult.
99 Sapna Maheshwari, "On YouTube Kids, Startling Videos Slip Past Filters," *New York Times*, 4 November 2017, https://www.nytimes.com/2017/11/04/business/media/youtube-kids-paw-patrol.html; James Bridle, "There Is Something Wrong on the Internet," *Medium*, 6 November 2017, https://medium.com/@jamesbridle/something-is-wrong-on-the-internet-c39c471271d2.
100 Brian Koerber, "Gaming the System: How Creepy YouTube Channels Trick Kids into Watching Violent Videos," *Mashable*, 10 October 2017, https://mashable.com/2017/10/22/youtube-kids-app-violent-videos-seo-keywords/#myVluH.T1aqq.
101 Gillespie, *Custodians of the Internet*, 88. Motivating this approach is the sheer quantity of the user-generated content the platform hosts (five hundred hours of video are uploaded to the site every minute, as of 2020). Also important is the company's interest in minimizing the labor costs of content moderation.
102 Noah Kulwin, "YouTube Kills Ads on 50,000 Channels as Advertisers Flee over Disturbing Child Content," *Vice*, 27 November 2017, https://www.vice.com/en_us/article/5955xd/youtube-kills-ads-on-50000-channels-as-advertisers-flee-over-disturbing-child-content.

103 Sara Ashley O'Brien, "Google Cracks Down on Disturbing Cartoons on YouTube Kids," CNN, 10 November 2017, https://money.cnn.com/2017/11/10/technology/youtube-age-restriction/; K. G. Orphanides, "Children's YouTube Is Still Churning Out Blood, Suicide, and Cannibalism," *Wired UK*, 23 March 2018, https://www.wired.co.uk/article/youtube-for-kids-videos-problems-algorithm-recommend.

104 Edelman, *No Future*.

105 Edelman, *No Future*, 3.

106 Muñoz, *Cruising Utopia*, 94.

107 See Renfro, *Stranger Danger*.

108 Spotify, "Introducing Spotify Kids, A New Standalone App for the Next Generation of Listeners," 30 October 2019, https://newsroom.spotify.com/2019-10-30/introducing-spotify-kids-a-new-standalone-app-for-the-next-generation-of-listeners/.

109 u/Con-Struct, "Save us parents from the horrors of kids music," Reddit post, 2 May 2020, https://www.reddit.com/r/spotify/comments/gcam4g/save_us_parents_from_the_horrors_of_kids_music/.

110 An ancillary benefit of Spotify's strategic partnership with Disney stems from the fact that Disney Music Group isn't a major label, despite being owned by one of the largest entertainment conglomerates in the world. Hence, the more traffic Spotify directs to Disney's music, the more leverage it gains relative to the three majors.

111 Spotify, "Your Daily Routine," playlist, accessed 22 November 2020. https://open.spotify.com/playlist/37i9dQZF1DWWVwtV5Pv39d.

112 Baumol and Bowen, *Performing Arts*, 164.

113 Donath, "Other Economy," 119.

114 This distinction is derived from Tronto, *Moral Boundaries*, ch. 4.

115 Wajcman, *Pressed for Time*, 129.

116 England, Budig, and Folbre, "Wages of Virtue"; Razavi and Staab, "Underpaid and Overworked"; Barron and West, "Financial Costs of Caring"; Folbre, "Care Penalty."

117 Baumol, *Cost Disease*, 19.

118 Rebecca Strong, "PureTech Launches Music-for-Health Startup, the Sync Project," *BostInno*, 11 March 2015, https://www.bizjournals.com/boston/inno/stories/news/2015/03/11/puretech-launches-music-for-health-startup-the.html.

119 Marko Ahtisaari, "Music as Precision Medicine," Sync Project, accessed 9 September 2020, http://syncproject.co/blog/markoahtisaari-qanda.

120 Ketki Karanam, "Music for Pain Management," Sync Project, accessed 9 September 2020, http://syncproject.co/blog/2016/7/26/music-for-pain-management; Ketki Karanam, "The Many Ways Music Supports Memory in Alzheimer's," http://syncproject.co/blog/2016/8/2/many-ways-music-supports-memory-in-alzheimers; Ketki Kara-

nam, "Music Training as Rehabilitation for Developmental Dyslexia," accessed 9 September 2020, http://syncproject.co/blog/2015/10/25/music-training-as-rehabilitation-for-developmental-dyslexia; Andrew Zannetos, "Body in Tune: Music and the Immune System," accessed 9 September 2020, http://syncproject.co/blog/2017/8/23/music-and-the-immune-system.

121 "Sync Project Announces New Investors and Accelerates Development of Personalized Music Health Platform," *Business Wire*, 17 May 2017, https://www.businesswire.com/news/home/20170516006817/en/.

122 Sync Project, "Could Music One Day Be Prescribed Like Conventional Medicine?," *Medium*, 1 November 2015, https://medium.com/sync-project/could-music-one-day-be-prescribed-like-conventional-medicine-10b7580866de.

123 According to Music and Memory's Registration Statement, the organization was first incorporated in Delaware before relocating to New York in 2014. New York State Office of the Attorney General, "Music & Memory," Charities (database), accessed 12 September 2020, https://www.charitiesnys.com/RegistrySearch/show_details.jsp?id={05FDABAE-F00A-4C31-A6DC-86FB175D1EF8}.

124 Music and Memory, "Our Mission," accessed 12 September 2020, https://musicandmemory.org/about/mission-and-vision/.

125 Music and Memory, *Making the Case for Personalised Music: A Guide for Care Professionals*, 2014, 4–5, https://musicandmemory.org/wp-content/uploads/2020/11/Making_the_Case_for_Personalized_Music-A_Guide_for_Caregivers_2020_Edition.pdf.

126 Music and Memory, "Music & Memory Certification Training," accessed 22 April 2023, https://musicandmemory.org/get-trained/certification-training/.

127 See, for instance, Wisconsin Department of Health Services, Joint Committee on Finance, "Long-Term Care Expansion Report" (2013), https://www.dhs.wisconsin.gov/publications/p0/p00590.pdf.

128 Wisconsin Department of Health Services, "Music and Memory Program Overview," accessed 12 September 2020, https://www.dhs.wisconsin.gov/music-memory/overview.htm.

129 G.M., "How Personalised Music Can Be Used in Healthcare," *Economist*, 15 May 2017, https://www.economist.com/prospero/2017/05/15/how-personalised-music-can-be-used-in-health-care.

130 G.M., "How Personalised Music Can Be Used."

131 All-Party Parliamentary Group on Arts, Health, and Wellbeing, *Creative Health: The Arts for Health and Wellbeing*, Culture, Health and Wellbeing Alliance, 2017, https://www.culturehealthandwellbeing.org.uk/appg-inquiry/.

132   See, for instance, Chris Curtis, "Brits Still Love the NHS, but They Are Nervous about Its Future," *YouGov*, 4 July 2018, https://yougov.co.uk/topics/politics/articles-reports/2018/07/04/brits-still-love-nhs-they-are-nervous-about-its-fu. See also King's Fund, "British Public's Satisfaction with the NHS at Lowest Level in over a Decade," 7 March 2019, https://www.kingsfund.org.uk/press/press-releases/british-public-satisfaction-nhs-lowest-decade.

133   See Toynbee, "NHS"; and Abi Rimmer, "Health and Social Care Spending Cuts Linked to 120,000 Excess Deaths in England," *BMJ Open* 15 (2017), https://www.bmj.com/company/newsroom/health-and-social-care-spending-cuts-linked-to-120000-excess-deaths-in-england/.

134   All-Party Parliamentary Group on Arts, Health, and Wellbeing, *Creative Health*, 37.

135   All-Party Parliamentary Group on Arts, Health, and Wellbeing, *Creative Health*, 5.

136   All-Party Parliamentary Group on Arts, Health, and Wellbeing, *Creative Health*, 8.

137   All-Party Parliamentary Group on Arts, Health, and Wellbeing, *Creative Health*, 68.

138   Leary, *Keywords*, 176.

139   Judith Pinkerton, "Music Wellness Programs: Merging Self-Responsible Strategies," *Corporate Wellness Magazine*, 29 January 2014, https://www.corporatewellnessmagazine.com/article/music-wellness-programs-merging.

140   Pinkerton, "Music Wellness Programs."

141   Pinkerton, "Music Wellness Programs."

142   Beth McGroarty, "Wellness Music," Global Wellness Summit, https://www.globalwellnesssummit.com/2020-global-wellness-trends/wellness-music/.

143   McGroarty, "Wellness Music."

144   See, for instance, Jessica Roiz, "'Medicine for the Soul': How Music Heals During a Global Pandemic," *Billboard*, 8 April 2020, https://www.billboard.com/articles/columns/latin/9353932/music-coronavirus-pandemic; and Cathy Applefeld Olson, "Meeting of the Minds: Why the Music and Mental Wellness Industries Are Syncing Up Now More than Ever," *Forbes*, 18 August 2020, https://www.forbes.com/sites/cathyolson/2020/08/18/meeting-of-the-minds-why-the-music-mental-wellness-industries-are-syncing-up-now-more-than-ever/. On music's enlistment for social reproduction in response to COVID-19, see Thompson and Drott, "Music Is Still at Work."

145   Alan Taylor, "Music and Encouragement from around the World," *Atlantic*, 24 March 2020, https://www.theatlantic.com/photo/2020/03/music-and-encouragement-from-balconies-around-world/608668/; Pam Kragen, "Music a Healing Balm for Hospitalized COVID Patients,"

Medical Express, 29 July 2020, https://medicalxpress.com/news/2020-07-music-balm-hospitalized-covid-patients.html.

146 Musicians on Call, "Musicians on Call Expands Music Pharmacy Program to Bring Music to Thousands during Pandemic," accessed 10 September 2020, https://www.musiciansoncall.org/musicians-on-call-expands-music-pharmacy-program-to-bring-music-to-thousands-during-pandemic/.

147 Deezer, "We just launched our 'Stay at home' channel to keep you company while you spend your days at home. There's playlists, podcasts and radio content to keep . . . ," Facebook post, 23 March 2020, https://www.facebook.com/Deezer/posts/we-just-launched-our-stay-at-home-channel-to-keep-you-company-while-you-spend-yo/10151196853709982/. For the "Dancing with Myself" playlist, see https://www.deezer.com/en/playlist/7427160544, accessed 10 September 2020 (note that the playlist's title has since changed to the more general and anodyne "Birthday Party," most likely in response to the end of social distancing measures).

148 Spotify, "Audio Connects Us All in Spotify's Newest Campaign, 'Listening Together,'" 7 May 2020, https://newsroom.spotify.com/2020-05-07/audio-connects-us-all-in-spotifys-newest-campaign-listening-together/.

149 Spotify, "Audio Connects Us All."

150 Hesmondhalgh, "Is Music Streaming Bad?"

151 See Brook, O'Brien, and Taylor, *Culture Is Bad for You*, 158–59. See also Deresiewicz, *Death of the Artist*, ch. 4.

Epilogue

1 See Marshall, "'Let's Keep Music Special.'"

2 Action Network, "Tell Spotify to Stop Exploiting Musicians during the COVID-19 Outbreak," accessed 7 May 2023, https://actionnetwork.org/petitions/tell-spotify-to-stop-exploiting-musicians-during-the-covid-19-outbreak.

3 Matthew Strauss, "SXSW Under Fire over Artist Deportation Contract Clause," *Pitchfork*, 2 March 2017, https://pitchfork.com/news/72013-sxsw-under-fire-over-artist-deportation-contract-clause/.

4 Tom Gray (@MrTomGray), "It's a #brokenrecord business," Twitter, 13 April 2020, 9:22 a.m., https://twitter.com/MrTomGray/status/1249689366630404098

5 Tom Gray, "It's a #brokenrecord business."

6 Ivors Academy, "The Ivors Academy and Musicians' Union Launch Keep Music Alive Campaign to 'Fix Streaming Now,'" 11 May 2020, https://ivorsacademy.com/news/the-ivors-academy-and-musicians-union-launch-keep-music-alive-campaign-to-fix-streaming-now/.

7   Digital, Culture, Media and Sport Committee, *Economics of Music Streaming*, UK Parliament, 15 July 2021, https://committees.parliament.uk/work/646/economics-of-music-streaming/.
8   Scholz, *Ours to Hack and to Own*.
9   Peter Harris, "The Story behind Resonate," *Medium*, 29 March 2016, https://medium.com/resonatecoop/the-story-behind-resonate-4b1658677663.
10 Resonate, "Why We're a Cooperative," 19 September 2015, https://resonate.is/why-were-a-cooperative/.
11 Resonate, "Stream It Till You Own It," 4 May 2015, https://web.archive.org/web/20190316151852/https://resonate.is/stream2own/.
12 Resonate, "Why We're a Cooperative."
13 Rhian Jones, "Audius Has Raised Nearly $10m for Its Spotify Rival. Can Its Blockchain-Based Model Change the Game for Artist Payments?," *Music Business Worldwide*, 20 January 2021, https://www.musicbusinessworldwide.com/audius-has-raised-nearly-10m-for-its-spotify-rival-can-its-model-change-the-game-for-artist-payments/.
14 Roneil Rumburg, Sid Sethi, and Hareesh Nagaraj, "Audius: A Decentralized Protocol for Audio Content," last updated 8 October 2020, 11, https://whitepaper.audius.co/.
15 Quoted in Trotsky, *Revolution Betrayed*, 220. The original quote (from Marx's *Critique of the Gotha Program*) is usually translated as "From each according to his ability, to each according to his needs."
16 Muikku, *Pro Rata and User Centric Distribution Models*; Page and Safir, "Money in, Money Out"; Pedersen, *A Meta-Study*.
17 Tim Ingham, "SoundCloud Is About to Revolutionize Streaming Payouts, Launching User-Centric Royalties for 100,000 Indie Artists," *Music Business Worldwide*, 2 March 2021, https://www.musicbusinessworldwide.com/soundcloud-is-about-to-revolutionize-streaming-payouts-launching-user-centric-royalties-for-100000-indie-artists/.
18 Murray Stassen, "135,000 Artists Are Now Getting Paid through SoundCloud's Fan-Powered Royalties Platform," *Music Business Worldwide*, 26 April 2022, https://www.musicbusinessworldwide.com/135000-artists-are-now-getting-paid-through-soundclouds-fan-powered-royalties-platform1/.
19 SoundCloud, "SoundCloud and Warner Music Group Announce Global Licensing Deal Bringing Fan-Powered Royalties to Major Label Artists," 21 July 2022, https://press.soundcloud.com/216750-soundcloud-and-warner-music-group-announce-global-licensing-deal-bringing-fan-powered-royalties-to-major-label-artists. Tim Ingham, "Sir Lucian Grainge: Music Needs a New Streaming Payout Model . . . and We're Working on It," *Music Business Worldwide*, 11 January 2023, https://

20. www.musicbusinessworldwide.com/sir-lucian-grainge-music-needs-a-new-streaming-payout/.

21. For its part, Sony in the past has also expressed guarded interest in UCD; see Stuart Dredge, "Major Labels Talk User-Centric Payouts and Equitable Remuneration," *Music Ally*, 24 February 2021, https://musically.com/2021/02/24/major-labels-talk-user-centric-payouts-and-equitable-remuneration/.

22. Mark Mulligan, "What Is the Value of Exposure," Midia Research, 6 May 2020, https://www.midiaresearch.com/blog/what-is-the-value-of-exposure-when-exposure-is-all-there-is.

23. Mulligan, "What Is the Value of Exposure."

24. Union of Musicians and Allied Workers, "Justice at Spotify," accessed 7 May 2023, https://www.unionofmusicians.org/justice-at-spotify-demands.

25. Andy Cush, "How Musicians Are Fighting for Streaming Pay during the Pandemic," *Pitchfork*, 29 June 2020, https://pitchfork.com/features/article/how-musicians-are-fighting-for-streaming-pay-during-the-pandemic/.

26. Rosa Luxemburg, for one, argued that cooperative enterprises represent "small units of socialized production within capitalist exchange." The problem, however, is that "in capitalist economy exchange dominates production." Luxemburg, *Reform or Revolution*, 47.

27. On this point, see International Co-operative Alliance, "International Co-operative Alliance," 21.

28. Thomas Hanna, Mathew Lawrence, and Nils Peters, "A Common Platform," December 2020, 6, https://www.common-wealth.co.uk/reports/common-platform-tech-utility-antitrust.

29. Meyne, quoted in Oliver Sylvester-Bradley, "Scaling Platform Co-Ops—Lessons from Resonate.is," *Open*, 29 April 2020, https://open.coop/2020/04/29/scaling-platform-co-ops-lessons-from-resonate-is/.

30. Sandoval, "Fighting Precarity," 64.

31. Digiconomist, "Cryptocurrency Energy Demand Is Still Underestimated," 4 August 2020, https://digiconomist.net/cryptocurrency-energy-demand-is-still-underestimated/.

32. Viljoen, "Democratic Data."

33. Sarah Roberts, "No, YouTube Is Not a Library—and Why It Matters," *Illusion of Volition*, 20 March 2018, https://illusionofvolition.com/2018/03/20/no-youtube-is-not-a-library-and-why-it-matters/.

34. Liz Pelly, "Socialized Streaming," *Real Life*, 16 February 2021, https://reallifemag.com/socialized-streaming/.

35. Felli, "On Climate Rent," 271.

36. As of 2021, Spotify claimed to host eight million "creators," though this figure combines both musicians and podcast producers. By contrast,

SoundCloud as of 2020 claimed to have twenty-five million artists on its service. For Spotify's figures, see US Securities and Exchange Commission, Amendment No. 3 to Form F-1 Registration Statement, Spotify Technology S. A., https://www.sec.gov/Archives/edgar/data/1639920/000119312518092759/d494294df1a.htm. For Soundcloud's figures, see Stuart Dredge, "12m SoundCloud Creators Get Heard Every Month (but 13m Don't)," *Music Ally*, 3 June 2020, https://musically.com/2020/06/03/12m-soundcloud-creators-get-heard-every-month-but-13m-dont/.

36 Joey La Neve DeFrancesco, interview, 8 December 2020, *Interdependence*, podcast, https://www.patreon.com/posts/justice-at-with-44808590.

37 DeFrancesco, interview.

38 Paul, "Enduring Ambiguities of Antitrust Liability."

39 Wright, *Classes*, 42–57.

40 Or, as DeFrancesco puts it, paraphrasing John Steinbeck: "Musicians see themselves not as an exploited proletariat, but as temporarily embarrassed pop stars." Joey La Neve De Francesco, "Musicians Can and Should Organize to Improve Their Pay and Working Conditions," *Jacobin*, February 2020, https://jacobinmag.com/2020/02/musicians-working-conditions-afm-amazon-sxsw-nomusicforice. For a discussion of recording musicians as aspiring rentiers, see Stahl, *Unfree Masters*, 99 and 230–31.

41 See Roberts, *Tell Tchaikovsky the News*, 76–78 and 90–92.

42 See, in this connection, Brouillette, "Creative Labor."

43 See Weeks, *Problem with Work*.

44 Care Collective, *Care Manifesto*, 94.

45 Mat Dryhurst, "Band Together: Why Musicians Must Strike a Collective Chord to Survive," *Guardian*, 9 April 2019, https://www.theguardian.com/music/2019/apr/09/experimental-musicians-must-strike-a-collective-chord-red-bull-music-academy-closing.

46 Anne Steele, "Apple Music Reveals How Much It Pays When You Stream a Song," *Wall Street Journal*, 16 April 2021, https://www.wsj.com/articles/apple-music-reveals-how-much-it-pays-when-you-stream-a-song-11618579800.

Bibliography

Abbing, Hans. *Why Are Artists Poor? The Exceptional Economy of the Arts.* Amsterdam: Amsterdam University Press, 2002.

Abraham, David. *Elements of Power: Gadgets, Guns, and the Struggle for a Sustainable Future in the Rare Metal Age.* New Haven, CT: Yale University Press, 2015.

Adkins, Lisa. *The Time of Money.* Stanford, CA: Stanford University Press, 2018.

Adkins, Lisa, Melinda Cooper, and Martijn Konings. *The Asset Economy.* Cambridge: Polity, 2020.

Adomavicius, Gediminas, Bamshad Mobasher, Francesco Ricci, and Alex Tuzhilin. "Context-Aware Recommendation Systems." *AI Magazine* 32, no. 3 (2011): 67–80.

Adorno, Theodor. *Essays on Music.* Edited by Richard Leppert. Berkeley: University of California Press, 2002.

Adorno, Theodor. *Introduction to the Sociology of Music.* Translated by E. B. Ashton. New York: Seabury Press, 1976.

Aegidius, Andreas Lenander. "The Music Streaming Metaphor and Its Tangle of Transcodes." *Popular Communication* 19, no. 1 (2020): 42–56.

Aitken, Rob. "'All Data Is Credit Data': Constituting the Unbanked." *Competition and Change* 21, no. 4 (2017): 274–300.

Alper, Neil, and Gregory Wassall. "Artists' Careers and Their Labor Markets." In *Handbook of the Economics of Arts and Culture*, vol. 1, edited by Victor Ginsburgh and David Throsby, 813–64. Amsterdam: North Holland, 2006.

Althusser, Louis. *On the Reproduction of Capitalism: Ideology and Ideological State Apparatuses.* Translated by G. M. Goshgarian. London: Verso, 2014.

Anderson, Chris. *The Long Tail: Why the Future of Business Is Selling More of Less.* New York: Hyperion, 2006.

Anderson, Jay. "Stream Capture: Returning Control of Digital Music to Users." *Harvard Journal of Law and Technology* 25, no. 1 (2011): 159–77.

Anderson, Paul Allen. "Neo-Muzak and the Business of Mood." *Critical Inquiry* 41, no. 4 (2015): 811–40.

Anderson, Tim. *Making Easy Listening: Material Culture and Postwar American Recording.* Minneapolis: University of Minnesota Press, 2006.

Anderson, Tim. *Popular Music in a Digital Music Economy: Problems and Practices for an Emerging Service Industry.* New York: Routledge, 2014.

Andrejevic, Mark. "Exploiting YouTube: Contradictions of User-Generated Labor." In *The YouTube Reader*, edited by Pelle Snickars and Patrick Vonderau, 406–23. Stockholm: National Library of Sweden, 2009.

Andrejevic, Mark. "Surveillance and Alienation in the Online Economy." *Surveillance and Society* 8, no. 3 (2011): 278–87.

Ang, Ien. *Desperately Seeking the Audience*. New York: Routledge, 1991.

Arditi, David. "Digital Subscriptions: The Unending Consumption of Music in the Digital Era." *Popular Music and Society* 41, no. 3 (2018): 302–18.

Arditi, David. "Disciplining the Consumer: File-Sharers under the Watchful Eye of the Music Industry." In *Internet and Surveillance: The Challenges of Web 2.0 and Social Media*, edited by Christian Fuchs, Kees Boersma, Anders Albrechtsund, and Marisol Sandoval, 170–86. New York: Routledge, 2012.

Arditi, David. *ITake-Over: The Recording Industry in the Streaming Era*. London: Lexington Books, 2020.

Attali, Jacques. *Noise: The Political Economy of Music*. Translated by Brian Massumi. Minneapolis: University of Minnesota Press, 1985.

Augé, Marc. *Non-Places: Introduction to an Anthropology of Supermodernity*. Translated by John Howe. London: Verso, 1995.

Austerberry, David. *The Technology of Video and Audio Streaming*. 2nd ed. New York: Focal, 2005.

Baade, Christina. "Lean Back: Songza, Ubiquitous Listening, and Internet Radio for the Masses." *Radio Journal* 16, no. 1 (2018): 9–27.

Bagley, Philip. *Extensions of Programming Language Concepts*. Philadelphia: University City Science Center, 1968.

Bakker, Karen. *An Uncooperative Commodity: Privatizing Water in England and Wales*. Oxford: Oxford University Press, 2003.

Barron, David, and Elizabeth West. "The Financial Costs of Caring in the British Labour Market: Is There a Wage Penalty for Workers in Caring Occupations?" *British Journal of Industrial Relations* 51, no. 1 (2013): 104–23.

Baumol, William. *The Cost Disease: Why Computers Get Cheaper and Health Care Doesn't*. New Haven, CT: Yale University Press, 2012.

Baumol, William, and William Bowen. *Performing Arts: The Economic Dilemma*. New York: Twentieth Century Fund, 1966.

Baym, Nancy. *Playing to the Crowd: Musicians, Audiences, and the Intimate Work of Connection*. New York: New York University Press, 2018.

Baym, Nancy, and Robert Burnett. "Amateur Experts: International Fan Labor in Swedish Independent Music." *International Journal of Cultural Studies* 12, no. 5 (2009): 433–49.

Beech, Dave. *Art and Value: Art's Economic Exceptionalism in Classical, Neoclassical, and Marxist Economics*. Leiden: Brill, 2015.

Beer, David. *Metric Power*. London: Palgrave, 2016.

Bellamy Foster, John, Brett Clark, and Richard York. *The Ecological Rift: Capitalism's War on the Earth*. New York: Monthly Review Press, 2010.

Bellamy Foster, John, and Robert McChesney. "Surveillance Capitalism." *Monthly Review* (July 2014): 1–31.

Bellamy Foster, John, Robert McChesney, and R. Jamil Jonna. "Monopoly and Competition in the Twenty-First Century." *Monthly Review* (April 2011): 1–39.

Benanav, Aaron. "Automation and the Future of Work—2." *New Left Review* 120 (November–December 2019): 117–46.

Benanav, Aaron, and John Clegg. "Misery and Debt: On the Logic and History of Surplus Populations and Surplus Capital." *Endnotes* 2 (2010).

Benjamin, Ruha. *Race after Technology: Abolitionist Tools for the New Jim Code*. Cambridge: Polity, 2019.

Benjamin, Walter. *The Work of Art in the Age of Its Technological Reproducibility, and Other Writings on Media*. Edited by Michael Jennings, Brigid Doherty, and Thomas Y. Levin. Cambridge, MA: Harvard University Press, 2008.

Bernards, Nick. "'Fintech' and Financial Inclusion." In *The Palgrave Handbook of Contemporary International Political Economy*, edited by Timothy M. Shaw, Laura C. Mahrenbach, Renu Modi, and Xu Yi-chong, 317–29. London: Palgrave, 2019.

Bhattacharya, Tithi, ed. *Social Reproduction Theory: Remapping Class, Recentering Oppression*. London: Pluto, 2017.

Birenbaum Quintero, Michael. "Late Capitalism, Affect, and the Algorithmic Self on Music Streaming Platforms." In *Sound and Affect: Voice, Music, World*, edited by Judith Lochhead, Eduardo Mendieta, and Stephen Decatur Smith, 159–95. Chicago: University of Chicago Press, 2021.

Bogost, Ian, and Nick Montfort. "Platform Studies: Frequently Questioned Answers." Paper presented at the Digital Arts and Culture Conference, University of California, Irvine, 2009. https://escholarship.org/uc/item/01r0k9br.

Bolter, Jay David, and Richard Grusin. *Remediation: Understanding New Media*. Cambridge, MA: MIT Press, 1999.

Born, Georgina. "Music and the Materialization of Identities." *Journal of Material Culture* 16, no. 4 (2011): 376–88.

Born, Georgina. "On Musical Mediation: Ontology, Technology, and Creativity." *Twentieth-Century Music* 2, no. 1 (2005): 7–36.

Bourdieu, Pierre. *Distinction: A Social Critique of the Judgment of Taste*. Translated by Richard Nice. Cambridge, MA: Harvard University Press, 1984.

Brackett, David. *Categorizing Sound: Genre and Twentieth-Century Popular Music*. Berkeley: University of California Press, 2016.

Brenner, Robert. *The Boom and the Bubble: The US in the Global Economy*. London: Verso, 2002.

Brodsky, Warren, Dana Olivieri, and Eugene Chekaluk. "Music Genre Induced Driver Aggression: A Case of Media Delinquency and Risk-Promoting Popular Culture." *Music and Science* 1 (2018): 1–17.

Brook, Orian, Dave O'Brien, and Mark Taylor. *Culture Is Bad for You*. Manchester: University of Manchester Press, 2020.

Brouillette, Sarah. "Creative Labor." *Mediations* 24, no. 2 (2009): 140–49.

Brown, Megan. "Taking Care of Business: Self-Help and Sleep Medicine in American Corporate Culture." *Journal of Medical Humanities* 25, no. 3 (2004): 173–87.

Browne, Simone. *Dark Matters: On the Surveillance of Blackness*. Durham, NC: Duke University Press, 2015.

Brunton, Finn. *Spam: A Shadow History of the Internet*. Cambridge, MA: MIT Press, 2013.

Bull, Michael. *Sound Moves: iPod Culture and Urban Experience*. London: Routledge, 2007.

Burkart, Patrick. *Music and Cyberliberties*. Middletown, CT: Wesleyan University Press, 2010.

Burkart, Patrick. "Music in the Cloud and the Digital Sublime." *Popular Music and Society* 37, no. 4 (2014): 393–407.

Buzzard, Karen. *Tracking the Audience: The Ratings Industry from Analog to Digital*. New York: Routledge, 2012.

Callon, Michel, Cécile Méadel, and Vololona Rabeharisoa. "The Economy of Qualities." *Economy and Society* 31, no. 2 (2002): 194–217.

Care Collective. *The Care Manifesto: The Politics of Interdependence*. London: Verso, 2020.

Carrington, Michal Jemma, Detlev Zwick, and Benjamin Neville. "The Ideology of the Ethical Consumption Gap." *Marketing Theory* 16, no. 1 (2016): 21–38.

Casilli, Antonio. "Digital Labor Studies Go Global: Toward a Digital Decolonial Turn." *International Journal of Communication* 11 (2017): 3934–54.

Caves, Richard. *Creative Industries: Contracts between Art and Commerce*. Cambridge, MA: Harvard University Press, 2000.

Celma, Oscar. *Music Recommendation and Discovery: The Long Tail, the Long Fail, and Long Play in the Digital Music Space*. Berlin: Springer, 2010.

Chastagner, Claude. "The Parents' Music Resource Center: From Information to Censorship." *Popular Music* 18, no. 2 (1999): 179–92.

Cheney-Lippold, John. *We Are Data: Algorithms and the Making of Our Digital Selves*. New York: New York University Press, 2017.

Christl, Wolfie. *Corporate Surveillance in Everyday Life*. Vienna: Cracked Labs, 2017.

Christophers, Brett. *Rentier Capitalism: Who Owns the Economy, and Who Pays for It?* London: Verso, 2020.

Citton, Yves. *The Ecology of Attention*. Translated by Barbara Malden. Cambridge: Polity, 2017.

Coalition for Innovative Media Measurement. *Enriching Media Data: Quality Is Key Requisite for Maximizing ROI*. June 2015. http://cimm-us.org/wp-content/uploads/2012/07/CIMM_Enriching-Media-Data-Quality-is-Key-for-ROI_June-20151.pdf.

Cohen, Nicole. "Commodifying Free Labor Online: Social Media, Audiences, and Advertising." In *The Routledge Companion to Advertising and Promotional Culture*, edited by Matthew Mcallister and Emily West, 177–91. New York: Routledge, 2013.

Cohen, Nicole. "The Valorization of Surveillance: Towards a Political Economy of Facebook." *Democratic Communiqué* 22, no. 1 (2008): 5–22.

Cooke, Chris. *Dissecting the Digital Dollar*. 2nd ed. London: Music Manager's Fund, 2018.

Cooper, Melinda. *Family Values: Between Neoliberalism and the New Social Conservatism*. New York: Zone Books, 2017.

Cowan, Ruth Schwartz. *More Work for Mother: The Ironies of Household Technology from the Open Hearth to the Microwave*. New York: Basic Books, 1983.

Coyle, Michael. "Hijacked Hits and Antic Authenticity: Cover Songs, Race, and Postwar Marketing." In *Rock over the Edge: Transformations in Popular Music Culture*, edited by Roger Beebe, Denise Fulbrook, and Ben Saunder, 133–57. Durham, NC: Duke University Press, 2002.

Crain, Matthew. "The Limits of Transparency: Data Brokers and Commodification." *New Media and Society* (2016): 1–17.

Crary, Jonathan. *Suspensions of Perception: Attention, Spectacle, and Modern Culture*. Cambridge, MA: MIT Press, 1999.

Crary, Jonathan. *24/7: Late Capitalism and the Ends of Sleep*. London: Verso, 2013.

Crawford, Kate, and Tarleton Gillespie. "What Is a Flag For? Social Media Reporting Tools and the Vocabulary of Complaint." *New Media and Society* 18, no. 3 (2016): 410–28.

Crawford, Matthew. *The World beyond Your Head: Becoming an Individual in an Age of Distraction*. New York: Farrar, Straus, and Giroux, 2015.

Crouch, Colin. "Privatised Keynesianism: An Unacknowledged Policy Regime." *BJPIR* 11 (2009): 382–99.

Cruz, Jon. *Culture on the Margins: The Black Spiritual and the Rise of American Cultural Interpretation*. Princeton, NJ: Princeton University Press, 1999.

Dannenberg, Roger, Jonathan Foote, George Tzanetakis, and Christopher Weare. "Panel: New Directions in Music Information Retrieval." In *Proceedings of the 2001 International Computer Music Conference*, 1–8. International Computer Music Association, 2001.

Daughtry, Martin. "Did Music Cause the End of the World?" *Transposition* (2020): 1–31.

Davenport, Thomas, and John Beck. *The Attention Economy: Understanding the New Currency of Business.* Boston: Harvard Business School Press, 2001.

Davies, Dan. *Lying for Money: How Legendary Frauds Reveal the Workings of Our World.* London: Profile Books, 2019.

Davies, Will. "Economics and the 'Nonsense' of Law: The Case of the Chicago Antitrust Revolution." *Economy and Society* 39, no. 1 (2010): 64–83.

DeAngelis, Massimo. "Does Capital Need a Commons Fix?" *ephemera* 13, no. 3 (2013): 603–15.

DeAngelis, Massimo. *Omnia Communis Sunt.* London: Zed Books, 2017.

de Cnudde, Sofie, Julie Moeyersoms, Marija Stankova, Ellen Tobback, Vinayak Javaly, and David Martens. "Who Cares about Your Facebook Friends? Credit Scoring for Microfinance." Working Paper No. D/2015/1169/018, University of Antwerp, Antwerp, Belgium, 2015.

Deleuze, Gilles. "Postscript on the Societies of Control." *October* 59 (Winter 1992): 1–5.

Demers, Joanna. *Steal This Music: How Intellectual Property Law Affects Musical Creativity.* Athens: University of Georgia Press, 2006.

DeNora, Tia. "Music as a Technology of the Self." *Poetics* 27 (1999): 31–56.

DeNora, Tia. *Music in Everyday Life.* Cambridge: Cambridge University Press, 2000.

Deresiewicz, William. *Death of the Artist: How Creators Are Struggling to Survive in the Age of Billionaires and Big Tech.* New York: Henry Holt, 2020.

Devine, Kyle. *Decomposed: The Political Ecology of Music.* Cambridge, MA: MIT Press, 2019.

Devine, Kyle. "Musicology without Music." In *On Popular Music and Its Unruly Entanglements*, edited by Nick Braae and Kai Arne Hansen, 15–38. Cham, Switzerland: Palgrave Macmillan, 2019.

DeWaard, Andrew. "Derivative Media: The Financialization of Film, Television, and Popular Music, 2004–2016." PhD diss., University of California, Los Angeles, 2017.

DeWaard, Andrew. "Wall Street's Content Wars: Financing Media Consolidation." Working Paper, 2021. https://escholarship.org/uc/item/7m6819ch.

Dimitrakaki, Angela, and Kirsten Lloyd. "Social Reproduction Struggles and Art History: An Introduction." *Third Text* 31, no. 1 (2017): 1–14.

Dixon, Pam, and Robert Gellman. *The Scoring of America: How Secret Consumer Scores Threaten Your Privacy and Your Future.* World Privacy Forum, 2014.

Doganova, Liliana. "Discounting the Future: A Political Technology." *Economic Sociology* 19, no. 2 (2018): 4–9.

Dolan, Emily. "Musicology in the Garden." *Representations* 132, no. 1 (2015): 88–94.

Donath, Judith. "Identity and Deception in the Virtual Community." In *Communities in Cyberspace*, edited by Marc Smith and Peter Kollock, 27–58. London: Routledge, 1999.

Donath, Susan. "The Other Economy: A Suggestion for a Distinctively Feminist Economics." *Feminist Economics* 6, no. 1 (2000): 115–23.

Dörr, Jonathan, Thomas Wagner, Thomas Hess, and Alexander Benlian. "Music as a Service as an Alternative to Music Piracy?" *Business and Information Systems Engineering* 5, no. 6 (2013): 383–96.

Drott, Eric. "Copyright, Compensation, and Commons in the Music AI Industry." *Creative Industries Journal* 14, no. 2 (2021): 190–207.

Drott, Eric. *Music and the Elusive Revolution: Cultural Politics and Political Culture in France, 1968–1981.* Berkeley: University of California Press, 2011.

Drott, Eric. "Music in the Work of Social Reproduction." *Cultural Politics* 15, no. 2 (2019): 162–83.

Drott, Eric. "Why the Next Song Matters: Streaming, Recommendation, Scarcity." *Twentieth-Century Music* 15, no. 3 (2018): 325–57.

Drott, Eric, and Marie Thompson. "'Is Your Baby Getting Enough Music?' Musical Interventions into Gestational Labor." *Women and Music* 26 (2022): 125–47.

Duffy, Mignon, Randy Albelda, and Clare Hammonds. "Counting Care Work: The Empirical and Policy Applications of Care Theory." *Social Problems* 60, no. 2 (2013): 145–67.

Duinker, Ben. "Song Form and the Mainstreaming of Hip Hop." *Current Musicology* 107 (2020): 93–135.

Durham, Blake. "Circulatory Maintenance: The Entailments of Participation in Digital Music Platforms." *American Music* 38, no. 2 (2020): 197–216.

Dymski, Gary, and John E. Elliott. "The Taxonomy of Primary Exploitation." *Review of Social Economy* 47, no. 4 (1989): 338–76.

Easterling, Keller. *Extrastatecraft: The Power of Infrastructure Space.* London: Verso, 2014.

Edelman, Lee. *No Future: Queer Theory and the Death Drive.* Durham, NC: Duke University Press, 2004.

Eideldinger, Jean-Jacques. *Chopin, âme des salons parisiens.* Paris: Fayard, 2013.

Eisenberg, Evan. *The Recording Angel: Music, Records and Culture from Aristotle to Zappa.* 2nd ed. New Haven, CT: Yale University Press, 2005.

Eisenmann, Thomas, Geoffrey Parker, and Marshall Van Alstyne. "Strategies for Two-Sided Markets." *Harvard Business Review* 84, no. 10 (October 2006): 92–101.

Elberse, Anita. *Blockbusters: Hit-Making, Risk-Taking, and the Big Business of Entertainment.* New York: Henry Holt, 2013.

Endnotes Collective. "The Logic of Gender." *Endnotes* 3 (September 2013). https://endnotes.org.uk/articles/the-logic-of-gender.

England, Paula, Michelle Budig, and Nancy Folbre. "Wages of Virtue: The Relative Pay of Care Work." *Social Problems* 49, no. 4 (2002): 455–73.

Eriksson, Maria. "Close Reading Big Data: Echo Nest and the Production of (Rotten) Music Metadata." *First Monday* 21, no. 7 (2016).

Eriksson, Maria. "The Editorial Playlist as Container Technology: On Spotify and the Logistical Role of Digital Music Packages." *Journal of Cultural Economy* 13, no. 4 (2020): 415–27.

Eriksson, Maria. "Online Music Distribution and the Unpredictability of Software Logistics." PhD diss., Umea University, 2019.

Eriksson, Maria, Rasmus Fleischer, Anna Johansson, Pelle Snickars, and Patrick Vonderau. *Spotify Teardown: Inside the Black Box of Streaming Music*. Cambridge, MA: MIT Press, 2019.

Eriksson, Maria, and Anna Johansson. "'Keep Smiling!': Time, Functionality, and Intimacy in Spotify's Featured Playlists." *Cultural Analysis* 16, no. 1 (2017): 67–82.

European Commission, International Monetary Fund, Organisation for Economic Co-operation and Development, United Nations, and World Bank. *System of National Accounts 2008*. New York: United Nations, 2009.

Evans, David, and Richard Schmalensee. *Matchmakers: The New Economics of Multisided Platforms*. Boston: Harvard Business Review Press, 2016.

Fanen, Sophian. *Boulevard du stream: Du mp3 à Deezer, la musique libérée*. Paris: Le Castor Astral, 2017.

Farooqi, Shehroze, Guillaume Jourjon, Muhammad Ikram, Mohamed Ali Kaafar, Emiliano De Cristofaro, Zubair Shafiq, Arik Friedman, and Fareed Zaffar. "Characterizing Key Stakeholders in an Online Black-Hat Marketplace." In *2017 APWG Symposium on Electronic Crime Research (eCrime)*, 17–27. New York: Institute of Electrical and Electronics Engineers, 2017.

Faulkner, Robert, and Andy B. Anderson. "Short-Term Projects and Emergent Careers: Evidence from Hollywood." *American Journal of Sociology* 92, no. 4 (1987): 879–909.

Federici, Silvia. *Revolution at Point Zero: Housework, Reproduction, and Feminist Struggle*. Oakland, CA: PM Press, 2012.

Felli, Romain. "On Climate Rent." *Historical Materialism* 22, nos. 3–4 (2014): 251–80.

Fergus, Devlin. "The Ghetto Tax: Auto Insurance, Postal Code Profiling, and the Hidden Transfer of Wealth." In *Beyond Discrimination: Racial Inequality in a Post-Racial Era*, edited by Frederick Harris and Robert Lieberman, 277–316. New York: Russell Sage Foundation, 2013.

Ferreboeuf, Hugues, and Lean ICT Working Group. *Lean ICT: Towards Digital Sobriety*. Shift Project, March 2019. https://theshiftproject.org/wp-content/uploads/2019/03/Lean-ICT-Report_The-Shift-Project_2019.pdf.

Fink, Robert. *Repeating Ourselves: American Minimal Music as Cultural Practice*. Berkeley: University of California Press, 2004.

Fisher, Irving. *The Nature of Capital and Income*. New York: Macmillan, 1906.

Fleischer, Rasmus. "If the Song Has No Price, Is It Still a Commodity? Rethinking the Commodification of Digital Music." *Culture Unbound* 9, no. 2 (2017): 146–62.

Folbre, Nancy. "The Care Penalty and Gender Inequality." In *The Oxford Handbook of Women and Economy*, edited by Susan Averett, Laura Argys, and Saul Hoffman, 749–66. Oxford: Oxford University Press, 2017.

Fortunati, Leopoldina. *The Arcane of Reproduction: Housework, Prostitution, Labor and Capital*. Brooklyn: Autonomedia, 1995.

Frank, Georg. "The Economy of Attention." *Telepolis*, 7 December 1999. https://www.heise.de/tp/features/The-Economy-of-Attention-3444929.html.

Frank, Robert, and Philip Cook. *The Winner-Take-All Society: Why the Few at the Top Get So Much More Than the Rest of Us*. New York: Random House, 1995.

Fraser, Nancy. "Behind Marx's Hidden Abode." *New Left Review* 86 (March–April 2014): 55–72.

Fraser, Nancy. "Capitalism's Crisis of Care." *Dissent* 63, no. 4 (2016): 30–37.

Fraser, Nancy, and Rahel Jaeggi. *Capitalism: A Conversation in Critical Theory*. Cambridge: Polity, 2017.

Fridell, Gavin. "Fair-Trade Coffee and Commodity Fetishism: The Limits of Market-Driven Social Justice." *Historical Materialism* 15 (2007): 79–104.

Frith, Simon. "Copyright and the Music Business." *Popular Music* 7, no. 1 (1988): 57–75.

Frith, Simon. "Music and Identity." In *Questions of Cultural Identity*, edited by Stuart Hall and Paul Du Gay, 108–27. London: Sage, 1996.

Fuchs, Christian. "Dallas Smythe and Digital Labor." In *Routledge Companion to Labor and Media*, edited by Richard Maxwell, 51–62. New York: Routledge, 2015.

Fuchs, Christian. *Social Media: A Critical Introduction*. London: Sage, 2014.

Galloway, Alexander. *The Interface Effect*. Cambridge: Polity, 2012.

Galuszka, Patryk. "Music Aggregators and Intermediation in the Digital Music Market." *International Journal of Communication* 9 (2015): 254–73.

Gaquin, Deirdre. *Artists in the Workforce: 1990 to 2005*. Research Report no. 48. Washington, DC: National Endowment for the Arts, 2008.

Gawer, Annabelle, ed. *Platforms, Markets, and Innovation*. Cheltenham, UK: Edward Elgar, 2009.

Gibson-Graham, J. K. *The End of Capitalism (As We Knew It): A Feminist Critique of Political Economy*. 2nd ed. Minneapolis: University of Minnesota Press, 2006.

Gibson-Graham, J. K. *A Postcapitalist Politics*. Minneapolis: University of Minnesota Press, 2006.

Gillespie, Tarleton. *Custodians of the Internet: Platforms, Content Moderation, and the Hidden Decisions That Shape Social Media.* New Haven, CT: Yale University Press, 2018.

Gillespie, Tarleton. "The Politics of 'Platforms.'" *New Media and Society* 12, no. 3 (2010): 349–50.

Gillespie, Tarleton. "Regulation of and by Platforms." In *The Sage Handbook of Social Media*, edited by Jean Burgess, Alice Marwick, and Thomas Poell, 254–78. London: Sage, 2018.

Gillespie, Tarleton. *Wired Shut: Copyright and the Shape of Digital Culture.* Cambridge, MA: MIT Press, 2009.

Gilliard, Chris. "Digital Redlining, Access, and Privacy." *Common Sense Education*, 24 May 2016. https://www.commonsense.org/education/articles/digital-redlining-access-and-privacy.

Gitelman, Lisa, and Virginia Jackson. "Introduction." In *Raw Data Is an Oxymoron*, edited by Lisa Gitelman, 1–14. Cambridge, MA: MIT Press, 2013.

Glenn, Evelyn Nakano. *Forced to Care: Coercion and Caregiving in America.* Cambridge, MA: Harvard University Press, 2010.

Goffman, Erving. *The Presentation of Self in Everyday Life.* New York: Anchor, 1958.

Goldhaber, Michael. "The Attention Economy and the Net." *First Monday* 2, no. 4 (7 April 1997). http://firstmonday.org/ojs/index.php/fm/article/view/519/440.

Goldschmitt, K. E. "The Long History of the 2017 Spotify 'Fake Music' Scandal." *American Music* 38, no. 2 (2020): 131–52.

Goldschmitt, K. E., and Nick Seaver. "Shaping the Stream: Techniques and Troubles of Algorithmic Recommendation." In *The Cambridge Companion to Music in Digital Culture*, edited by Nicholas Cook, Monique Ingalls, and David Trippett, 63–85. Cambridge: Cambridge University Press, 2019.

Goodman, David. "Distracted Listening: On Not Making Sound Choices in the 1930s." In *Sound in the Age of Mechanical Reproduction*, edited by David Suisman and Susan Strasser, 15–46. Philadelphia: University of Pennsylvania Press, 2011.

Gopinath, Sumanth. *The Ringtone Dialectic: Economy and Cultural Form.* Cambridge, MA: MIT Press, 2013.

Gopinath, Sumanth, and Jason Stanyek. "Anytime, Anywhere? An Introduction to Devices, Markets and Theories of Mobile Music." In *The Oxford Handbook of Mobile Music*, vol. 1, edited by Sumanth Gopinath and Jason Stanyek, 1–36. Oxford: Oxford University Press, 2014.

Gopinath, Sumanth, and Jason Stanyek. "Tuning the Human Race: Athletic Capitalism and the Nike+ Sport Kit." In *Music, Sound and Space: Transformations of Public and Private Experience*, edited by Georgina Born, 128–48. Cambridge: Cambridge University Press, 2013.

Gracyk, Theodore. "Covers and Communicative Intentions." *JMM: The Journal of Music and Meaning* 11 (2012–2013): 22–46.

Graeber, David. *Debt: The First 5,000 Years*. New York: Melville House, 2011.

Green, Lucy. "Musical Meaning and Social Reproduction: A Case for Retrieving Autonomy." *Educational Philosophy and Theory* 37, no. 1 (2005): 77–92.

Gross, Sally Anne, and George Musgrave. *Can Music Make You Sick? Measuring the Price of Musical Ambition*. London: University of Westminster Press, 2020.

Groys, Boris. *Art Power*. Cambridge, MA: MIT Press, 2008.

Guinan, Joe. "Socialising Capital: Looking Back on the Meidner Plan." *International Journal of Public Policy* 15, nos. 1–2 (2019): 38–58.

Gunderson, Ryan. "Problems with the Defetishization Thesis: Ethical Consumerism, Alternative Food Systems, and Commodity Fetishism." *Agriculture and Human Values* 31, no. 1 (2014): 109–17.

Guyer, Jane. "Obligation, Binding, Debt and Responsibility: Provocations about Temporality from Two New Sources." *Social Anthropology/Anthropologie Sociale* 20 (2012): 491–501.

Hagen, Anja Nylund. "The Playlist Experience: Personal Playlists in Music Streaming Services." *Popular Music and Society* 38, no. 5 (2015): 625–45.

Hammel, Stephan. "Music, the Realist Conception of Art, and the Materialist Conception of History." *Twentieth-Century Music* 16, no. 1 (2019): 33–50.

Hardin, Garrett. "The Tragedy of the Commons." *Science* 162, no. 3859 (1968): 1243–48.

Hariri, Negar, Bamshad Mobasher, and Robin Burke. "Context-Aware Music Recommendation Based on Latent Topic Sequential Patterns." In *Proceedings of the Sixth ACM Conference on Recommender Systems*, 131–38. Association for Computing Machinery, 2012.

Hartson, Rex, and Pardha Pyla. *The UX Book: Agile UX Design for a Quality User Experience*. Cambridge, MA: Elsevier, 2018.

Harvey, David. *Marx, Capital and the Madness of Economic Reason*. Oxford: Oxford University Press, 2018.

Harvey, David. *The New Imperialism*. Oxford: Oxford University Press, 2003.

Harvey, David. "The 'New' Imperialism: Accumulation by Dispossession." *Socialist Register* 40 (2004): 63–87.

Haßlinger, Gerhard. "Efficiency of Caching and Content Delivery in Broadband Access Networks." In *Advanced Content Delivery, Streaming, and Cloud Services*, edited by Mukaddim Pathan, Ramesh K. Sitaraman, and Dom Robinson, 71–90. Hoboken, NJ: Wiley, 2014.

Heen, Mary. "Ending Jim Crow Life Insurance Rates." *Northwestern Journal of Law and Social Policy* 4, no. 2 (2009): 360–99.

Heidegger, Martin. *The Question concerning Technology and Other Essays*. Translated by William Lovitt. New York: Harper and Row, 1977.

Helfrich, Silke. "Common Goods Don't Simply Exist—They Are Created." In *The Wealth of Commons*, edited by David Bollier and Silke Helfrich, 61–67. Amherst, MA: Levellers Press, 2014.

Helmond, Anne. "The Platformization of the Web: Making Web Data Platform Ready." *Social Media + Society* 1, no. 2 (2015): 1–11.

Hesmondhalgh, David. *The Cultural Industries*. 2nd ed. London: Sage, 2007.

Hesmondhalgh, David. "Is Music Streaming Bad for Musicians? Problems of Evidence and Argument." *New Media and Society* (2020): 3593–615.

Hesmondhalgh, David, Richard Osborne, Hyojung Sun, and Kenny Barr. *Music Creators' Earnings in the Digital Era*. London: Intellectual Property Office.

Hester, Helen, and Nick Srnicek. "The Crisis of Social Reproduction and the End of Work." In *The Age of Perplexity: Rethinking the World We Knew*, translated by David George and Pilar Guerrero, 335–51. Madrid: BBVA, 2017.

Hill, Peter. "On Goods and Services." *Review of Income and Wealth* 23, no. 4 (1977): 315–38.

Hill, Peter. "Tangibles, Intangibles, and Services: A New Taxonomy for the Classification of Output." *Canadian Journal of Economics/Revue canadienne d'Economique* 32, no. 2 (1999): 426–46.

Hochschild, Arlie Russell. "Global Care Chains and Emotional Surplus Value." In *Justice, Politics, and the Family*, edited by Daniel Engster and Tamara Metz, 249–61. London: Routledge, 2015.

Horkheimer, Max, and Theodor Adorno. *Dialectic of Enlightenment*. Translated by John Cumming. New York: Continuum, 1999.

Hu, Tung-Hui. *A Prehistory of the Cloud*. Cambridge, MA: MIT Press, 2015.

Hubbs, Graham. "Digital Music and Public Goods." In *21st Century Perspectives on Music, Technology, and Culture: Listening Spaces*, edited by Richard Purcell and Richard Randall, 134–52. New York: Palgrave Macmillan, 2016.

Hurley, Mikkela, and Julius Adebayo. "Credit Scoring in the Era of Big Data." *Yale Journal of Law and Technology* 18, no. 1 (2016): 148–216.

Hwang, Tim. *Subprime Attention Crisis: Advertising and the Time Bomb at the Heart of the Internet*. New York: FSG Originals X Logic, 2020.

Ihde, Don. *Technology and the Lifeworld: From Garden to Earth*. Bloomington: Indiana University Press, 1990.

Inglis, Ian. "Embassy Records: Covering the Market, Marketing the Cover." *Popular Music and Society* 28, no. 2 (2005): 163–70.

International Co-operative Alliance. "The International Co-operative Alliance and Platform Co-ops." Discussion paper, February 2019.

International Federation of Phonographic Industries. *The IFPI Global Music Report 2022: The State of the Industry*. London: IFPI, 2022.

James, Robin. "Is the Post- in Post-Identity the Post- in Post-Genre?" *Popular Music* 36, no. 1 (2017): 21–32.

Jameson, Fredric. *Postmodernism, or the Cultural Logic of Late Capitalism.* Durham, NC: Duke University Press, 1991.

Jappe, Anselm. *Les aventures de la marchandise: Pour une critique de la valeur.* Paris: La Découverte, 2017.

Johansson, Sophia, Ann Werner, Patrik Åker, and Greg Goldenzwaig. *Streaming Music: Practices, Media, Cultures.* London: Routledge, 2018.

Johnson, James H. *Listening in Paris: A Cultural History.* Berkeley: University of California Press, 1995.

Johnson, Tom. "Analyzing Genre in Post-Millennial Popular Music." PhD diss., City University of New York, 2018.

Jones, Phil. *Work without the Worker: Labour in the Age of Platform Capitalism.* London: Verso, 2021.

Jutla, Sukhi, and Narendiran Sundararajan. "India's FinTech Ecosystem." In *The FinTech Book*, edited by Susanne Chishti and Janos Barberis, 56–57. Hoboken, NJ: Wiley, 2016.

Kallis, Giorgos. *Degrowth.* Newcastle upon Tyne, UK: Agenda, 2018.

Kassabian, Anahid. "Music for Sleeping." In *Sound, Music, Affect: Theorizing Sonic Experience*, edited by Marie Thompson and Ian Biddle, 165–81. New York: Bloomsbury, 2014.

Kassabian, Anahid. *Ubiquitous Listening: Affect, Attention and Distributed Subjectivity.* Berkeley: University of California Press, 2013.

Katz, Mark. *Capturing Sound: How Technology Has Changed Music.* 2nd ed. Berkeley: University of California Press, 2010.

Kay, Peter, Yi Yuan Ting, and Kok Yang Tan. "Sex and Care: The Evolutionary Psychological Explanations for Sex Differences in Formal Care Occupations." *Frontiers in Psychology* 10 (2019): 1–7.

Keightley, Keir. "Music for Middlebrows: Defining the Easy-Listening Era, 1946–1966." *American Music* 26, no. 3 (2008): 309–35.

Keightley, Keir. "'Turn It Down!' She Shrieked: Gender, Domestic Space, and High Fidelity, 1948–1959." *Popular Music* 15, no. 2 (1995): 149–77.

Keil, Charles. "Motion and Feeling through Music." *Journal of Aesthetics and Art Criticism* 24, no. 3 (1966): 337–49.

Kelley, Norman, ed. *Rhythm and Business: The Political Economy of Black Music.* New York: Akashic, 2005.

Khamis, Susie. "The Aestheticization of Restraint: The Popular Appeal of Decluttering after the Global Financial Crisis." *Journal of Consumer Culture* 19, no. 4 (2019): 513–31.

Khan, Lina. "Amazon's Antitrust Paradox." *Yale Law Journal* 126 (2016): 710–805.

Kjøsen, Atle Mikkola. "An Accident of Value: A Marxist-Virilian Analysis of Digital Piracy." MA thesis, University of Western Ontario, 2010.

Klein, Bethany. "'The New Radio': Music Licensing as a Response to Industry Woe." *Media, Culture and Society* 30, no. 4 (2008): 463–78.

Klein, Bethany. *Selling Out: Culture, Commerce, and Popular Music*. London: Bloomsbury, 2020.

Kopytoff, Igor. "The Cultural Biography of Things: Commoditization as Process." In *The Social Life of Things: Commodities in Cultural Perspective*, edited by Arjun Appadurai, 64–91. Cambridge: Cambridge University Press, 1986.

Kramer, Lawrence. *Why Classical Music Still Matters*. Berkeley: University of California Press, 2007.

Kreidler, John. "Leverage Lost: The Non-profit Arts in the Post-Ford Era." *Journal of Arts Management, Law, and Society* 26, no. 2 (1996): 79–100.

Krueger, Alan. *Rockonomics: A Backstage Tour of What the Music Industry Can Teach Us about Economics and Life*. New York: Currency, 2019.

Kusek, David, and Gerd Leonhard. *The Future of Music: Manifesto for the Digital Music Revolution*. Boston: Berklee Press, 2005.

La Berge, Leigh Clare. "Decommodified Labor: Conceptualizing Work after the Wage." *Lateral* 7, no. 1 (2018).

Langley, Paul, and Andrew Leyshon. "Platform Capitalism: The Intermediation and Capitalisation of Digital Economic Circulation." *Finance and Society* 3, no. 1 (2016): 1–21.

Larson, Rob. *Bit Tyrants: The Political Economy of Silicon Valley*. Chicago: Haymarket, 2020.

Lauer, Josh. "Plastic Surveillance: Payment Cards and the History of Transactional Data, 1888 to Present." *Big Data and Society* (2020): 1–14.

Lazzarato, Maurizio. *Governing by Debt*. Translated by Joshua David Jordan. Los Angeles: Semiotext(e), 2015.

Lazzarato, Maurizio. *The Making of the Indebted Man: An Essay on the Neoliberal Condition*. Translated by Joshua David Jordan. Los Angeles: Semiotext(e), 2012.

Leary, John Patrick. *Keywords: The New Language of Capitalism*. Chicago: Haymarket, 2018.

Lehdonvirta, Vili, Isis Hjorth, Mark Graham, and Helena Barnard. "Online Labour Markets and the Persistence of Personal Networks: Evidence from Workers in Southeast Asia." Paper presented at the ASA Annual Meeting, Chicago, IL, 2015. http://vili.lehdonvirta.com/files/Online%20labour%20markets%20and%20personal%20networks%20ASA%202015.pdf.

Lehman, Frank. "Form and Ignorability in Ambient Music." Paper presented at the 2017 annual meeting of the Society for Music Theory, Arlington, VA, 2–5 November 2017.

Leppert, Richard. *Aesthetic Technologies of Modernity, Subjectivity, and Nature: Opera, Orchestra, Phonograph, Film*. Berkeley: University of California Press, 2015.

Leveillé Gauvin, Hubert. "Drawing Listener Attention in Popular Music: Testing Five Musical Features Arising from the Theory of the Attention Economy." *Musicae Scientiae* 22, no. 3 (2018): 291–304.

Lewis, Sophie. *Full Surrogacy Now: Feminism against Family*. London: Verso, 2019.

Leydon, Rebecca. "The Soft-Focus Sound: Reverb as a Gendered Attribute in Mid-Century Mood Music." *Perspectives of New Music* 39, no. 2 (2001): 96–107.

Leyshon, Andrew. *Reformatted: Code, Networks, and the Transformation of the Music Industry*. Oxford: Oxford University Press, 2014.

Linton, Jamie. *What Is Water?* Vancouver: UBC Press, 2010.

Lüders, Marika. "Ubiquitous Tunes, Virtuous Archiving, and Catering for Algorithms: The Tethered Affairs of People and Music Streaming Services." *Information, Communication and Society* (2020): 1–17.

Luxemburg, Rosa. *Reform or Revolution and Other Writings*. Mineola, NY: Dover, 2006.

Macleod, Kembrew. *Freedom of Expression®: Resistance and Repression in the Age of Intellectual Property*. Minneapolis: University of Minnesota Press, 2007.

Manabe, Noriko. "A Tale of Two Countries: Online Radio in the United States and Japan." In *The Oxford Handbook of Mobile Music*, vol. 1, edited by Sumanth Gopinath and Jason Stanyek, 456–95. Oxford: Oxford University Press, 2014.

Marshall, Lee. "Do People Value Recorded Music?" *Cultural Sociology* 13, no. 2 (2019): 141–58.

Marshall, Lee. "'Let's Keep Music Special. F—Spotify': On-Demand Streaming and the Controversy over Artist Royalties." *Creative Industries Journal* 8, no. 2 (2015): 177–89.

Marx, Karl. *Capital: A Critique of Political Economy*, vol. 1. Introduced by Ernest Mandel. Translated by Ben Fowkes. London: Penguin, 1976.

Marx, Karl. *Grundrisse: Foundations of the Critique of Political Economy*. Translated by Martin Nicolaus. London: Penguin, 1993.

Mayer-Schönberger, Victor, and Kenneth Cukier. *Big Data: A Revolution That Will Transform How We Live, Work, and Think*. New York: Houghton Mifflin, 2013.

McChesney, Robert. *Digital Disconnect*. New York: New Press, 2013.

McCourt, Tom, and Eric Rothenbuhler. "SoundScan and the Consolidation of Control in the Popular Music Industry." *Media Culture Society* 19 (1997): 201–18.

McGowan, Todd. *Capitalism and Desire: The Psychic Cost of Free Markets*. New York: Columbia University Press, 2016.

McKelvey, Fenwick, and Robert Hunt. "Discoverability: Toward a Definition of Content Discovery through Platforms." *Social Media and Society* 5, no. 1 (2019): 1–15.

Meehan, Eileen. "Ratings and the Institutional Approach: A Third Answer to the Commodity Question." *Critical Studies in Mass Communication* 1, no. 2 (1984): 216–25.

Meier, Leslie. *Popular Music as Promotion: Music and Branding in the Digital Age*. Cambridge: Polity, 2017.

Meier, Leslie, and Vincent Manzerolle. "Rising Tides? Data Capture, Platform Accumulation, and New Monopolies in the Digital Music Economy." *New Media and Society* 21, no. 3 (2018): 543–61.

Meinel, Christoph, and Harald Sack. *Internetworking: Technological Foundations and Applications*. Berlin: Springer, 2013.

Menger, Pierre-Michel. "Artistic Labor Markets and Careers." *Annual Review of Sociology* 25, no. 1 (1999): 541–74.

Menger, Pierre-Michel. *Le travail créateur: S'accomplir dans l'incertain*. Paris: Gaillmard, 2009.

Midnight Notes Collective. "Introduction to the New Enclosures." *Midnight Notes* 10 (1990): 1–10.

Miller, Karl Hagstrom. *Segregating Sound: Inventing Folk and Pop Music in the Age of Jim Crow*. Durham, NC: Duke University Press, 2010.

Miller, Karl Hagstrom. "Working Musicians: Exploring the Rhetorical Ties between Musical Labor and Leisure." *Leisure Studies* 27, no. 4 (2018): 427–41.

Moazed, Alex, and Nicholas Johnson. *Modern Monopolies: What It Takes to Dominate the 21st-Century Economy*. New York: St. Martin's Press, 2016.

Moore, Jason. *Capitalism in the Web of Life: Ecology and the Accumulation of Capitalism*. London: Verso, 2015.

Morris, Jeremy Wade. "Artists as Entrepreneurs, Fans as Workers." *Popular Music and Society* 37, no. 3 (2014): 273–90.

Morris, Jeremy Wade. "Curation by Code: Infomediaries and the Data Mining of Taste." *European Journal of Cultural Studies* 18, nos. 4–5 (2015): 446–63.

Morris, Jeremy Wade. *Selling Digital Music, Formatting Culture*. Berkeley: University of California Press, 2015.

Morris, Jeremy Wade, and Devon Powers. "Control, Curation, and Musical Experience in Streaming Music Services." *Creative Industries Journal* 8, no. 2 (2015): 106–22.

Mosco, Vincent. *The Political Economy of Communication: Rethinking and Renewal*. London: Sage, 1996.

Moulier Boutang, Yann. *Cognitive Capitalism*. Translated by Ed Emery. Cambridge: Polity, 2011.

Mueller, Gavin. *Media Piracy in the Cultural Economy: Intellectual Property and Labor under Neoliberal Restructuring*. New York: Routledge, 2019.

Mühlbach, Saskia, and Payal Arora. "Behind the Music: How Labor Changed for Musicians through the Subscription Economy." *First Monday* 25, no. 4 (6 April 2020).

Muikku, Jari. *Metadata of Digital Music Files: Summary.* Helsinki: Digital Media Finland, 2017.

Muikku, Jari. *Pro Rata and User Centric Distribution Models: A Comparative Study.* Helsinki: Digital Media Finland, 2017.

Muñoz, José Esteban. *Cruising Utopia: The Then and There of Queer Futurity.* New York: New York University Press, 2009.

National Endowment for the Arts. *Artists in the Workforce, 1990–2005.* Research Report no. 48, May 2008.

Negus, Keith. "From Creator to Data: The Post-Record Music Industry and the Digital Conglomerates." *Media, Culture and Society* 41, no. 3 (2018): 367–84.

Nopper, Tamara K. "Digital Character in the 'Scored Society': FICO, Social Networks, and Competing Measurements of Creditworthiness." In *Captivating Technology: Race, Carceral Technoscience, and Liberatory Imagination in Everyday Life*, edited by Ruha Benjamin, 170–87. Durham, NC: Duke University Press, 2019.

North, Paul. *The Problem of Distraction.* Stanford, CA: Stanford University Press, 2012.

O'Brien, M. E. "To Abolish the Family." *Endnotes* 5 (2019).

Ohm, Paul, and Scott Peppet. "What If Everything Reveals Everything?" In *Big Data Is Not a Monolith*, edited by Cassidy Sugimoto, Hamid Ekbia, and Michael Mattioli, 45–60. Cambridge, MA: MIT Press, 2016.

Page, Will, and David Safir. "Money in, Money Out: Lessons from CMOs in Allocating and Distributing Licensing Revenue." *Music and Copyright Newsletter* 29 (2018): 23–31.

Parker, Geoffrey, Marshall Van Alstyne, and Sangeet Paul Choudary. *Platform Revolution: How Networked Markets Are Transforming the Economy and How to Make Them Work for You.* New York: Norton: 2016.

Parkhurst, Bryan. "Digital Information and Value: A Response to Jakob Rigi." *tripleC* 17, no. 1 (2019): 72–85.

Parkhurst, Bryan. "Music, Art, and Kinds of Use Values." *Critique: Journal of Socialist Theory* 48, nos. 2–3 (2020): 205–24.

Parkhurst, Bryan, and Stephan Hammel. "Pitch, Tone, and Note." In *The Oxford Handbook of Critical Concepts of Music Theory*, edited by Alexander Rehding and Steve Rings, 3–39. Oxford: Oxford University Press, 2018.

Passman, Donald. *All You Need to Know about the Music Business.* 10th ed. New York: Simon and Schuster, 2019.

Paul, Sanjukta. "The Enduring Ambiguities of Antitrust Liability for Worker Collective Action." *Loyola University Chicago Law Review* 47 (2015): 969–1048.

Pedersen, Rasmus Rex. *A Meta-Study of User-Centric Distribution for Music Streaming.* Roskilde University, 2020. https://www.koda.dk/media

/224782/meta-study-of-user-centric-distribution-model-for-music-streaming.pdf.

Perelman, Michael. "The Rise of Guard Labor." *Dollars and Sense* 286 (2010): 10–16.

Perzanowski, Aaron, and Jason Schultz. *The End of Ownership: Personal Property in the Digital Economy*. Cambridge, MA: MIT Press, 2016.

Peterson, Richard, and Albert Simkus. "How Musical Taste Groups Mark Occupational Status Groups." In *Cultivating Differences: Symbolic Boundaries and the Making of Inequality*, edited by Michele Lamont and Marcel Fournier, 152–68. Princeton, NJ: Princeton University Press, 1992.

Petre, Caitlin, Brooke Erin Duffy, and Emily Hund. "'Gaming the System': Platform Paternalism and the Politics of Algorithmic Visibility." *Social Media + Society* (2019): 1–12.

Phillips, Natalie. *Distraction: Problems of Attention in Eighteenth Century Literature*. Baltimore: Johns Hopkins University Press, 2016.

Phillips, Whitney, and Ryan Milner. *The Ambivalent Internet: Mischief, Oddity, and Antagonism Online*. Cambridge: Polity, 2017.

Pongratz, Hans. "Of Crowds and Talents: Discursive Constructions of Global Online Labour." *New Technology, Work, and Employment* 33, no. 1 (2018): 58–73.

Powers, Devon. "Lost in the Shuffle: Technology, History, and the Idea of Musical Randomness." *Critical Studies in Media Communication* 31, no. 3 (2014): 244–64.

Prey, Robert. "Locating Power in Platformization: Music Streaming Playlists and Curatorial Power." *Social Media + Society* (2020): 1–11.

Prey, Robert. "Music Analytica: The Datafication of Listening." In *Networked Music Cultures: Contemporary Approaches, Emerging Issues*, edited by Raphaël Nowak and Andrew Whelan, 31–48. London: Palgrave Macmillan, 2016.

Prey, Robert. "Nothing Personal: Algorithmic Individuation on Music Streaming Platforms." *Media, Culture and Society* 39 (2017): 1–15.

Prey, Robert. "'Now Playing. You': Big Data and the Production of Music Streaming Space." PhD diss., Simon Fraser University, 2015.

Prior, Nick. *Popular Music, Digital Technology, and Society*. London: Sage, 2018.

Qu, Shuwen, David Hesmondhalgh, and Jian Xiao. "Music Streaming Platforms and Self-Releasing Musicians: The Case of China." *Information, Communication and Society* (2021): 1–17.

Rai, Shirin, Catherine Hoskyns, and Dania Thomas. "Depletion: The Cost of Social Reproduction." *International Feminist Journal of Politics* 16, no. 1 (2014): 86–105.

"The Rate of Exploitation (the Case of the iPhone)." *Tricontinental: Institute for Social Research*, Notebook no. 2 (2019). https://www

.thetricontinental.org/wp-content/uploads/2019/09/190928_Notebook-2_EN_Final_Web.pdf.

Ratliff, Ben. *Every Song Ever: Twenty Ways to Listen in an Age of Musical Plenty*. New York: Farrar, Straus, and Giroux, 2016.

Razavi, Shahra, and Silke Staab. "Underpaid and Overworked: A Cross-National Perspective on Care Workers." *International Labour Review* 149, no. 4 (2010): 407–22.

Rekret, Paul. "'Melodies Wander Around as Ghosts: On Playlist as Cultural Form." *Critical Quarterly* 61, no. 2 (2019): 56–76.

Renfro, Paul. *Stranger Danger: Family Values, Childhood, and the American Carceral State*. Oxford: Oxford University Press, 2020.

Ricardo, David. *On the Principles of Political Economy and Taxation*. London: John Murray, 1821.

Roberts, Michael. *Tell Tchaikovsky the News: Rock'n'Roll, the Labor Question, and the Musicians' Union*. Durham, NC: Duke University Press, 2014.

Robinson, Dom. *Content Delivery Networks: Fundamentals, Design, and Evolution*. Hoboken, NJ: Wiley, 2017.

Robinson, Michael, and Sarah Montgomery. "The Time Allocation and Earnings of Artists." *Industrial Relations* 39, no. 3 (2000): 525–34.

Rochet, Jean-Charles, and Jean Tirole. "Platform Competition in Two-Sided Markets." *Journal of the European Economic Association* 1, no. 4 (2003): 990–1029.

Rogers, Jim. *The Death and Life of the Music Industry in the Digital Age*. London: Bloomsbury, 2013.

Rónai, András. "Frictionless Platforms, Frictionless Music: The Utopia of Streaming in Music Industry Press Narratives." In *Popular Music, Technology, and the Changing Media Ecosystem*, edited by Tamas Tofalvy and Emília Barna, 97–113. Cham, Switzerland: Palgrave, 2020.

Rosa, Hartmut. *Social Acceleration: A New Theory of Modernity*. Translated by Jonathan Trejo-Mathys. New York: Columbia University Press, 2013.

Rosen, Sherwin. "The Economics of Superstars." *American Economic Review* 71, no. 5 (1981): 845–58.

Rossiter, Ned. *Software, Infrastructure, Labor: A Media Theory of Logistical Nightmares*. London: Routledge, 2016.

Ryan, Bill. *Making Capital from Culture: The Corporate Form of Capitalist Cultural Production*. Berlin: De Gruyter, 1992.

Sadowski, Jathan. "The Internet of Landlords: Digital Platforms and the New Mechanisms of Rentier Capitalism." *Antipode* 52, no. 2 (2020): 562–80.

Samarotto, Frank. "The Trope of Expectancy/Infinity in the Music of the Beatles and Others." Paper presented at the annual meeting of the Society for Music Theory, New Orleans, LA, 1–4 November 2012.

Sandoval, Marisol. "Fighting Precarity with Co-Operation? Worker Co-Operatives in the Cultural Sector." *New Formations* 88 (2016): 51–68.

Sargeson, Sally. "The Demise of China's Peasantry as a Class." *Asia-Pacific Journal* 14, no. 13/1 (2016): 1–22.

Satyal, Kalyan. *Rethinking Capitalist Development: Primitive Accumulation, Governmentality and Post-colonial Capitalism*. Abingdon, UK: Routledge, 2007.

Say, Jean-Baptiste. *A Treatise on Political Economy*, vol. 1. Translated by C. R. Prinsep. London: Longman Hurst, 1821.

Scherzinger, Martin. "From Torrent to Stream: Economies of Digital Music." *Transposition* 6 (2016).

Scherzinger, Martin. "The Political Economy of Streaming." In *The Cambridge Companion to Music in Digital Culture*, edited by Nicholas Cook, Monique Ingalls, and David Trippett, 274–97. Cambridge: Cambridge University Press, 2019.

Scherzinger, Martin. "Towards a History of Digital Music." In *The Cambridge Companion to Music in Digital Culture*, edited by Nicholas Cook, Monique Ingalls, and David Trippett, 33–57. Cambridge: Cambridge University Press, 2019.

Scholz, Trebor. "Market Ideology and the Myths of Web 2.0." *First Monday* 13, no. 3 (2008).

Scholz, Trebor. *Ours to Hack and to Own: The Rise of Platform Cooperativism, a New Vision for the Future of Work and a Fairer Internet*. New York: OR Books, 2017.

Schotzko, T. Nikki Cesare. "A Sufficiently Advanced Racket: Performance on the Margins of Art and Commerce." *Canadian Theatre Review* 162 (Spring 2015): 52–57.

Schrift, Alan, ed. *The Logic of the Gift: Toward an Ethic of Generosity*. London: Routledge, 1997.

Seaver, Nick. "Captivating Algorithms: Recommender Systems as Traps." *Journal of Material Culture* 24, no. 4 (2019): 421–36.

Seaver, Nick. "Seeing Like an Infrastructure: Avidity and Difference in Algorithmic Recommendation." *Cultural Studies* 35, nos. 4–5 (2021): 771–91.

Segrave, Kerry. *Payola in the Music Industry: A History, 1880–1991*. Jefferson, NC: McFarland, 1994.

Shuker, Roy. *Wax Trash and Vinyl Treasures: Record Collecting as a Social Practice*. Farnham, UK: Ashgate, 2010.

Sicker, Douglas, Paul Ohm, and Shannon Gunaji. "The Analog Hole and the Price of Music: An Empirical Study." *Journal of Telecommunications and High Technology Law* 5 (2007): 573–87.

Simon, Herbert. "Designing Organizations for an Information-Rich World." In *Computers, Communication, and the Public Interest*, edited by Martin Greenberger, 38–72. Baltimore: Johns Hopkins University Press, 1971.

Simpson, Kim. *Early 70s Radio: The American Format Revolution*. London: Continuum, 2011.

Sinnreich, Aram. *Mashed Up: Music, Technology, and the Rise of Configurable Culture.* Boston: University of Massachusetts Press, 2010.

Sinnreich, Aram. "Music Cartels and the Dematerialization of Power." In *The Sage Handbook of Popular Music*, edited by Andy Bennett and Steve Waksman, 613–28. London: Sage, 2015.

Sinnreich, Aram. *The Piracy Crusade: How the Music Industry's War on Sharing Destroys Markets and Erodes Civil Liberties.* Amherst: University of Massachusetts Press, 2013.

Sinnreich, Aram. "Slicing the Pie: The Search for an Equitable Recorded Music Economy." In *Business Innovation and Disruption in the Music Industry*, edited by Patrik Wikström and Robert DeFillippi, 153–74. Cheltenham, UK: Elgar, 2016.

Smith, Adam. *An Inquiry into the Nature and Causes of the Wealth of Nations*, vol. 1. London: Strahan and Caddell, 1776.

Smythe, Dallas W. "Communications: Blindspot of Western Marxism." *Canadian Journal of Political and Social Theory* 1/3 (1977): 1–27.

Smythe, Dallas W. *Dependency Road.* Norwood, NJ: Ablex, 1981.

Snickars, Pelle. "More Music Is Better Music." In *Business Innovation and Disruption in the Music Industry*, edited by Patrik Wikström and Robert DeFillippi, 191–210. Cheltenham, UK: Elgar, 2016.

Soederberg, Susanne. *Debtfare States and the Poverty Industry: Money, Discipline, and the Surplus Population.* London: Routledge, 2014.

Solie, Ruth. *Music in Other Words: Victorian Conversations.* Berkeley: University of California Press, 2004.

Solis, Gabriel. "I Did It My Way: Rock and the Logic of Covers." *Popular Music and Society* 33, no. 3 (2010): 297–318.

Srnicek, Nick. *Platform Capitalism.* Cambridge: Polity, 2017.

Stahl, Matt. *Unfree Masters: Recording Artists and the Politics of Work.* Durham, NC: Duke University Press, 2013.

Stahl, Matt, and Leslie Meier. "The Firm Foundation of Organizational Flexibility: The 360 Contract in the Digitalizing Music Industry." *Canadian Journal of Communication* 37 (2012): 441–58.

Steingo, Gavin. "Sound and Circulation: Immobility and Obduracy in South African Electronic Music." *Ethnomusicology Forum* 24, no. 1 (2015): 102–23.

Sterne, Jonathan. *MP3: The Meaning of a Format.* Durham, NC: Duke University Press, 2012.

Sterne, Jonathan. "What's Digital in Digital Music?" In *Digital Media: Transformations in Human Communication*, edited by Paul Messaris and Lee Humphreys, 95–110. New York: Peter Lang, 2006.

Steyerl, Hito. "Digital Debris: Spam and Scam." *October* 138 (2011): 70–80.

Stockfelt, Ola. "Adequate Modes of Listening." In *Keeping Score: Music, Disciplinarity, Culture*, edited by David Schwarz, Anahid Kassabian, Lawrence Siegel, 129–46. Charlottesville: University of Virginia Press, 1997.

Straw, Will. "Sizing Up Record Collections." In *Sexing the Groove: Popular Music and Gender*, edited by Sheila Whiteley, 3–16. New York: Routledge, 1997.

Summach, Jay. "Form in Top-20 Rock Music, 1955–1989." PhD diss., Yale University, 2012.

Taylor, Timothy. "The Commodification of Music at the Dawn of the Era of 'Mechanical Music.'" *Ethnomusicology* 51, no. 2 (2007): 281–305.

Taylor, Timothy. *Music and Capitalism: A History of the Present*. Chicago: University of Chicago, 2016.

Taylor, Timothy. *The Sounds of Capitalism: Advertising, Music, and the Conquest of Culture*. Chicago: University of Chicago, 2012.

Tchernova, Pavlina. *The Case for a Job Guarantee*. Cambridge: Polity, 2020.

Terranova, Tiziana. "Free Labor: Producing Culture for the Digital Economy." *Social Text* 18, no. 2 (2000): 33–58.

Thompson, Emily. "Machines, Music, and the Quest for Fidelity: Marketing the Edison Phonograph in America, 1877–1925." *Musical Quarterly* 79 (1995): 131–71.

Thompson, Marie. "Music in the Post-Mom Economy." Lecture presented at the 56th Annual Conference of the RMA, 8 September 2020.

Thompson, Marie. "Sounding the Arcane: Contemporary Music, Gender and Reproduction." *Contemporary Music Review* 39, no. 2 (2020): 273–92.

Thompson, Marie. "Your Womb, The Perfect Classroom: Pre-Natal Soundsystems and Uterine Audiophilia." *Feminist Review* 127, no. 1 (2021): 73–89.

Thompson, Marie, and Eric Drott. "Music Is Still At Work Even if Musicians Aren't: Care, Reproduction, Crisis." *Working in Music*, 13 August 2020. https://wim.hypotheses.org/1430.

Throsby, David. *Economics and Culture*. Cambridge: Cambridge University Press, 2001.

Till, Nicholas. "The Operatic Event: Opera Houses and Opera Audiences." In *The Cambridge Companion to Opera Studies*, edited by Nicholas Till, 70–92. Cambridge: Cambridge University Press, 2012.

Toynbee, Polly. "NHS: The Blair Years." *BMJ* 334, no. 7602 (2007): 1030–31.

Tronto, Joan. *Moral Boundaries: A Political Argument for an Ethic of Care*. London: Routledge, 1993.

Trotsky, Leon. *The Revolution Betrayed: What Is the Soviet Union and Where Is It Going?* Detroit, MI: Labor Publications, 1991.

Tsing, Anna. "Supply Chains and the Human Condition." *Rethinking Marxism* 21, no. 2 (2009): 148–76.

Tzuo, Tien. *Subscribed: Why the Subscription Model Will Be Your Company's Future—and What to Do about It*. New York: Portfolio, 2018.

van Bohemen, Samira, Julian Schaap, and Pauwke Berkers. "The Sex Playlist: How Race and Ethnicity Mediate Musically 'Composed' Sexual Self-

Formation." In *Popular Music, Technology, and the Changing Media Ecosystem: From Cassettes to Stream*, edited by Tamas Tofalvy and Emília Barna, 115–28. Cham, Switzerland: Palgrave, 2020.

van Dijck, José. "Datafication, Dataism and Dataveillance: Data between Scientific Paradigm and Ideology." *Surveillance and Society* 12, no. 2 (2014): 197–208.

van Dijck, José, Thomas Poell, and Martijn de Waal. *The Platform Society: Public Values in a Connected World*. Oxford: Oxford University Press, 2018.

Varol, Onur, Emilio Ferrara, Clayton Davis, Filippo Menczer, and Alessandro Flammini. "Online Human-Bot Interactions: Detection, Estimation, and Characterization." *Proceedings of the International AAAI Conference on Web and Social Media* 11, no. 1 (2017): 280–89.

Viljoen, Salomé. "Democratic Data: A Relational Theory of Data Governance." *Yale Law Journal* 131, no. 2 (2021): 573–654.

Vogel, Lise. *Marxism and the Oppression of Women: Toward a Unitary Theory*. London: Pluto Press, 1983.

Vonderau, Patrick. "The Politics of Content Aggregation." *Television and New Media* 16, no. 8 (2015): 717–33.

Vonderau, Patrick. "The Spotify Effect: Digital Distribution and Financial Growth." *Television and New Media* 20, no. 1 (2019): 3–19.

Wajcman, Judy. *Pressed for Time: The Acceleration of Life in Digital Capitalism*. Chicago: University of Chicago Press, 2015.

Wallerstein, Immanuel. "The Bourgeois(ie) in Concept and Reality." *New Left Review* 167, no. 1 (1988): 91–106.

Warner, Michael. *Publics and Counterpublics*. New York: Zone Books, 2002.

Warrillow, John. *The Automatic Customer: Creating a Subscription Business in Any Industry*. New York: Portfolio, 2015.

Washburne, Christopher, and Maiken Derno, eds. *Bad Music: The Music We Love to Hate*. New York: Routledge, 2004.

Weber, William. "Did People Listen in the Eighteenth Century?" *Early Music* 25, no. 4 (November 1997): 678–91.

Weeks, Kathi. *The Problem with Work: Feminism, Marxism, Antiwork Politics, and Postwork Imaginaries*. Durham, NC: Duke University Press, 2011.

Weinstein, Deena. "The History of Rock's Pasts through Rock Covers." In *Mapping the Beat: Popular Music and Contemporary Theory*, edited by Andrew Herman, John Sloop, and Thomas Swiss, 137–52. Malden, MA: Blackwell, 1998.

Weisbard, Eric. *Top 40 Democracy: The Rival Mainstreams of American Popular Music*. Chicago: University of Chicago, 2014.

Werner, Ann. "Organizing Music, Organizing Gender: Algorithmic Culture and Spotify Recommendations." *Popular Communication* 18, no. 1 (2020): 78–90.

Wikström, Patrik. *The Music Industry: Music in the Cloud*, 3rd ed. Cambridge: Polity, 2019.

Wikström, Patrik, and Robert DeFillippi. "Introduction." In *Business Innovation and Disruption in the Music Industry*, edited by Patrik Wikström and Robert DeFillippi, 1–12. Cheltenham, UK: Edward Elgar, 2016.

Williams, Raymond. *Television: Technology and Cultural Form*. New York: Schocken, 1975.

Williams, Raymond. *Television: Technology and Cultural Form*. 2nd ed. New York: Routledge, 1990.

Williams, Simon. *The Politics of Sleep: Governing (Un)consciousness in the Late Modern Age*. London: Palgrave, 2011.

Winston, Emma, and Laurence Saywood. "Beats to Relax/Study to: Contradiction and Paradox in Lofi Hip Hop." *IASPM Journal* 9, no. 2 (2019): 40–54.

Wright, Erik Olin. *Classes*. London: Verso, 1984.

Wu, Tim. "Blind Spot: The Attention Economy and the Law." *Antitrust Law Journal* 82, no. 3 (2019): 771–806.

Yanggratoke, Rerngvit, Gunnar Kreitz, Mikael Goldmann, and Rolf Stadler. "Predicting Response Times for the Spotify Backend." In *Proceedings of the 8th International Conference on Network and Service Management (CNSM)*, edited by Jorge Lobo, Philippe Owezarski, Hui Zhang, and Deep Medhi, 117–25. New York: Institute of Electrical and Electronics Engineers, 2012.

Young, Katie. "Market-Mediated, Access-Based Consumption of Digital Music." *Journal of Promotional Communications* 1, no. 1 (2013): 68–84.

Yúdice, George. *The Expediency of Culture: Uses of Culture in the Global Era*. Durham, NC: Duke University Press, 2003.

Zielinski, Siegfried. "Art and Apparatus (a Flusserian Theme): Plea for the Dramatization of the Interface." *Interface Critique* 1 (2018).

Zuboff, Shoshana. *The Age of Surveillance Capitalism: The Fight for a Human Future at the New Frontier of Power*. New York: PublicAffairs, 2019.

Index

Page numbers in italics refer to figures.

AAC, 30
ABBA, 38
Abbing, Hans, 296n40
access model, 2–3
accumulation by dispossession, 82, 269n54
"Ada Diri-Mu," 34
Adkins, Lisa, 69
administrative metadata, 36
Adorno, Theodor, 65, 77; on listeners, 153–54
adtech, 135
Ad Training Summit (ATS), 122
Advanced Research Projects Agency Network (ARPANET), 48
Advertising Age, 117–18
Aegidius, Andreas, 56, 62
affect, waning of, 127–28
AI (artificial intelligence), 188–90, 232
Aitken, Rob, 136
Akamai, 32
algorithms: Pandora, 114; Spotify, 115–16, 126–27, 163
Alphabet, 222
alternative data, 137–38
Althusser, Louis, 197, 199
Amazon, 8, 212, 232–33
Amazon Echo, 134, 158
Amazon Music, 22, 32, 112–13; advertising on, 117; market share, 73, 75; playlists, 117–18, 201, 217; user interface, 43
"Amazon Music Experts," 43
American Girl, 161
Amnesty International, 141–42
Ancestry.com, 133
Anchor Media, 105

Anderson, Chris, 172
Anderson, Paul Allen, 129
Anderson, Tim, 102, 109–10
Andrejevic, Mark, 110
Ang, Ien, 109
antitrust law, 249
APIs (application programming interfaces), 14
Apple, 1, 38, 212
Apple Music, 2, 22, 134, 164, 252; advertisements, *23*; market share of, 73, 75; playlists, 201; promotion of human curation, 114, 219
Apple Music Kids, 220
application programming interfaces (APIs), 14
Arbitron, 109
Arditi, David, 264n124
Arora, Payal, 271n98
ARPANET (Advanced Research Projects Agency Network), 48
artificial intelligence (AI), 188–90, 232
artistic practice, 90
Assai, 38
asset economy: data in, 103; guard labor in, 71; Marxian accounts of, 71–72; platforms in, 67–72, 78–79, 110
Asset Economy, The (Adkins, Cooper, and Konings), 69
assetization, 78–79, 86, 106
asset price Keynesianism, 104, 212
assets, valorization of, 69
ATS (Ad Training Summit), 122
AT&T, 106
Attali, Jacques, 57, 264nn126–27

attention, 107, 109; authentication of, 147; Citton on, 175; commodification of, 168, 266n8; Crary on, 152; ecology of, 175; illusory, 284n23; inattention and, 165–66; monetization of, 170

attention economy, 148; foundational texts of, 284n12; platforms in, 149

Attention Economy, The (Davenport and Beck), 153

Auddly, 38

audience, commodification of, 266n8

audience labor, 275n45

audience power, 111, 275n45

Audius, 239–40, 243, 245

aura, 12

Austerberry, David, 50–51; on streaming, 49

Australasian Performing Right Association, 85

authenticity, 186

automotive insurance, 139–41

Bagley, Philip, 36
Baidu, 28
Bandcamp, 253–54
banner ads, 105
Basanta, Adam, 194
Basinski, William, 194
Baumol, William, 149, 207, 208, 263n90
Baym, Nancy, 150
Beats Music, 219
Beck, John, 153, 155
Beech, Dave, 205, 296n40
Benanav, Aaron, 208
Benedik, Brian, 117
Benjamin, Ruha, 141
Benjamin, Walter, 12
Bernards, Nick, 281n142
Beyoncé, 174
Bhattacharya, Tithi, 199
biases, in metadata, 40
Bibio, 188
Bieber, Justin, 132
Birenbaum Quintero, Michael, 298n81
Birthday Bunch, the, 157

black-hat marketplaces, 169
BlackRock, 70
blockchain, 239, 242; carbon emissions of, 245
"Blue in Green," 44
Bocelli, Andrea, 140
Bolter, Jay, 263n88
Boomplay, 23
Born, Georgina, 17, 24
Bose, 232–33
bots, on Twitter, 170
Bourdieu, Pierre, 200, 249
Bowen, William, 149, 207, 208, 263n90
Bowie, David, 63, 235
Brenner, Robert, 212
British Musicians' Union, 236
Broadcast Data Systems, 109
#BrokenRecord campaign, 236, 248, 249
Brown, Megan, 195
Brunton, Finn, 166, 181
Bulgarian Spotify Scam, 178–80
bundling, 174

"Cake by the Ocean," 221
Calm, 232
Cambridge Analytica, 124, 142
Capital (Marx), 69, 72
capitalism: competition under, 6–7; exploitation of natural resources under, 9–10, 202; non-economic background conditions for, 10–11; social reproduction under, 10, 202–3; supply chain, 53; surveillance, 273. *See also* platform capitalism
capitalocentric discourse, 8–9
Caramanica, Joe, 128
carbon emissions: of blockchain, 245; of Spotify, 33
Care Collective, 251
care work, 200, 202–3, 208; cost disease and, 226; inflationary trends in, *228*; under neoliberalism, 220, 228–29
Cashless Consumer, 137
CASH Music Summit, 44
Casilli, Antonio, 184

Caves, Richard, 290n117
CD Baby, 2, 152
CDDB (Compact Disc Database), 37, 260n46
CDNs. *See* content delivery networks
CDs, 30, 70, 98–99; metadata, 37
Celma, Òscar, 172
Change.org, 44
Chartmetric, 38, 131, 215
chattel slavery, 274n27
cheap music, 204–10; subsidizing, 210–13
Cheney-Lippold, John, 192
childcare, 200
children, moral panic and, 222–23
ChilledCow, 130
Chillhop, 130
China, 211–12
choruses, 126, 279n98
Christophers, Brett, 6
circuit of capital: commodities exiting, 83; expanded, 77
Citton, Yves, 175
Clairo, 128
Clear Channel, 7
Clegg, John, 208
click farms, 183–86
climate change, 94
cloners, 157
club goods, 88; streamed music as, 89
Coalition for Innovative Media Measurement, 112
Coca-Cola, 118
Cohen, Nicole, 72
Cole, Henderson, 246–47
College Music, 130, 131
commodification, 12–13, 18, 78–79; of attention, 168, 266n8; of audiences, 266n8; culture and, 65; of music, 73, 77, 96–97; of recorded sound, 2, 208; of social reproduction, 203
commodities: commodity fetishism, 96; cybernetic, 72; data as, 103; exiting circuit of capital, 83; on platforms, 65
common goods, 88
Commonsense Media, 221

communism, "actually existing," 82
Compact Disc Database (CDDB), 37, 260n46
compression: formats, 30; streaming and, 44–45. *See also specific types*
Concord Music Group, 70
consumer surplus, 215
content delivery networks (CDNs): privately owned, 32–33; third-party, 32–33
Content Delivery Networks (Robinson), 48
contextualization: of music, 31; streaming and, 44
contextual playlists, 214–17
continuous access, 54–55, 57
Cook, Jean, 44
Cook, Philip, 173–74
Cooper, Melinda, 69
co-ops, 238–39, 242–43, 253
copyright, 12, 63, 83, 92–93; infringement, 84–85
Copyright Royalty Board (CRB), 29, 75
coronavirus pandemic, 235–36
Corporate Wellness Magazine, 232
correlation, data and, 116, 135–36
cost disease, 207, 229, 263n90; care work and, 226; in performing arts, 149–50; social reproduction and, 227
cover songs, 161; soundalikes contrasted with, 162
Cowan, Ruth Schwartz, 208
Coyle, Michael, 161
Crain, Matthew, 111
Crary, Jonathan, 149; on attention, 152; on sleep, 195
Crawford, Kate, 155, 211
Crawford, Matthew, 148–49
CRB (Copyright Royalty Board), 29, 75
Creative Health, 231
credit scoring, 138; data in, 135–36
CreditVidya, 137
critical sociology, 200
CrowdFlower, 169
crypto, 239
Cubitt, Sean, 210
Cumulus, 7

Index → 333

curation: as care, 218–26; by Spotify, 81
Cush, Andy, 241–42
cybernetic assets, 78
cybernetic commodity, 72

data, 4–5; alternative, 137–38; in asset economy, 103; collection of, 84; as commodity, 103; correlation and, 116, 135–36; corruption of, 146; in credit scoring, 135–36; devaluation of, 146; as factor of production, 103; monetization of, 103–4; music as, 30–34; Pandora and, 143; beyond platforms, 132–43; Spotify and, 101–2, 105–6, 143; streaming, 192; surveillance and collection of, 106; user, 101–3, 115–16, 117. *See also* metadata
data aggregators, 78, 134–35
data analytics, 135; platforms and, 113–14
data brokers, 4, 18, 64, 78, 106, 111, 113; surveillance and, 141–42
data management platforms (DMPs), 134–35
data quality management, 112
Daughtry, Martin, 15–16, 137
Davenport, Thomas, 153, 155
Davies, Dan, 158
DAWs (digital audio workstations), 206
DCMS Committee, 256n9
DDEX (Digital Data Exchange), 39
DeAngelis, Massimo, 92
debt, subscriptions and, 57–59
decommodification, 86, 95; of music, 64–65, 96–97, 99–100, 253
Deezer, 1, 18, 23, 28, 35, 78, 133–34, 212, 233; architecture of, 32; complaints on community forum, 221; Flow, 149; unlicensed music on, 28
DeFrancesco, Joey La Neve, 248, 306n40
degeneration thesis, 242–43
Deleuze, Gilles, 111
Del Ray, Lana, 128
dementia, 230
demonetization, 86–87
DeNora, Tia, 124, 201, 215
Department of Health Services, 230
descriptive metadata, 36

Devine, Kyle, 15, 33, 210
digital assets, 78
digital audio workstations (DAWs), 206
Digital Data Exchange (DDEX), 39
digital distribution, 171–72
digital downloads, 1; streaming compared with, 54–56
digital footprints, 142
digital reproduction, 31, 162–63, 209; materiality and, 33; subsidizing, 210–11
digital traces, 151–52
digitization, 13, 92, 209–10; materiality and, 33; piracy and, 79–80
discoverability, 19
displacement, via spam, 159–60
disruption, 80
DistroKid, 2, 206
dividuals, 111–12
Dizzee Rascal, 140
DMPs (data management platforms), 134–35
DNA testing, 133
DNCE, 221
Donath, Susan, 226–27
Donnath, Judith, 164
"Don't Speak," 165
dot-com boom, 284n12
Dredge, Stuart, 189
DRM, 50, 56, 84, 86, 209
DropLabs, 232
Dryhurst, Mat, 251
Duinker, Ben, 279n100
Dylan, Bob, 70

Echo Nest, 38, 123, 171, 263n89
economic exceptionalism, music and, 204–7; defining, 296n40
ecosocialism, 15
Edelman, Lee, 222
Eight Mile Style, 29
Eilish, Billie, 128
Ek, Daniel, 64, 67, 101
Elberse, Anita, 175
email spam, 159
Embassy, 162
EMI, 28

Eminem, 29, 140
Endel, 232
Endnotes Collective, 199
end user license agreement (EULA), 30; shrink-wrap, 46
Energy, 34, 260n38
energy, cheap, 210
engagement metrics, 146–47
England, Nancy, 227
Enlightenment, the, 123
Eno, Brian, 188
Enriching Media Data, 112
Entrepreneur, 194–95
environmental impacts, of streaming, 245
Epidemic Sound, 187–88, 293n165
Equal Credit Opportunity Act, 138
Eriksson, Maria, 36, 214
EULA. *See* end user license agreement
exchange value, 89–90, 91; use value decoupled from, 99, 198
expanded circuit of capital, 77
Experian, 142
expropriation, 82
externalities, 89–90
extradependences, 252–53

Facebook, 8, 103, 106, 133, 169
fair-trade networks, 98
fake artists, 186–91; on Spotify, 147–48
fake streams, 169–85
family, the, 220–21
"fans also like" feature, 47
Farley, Matt, 286n69
Fast Company, 189
Federal Reserve, US, 104, 212
Federal Trade Commission (FTC), 7
Federici, Silvia, 199
Fergus, Devlin, 139
file sharing, 27–28, 31
file transfer, 48–49
financial crisis of 2008, 6
fintech, 135, 136, 281n142
Fisher, Irving, 52
Fiverr, 169
fiveup.com, 182

flat-fee utility models, 67
Fleischer, Rasmus, 86
flows, 51–52, 56; platforms managing, 81
Flying Lotus, 130
Folbre, Nancy, 227
folklore, 131–32
Fordism, 223
format replacement cycles, 70, 154
Foxconn, 252
Frank, Georg, 149
Frank, Robert, 173–74
Fraser, Nancy, 10, 203, 213; on expropriation, 296n39
fraud, 158, 180
free gifts of nature, 9–10, 90, 203, 211; music as, 213; water as, 95
free labor, 275n31
freelancer.com, 291n145
free lunch, 107
free markets, under neoliberalism, 7
freemium services, 64, 68, 86, 98, 150–51; Amazon, 117
friction: defining, 41–42; in interfaces, 46–47
frictionless UX, 41
Frith, Simon, 27
FTC (Federal Trade Commission), 7

Galloway, Alex, 45
gatekeepers, 171
gender, 217–18; metadata and, 261n64; music and, 200–201, 215–16
genre tags, on Spotify, 40–41
German Romantics, on music, 123
Gibson, Katherine, 8
Gibson-Graham, J. K., 8
Gillespie, Tarleton, 68, 155, 180, 222, 288n87
Gimlet, 105
Glenn, Evelyn Nakano, 200
global market share, *74, 75*
Global Wellness Summit, 232–33
Goldhaber, Michael, 284n12
Goldman Sachs, 103–4
Goldschmitt, K. E., 292n160
Gomez, 236

Index → 335

Google, 8, 29, 103, 133, 212
Google Cloud, 32
Google Home, 158
Google Play Music, 119, 134; mood and activity recommendations on, *120*
Gopinath, Sumanth, 120
Goulding, Ellie, 233
Graeber, David, 82
Graham, Julie, 8
Grange, Lucian, 240–41
Gray, Tom, 236
Great Recession, 42–43
Grooveshark, 28
Grusin, Richard, 263n88
guard labor, in asset economy, 71
Guetta, David, 70

Hagen, Anja Nylund, 87
"Hallucinate," 127, *128*
Hanna, Thomas, 243
"Happy Birthday," 160
"Happy Roadtrip," 221
Hardin, Garrett, 88
Harding, Charlie, 126
Harvey, David, 296n31
Hassan, Aisha, 126
Havighurst, Craig, 44
Headspace, 232
Heemann, Christoph, 194
Helfrich, Silke, 94
Hesmondhalgh, David, 234
"Hey Jude," 125
Hill, Peter, 52–53
Hipgnosis, 70–71
hip-hop, 279n100; lo-fi, 130–31
hits, 172
Hoffman, E. T. A., 123
Höglund, Oscar, 187
Hopkins, Harry, 4, 256n11
"Human," 165, 168
hypodermic needle theory, 122–23

ID3 tags, 37
identity: music and, 123; online, 177–78
ideology, of streaming, 55–56

IDM (intelligent dance music), 171
IFPI (International Federation of the Phonographic Industry), 28, 84–85
Ihde, Don, 130
illusory attention, 284n23
immaterial labor, 11
impressions, 152
inattention, 165–66
independent contractors, 248–49
independent musicians, 206–7
Indify, 38
infomediation, 114
"Ingiusta," 34
innovation, 69
Instagram, 29, 169
InsurTech, 139–40
intellectual property, 77; music as, 27–30; in music industry, 27
intelligent dance music (IDM), 171
Interactive Advertising Bureau, 105
interactive technology, 109–10
interdependence, 251–52
interface: defining, 45; interfaceless interfaces, 263n88; music as, 41–48
interfaces: friction in, 46–47; minimalism of, 45–46
International Federation of the Phonographic Industry (IFPI), 28, 84–85
International Standard Recording Code (ISRC), 36
invisibilities, 89–90
iPhones, 212
iPod, 55
ISRC (International Standard Recording Code), 36
ISWC (Standard Musical Work Code), 36
iTunes Store, 1, 3, 75, 86–87
Ivors Academy, 236

Jaak, 38
Jakovljevic, Jana, 122
Jameson, Fredric, 127–28
Japan: listening in, 119; radio broadcast in, 119
Jay-Z, 98, 140

jazz, 44
J Dilla, 130
Jenkins, Chaz, 131
JioSaavn, 22, 176
Johansson, Anna, 214
Johnson, Maura, 163
Johnson, Tom, 40
Joler, Vladan, 211
Jones, John "The Ragin' Cajun," 168
Joyeux Anniversaire, 160
Jukedeck, 190
June Jett, 164
Justice at Spotify campaign, 236–37, 244

Kaiser Permanente, 232
Kallis, Giorgis, 218
Kant, Immanuel, 197
karaoke, 167
Kassabian, Anahid, 118
Katz, Mark, 279n96
Kazaa, 31
Keep Music Alive campaign, 236
Keil, Charles, 154
Keynes, John Maynard, 61–62
Keynesianism, asset price, 104, 212
Konings, Martijn, 69
Kopf, Dan, 126
Kosinski, Michal, 142
Kreidler, John, 205–6
Krueger, Alan, 87
Krukowski, Damon, 99
Krux, 134
Kusek, David, 64–65, 67–68, 88, 92, 93, 270n91

La Berge, Leigh Claire, 97–98
labor: cheap, 210–13; free, 275n31; immaterial, 11; manual, 11; mobilization, 248
Lamere, Paul, 263n89
Lauv, 131–32
Lawrence, Mathew, 243
Leary, John Patrick, 231–32
Lee, Danielle, 121–22; on streaming, 124
Lehman, Frank, 130
leisure, productivity and, 217

Lemonade, 174
Lenddo, 136
Leonhard, Gerd, 64–65, 67–68, 88, 92, 93, 270n91
Leppert, Richard, 208
libertarianism, 180
libraries, streaming services as, 246
licensing agreements, 3, 28–29, 76
Liebling, A. J., 107
Life of Pablo, The, 102, 174
Limelight, 32
Liminal Sleep, 194
liner notes, 44
LinkedIn, 177
Linton, Jamie, 94
Lipa, Dua, 127, *128*
listeners: Adorno on, 153–54; disengagement of, 190; emotional, 154; engagement of, 155; expert, 153–54; renting, 107–12
listening: active v. passive, 119; in Japan, 119; legitimate listening behavior, 154; machine, 126–27; ubiquitous, 118–19
Little, Tasmin, 242
Live Nation, 7
local lengthening, 184
Lofi Fruits, 131
lo-fi hip-hop, 130–31
long tail, 156, 172
look-alikes, identification of, 138
Luxemburg, Rosa, 305n25
lyrics, 44–45

machine listening, 126–27
Madlib, 130
Maitland, James, 91
Manabe, Noriko, 119
Mandel, Aaron, 157
manual labor, 11
Manzerolle, Vincent, 268n44
Maples, Jon, 157
Marconi Union, 194
Marshall, Lee, 98, 271n106
Martin, Max, 38
Marx, Karl, 60, 69, 91, 95–96, 197, 240; expanded circuit of capital formula, 77

Index → 337

Marxian analysis, of asset economy, 71–72
Marxist feminism, 199
Mass Media+, 176–77
master rights, 29
Mathew effect, 176–77
MBW (*Music Business Worldwide*), 186
mechanical reproduction, 12, 209
Mechanical Turk, 169
mediality, 51
media saturation, 148
Meehan, Eileen, 109
Megaphone, 105
Meidner plan, 247, 272n109
Meier, Leslie, 268n44
mental shelf space, 173
mergers, 7
Merton, Robert, 177
metadata, 26; administrative, 36; biases in, 40; CDs, 37; collection of, 37–38; defining, 36; descriptive, 36; faulty, 40; gender and, 261n64; industry problems with, 37; music as, 34–41; ownership, 36; racialization and, 261n64; standardization of, 38–39; startups, 38; types of, 36–37
metric power, 76
microlabor platforms, 169
micropayments, 4
Middleton, Tom, 194
Migos, 233
Milner, Ryan, 177
Milton, John, 95
minimalism, 43; of interfaces, 45–46
MIR (music information retrieval), 37, 188
Mixtronic, 160
MMA (Music Modernization Act), 29
Moffitt, Barak, 39
Molinder, Niclas, 38
Mondragon Corporation, 243
monetary stimulus, 212
money, cheap, 210–13
monopoly, 6–7, 8, 77–78; online advertising, 105
mood EPs, 131–32
mood playlists, 127–28, 187–89, 216
Moore, Jason, 89, 202, 210

Morris, Jeremy Wade, 30, 51, 96–97, 114
Mosco, Vincent, 72
MP3s, 2, 30, 49, 56, 84, 86–87; sale of, 3
Mubert, 232
Mueller, Gavin, 53–54
Mühlbach, Saskia, 271n98
Mulligan, Mark, 61, 63, 106, 156, 173, 190; on UCD, 241
multisided markets, 18, 77; platforms as, 68–69
Muñoz, Esteban, 223
music: analytics, 37–39; cheap, 204–10; as club good, 89; commodification of, 73, 77, 96–97; as consumer surplus, 215; contextualization of, 31; as data, 30–34; decommodification of, 64–65, 96–97, 99–100, 253; as economic exception, 11–12; economic exceptionalism of, 204–7; as free gift, 213; future of, 65–67; gender and, 200–201, 215–16; German Romantics on, 123; identity and, 123; as intellectual property, 27–30; as interface, 41–48; intergenerational reproduction of class and, 200; as metadata, 34–41; as passion point, 122; platform capitalism and, 72–82, 244–54; as predictor of dispositions, 124; as private good, 88–89, 253–54; as public good, 88–89, 246–47, 253; racialization of, 139–41, 215–16; renting, 107–12; as service, 55–56; social reproduction and, 11–12, 197, 198–204; as stream, 48–62; for surveillance, 125–32, 274n27; as utility, 96–97; utopian potential of, 251; as water, 63–64, 66–67, 91, 93–96. *See also specific topics*
musical reproduction, crisis of, 226–33. *See also* digital reproduction; mechanical reproduction
musical spam, 147, 155–69
Music and Memory, 229–30
Music Business Worldwide (MBW), 186
Music Consumer Insight Report, 84–85
Music Genome Project, 37
musicians: class position of, 250–51; income of, 205–6
Musicians on Call, 232–33

music industry, intellectual property in, 27
music information retrieval (MIR), 37, 188
Musicmetric, 38
Music Modernization Act (MMA), 29
Music Search Engine, 37
Musimap, 38
Muslims, 142
myndstream, 232

Napster, 1, 27–28, 31, 84; piracy epidemic and, 2
National Endowment for the Arts, 205
National Security Agency (NSA), 141
natural resources, exploitation of, 9–10, 202
nature: cheap, 210–13; free gifts of, 9–10, 90, 95, 203, 211
neoliberalism, 217; care work under, 220, 228–29; free markets under, 7; social reproduction under, 203
neo-Muzak, 20, 129
Netflix, 8, 106, 186
Network of Music Partners, 39–40
Newton-Rex, Ed, 190
New York Advertising Week, 121
New York Stock Exchange, 79; Spotify on, 103–4
Next Big Sound, 38
NextMark, 142
niches, *versus* hits, 172
Nielsen, 109
No Doubt, 165
noncapitalist economies, 82–83
noncommodities, on platforms, 65
noncommodity fetishism, 90–96
nonprofits, 229
Norström, Alex, 223
NSA (National Security Agency), 141

offshoring, 183
Ohm, Paul, 135
oligopoly, 73–74
oligopsony, 73–74
online advertising, monopolization of, 105
ownership metadata, 36
ownership model, 2–3, 244

Pachet, François, 188–89, 293n175
Pandora, 18, 37, 102, 109–10, 112–13, 172, 219, 276n52; algorithms, 114; architecture of, 32; data and, 143; political ads on, 124; user data, 115–16
Pandora for Brands, 114–15
paratexts, 43
Parkhurst, Bryan, 297n52, 297n60
patronage, 207
"Payson," 34
peak streaming, 1
Pearl River Delta, 211–12
peer-to-peer networks, 32
Pelly, Liz, 128, 246–47
Peppet, Scott, 135
performance, 15–16
performing arts, cost disease in, 149–50
personalization, 17, 219–20, 229
personalized music, 160–61
personalized risk assessment, 139
Peters, Nils, 243
Philippines, 136, 183–85
Phillips, Natalie, 153
Phillips, Whitney, 177
phonograph, 217–18
phonograph effect, 279n96
Pickwick Records, 162
piracy: digitization and, 79–80; Napster and, 2
Pitchfork, 163
platform capitalism, 7–8, 14–15; music and, 72–82, 244–54
platformization, 7–8, 14, 59
platforms, 62; in asset economy, 67–72, 78–79, 110; in attention economy, 149; commodities and noncommodities on, 65; competition on, 113; co-op, 238–39, 242–43, 253; data analytics and, 113–14; data beyond, 132–43; flows managed by, 81; microlabor, 169; as multisided markets, 68–69; outputs, 81; product differentiation on, 113–14; record labels interacting with, 76–77; winner-take-all tendencies on, 173–74

Index → 339

playlists, 19, 20, 51; Amazon, 117–18; contextual, 214–17; mood, 127–28, 187–89, 216; showering, 122; for social reproductive activities, 201; Spotify, 117–18, 122, 176

Pokémon, 225

political ads, on Pandora, 124

political economy, 6–13

Polnareff, Michel, 265n2

Polo G, 233

Popjustice, 293n175

pop music, 69

Powers, Devon, 51, 96–97

preferential ranking, 256n11

Prey, Robert, 81, 135–36

PRISM program, 141

privacy: on Spotify, 101–2; Supreme Court on, 141

private goods, 92, 209–10; music as, 88–89, 253–54; water as, 94

private property, 247

profiles, 111

Progression, 260n38

proletarianization, 60

pro rata model, 237–40, 290n133; on Spotify, 179

pseudopersonalized music, 157

public goods, 209–10; defining, 88; music as, 88–89, 246–47, 253

public libraries, 93

PureTech Health, 229

QAnon, 223

Qobuz, 54–55

quantification, 151–52

racialization: metadata and, 261n64; of music, 139–41; music and, 215–16

"Radio" (song by Michel Polnareff), 265n2

radio broadcast, 88; in Japan, 119

Rag'n'Bone Man, 165, 168

rare earth metals, 211

Raymond, Adam, 156, 186

Rdio, 22

real subsumption, 205

recommendations, 4–5, 47–48; mood and emotion-based, 114–16; personalized, 148–49

recorded sound, commodification of, 2, 208

Recording Industry Association of America (RIAA), 28, 85

record labels: licensing agreements with, 28–29; major labels and monopoly power, 7; platforms interacting with, 76–77; pro rata model and, 179; responses to file sharing, 12; shift from manufacture to rights management, 27; streaming fraud and, 174

Reflective Ventures, 239

reforms, 237–39

Rekret, Paul, 127–28

rental services, 59

rent extraction, 7–8

rents, 70

repetition, 286n68

Resonate, 238, 243

revenue from streaming, 3–4, 60–61. *See also specific topics*

revenue-sharing models, 76, 247

Rhapsody, 157

RIAA (Recording Industry Association of America), 28, 85

Ricardo, David, 91

Rich, Robert, 194

Rihanna, 40–41, 165

ringtones, 12

Roberts, Sarah, 246

Robinson, Dom, 50, 54; on streaming, 48–49

Rónai, András, 268n44

royalties, 3, 46, 178; Spotify payments, 78, 237–38

Ryan, Bill, 205

sampling (musical), 83

Samsung, 106

Sandoval, Marisol, 244

Say, Jean-Baptiste, 91

scarcity, 13; artificiallly imposed by copyright, 27; superstar economies and, 173; of water, 270n91

Schotzko, T. Nikki Cesare, 145
search results, on Spotify, 34–35
Seed Scientific, 38
self-identification, 79
Senzari, 38
SEOClerk.com, 169–70, 174, 182
services, goods contrasted with, 52–54
service work, 208
sheet music, 62
Shenzhen, 211–12
Shift Project, 210–11
showering playlists, 122
shrink-wrap licenses, 26
Sigur Rós, 194
Silicon Valley, 42, 79
Simon, Herbert, 148
Sirius XM, 18, 29
slavery, 274n27
Sleep, 194
sleep, 194; Crary on, 195
Sleep Better, 194
Sleepify, 144, 152, 178, 181, 194; Spotify removing, 145–47
Sloan, Nate, 126
smartphones, 211; UI on, 43
Smith, Adam, 55, 91
Smokey and the Mirror, 152, 155
Smythe, Dallas, 107–8, 111, 275n31
Snickars, Pelle, 144–45, 158
Snowden, Edward, 141
social circulation, 82–90
social class: intergenerational reproduction of, 200; musician class position, 250–51
social media, 124
social reproduction, 11, 15, 89, 196, 207–8, 217, 251; under capitalism, 10, 202–3; commodification of, 203; cost disease and, 227; crisis of, 226–33; defining, 198–99; music and, 11–12, 197; under neoliberalism, 203; playlists for activities of, 201; playlists for tasks of, 201; systematic neglect of, 199
Sodatone, 38
Solis, Gabriel, 162
Sony, 28
Sony ATV, 73

Sony Music, 188–89; Spotify Contract with, 49–50, 76
soundalikes, 155–69; cover songs contrasted with, 162; naming of, 164–65; on Spotify, 163–64
Soundcharts, 38
SoundCloud, 2, 110, 176, 185; artists on, 305–6n35; UCD of, 240
Soundstr, 38
spam, 19; defining, 155, 159; displacement via, 159–60; email, 159; filters, 181; identification of, 157–58; income siphoned by, 168; labeling of, 166–67; musical, 147, 155–69; removal of, 158
special economic zones, 53
species being, 95
Spotify, 1, 8, 18, 28, 207, 212, 220, 241; acquisition of, 106; algorithms, 115–16, 126–27, 163; architecture of, 32; Browse page, 193; Bulgarian Spotify Scam, 178–80; carbon emissions of, 33; creators on, 305–6n35; curatorial power of, 81; data and, 101–2, 105–6, 143; DeFrancesco on, 248; Design Blog, 41; Dinner category, 214; Discover Weekly, 149; DNA testing and, 133; fake artists on, 147–48; first-time visitors pitch, 22–23; genre tags on, 40–41; lawsuits against, 29; losses, 241; mood and activity recommendations on, *120*; on New York Stock Exchange, 103–4; original content on, 186; petitions against, 235–36; playlists, 117–18, 122, 176, 178; preferential ranking on, 256n11; privacy policy on, 101–2; profitability of, 103–4; pro rata model of, 179; royalty payments, 78, 237–38; search results on, 34–35; segments on, 277n67; self-valorization of, 79–80; Sleep category on, 193–96, 200; *Sleepify* removed by, 145–47; songs purged from, 291n139; Sony Music contract with, 49–50, 76; soundalikes on, 163–64; subscription model, 86; *Thin Black Line* removed from, 152; trusted business partners, 102; UMAW critique of, 241–42; user base of, 104–5; user data, 117; UX, 41–42

Spotify Audience Network, 105
Spotify Community Forum, 156, 158, 163
Spotifycore, 128–29
Spotify for Artists, 175–76
Spotify for Brands, 121
Spotify Kids, 223–26
Spotify Teardown, 68, 79
Spotviewbot, 181, *182*
Srnicek, Nick, 59
standardization of metadata, 38–39
Standard Musical Work Code (ISWC), 36
Stanyek, Jason, 120
statistical sampling, 109
Sterne, Jonathan, 50–51, 86–87
Steyerl, Hito, 159
stockpiling, 57, 264nn126–27
stocks, 51–52
Stratton, Jack, 144–45
stream, the: defining, 1; music as, 48–62
stream2own payment model, 238
streambait pop, 128
Streamify, 177, 183
streaming: abusive, 152, 154; adaptation of, 16; Austerberry on, 49; benefits of, 2; compression and, 44–45; contextualization and, 44; data, 192; defining, 48–50; digital downloads compared with, 54–56; ecosystem, 13–22; environmental impacts of, 245; gaming, 156; growth of, 22; ideology of, 55–56, 60, 62; impact of, 1–2; Lee on, 124; as library, 246–47; as metaphor, 51; as mirror, 124; Mueller on, 53–54; phenomenology of, 26; polysemic richness of, 51; revenue from, 3–4, 60–61; rhetoric of, 22–23; Robinson on, 48–49; as service, 51–52; transformation of music into, 26
stream ripping, 85
Streisand, Barbra, 140
subscriptions: consumer preferences and, 59–60; as debt, 57–59; Spotify model for, 86
Summach, Jay, 279n98
Super Fitness Music, 166
supply chain capitalism, 53

supply chains, 184
Supreme Court, US, 141
surplus population, 170, 206
surplus use values, 214–18
surveillance, 18, 121; capitalism, 273; data brokers and, 141–42; data collection and, 106; music for, 125–32, 274n27; outsourcing, 141
Sweden, 247
Swift, Taylor, 97–98, 131–32, 161, 164
Swing, Tanya, 161, 164
sync licensing, 12
Sync Project, 229

Tame Impala, 40
Technology of Video and Audio Streaming, The (Austerberry), 49
Telecommunications Act of 1996, 7
"Tempo 106," 34
temporality, 46, 51–52, 70–71
Tencent, 106
Tesla, 133
"Theme from *Shaft*," 125
Thin Black Line, 152
Thinnen, 256n11
third-party partnerships, 78
Thompson, Marie, 215, 218
Ticketmaster, 7
Tidal, 22, 31, 32, 98, 102, 191
Tiësto, 260n38
Tinder, 133
Tops, 162, 287n76
tragedy of the commons, 88
transparency, 138–39
Tranter, Justin, 29
Trump, Donald, 124, 141–42
Tsing, Anna, 53
23andMe, 133
24/7 (Crary), 195
Twitter, 169; bots on, 170

Uber, 67–68, 80
ubiquitous listening, 118
UCD. *See* user-centric distribution model
UI (user interface), 43

Ulvaeus, Björn, 38
UMAW. *See* Union of Musicians and Allied Workers
unionization, 97–98
Union of Musicians and Allied Workers (UMAW), 236, 244, 249, 253; Spotify critiqued by, 241–42
United States Trade Representative, 85
Universal, 28, 73
Universal Product Code (UPC), 36
user-centric distribution model (UCD), 179, 237; Mulligan on, 241; of SoundCloud, 240–41
user data, 101–3; Pandora, 115–16; Spotify, 117
user experience (UX): frictionless, 41; of Spotify, 41–42
user interface (UI), on smartphones, 43
user splitting, 276n56
use value, 89–90, 91, 213; exchange value decoupled from, 99, 198; production-tracking, 297n52
utilities, music as, 96–97
utopianism, 251, 254
UX. *See* user experience

valorization: of assets, 69; self-valorization of spotify, 79–80
Verge, The, 37
Victorian era, 217
vinyl records, 70, 253–54
Virgin Airlines, 133
Vogel, Lise, 199
Vulfpeck, 144–46, 152, 178, 181, 194

Wackenroder, W. H., 123
Wajcman, Judy, 227
Walker, Scott, 230
walled gardens, 54, 71, 85–86
Wallerstein, Immanuel, 7
Warner, Michael, 108
Warner Chappell, 73
Warner Music Group, 28
Warrillow, John, 60
Warwick, 162
water: as free gift of nature, 95; music as, 63–64, 66–67, 91, 93–96; political economy of, 91; as private good, 94; scarcity, 270n91
water rights, 66–67
Watkins, Holly, 123
Wbix, 183
Wealth of Nations, The, 91
"We Are Never Ever Getting Back Together," 161
Weav, 232
Webern, Anton, 154
wellness, 231–32
West, Kanye, 102, 174
Western classical music, 44, 90, 207
"Where Have You Been," 165
Whitman, Brian, 123, 171–72
Williams, Raymond, 51
Williams, Simon, 194
World Privacy Forum, 138
Wright, Erik Olin, 249
Wu, Tim, 148

Young, Jonathan, 286n68
YouTube, 32, 110, 130–31, 246
YouTube Kids, 221–22
YouTubNow, 85

Zest Finance, 135
Zielinski, Siegfried, 45
Zouk, 34, 35

Index → 343

Printed and bound by CPI Group (UK) Ltd, Croydon, CR0 4YY
23/01/2024
08225977-0001